PIERRE D'AILLY
AND
THE BLANCHARD AFFAIR

STUDIES
IN MEDIEVAL AND
REFORMATION THOUGHT

EDITED BY

HEIKO A. OBERMAN, Tübingen

IN COOPERATION WITH

E. JANE DEMPSEY DOUGLASS, Claremont, California
LEIF GRANE, Copenhagen
GUILLAUME H. M. POSTHUMUS MEYJES, Leiden
ANTON G. WEILER, Nijmegen

VOLUME XXIV

ALAN E. BERNSTEIN
PIERRE D'AILLY
AND
THE BLANCHARD AFFAIR

LEIDEN
E. J. BRILL
1978

PIERRE D'AILLY
AND
THE BLANCHARD AFFAIR

University and Chancellor of Paris
at the Beginning of the Great Schism

BY

ALAN E. BERNSTEIN

LEIDEN
E. J. BRILL
1978

ISBN   90 04 05712 9

PRINTED IN THE NETHERLANDS

To the Memory of E. B.

CONTENTS

PREFACE

Much fruitful study has elucidated the emergence and early history of the University of Paris in the twelfth and thirteenth centuries, but relatively little attention has been paid to its maturity, even though the documentation for the fourteenth century is much fuller. One of the most complete dossiers in the later period is a product of the rebellion that dislodged the capricious and corrupt John Blanchard from his position as Chancellor of Paris in 1386. In the course of that conflict, the university masters promulgated statutes forbidding the chancellor's alleged abuses, the pope sent a delegate to investigate, the opposing sides drew up position papers, and eighty witnesses testified on them. The case then moved to the Parlement of Paris, where more testimony was heard. The resulting documentation, permits the most detailed picture of the university available since the end of its formative stage in the mendicant controversy.

The issues debated in the Blanchard affair are fundamental to an understanding of the university, its self-government, its relationship to the chancellor and to the pope. But beyond institutional history, the affair has connections with the crises swirling about France and the Church at that time, the Great Schism and the power struggle early in the reign of Charles VI. In addition, the university's spokesman throughout the conflict was the outstanding Paris theologian, Pierre d'Ailly. The reform provides an excellent look at his early career, while he was in the process of using the university as a springboard to preferment in the ecclesiastical hierarchy and into politics, where he would eventually become a figure of European importance. In the two speeches against the chancellor edited in the Appendix and analyzed in Chapter VI, we see how he sprang into the limelight; how he adapted the principles of university autonomy not only to oppose Blanchard, but also to work out larger ecclesiological ideas drawing on Gallicanism and conciliarism.

In the study that follows, the Blanchard affair is analyzed as a phenomenon in its own right, but also as inhering within a historical, political, institutional, and intellectual context that affects and informs it. The exposition proceeds from context to core: from the history of the license to teach, the political crisis imposed by the Great Schism, and the intellectual ferment that helped prepare the Church for the councils of Pisa and Constance; to Blanchard's administration as chancellor, the attack mounted against him, and his defense; and finally to the speeches themselves.

In presenting the revolt against Blanchard, I seeks also to describe the connection between internal university affairs and the broader movements of politics, reform, and ideology in France and the Church at the beginning of the Great Schism.

The debts incurred in writing this book are many. I am grateful to the Fulbright-Hays Commission, the President's Fellowship Committee of Columbia University, and Stanford University for material support provided at various stages in the research, writing, and publication of this work. My chief debt, however, is to the friends who have counseled and sustained me throughout its production. The first is Gilbert Ouy, who encouraged me to study Pierre d'Ailly and his manuscripts and who has shared with me countless facts and ideas throughout a long and stimulating relationship.

John Hine Mundy and Paul Oskar Kristeller of Columbia University helped me to advance the topic to the doctoral level and beyond with personal encouragement and technical advice. The incisive questions of my colleagues and students at Stanford University have kept me aware of what my subject looks like to those unfamiliar with its intricacies. Elmer Grieder, formerly of the Stanford University Library, devoted hours to providing the material support, in the form of books, that made possible research and teaching in the field of meddieval universities. To Heiko Oberman I am indebted for the encouragement manifested by his decision to publish my work in this series.

I wish also to thank Elissa Lewis and Robert H. Rodgers for carefully reading and criticizing the appendix. Gavin Langmuir, Howard Kaminsky, and Philip Lewis have all read the penultimate draft of my manuscript and generously shared their detailed observations. The final version has benefited much from their comments, and I recall their exertions with deep gratitude. Of course I assume full responsibility for whatever faults remain. My thanks go also to Muriel Bell, who read the final manuscript with an eye equally alert to detail and to argument.

Above all, I wish to thank my wife, JoAnne Gitlin Bernstein, a scholar in her own right. Through the vicissitudes of this prolonged effort her steadfast confidence, good judgment, scholarly experience, and reasoned patience have contributed immeasurably to its realization.

Stanford University   A.E.B.
January, 1978

CHAPTER ONE

LICENSE AND MAGISTERIUM

Historians of the medieval University of Paris have traditionally located the key to its development in the professors' struggle against the Chancellor of Notre-Dame for the self-government of their fledgling association. This view is essentially correct; without the masters' victory in this initial conflict, the university might never have evolved as it did. Yet, in this unqualified form, the theory fully describes only the period from about 1200 to 1231, and it overlooks the risks that papal support later entailed for the professors. In the first decades of the thirteenth century, the chancellor disputed the university's very right to exist and claimed to be the *judex ordinarius* of scholars, with the power to excommunicate and jail them. Following appeals to the popes, the masters obtained relief from the chancellor's monopolistic practices and unrestricted power.[1] In the second half of the thirteenth century, the masters came to recognize that the source of their protection from the chancellor could itself pose a threat to their liberty. Consequently they learned to steer a middle course in ecclesiastical politics, between the proprietary parochialism of the chancellor and the paternalism of the pope. In discussing the formation of university autonomy, therefore, we must take into account not only the struggle for immunity from the chancellor's power, but· also the professors' growing fear of unrestricted papal domination.

The best index of the professors' autonomy lies in the growth of their control over admission to their professional organization, the university; but this movement must be understood in the context of the cathedral school, and the exclusive jurisdiction over education and the teacher's license earlier conceded to episcopal authority. Gregory VII, greatest of the eleventh century's reforming popes, who sought to remove the Church from lay control and consolidate it under papal direction, made education the responsibility of each

---

[1] H. Rashdall, *The Universities of Europe in the Middle Ages*, new ed. by F. M. Powicke and A. B. Emden, eds., 3 vols. (London, 1935), I, 304-5. Especially illustrative of the extent of the chancellor's claims is *Chartularium Universitatis Parisiensis*, ed. H. Denifle & E. Châtelain, 4 vols. (Paris, 1889-97), vol. I, no. 45, pp. 102-4. (Hereafter cited as *Chart.*)

bishop, ordering in 1079 that "all bishops should cause the discipline of letters to be taught in their churches." [2] Thus the diocesan schools, which became the institutional antecedents of the early universities, had themselves received formative impetus from papal efforts to promote education in Latin Christendom. Gregory's legislation naturally obtained uneven results, but within the next century schools such as those at Laon, Reims, Orleans, Paris, and Chartres in Northern France, and Winchester, London, York, and Lincoln in England became the most advanced educational institutions in Europe, at least for the study of philosophy, literature, and theology. These schools were usually administered either by the bishop himself or by a subordinate official in the cathedral chapter, such as the archdeacon or chancellor (as at Paris). In other chapters a canon might be promoted to the office of *scholasticus*, *magister scholarum*, or *caput scholae*. Because education was an episcopal responsibility, the chancellor or school-master had a monopoly over instruction in the diocese. [3] Philippe Delhaye cites papal confirmations of the chancellor's exclusive rights dated 1139 and 1169. [4] The schoolmaster's monopoly was also central to the career of Abelard, for one of this brilliant gadfly's most resented actions was his expounding of Ezekiel in the territory of Anselm of Laon without the latter's permission. [5] However, not all schoolmasters were episcopal functionaries. Some belonged to monasteries or collegiate churches and directed schools exempted by papal privilege from episcopal jurisdiction. The school of the Canons Regular of Ste-Geneviève in Paris is an important exception of this type. [6] The

---

[2] "Ut omnes episcopi artes litterarum in suis ecclesiis docere faciant." J. D. Mansi (cont. I. B. Martin, L. Petit), *Sacrorum conciliorum nova et amplissima collectio...*, 53 vols. (Florentiae-Venetiis-Parisiis-Lipsiae, 1759-1927), XX, 50. Quoted in P. Delhaye, "L'Organisation des écoles au XIIe s.," *Traditio*, V (1947), 240.

[3] All these terms are synonymous, varying only by local custom. I shall use "schoolmaster" to refer generically to this office in any diocese, and "chancellor" to refer specifically to the delegate of the Bishop of Paris.

[4] Delhaye, p. 254; Rashdall, I, 281.

[5] This point is discussed at length by Delhaye, p. 257, but was noticed earlier by Rashdall, I, 283-84. Most information about Abelard's career derives from the "Historia Calamitatum" or first letter in the correspondence attributed to Abelard and Eloise. Serious, new challenges to the authenticity of the collection have been raised by J. Benton, "Fraud, Fiction and Borrowing in the Correspondence of Abelard and Héloïse," in *Pierre Abélard, Pierre le Vénérable; Les Courants philosophiques, littéraires et artistiques en occident au milieu du XIIe s. Abbaye de Cluny 2 au 9 juillet, 1972*, Colloques internationaux du CNRS, no. 546 (Paris, 1975), 469-506.

[6] H. Denifle, *Die Entstehung der Universitäten des Mittelalters bis 1400* (Berlin, 1885; reissue Graz, 1956), pp. 655-94.

rule nonetheless holds that to teach in the district of a particular schoolmaster, one needed his permission, or license.

As the twelfth century progressed, the growth in population, commerce, interregional communication, and urbanization that had begun in the previous century continued apace, and so, accordingly, did the need for literacy, administrative skills, jurisprudence, logic, rhetoric, and preaching (theology). The pressure to increase the number of teachers and the schoolmaster's advantage in maintaining the status quo were already in conflict. By the second quarter of the century at the latest, therefore, future teachers were paying for the license to teach in anticipation of profitable careers.[7] This was explicitly true of Paris. Around 1170-72, Pope Alexander III issued the decretal *Quanto Gallicana*, in which he ordered that the "depraved" custom of exacting a payment for the license to teach be ended and that "any competent and lettered men who may wish to teach (*regere studia litterarum*) be permitted to do so (*scholas regere*) without any molestation or exaction."[8] An early thirteenth-century gloss attributed to Vincent of Spain states that this decretal was aimed at the Chancellor of Paris, "who was accustomed to exact a mark from every teacher." [9]

Once he had paid a fee and been licensed by the schoolmaster, the new teacher would support himself from payments made by his

---

[7] G. Post, "Alexander III, the *Licentia Docendi*, and the Rise of the Universities," in *Anniversary Essays in Mediaeval History by Students of Charles Homer Haskins* (Boston and New York, 1929), p. 258. See also A. L. Gabriel, *Garlandia* (Notre Dame, Ind., 1969), ch. II, "The Cathedral Schools of Notre-Dame and the Beginning of the University of Paris," pp. 39-64.

[8] J. P. Migne, *Patrologiae cursus completus. Series latina* (hereafter PL), 221 vols., (Parisiis, 1864-68), 200, 741-42: "Dignum admiratione videtur, quod illi, qui nomen magistri (ed.: magisterii) scholarum, et dignitatem in ecclesiis vestris assumunt, sine certo pretio ecclesiasticis viris docendi alios licentiam non impendunt.... Nos quoque ... per apostolica scripta mandamus, quatenus sub anathematis interminatione prohibere curetis, ne qui dignitate illa... pro praestanda licentia docendi alios ab aliquo quidquam amodo exigere audeant vel extorquere; sed eis districte praecipiatis, ut quicunque viri idonei et litterati voluerint studia regere litterarum, eos sine molestia et exactione qualibet scholas regere patiantur." Cf. Ph. Jaffe & G. Wattenbach, eds., *Regesta Pontificum Romanorum*, 2ᵈ ed., 2 vols. (Leipzig, 1885, 1888), vol. II, no. 11925, and *Corpus Juris Canonici*, X. 5, 5, 3; ed. E. Friedberg, 2 vols. (Leipzig, 1879), II, 769, which latter gives the reading "qui nomen magistri scholarum... assumunt."

[9] Vincentius Hispanus, *Apparatus ad Compilationem Primam*, Vat. lat. 1377, in 5. 4. 3. Bernard of Parma included Vincent's observation in his gloss on the Decretals; *Gregorii Papae IX Libri V Decretalium cum Glossis* (Romae, 1582), col. 1651. This gloss was known to d'Ailly; see below, p. 173. Post ("Alexander III," p. 260, n. 23) cites the gloss as it appears in *Chart.*, I, p. 5.

students. An obvious consequence of this arrangement was that those who could not afford to pay could not study. In 1179 Alexander III sought to remove that difficulty. In his canon *Quoniam Ecclesia,* he ordered bishops to establish an ecclesiastical benefice in every diocese for a teacher who, supported by his prebend, would thus be relieved of the need to charge his students.[10] Consequently, there developed in the last quarter of the twelfth century a distinction between those teachers who were supported by their students' payments and those who were supported by the Church and taught gratis.

From the former, the schoolmaster had always exacted a fee for granting the license. The new teacher for needy students, however, would live on an ecclesiastical benefice that, in theory, was only large enough to provide him with the necessities of life. Alexander may have reasoned that such a teacher would have no excess revenue with which to pay the schoolmaster a fee. Furthermore, we know that Alexander considered the imposition of a fee for the license to teach inappropriate, verging on simony, for he had also written that "knowledge of letters is a gift of God ... therefore that which is acquired by the gift of heavenly grace ought not to be exposed for sale; but ought to be produced freely for all, so that what is written may be fulfilled: 'Freely you have received, freely give.'" (Matt. 10:8) [11] Acting on this consideration, he had already forbidden the demand of a payment in *Quanto Gallicana.* He therefore took the new opportunity to insist on the elimination of a custom that "proceeded from the root of cupidity," [12] and that endangered the effectiveness of his new institution. He provided under the penalty of deprivation of benefices [13] that "absolutely no one should exact a price for

---

[10] *Conciliorum Oecumenicorum Decreta,* ed. J. Alberigo, J. A. Dossetti, P. Joannou, et al., 3ª ed. (Bologna, 1973), p. 220: "ne pauperibus, qui parentum opibus iuvari non possunt, legendi et proficiendi opportunitas subtrahatur, per unamquamque ecclesiam cathedralem magistro, qui clericos eiusdem ecclesiae et scholares pauperes gratis doceat, competens aliquod beneficium assignetur, quo docentis necessitas sublevetur et discentibus via pateat ad doctrinam." Cf. X. 5, 5, 1; ed. E. Friedberg, II, 768-69.

[11] "... quoniam, cum donum Dei sit scientia litterarum, ... non enim debet venale exponi, quod munere gratiae coelestis acquiritur: sed gratis debet omnibus exhiberi, ut impleatur quod scriptum est: 'Gratis accepistis, gratis date.'" Migne, *PL,* vol. 200, col. 840. Jaffe no. 12096. Quoted by Post, p. 257, n. 11. Cf. the use of Matthew 10:8 by Alexander in X. 5, 5, 2 and by d'Ailly in Chapter VI below.

[12] Alexander's phrase in X. 5, 5, 3, *Quanto Gallicana;* ed. Friedberg, II, 769. Cf. Migne, *PL,* vol. 200, col. 742.

[13] "Qui autem contra hoc venire praesumpserit, ab ecclesiastico fiat beneficio alienus," X. 5, 5, 1.

the license to teach." [14] The decretal continues, "nor should [anyone] ask anything from those who teach, under the pretext of some custom." [15] Alexander further required the chancellor or *scholasticus* to grant the license to any competent person who sought it.[16]

Alexander's decretal gives no indication how the candidate's competence is to be determined. Should the chancellor make the decision alone, or should the opinion of other teachers be taken into account? None of the documents cited above refers to any participation by those actually teaching in the process of selecting new professors.[17] This silence is especially surprising because in this age of association, like all other men related by profession, from knights to guild merchants, the masters must have begun to initiate newly licensed teachers into their number sometime in the twelfth century. The honor of admission into the guild of masters was called the *magisterium* and it was awarded in a ceremony called "inception." The inception began with the new licentiate's former professor saying a blessing, then placing a ring on his finger, a beret on his head, an open book on his lap, and a kiss on both cheeks. From the book the licentiate would deliver his inaugural lecture and thus "commence" the actual exercise of his new profession in the presence of his colleagues. A banquet provided by the "inceptor" would conclude the ceremony. The new master would also give traditional gifts, usually of clothes, to his sponsor, as a token of his appreciation for the guidance he had received.[18]

The introduction of inception and the magisterium marks the

---

[14] "Pro licentia vero docendi nullus omnino pretium exigat." X. 5, 5, 1. In discussing this provision, Post confuses the *magister scholarum* or chancellor mentioned in *Quanto Gallicana* with the ordinary master (p. 261). The distinction made by Tancred's commentary on *Quoniam Ecclesia*, which Post cites (p. 263, n. 30), is between beneficed masters who may not charge fees and nonbeneficed masters who may. But this does not mean that the chancellor could charge a fee from licentiates who will themselves charge fees and not from those who will hold benefices. *Quanto Gallicana* and *Quoniam Ecclesia* are equally absolute in prohibiting exactions for the license to teach. The right of the two kinds of masters to charge their students is a different question.

[15] "... vel sub obtentu alicuius consuetudinis ab eis, qui docent, aliquid quaerat." X. 5, 5, 1.

[16] *Ibid.*: "... nec docere quemquam, qui sit idoneus, petita licentia, interdicat."

[17] In the middle ages, the terms "professor," "master," and "doctor" were synonymous. Students were called "scholars," and student-teachers "bachelors."

[18] Rashdall, I, 283-87. For an allusion to the gift of clothing see below, p. 134. Of course we do not know to what extent all the details of later inception ceremonies were included in those of the twelfth century.

emergence of the masters teaching in Paris from a mere coterie of similarly employed men into at least a primitive formal association, guild, or corporation. It is precisely upon this process of incorporation that Rashdall bases his history of the University of Paris, thus laying the foundation for an interpretation that has justifiably supported successive contributions ever since.[19] Rashdall's contention is that as the masters perceived their common interests more clearly, they followed the example already established by many communes, guilds, and religious confraternities, and modeled their association after the pattern of a corporation as described in Roman law. He traces the university's evolution toward the full status of a corporation having the privileges of a collective legal person: the right to make its own bylaws, elect its own officers, have a seal, and be represented at law.[20] In fact, throughout the early history of the university, its members described their community in terms that ultimately derive from Justinian's *Corpus Juris Civilis*: *universitas, societas, collegium*.[21] The earliest surviving term used to describe the Parisian teachers as a group is "consortium." [22]

The license and the magisterium, therefore, were two different things. The license represented a permission to teach granted by ecclesiastical authority. It certified satisfactory completion of a course of studies. It was granted by the chancellor in the name of the bishop, ultimately representing the pope, at the recommendation of the professors or at the will of the chancellor, and it always preceded the magisterium. The latter term signified membership in the guild of masters and implied both the masters' approval of the inceptor and

---

[19] Rashdall, I, 5, 292-94, and 298 *sqq.*

[20] Rashdall, I, 299-315. Rashdall's treatment is reviewed in detail by G. Post, "Parisian Masters as a Corporation, 1200-1246," *Speculum*, 9 (1934), 421-45. See also G. Leff, *Paris and Oxford Universities in the Thirteenth and Fourteenth Centuries* (New York, 1968), p. 17; J. Verger, *Les Universités au Moyen Age* (Paris, 1973), pp. 25-36; and A. B. Cobban, *The Medieval Universities* (London, 1975), pp. 81-84.

[21] Digest, III, 4, 1, and *Chart.*, vol. I, no. 256, p. 293. Cf. Rashdall, I, 164, and n. 1, where he cites Code, III, Tit. XIII. For a more thorough discussion of the *universitas* in Roman law, see R. E. Korneman, "Leges Collegiorum" in A. F. von Pauly, *Real-Enzyklopädie der klassischen Altertumswissenschaft*, ed. G. Wissowa (Stuttgart, 1894-1903), IV, 415 *sqq.*

[22] T. Walsingham, *Gesta Abbatum Monasterii Sancti Albani*, ed. Riley ("Rerum Britannicarum Medii Aevi Scriptores," no. 28, vol. 4, pt. 1; London, 1867), p. 217, where it is said of John, Abbot of St-Albans, 1195-1214, "Hic, in juventute scholarum Parisiensium frequentator assiduus, ad *electorum consortium magistrorum* meruit attingere." Also cited in *Chart.*, I, p. ix.

the newcomer's acceptance under oath of the bylaws, jurisdiction, and officers of the corporation.[23]

With the gradual evolution of the university into an autonomous corporation whose membership card was the magisterium, the masters were increasingly able to review the men licensed by the chancellor. The licentiate had to meet a series of requirements and examinations before he was accorded the magisterium. In the Faculty of Arts, after the chancellor's examination and the granting of the license, candidates for the magisterium had to wait from six months to as much as three years, depending on the period in question.[24] Much later, after the reform instituted by Urban V's two legates in 1366, licentiates in arts were not allowed to apply for the magisterium until they had returned to the schools and studied Aristotle's *Ethics* and *On Meteors*.[25] On the evening before his inaugural lecture, the candidate had to take part in the "vespers," a final, formal disputation.[26]

In the Faculty of Theology, the procedure was even more complicated. On the eve of his inception, the licentiate took part in a solemn disputation also called vespers. The next day, in the bishop's hall, the chancellor placed the master's beret upon his head (his participation being a token, perhaps, of the earliest days of university history, when the chancellor's approval alone sufficed), and a new disputation known as the *aulica* was conducted. Senior masters were expected to debate with the *aulandus* on this occasion. These two disputations took place in the spring. Hence, although technically now a master, it was only in the following autumn, by means of the *resumptio*, in which he replied to points raised in the earlier debates, that he actually began to teach.[27]

---

[23] Gradually, this oath came to be exacted even earlier than the master's inception, at the point when a student became a bachelor and began his career as a student-teacher. Although the teaching by bachelors *cursorie* and that by doctors *ordinarie* were carefully distinguished, the concept of the teaching profession here is the same as in the primitive university: no one shall actually lecture, even as a student-teacher, unless he has accepted the authority of the corporation of masters, or at least of the masters in his faculty. For the oaths sworn by bachelors about to "determine," see *Chart.*, I, nos. 201 and 501.

[24] Rashdall, I, 461, and n. 2.

[25] *Chart.*, III, no. 1319, p. 145.

[26] Rashdall, I, 461.

[27] *Ibid.*, 484-86. I have only sketched the barest essentials of the organization of teaching and testing at Paris. For more detail, see L. J. Paetow, *The Arts Course at Medieval Universities* (Urbana-Champaign, Ill., 1910); C. Thurot, *De l'Organisation de l'enseignement dans l'Université de Paris au moyen âge* (Paris-Besançon, 1850); and P. Glorieux, "L'Enseignement au moyen âge: techniques et méthodes en usage à la Faculté de Théologie de Paris au XIIIe s.," *Archives d'Histoire Doctrinale et Littéraire du Moyen Age*, XXXV (1968), esp. 141-47 and 168-74.

Nor was progress through these disputations automatic. In 1387 a Dominican Friar named Juan de Monzon asserted in his vespers that it was against the faith to say the Virgin Mary had not contracted original sin. When he defended this view in his *resumptio*, he was attacked by the Faculty of Theology and never gained admission to the university.[28]

The license, or ecclesiastical permission to teach, therefore, was no guarantee of eventual membership in the professors' guild at Paris and without the magisterium a teaching career there would be very difficult. Although the masters could not actually prevent a licentiate from lecturing, they could boycott him and threaten his students with eventual exclusion from the guild. The control that the masters gradually obtained over the admission of members to the teaching corps at Paris depended upon the magisterium's not being just a routine complement to the license. Even the early use of the term "consortium" referred specifically to a body of "chosen masters."[29]

The distinction between the license and the magisterium, therefore, depended upon an intervening autonomous exercise of deliberate review and approbation by the masters. Clearly, the magisterial honor would be debased if popes or chancellors could compel the professors to accept an outsider who had not observed the requirements outlined above or if the masters were forced to accept members who would not swear loyalty to the guild. For that reason we must consider briefly the status of a corporation within the thirteenth- and fourteenth-century Church.

The Church of the early thirteenth century has been characterized as "a federation of semi-autonomous units, a union of innumerable greater or lesser corporate bodies."[30] Evolving more and more into a corporation itself, the University of Paris had to jostle for position with collegiate entities of every kind, guilds, confraternities, religious orders, abbeys and bishoprics, all with collective rights defended by legal representatives, all jealous of their own autonomy but also seeking to elaborate the principles of their own internal structure. One of the great accomplishments of thirteenth-century jurisprudence was a clarification of corporation law that enabled the

---

[28] *Chart.*, III, nos. 1557-83. For other men who encountered difficulties in their vespers, see Glorieux, p. 170, n. 89 and p. 177, notes 123 and 127.

[29] See n. 22 above, and Rashdall, I, 305-6.

[30] B. Tierney, *Foundations of the Conciliar Theory* (Cambridge, Eng., 1955), p. 97.

courts to handle suits brought by these special groups. In Roman law, the corporation was considered comparable to a state ("ad exemplum rei publicae"),[31] but imperial jurists also anticipated the paradigm preferred by the canonists—that of a body, whose internal structure was analyzed through an analogy to the relationship of head and members.[32] This frame of reference for intracorporational disputes anthropomorphizes the more abstract relationship of the parts to the whole, with one part, the head, given primacy.

The organic conception of the corporation led many thinkers to view the Church itself as a corporate body, and to superimpose the concomitant legal constructions upon the theological metaphors that, since St. Paul, had portrayed the community of Christians as a single body. Hostiensis, a product of the law schools of Bologna, who taught in Paris around 1239 and probably began his influential *Summa* there,[33] played an important role in applying the theory of ecclesiastical corporations to the whole Church.[34]

Evolving at the same time as these ideas, the organization of the University of Paris illustrates some of the practical problems they engendered. In the struggle with the chancellor, the university had to protect its integrity and defend its autonomy from the outside. In the internal constitutional struggle between nations and faculties, Rector of Arts and Dean of Theology, the relationship of head to members was elaborated. In the conflict with the mendicants, the university had to appeal to the pope, head of the whole Church, to adjudicate the relative rights of "members" in conflict. Finally, in opposition to the pope, it contributed to the historic debate about the relationship between head and members in the Church Universal.

Because of the university's own structure, corporation law was no mere theoretical abstraction for professors of the Parisian *studium*.

---

[31] *Corpus Juris Civilis*, D. 3. 4. 1.: "... quibus autem permissum est corpus habere collegii societatisve [read: sodaliciive, Cohn], sive cuiusque alterius eorum nomine proprium est ad exemplum rei publicae habere res communes, arcam communem, et actorem sive syndicum, per quem tanquam in republica, quod communiter agi fierique oporteat, agatur fiat." Here the metaphor of the body is juxtaposed with the simile of the republic, which is used twice.

[32] A. Ehrhardt, "Das Corpus Christi und die Korporationen im spätrömischen Recht," *Zeitschrift der Savigny-stiftung für Rechtsgeschichte. Romanistische Abteilung*, LXX (1953), 299-347; LXXI (1954), 25-40. Medieval developments of this theme are traced by Otto Gierke, *Das deutsche Genossenschaftsrecht*, 4 vols. (Berlin, 1868-1913), III, 517, n. 7; 546-550.

[33] C. Lefebvre, "Hostiensis," in R. Naz, ed., *Dictionnaire du Droit Canonique*, 7 vols. (Paris, 1935-65), V, 1211-27, at cols. 1212, 1216.

[34] Tierney, p. 147.

When they conceived of the Church as a corporate body, their experience within an analogous constitution tempted them into certain simplified formulas when dealing with questions of ecclesiastical politics. Their Alma Mater was itself a federation of collegiate bodies—nations, faculties, and colleges—and masters were well-schooled in both guiding the evolution and enduring the stress of conflicting collective interests. It is no accident, therefore, that university members tended to portray the studium as a microcosm of the whole Church, and to project the premises of corporation theory onto a wide variety of problems.

The trend toward corporate cohesion within the body of teachers at Paris became identifiable as a threat to the Chancellor of Paris very early in the thirteenth century. The data of *circa* 1210 may be taken as a *terminus ante quem* for the institution of the inception and boycott, because it was about then that the chancellor began to resist it. He sought to neutralize the masters' new veto power by demanding an oath of obedience from each new licentiate, so that, if necessary, he could compel the acceptance of all whom he licensed. The implications of the oath exacted by the chancellor were clear to the masters and they appealed to papal authority, the source of the initiative that had established the cathedral schools.[35] In 1213 Innocent III forced representatives of the university and the chancellor to work out a compromise, whose terms are listed in two groups. The first contains provisions that were to be observed "for all time." The chancellor was forbidden to demand an oath of fidelity, or money, or any substitute for money, in exchange for the license. Those who had been forced to swear fidelity to him were to be released from their oaths.[36] The provisions of the second group were to remain in effect only during the tenure of the current chancellor. They are extremely important because they provided the first opening for the masters to act as advisers to the chancellor. Here it was stipulated that, when a candidate seeking the license in either theology, law (Roman law was not prohibited at Paris until 1219), or medicine is recommended by a majority of the masters of his faculty, the chancellor may not deny him the license. At the same time, the chancellor remains free to license men not recommended by the masters.[37]

---

[35] Rashdall, I, 308.

[36] *Chart.*, I, no. 16, p. 75.

[37] *Ibid.*, pp. 75-76. And similarly, but with minor exceptions, for law and medicine.

This provision, I think, was intended less to preserve the chancellor's freedom than to reserve the possibility of his awarding the license without interference from the professors to men designated by the pope. It also shows, as Denifle suggests, that even at this early stage in university history, the chancellor could act as a representative of papal authority; he was no longer a mere diocesan official.[38]

The first instance of direct papal intervention in these licensing procedures was to support the masters. In 1218, Honorius III wrote to three Parisian masters of theology, authorizing them to examine a certain Matthew of Scotland and, if they found him worthy, so to advise the chancellor, who could then no longer delay in licensing him.[39] It is clear that in this case the three masters had petitioned the pope on Matthew's behalf. But later, as a consequence of the quarrel over the mendicants, to be discussed below, the popes dispensed with examination by the masters and both the chancellor and the masters were forced to accept papal protégés. Examples become more frequent toward the end of the century. In 1288, Nicholas IV had to be very insistent to obtain a license for John de Murro, O. F. M., and was aided in his efforts by the death of the reluctant Parisian chancellor, Nicholas of Nonacuria.[40] In his struggle with Philip IV, Boniface VIII suspended the right to confer the license anywhere in France.[41] Consequently, his successor, Benedict XI, had to confer the license personally upon two candidates and authorized Chancellor Simon to license two more, Boniface VIII's prohibition notwithstanding.[42] On April 18, 1304, Benedict restored normal operations.[43] Under John XXII and his successors, the licenses granted at special papal request became so numerous that masters who, by contrast, had earned their degrees within the Parisian system came to refer to the papally sponsored ones as *licentia bullata*.[44] The pact of 1213, therefore, provided two paths to the license: first, through normal

---

[38] Denifle, *Universitäten*, pp. 686-87.
[39] *Chart.*, I, no. 27, p. 85.
[40] *Ibid.*, II, nos. 548, 550, 551.
[41] *Ibid.*, no. 636, p. 104.
[42] *Ibid.*, nos. 639, 640, 643.
[43] *Ibid.*, no. 645, pp. 113-14.
[44] E. Delaruelle, E.-R. Labande, & P. Ourliac, *L'Église au temps du Grand Schisme et de la crise conciliare (1378-1449)*, vol. XIV of A. Fliche & V. Martin, eds., *Histoire de l'Église*, 2 vols. (Paris, 1962-64), II, 471-73. Note, however, that this practice did not await the outbreak of the Great Schism. For the pontificate of John XXII, many examples may be found in *Chart.*, II, beginning with no. 748.

academic procedures and the recommendations of the masters; second, through the chancellor's direct grant of the license to "men of his own choice" at papal "request." The position of the chancellor as a papal delegate was thus established as a convenient focus for influence from Rome or Avignon.

In the Faculty of Arts, the situation was different because the number of masters was so great. The compromise of 1213 stipulated that a majority of a panel of six masters, three named by the Faculty of Arts and three by the chancellor, should be empowered to make binding recommendations to the chancellor.[45] Thus the chancellor's control over candidates nominated by masters became only indirect, for his discretionary power extended only to the appointment of his three examiners, who still had to be Masters of Arts. Nor was there any guarantee that those licensed either on the recommendation of the panel or at the chancellor's personal initiative would be allowed to incept. Thus the terms elaborated in 1213 cut deeply into the chancellor's control of the license.

The last document emanating from the appeal of 1212 was handed down by the papal legate Robert of Courzon in 1215. His decision was later referred to as *Servus crucis* after its opening words. Robert of Courzon forbade the candidates to give money while ignoring the chancellor's tendency to demand it. The penalty for succumbing to this traditional practice was to be barred from inception. Thus it was the students' conduct, rather than the chancellor's, that Courzon sought to regulate. Even in so doing, however, he recognized the existence of the masters' association by distinguishing clearly between inception and the license when he said: "let no one licensed by the chancellor or another incept if he gave him money, swore an oath, or made some other agreement." [46]

For the Faculty of Arts, Courzon specified that the candidate was to be tested publicly and "examined according to the form ... contained in the peace [of 1213] between the chancellor and the scholars." For the Faculty of Theology, the statement is more vague, saying that only those men may solemnly lecture or preach in Paris who are of proven morals and learning.[47] Presumably, the proving

---

[45] *Chart.*, I, no. 16, p. 76.

[46] *Ibid.*, no. 20, p. 79: "Nullus incipiat licentiatus a cancellario vel ab alio data ei pecunia vel fide prestita, vel alia conventione habita."

[47] *Ibid.*, pp. 78-79. For a more detailed discussion of the combination of teaching and preaching, see below, pp. 157-8.

was to be done in the old style, in front of the chancellor. Thus, in the superior faculties, the masters of theology, law, and medicine lost their power to compel acceptance of recommended candidates.

The next important development is difficult to date. To escape the chancellor's fee and oath of obedience, many masters began to move their classes from the Île de la Cité, where Notre-Dame stands, to the left bank of the Seine, where they were outside the chancellor's jurisdiction. As had Abelard when William of Champeaux would not let him teach in his district, they placed themselves under the jurisdiction of the independent Congregation of Canons Regular of Ste-Geneviève. The chancellor countered by requiring those who sought the license to swear to teach only between the two bridges, linking the Île de la Cité to the right and left banks of the Seine, that is, within his jurisdiction. The masters appealed to the pope and, in 1227, Gregory IX confirmed the Abbot of Ste-Geneviève's immunity from episcopal authority and supported his right to license masters of theology, canon law, and arts.[48] By 1255 the abbot had appointed a Chancellor of Ste-Geneviève who swore an oath before the Faculty of Arts promising to examine candidates in good faith.[49] By 1366, the cardinals delegated by Urban V, John of Blandy and Giles of Montagu, prescribed the closest cooperation between the Chancellor of Ste-Geneviève and the Faculty of Arts. According to this reform, the examiners were to be drawn from among the masters, one examiner per nation, and these were to swear an oath of office before the faculty. The cardinals provided further that if the Chancellor of Ste-Geneviève, who must be a canon, was not a Master of Arts, a subchancellor was to be chosen from among the masters of theology, so that the arts students should never be examined by a simple canon with little formal education.[50] As it turned out, candidates in arts were the only ones to frequent the Chancellor of Ste-Geneviève, but they did it in such great numbers that he was nicknamed "Chancellor of Arts." [51]

The privilege *Servus crucis* and Gregory IX's renewal of the Abbot of Ste-Geneviève's rights confirm the existence of a pattern in the early history of the University of Paris. It proceeds from initiative to reaction, subsequent scandal or outrage, and finally to an appeal to

---

[48] *Chart.*, I, no. 55, p. 111.
[49] *Ibid.*, no. 260, p. 299; Rashdall, I, 340-41.
[50] *Chart.*, III, no. 1319, p. 145.
[51] Rashdall, I, 341.

Rome. The papal resolution of the crisis provides the document from which the story must be reconstructed. Occasionally the process started in the middle, with a scandal, as it did in 1229, when a carnival riot produced an appeal to the pope backed up by the Great Dispersion, in which University members boycotted the whole city and left Paris *en masse*.[52]

Gregory IX used this occasion to reconsider the nature of the university and how it should be run. The result of his reflections is the bull of April 13, 1231, *Parens scientiarum*. Here there is a significant change. Although no mention is made of the testing mechanism in the Faculty of Arts,[53] or of the compromise of 1213, the chancellor was forced to swear that he would grant the license only to worthy candidates following consultation with the masters. Thus, although the superior faculties could no longer actually dictate their choices to him, the chancellor was obliged to align his standards more closely with the masters'. For the Faculties of Arts and Medicine, Gregory said only that the chancellor must "consult the masters," but for Theology and Canon Law, he prescribed a complex and thorough investigation into the candidates' "morals, knowledge, and eloquence, as well as their plans and potential for advancement.... Within three months of the request for the license, [the chancellor] must take testimony not only from all the masters of theology present in the city, but also from other honest and literate men from whom the truth may be known" concerning the qualifications named above, and "when the investigation is finished, in the light of what in good faith seems decent and expedient, the chancellor may grant or deny the requested license according to his own conscience." To assure the validity of the investigation, Gregory provided that henceforth, when a new master incepted, he would have to swear publicly that he would provide honest testimony concerning petitioners for the license. In turn, the chancellor should promise not to reveal any detrimental testimony.[54] Although unfavorable reports were to be kept secret, it is hard to imagine that laudatory statements about a candidate

[52] Rashdall, I, 334-38, and P. Kibre, *Scholarly Privileges in the Middle Ages* (Cambridge, Mass., 1962), 92-94.

[53] This had been prescribed by Robert of Courzon. Furthermore, once the Abbot of Ste-Geneviève could confer the license, many candidates, especially in arts, never dealt with the Chancellor of Notre-Dame. Gregory IX's silence on this subject may be explained by a desire to see what the further consequences of his 1227 decision would be.

[54] *Chart.*, I, no. 79, p. 137.

refused by the chancellor would not quickly become known to all. It seems that, in reality, under the system established by *Parens scientiarum*, the chancellor could only exceptionally refuse a candidate recommended by a large plurality of masters. Finally, in a sweeping prohibition, Gregory IX told the chancellor that he must be content with the oath to testify truthfully about candidates, and that he could not "exact from those about to be licensed an oath of obedience or other caution, nor receive any emolument or promise, for granting the license." [55] The chancellor therefore retained relatively little of the discretionary power he had enjoyed at the turn of the century.

Thus *Parens scientiarum* ends the first phase of university history, a period characterized by the masters' efforts to escape from the chancellor's jurisdiction by asserting their corporate rights and, through their legal representative at Rome, appealing to the superior authority of the pope.

At mid-century, the dispute over the introduction of the mendicant orders into the university was to modify this relationship considerably. For now the popes were seen as misguided champions of the deeply distrusted friars, while the professors and chancellor, as well as other influential prelates from Northern France, joined forces against them. Until the arrival at the Parisian studium of the Dominicans in 1217 and the Franciscans in 1220, teaching at the University of Paris had been a monopoly of the secular clergy. It would be hard to overestimate the emotion felt by the professors when confronted by rival teachers belonging to the new orders. For the mendicant mentality fostered a radical reassessment of the clerical mission, founded on such sweeping self-abnegation that a friar could actually deny he had a will of his own, on the grounds that he had nothing of "his own." Thus the followers of Francis and Dominic renounced all property and rights and devoted themselves energetically to

---

[55] *Ibid.*, p. 138: "Nec cancellarius a licentiandis magistris juramentum vel obedientiam seu aliam exiget cautionem, nec aliquod emolumentum seu promissionem recipiet pro licentia concedenda, juramento superius nominato contentus." To understand the apparently anomalous expression "a licentiandis magistris," one must recall that *Parens scientiarum* is here dealing with the superior Faculties of Theology and Canon Law. Hence the candidates would necessarily also be Masters of Arts, and the phrase refers to masters (of Arts) about to be licensed. Cf. L. Thorndike's translation of this passage in *University Records and Life in the Middle Ages* (New York, 1944), p. 38.

preaching this new conception of Christian poverty, an interpretation the seculars considered a threat to their idea of the Church and the religious life.

Nonetheless, the popes encouraged the mendicants. Just as Innocent III, Honorius III, and Gregory IX had supported the university as a place where Catholic doctrine could be refined,[56] so these popes also encouraged the spread of two orders subjected directly to themselves and sworn to obedience, who through their preaching, hopefully underscored by their example, could spread this same purified doctrine. If Honorius III in 1219 could compare the studium to the source of a flowing river of doctrine that spreads everywhere to water and fertilize the land of the Universal Church,[57] then the mendicants must be considered boatmen plying the waterways to reach the people. From the papal perspective, the integration of the mendicants into the university was a foregone conclusion. This view, nonetheless, disregards the contrasts in outlook between the two groups. Conflict was inevitable.

As both papal support and popular acceptance of their mission increased, the mendicants began to hear confession, assign penance, and assume other sacramental functions of the parish clergy—activities interpreted by bishops and priests as an invasion of their own special area of competence. Thus the university masters were not alone in their opposition to the friars, and, on this issue, professors and chancellors were able to make common cause.

In 1229 the Bishop of Paris, William of Auvergne, over the head of his chancellor, gave the license in theology to Roland of Cremona, *lector* at the Dominican studium in Paris. Roland was then succeeded by another Dominican, Hugh of St-Cher. Next, Roland's teacher, John of St-Giles, already a master in the Faculty of Theology, joined the Dominican order and kept his chair. Then another master, Alexander of Hales, was converted to the Order of Friars Minor. By 1231, three chairs out of twelve belonged to mendicants. One sign that bode ill for the future was the promotion of these men during the university's Great Dispersion. By remaining aloof from the boycott, the mendicants evinced a deeper loyalty to their orders than to the corporation of masters. In addition, their behavior

---

[56] This image comes from Gregory IX's preamble to *Parens scientiarum*, *Chart.*, I, no. 79, pp. 136-37.

[57] *Chart.*, I, no. 31, p. 88.

aroused the suspicion that they had deliberately remained in Paris to take advantage of the seculars' absence.[58]

As time passed and William of Auvergne died, suspicion of the friars remained unallayed. In 1250, Innocent IV learned the Chancellor of Paris, Aimery of Veire, was cooperating with the masters and exploiting a technicality to withhold the license from mendicants. One consequence of the friars' renunciation of will was their refusal to petition for the license to teach. Pointing to *Parens scientiarum*, Aimery was able to show that Gregory IX had referred to the "requested license," and he maintained that because the friars would not request the license, he could not award it to them. Innocent IV undercut this excuse, saying that "the act of petitioning makes no one more worthy of having the license," and therefore the chancellor henceforth is to license those whom he finds worthy according to the formula of Gregory IX, even when the scholar does not actually seek the honor.[59]

In 1252, when the mendicants again refused to support a university-ordered dispersion, the seculars resolved that thereafter no one could be admitted to the magisterium nor any bachelor begin his student-teaching unless he had sworn to observe all the university's statutes, including the rule that duly voted boycotts be honored by all.[60] When the Dominican masters refused to swear the oath, they were excluded from the university.[61] Lawsuits followed. Although the university's proctor at Rome, William of St-Amour, was able to win an initial victory from Innocent IV (*Etsi animarum*, May 10, 1254), just before the latter's death,[62] the new pope, Alexander IV, who had been cardinal protector of the Franciscans, reversed his predecessor's judgment immediately after taking office. In *Quasi lignum vitae*, issued April 14, 1255, Alexander spelled out the papal

---

[58] Rashdall, I, pp. 370-76. See also the discussion of this first phase of the masters' conflict with the mendicants in Leff, pp. 34-47 (an extremely valuable sketch); Kibre, pp. 103-17; Verger, pp. 83-91; Cobban, pp. 90-94; and P. R. McKeon, "The Status of the University of Paris as *Parens Scientiarum*: An Episode in the Development of its Autonomy," *Speculum*, 39 (1964), 651-75. None of these treatments, however, can match the new, magisterial *Guillaume de Saint-Amour et la polémique universitaire parisienne, 1250-1259* by M.-M. Dufeil (Paris: Picard, 1972), esp. pp. 146-282.

[59] *Chart.*, I, no. 191, p. 219, and n. 2.

[60] *Ibid.*, no. 219, p. 243.

[61] *Ibid.*, no. 230, p. 255.

[62] *Ibid.*, no. 240, pp. 267-70.

conception of the magisterium, a conception deeply antithetical to that of the masters.

Alexander annulled the masters' legislation against the friars and, *de potestatis plenitudine*, ordered the reinstatement of the Dominican masters to their chairs.[63] Moreover, for the future, he authorized *the chancellor* to offer the magisterial title as an enticement to those who are naturally gifted for learning and would be suited to Church government.[64] Thus the obstacles formerly placed in the way of the mendicants are to be removed "if the chancellor determines that the license . . . ought to be awarded to those who have been examined in all that ought to be considered." The things that "ought to be considered" are the criteria for the license described in *Parens scientiarum*, which Alexander quoted at length in the immediately preceding passage. Therefore his licensing procedure should theoretically include the testimony of the masters also required in that privilege, but *Quasi lignum vitae* certainly put greater stress on the chancellor's judgment ("si . . . licenciam . . . viderit . . . concedendam") than upon the survey of opinion mentioned in *Parens scientiarum*.[65]

Even more ominous for the masters was the use of "magisterium" and "license" in analogous positions in consecutive sentences, as if the two words were synonymous. *Servus crucis*, which implicitly recognized the distinction between the license and the magisterium, only authorized the chancellor to *license* men of his own choice. Here, in *Quasi lignum vitae*, the chancellor is urged to tempt potential scholars

---

[63] *Chart.*, I, no. 247, pp. 279-85, at p. 284: "Predictos insuper Predicatorum Ordinis fratres theologice facultatis magistros ad magistrorum consorcium ipsosque ac auditores eorum ad Universitatis collegium de nostre potestatis plenitudine restituentes omnino et decernentes, ad eadem consorcium et collegium a vobis in dulcedinis ubere sine difficultate admittendos."

[64] *Ibid.*, p. 283: "Et hiis, quos . . . viderit ad magisterium promovendos, sic faveat, quod capacem sensum a natura sortiti ad profectum scientie, proposito studiosis magistralis tituli premio provocentur."

[65] *Ibid.*: "Nolemus ex hoc viam aliquem vel plures habendi precludi, si cancellarius omnibus que considerari debentins pectis . . . licenciam eis viderit . . . concedendam." In interpreting *Quasi lignum*, Dufeil stresses the fact that Alexander compelled the mendicants to participate in boycotts voted in the future (p. 155). But he relegates to a footnote the fact emphasized by McKeon (p. 658) that these future boycotts must now be approved by a two-thirds majority in each faculty. Since the mendicants comprised more than a third of the Faculty of Theology (assuming their readmission according to the terms of *Quasi lignum*) they would have a veto over the university's exercise of the right to suspend lectures assured in *Parens scientiarum*. However crippling this consequence, it seems to me to derive from the more fundamental loss of the control over membership, since only members vote on boycotts. Cf. Rashdall, I, 383; Leff, p. 42.

and leaders with the title of master, thus disregarding the professors' former control over its award. When Alexander reinstated the two Dominicans, he effectively overrode the masters' traditional review of licentiates and awarded the magisterium directly. Why could his deputy do less?

The masters' struggle with Innocent IV and Alexander IV over the entry of the mendicants into the Faculty of Theology elicited an authoritative papal interpretation of the corporation's rights that was sharply opposed to their own. On the basis of *Quasi lignum vitae*, the chancellor was forced to license, almost automatically, any friar who had completed his studies under a mendicant teacher, and the masters were forced to accept as colleagues men they would never have recommended for the license. Invoking papal plenitude of power, Alexander cut through the university's corporate autonomy and appointed university professors just as he would any other officer in the Church.

To resist Alexander's imposition of unwanted members upon the corporation, the masters took an unprecedented action. They dissolved the university. Emphasizing the voluntary nature of their society and its separation from men who do not meet its standards or support its goals, the masters asserted that the disadvantages of involuntary association with the friars outweighed the advantages of unity and renounced the privileges and benefits of their consortium. The impact of this symbolic action was more dramatic in words than in practice, for the corporation did not break up into so many individuals. Instead, renouncing the common seal of the university, the masters affixed to their letter of dissolution the seals of the four nations.[66] Thus a larger confederation was separated into its constituent parts and, for a time, the university operated through the nations' representatives.

In addition to this dramatic gesture, aimed at impressing contemporary opinion, the masters sought allies outside the studium, not only defending the autonomy of their own corporation, but also taking on the role of spokesmen for all seculars who felt their rights imperiled by the pope's support of the mendicants. The most articulate opponent of Alexander IV and the friars was William of St-Amour, whose writings illustrate the rationale of seculars both inside and outside the university. His discussion is noteworthy for its assump-

---

[66] Rashdall, I, 348.

2

tions about the inviolability of parts in a corporate whole. This is ironic because the masters were complaining bitterly that the mendicants had constituted themselves a separate part working against the university as a whole.[67]

In his appeal for support from the offended prelates of France, William of St-Amour stressed the separateness of each distinct jurisdiction within the Church, whether bishopric, parish, or corporation. Just as the pope acted unjustly in imposing the friars upon the university, William argued, so he errs in allowing them to preach at will in dioceses and parishes without the permission of bishop or priest:

> We do not wish to dispute about the power of the lord pope or of the bishops, but nonetheless, according to both divine and human law, there may be only one priest in a church, otherwise the church would be not a bride but a harlot (C.21 q.2 c.4), nor should there be many heads in one church, lest it be made a monster (X. 1. 31. 14.). Moreover, since the office of preacher is chief in the rule of churches (X. 5. 7. 12.), if the lord pope grants to some people the power to preach everywhere, it must be understood to mean, "where they are invited to do so," because even bishops ought not to approach ecclesiastical matters outside their own diocese unless they have been so invited (C.9 q.2 c.9).[68]

Thus for William the Church is a honeycomb of particularisms, each with very firm boundaries that cannot be broached without violence.

The question is how to determine who is an outsider. Can a papal license to preach in someone else's parish or diocese remove the stigma? The answer for William lies in understanding the correct distribution of functions within the Church. These were laid down by Christ himself, when He chose the twelve Apostles, who prefigure the bishops, and the 72 disciples, who were succeeded by the parish priests. Later, "helpers" were instituted to aid the others. And these have been established and are regulated by fixed procedures. But if the lord pope were to allow an infinite and undetermined number of men, unknown to himself and not elected, to preach, hear confessions, and enjoin penances (which functions constitute for the most part the cure of souls), it is unlikely that he would understand these men to be general apostles or helpers able to operate anywhere

---

[67] *Chart.*, I, no. 230, p. 255.

[68] *De Periculis Novissimorum Temporum*, ed. M. Bierbaum, in *Bettelorden und Weltgeistlichkeit an der Universität Paris* (Münster-in-Westf., 1920), pp. 10-11.

in the Church uninvited or unwanted by the regularly constituted prelates, because Christ, whose vicar he is and whom he should therefore imitate, only sent out certain persons chosen individually by Him, that is, the twelve Apostles and 72 disciples.[69] Thus, the precincts of the Church were firmly established and the proper personnel sent by Christ himself to administer to the spiritual needs of residents within each district. No pope, therefore, can legitimately send newcomers to do the same work because this would trespass over an inviolable boundary and usurp a function already delegated by Christ. In a corporate body, the head cannot intervene in affairs proper to one member. Even a secular ruler knows better than to do this, for, says William, quoting Roman law, "a prince does not wish to prejudice the jurisdiction of another by his mandates (X. 1. 8. 5; 1. 31. 12; D § 16. 43. lex 8) lest, God forbid, injustice might seem to arise from the very place where rights are born (C. 8. 4. lex 6; X. 5. 1. 24)."[70] Local or corporate self-determination is therefore the ideal that William opposed to the universal authority invoked by Alexander IV. But the locality need not always be as restricted as a parish or diocese, as William's reference to a prince suggests. Indeed, as the controversy with the mendicants progressed in waves through the thirteenth century, the university masters and prelates of Northern France (Archbishop of Reims, bishops of Bourges, Amiens) worked more and more closely together. Two years after Clement IV issued *Quidam temere sentientes* in 1265, freeing friars from the need to seek the permission of the parish priest before preaching in his parish, a council at Reims declared its opposition, and Master Gérard d'Abbeville was its spokesman. After Martin IV's *Ad fructus uberes* of 1282, which gave sole supervision of the friars' pastoral work to the heads of the mendicant orders, Masters Henry of Ghent and Godfrey of Fountains cooperated with William of Mâcon, Bishop of Amiens, to seek its reversal.[71] In short, the community of dissident prelates emerging in Northern France could hardly help feeling that a King of France might be a more reliable

---

[69] *Collectiones Catholicae et Canonicae Scripturae* in Guillaume de St-Amour, *Opera* (Constance, 1632, pp. 144, sqq.) quoted in Y. M.-J. Congar, "Aspects Ecclésiologiques de la querelle entre mendiants et séculiers...," *AHDLMA*, 35 (1960), 54, n. 34a.

[70] *De Periculis*, p. 10.

[71] D. L. Douie, *The Conflict Between the Seculars and the Mendicants at the University of Paris in the Thirteenth Century* (Aquinas Society of London, Aquinas Paper no. 23; London, 1954), pp. 17-30.

defender than the pope. At the turn of the century Philip IV initiated actions designed to incorporate the French clergy into the realm, by consulting them in embryonic representative assemblies, taxing them, and seeking their approval of actions aimed against Pope Boniface VIII.[72] Earlier in his career Benedict Gaetani (who would become Pope Boniface VIII) distinguished himself by delivering the most resounding insult to the masters in a half-century of litigation over the friars. As a legate of Nicholas IV, in 1290 Gaetani was in Paris to mediate between the kings of England, France, and Aragon. When William of Mâcon approached him to consider a revocation of *Ad fructus uberes*, the legate quashed all the acts of the French synods that had opposed it and forbade any further discussion of the bull. He suspended Henry of Ghent from teaching for questioning so complete a rejection. Then, when delegates of the four faculties sought to mitigate this punishment, Benedict denounced the university and praised the mendicants as the only sound member of the Church.[73]

As pope, Boniface modified his position. In his bull of 1300, *Super cathedram*, he granted the seculars concessions they had long sought. Mendicants could preach in the streets only when it did not conflict with the parish priest's sermon and in churches only with the priest's permission. Only those friars could hear confession and assign penances who had been chosen by their order and licensed by the bishop of each diocese. Absolution of the most serious sins— incest, rape, murder, sodomy, etc.—was reserved to the bishop and could no longer be dealt with by friars. When people desired to be buried on the grounds of a friary, the mendicants would give one-quarter of the customary payment to the parish.[74]

But Boniface did not recover the loyalty of the French clergy with these moves, however welcome they were. In the historic conflict between Boniface VIII and Philip IV that was already under way, the French clergy and university generally worked together in

---

[72] K. Schleyer, *Anfänge des Gallikanismus im 13. Jht. Der Widerstand des fran-zösischen Klerus gegen die Privilegierung der Bettelorden* ("Historische Studien," Heft. 314; Berlin, 1937), pp. 56 sqq.; Rashdall, I, 395; Leff, p. 48.

[73] P. Glorieux, "Prélats français contre religieux mendiants," *Revue d'Histoire de l'Église de France*, XI (1925), 309-31; 471-95, esp. 491 sqq. The cardinal's words may be found in C.-J. Hefele, *Histoire des Conciles*, ed. H. Leclercq, vol. VI, pt. 2 (Paris, 1915), 1478-80.

[74] *Corpus Juris Canonici, Constitutiones Clementis Papae V*, 3. 7. 2.; ed. Fried-berg, II, 1162-64.

support of the king. Although Philip had to exert pressure to obtain university concurrence in the condemnation of the Templars, when Boniface excommunicated adherents of the king, three faculties out of four supported the effort to try the pope before a general council.[75]

The last half of the thirteenth century and the first decade of the fourteenth, therefore, saw the prelates and professors of Northern France forming an increasingly coherent coalition against the universal authority of popes defending the ecumenical mendicant orders. The fundamental premise that underlay their position was a belief in the distinctness and inviolability of the discrete parts of a whole, or, in less abstract terms, the autonomy of local administrative districts. They portrayed their opponents as intruders upon their territory or usurpers of their rights. As the thirteenth century came to a close, however, and the French monarchs established a more widespread and reliable civil order, there developed a new loyalty to another sub-ecumenical entity, the French, or Gallican, church. Benefiting from the attitude toward the monarch fostered by Roman law, illustrated earlier in the quotations offered by William of St-Amour, and increasingly desirous of turning the wealth of the clergy to his own ends, a king like Philip IV could pose as a defender of the local rights of the French clergy against the fiscal exactions of Roman popes. Even though the king demanded taxes too, French prelates were inclined to look to him for protection against a Roman see that, over the last half-century, had seemed to violate their rights and contravene their interests consistently. The new loyalty, called Gallicanism, may be defined, therefore, as the consciousness of a viable, particular, French church, united in defense of local rights, and protected by the King of France.[76]

Even though secular resistance to the mendicants continued throughout the second half of the thirteenth century, as early as 1255 the university professors had to acknowledge a bitter truth. Their former protectors could exercise uncomfortable pressures and even require quick compliance in return for earlier favors. It was the disappointment of this experience that identified for the professors

---

[75] *Chart.*, II, no. 634, pp. 101-2; Rashdall, I, 412.

[76] Cf. V. Martin, *Les Origines du Gallicanisme*, 2 vols. (Paris, 1939), I, 31. On p. 34, Martin maintains that the invocation of Gallican liberties around 1300 was against the lay aristocracy, "Aucun souci de se défendre contre le pape."

their papal Scylla opposite the chancellorial Charybdis. Obviously, the university could never stray too far from the papacy, whose patronage was taking more varied and subtle forms as the thirteenth century progressed, but from then on the masters' view of the popes had to be cautiously ambivalent: popes could be a source of danger as well as defense.

In one important regard, however, the conflict yielded a valuable result for the corporation. In April 1253, the masters adopted the strategem of requiring all members and all who would become members of their consortium to swear an oath to obey the statutes and officers of the university and to preserve its customs.[77] The purpose of this oath was to exclude the mendicants, for whom it would be unacceptable. In desperation, the masters had enlarged considerably upon the oath-exacting power given them by Robert of Courzon.[78] Yet this oath was to have a proud future.[79] The masters' oath had a parallel in the oath sworn by bachelors in the Faculty of Arts as early as 1252 to the effect that each would obey the rector "as long as he should profess the Faculty of Arts." [80] Around 1256 the oath was changed so that the bachelor swore to obey the rector "to whatever state [he, the bachelor] might come." [81] Obedience to the rector was specified because he was elected by the four nations and, as head of the Faculty of Arts, the largest at Paris, he was emerging as head of the whole university. The rector presided over assemblies in which university policy was made.[82] Thus the oath of obedience to the rector was a means of subjecting bachelors to the university in general. Moreover, because the Faculty of Arts was

---

[77] Rashdall, I, 378; cf. *Chart.*, I, no. 219.

[78] *Chart.*, I, no. 20, pp. 78-79: "Item facere possunt magistri et scolares, tam per se quam cum aliis obligationes et constitutiones fide vel pena vel juramento vallatas in hiis casibus, scilicet in interfectione vel mutilatione scolaris, vel in atroci injuria illata scolari, si defuerit justitia, pro taxandis pretiis hospitiorum, de habitu, de sepultura, de lectionibus et disputationibus, ita tamen, quod propter hec studium non dissolvatur aut destruatur."

[79] P. Kibre, "Academic Oaths at the University of Paris in the Middle Ages," in *Essays in Medieval Life and Thought Presented in Honor of Austin Patterson Evans*, ed. J. H. Mundy, R. W. Emery, and B. N. Nelson (New York, 1955), pp. 123-37, especially p. 126, n. 9.

[80] Rashdall, I, 328, quoting *Chart.*, I, no. 201.

[81] *Ibid.*, quoting *Chart.*, I, no. 501, which dates from *circa* 1280.

[82] The rector met sporadic challenges from the Proctor of the French nation for headship over the Faculty of Arts and from the Dean of Theology for preeminence as university spokesman; his ascendency was not certain until the end of the century. Rashdall, I, 299-332; 398-415. See also G. C. Boyce, *The English-German Nation in the University of Paris* (Bruges, 1927), 41-73.

considered preparatory for the higher faculties, it was believed that, except for the regular clergy, virtually all masters at Paris would at one time have taught in arts and sworn this oath. Later those graduates who went on to attain influential positions outside the university (nonregent masters, as opposed to regent masters, who remained in teaching positions) could be reminded of their oath as bachelors and threatened with the penalties for perjury if they opposed either the rector or the university's interests. The chancellor previously had tried to exact an oath of this sort, but it was considered a kind of "price for the license" and prohibited in 1213. Papal tolerance of the rector's new oath gave the masters a decided advantage, all the greater because many future chancellors would have been masters of arts and sworn this oath. Future chancellors would thus find themselves bound by old ties of loyalty to the rector.[83]

An instance of the importance attached to oaths in the medieval University of Paris will illustrate the balanced opposition between masters and chancellor that had evolved by the 1260's, a balance upon which the daily functioning of the studium was poised. The dispute concerns nothing less than the master's oath stipulated in *Parens scientiarum* to testify truthfully concerning the competence of the bachelors seeking the license. Apparently, it was not until after he became chancellor that Stephen Tempier decided in 1264 that he wanted to teach in the Faculty of Theology. When the time came for his inception, however, he refused, as chancellor, to swear the oath. The jurisdiction of the faculty and, by implication, the university, over its masters was at stake. The masters recognized that the chancellor's case was special, and agreed that he would not actually have to testify—since he would in effect be testifying to himself—as long as he would swear the oath. Reluctant to establish the precedent of a chancellor's swearing more than his oath of office to the faculty, Stephen continued to refuse. The theologians then denied him entry to the faculty and, because Stephen's reprisals almost brought the studium to a standstill, they appealed to the pope. On May 26, 1264, Urban IV supported the compromise solution offered by the masters. This meant that if Stephen wanted to teach, he would have to swear the oath, but since he was chancellor, he would

---

[83] Pierre d'Ailly and the Faculty of Arts employed the same tactic against the chancellor, John Blanchard, in 1385-86. See below, pp. 74, 167. For other examples, see Kibre, "Academic Oaths."

be excused from the obligation to testify. Again, papal authority supported the corporate nature of the university, exempting not even the chancellor should he wish to share in its functions and privileges. At the same time, both the pope and the masters recognized the special role of the chancellor as grantor of the license.[84]

A summary of the cumulative constitutional effect of papal judgments concerning the University of Paris shows that, during the thirteenth century, the masters acquired considerable control over the selection of teachers at the chancellor's expense. In the Faculty of Arts, students could avoid him altogether by going to Ste-Geneviève, whose chancellor swore an oath of office to the faculty and whose examiners were named by the masters. Those in arts who wished to be examined at Notre-Dame came before a panel of six, three named by the masters and three by the chancellor, according to the compromise formula of 1213. The chancellor was bound by the majority of this panel. In the superior faculties, he was bound by *Parens scientiarum*, whose restrictive impact upon the chancellor has been discussed.

But one aspect of papal legislation limited the masters as much as the chancellor, namely the provisions for papally initiated awards of the license (the licentia bullata) and, exceptionally, the magisterium. This danger was hidden from the beginning in the fact that both masters and chancellors had appealed to a papal authority that all contenders had implicitly acknowledged to be superior. One clause in the compromise of 1213 seemed to give the chancellor the liberty to license men of his own choosing, regardless of the masters. But as early as 1218 the chancellor saw himself compelled to license a man named by the pope conditional upon the masters' approval. As a result of *Quasi lignum vitae*, in 1255 both masters and chancellor saw their relative positions weakened when Alexander IV insisted that a candidate's merit should outweigh the interest of either participant in the rivalry, and thus the discretion of both was limited. Nonetheless, the cumulative loss over the century was greater for the chancellor.

Not even Nicholas IV's conferral in 1292 of the *ius ubique docendi*, which gave the license granted at Paris universal validity, could enhance the prestige of the chancellor, who was by then locked into

---

[84] *Chart.*, I, no. 396, p. 438. It was my student Frank Marmolejo who noticed how neatly the institutional history of the university is encapsulated in this single document.

a network of allegiances and jurisdictions (seen in the quarrel with Stephen Tempier) that routinized his function and subjected it to the greater ends of either the university or the pope. Nicholas IV's own document reveals how greatly the masters had limited the impact of their rival's former authority. First, it should be mentioned that this privilege was granted to Paris more than half a century after it had been granted to the University of Toulouse in 1233,[85] and eight months after its conferral upon the University of Bologna.[86] Second, the document is addressed not to the chancellor, but to the "university of masters and students of Paris." Finally, the privilege is not bestowed upon the license or the man who confers it, but upon those who attain it, "so that whoever is examined and approved ... from now on has the unrestricted right to teach in any place outside [Paris] without public or private examination or approbation or any other new formality."[87] The *ius ubique docendi* exalts the Parisian license in theory, but in recognition of the training received there rather than the prestige of the chancellor.

At the same time, the masters had also lost some of the control they had accumulated through *Parens scientiarum*, and it was reduced by the very agency that earlier had granted it to them. In the popes' defense of the mendicants, especially Alexander IV's *Quasi lignum vitae*, they buttressed the independent approach to the license and compelled the Faculty of Theology to award the magisterium to friars trained outside the university. The masters' actions in opposition showed that they were not standing alone, and that the corporation's spokesmen advanced not only their own interests, but those of an important segment of the French higher clergy as well.

If the pope could impose his conception of the magisterium, appointing masters against the will of the university, he could send intruders to preach in another's parish. With the recognition of this common interest, the masters and Northern French prelates together learned to take a more independent look at Roman primacy and the theories describing the authority of a corporation's head over its members.

---

[85] Rashdall, II, 165-66. For a general discussion of the *ius ubique docendi*, see Cobban, pp. 27-35.

[86] *Chart.*, I, 402, n. 1.

[87] *Chart.*, II, no. 578, p. 55.

CHAPTER TWO

THE UNIVERSITY OF PARIS AND THE GREAT SCHISM

The year 1378 saw the University of Paris at the height if its prestige. Its service to the kings of France had been proved during the reign of Philip IV, when the university supported his position against Boniface VIII and participated, however reluctantly, in the trial of the Templars.[1] Philip exempted the university masters from taxation, thus preserving for them a privilege that once had been enjoyed by the entire clergy.[2] The distinction between the clergy in general and the university clerics was also recognized during the Estates General of 1358 in the aftermath of the uprising led by Etienne Marcel, when the university masters were called upon to serve as intermediaries between court and Estates.[3] In recognition, Charles V, who as dauphin had seen his authority severely challenged during this crisis, awarded the university the right to style itself the Eldest Daughter of the King, that is, an institution naturally entitled to his paternal protection.[4] French kings also exempted students from guard duty on the walls of Paris, and from the jurisdiction of civil magistrates. They allowed students from foreign countries, even countries at war with France, to circulate freely in the kingdom.[5] This privilege contributed to the university's international standing and cosmopolitan membership.

The university was supported by the aristocracy as well as the king, and material evidence of this favor was increasingly evident during the first three-quarters of the fourteenth century. Thirty-four colleges had been established between 1300 and 1370, as compared to only eighteen during the preceding history of the university.[6] (The first, the Collège des Dix-huit, founded in 1180, was older than the university itself.) The masters' relations with the papacy were not

---

[1] P. Kibre, *Scholarly Privileges in the Middle Ages* (Cambridge, Mass., 1962), p. 132; on Templars, *Chartularium Universitatis Parisiensis*, ed. H. Denifle and E. Châtelain, 4 vols. (Paris, 1889-97), II, nos. 664, 666. (Hereafter cited as *Chart.*)

[2] *Ibid.*, no. 644, p. 113.

[3] H. Rashdall, *The Universities of Europe in the Middle Ages*, new ed. by F. M. Powicke and A. B. Emden, 3 vols. (London, 1935), I, 542.

[4] *Ibid.*

[5] *Chart.*, II, no. 601; Kibre, *Scholarly Privileges*, 86, 129-30, 133, *et passim*.

[6] Rashdall, I, 536-39. These statistics exclude mendicant houses.

nearly as stormy as might have been anticipated after the encounter with Boniface VIII. True, in 1333-34, the Faculty of Theology, backed by King Philip VI, forced Pope John XXII to accept its correction of his pronouncement on the Beatific Vision,[7] but in the long run, the popes at Avignon were the beneficiaries and not the objects of the masters' zeal for detecting errors. During the first three-quarters of the century, they censured those of Marguerite Porette (1310),[8] Peter John Olivi (1318-20),[9] Meister Eckhardt (1329),[10] William of Ockham (1339),[11] Nicholas of Autrecourt (1346),[12] John of Mirecourt (1347),[13] and the flagellants (1349),[14] and searched out translations of the condemned *Defensor Pacis* (1375).[15]

In return for such cooperation, the popes offered their strong, general support of the university. They showered the university and its masters with resounding compliments in the prefaces to documents. Consider this relatively measured tribute by Urban VI:

> As we intently focus our vision upon the splendid Parisian studium, which, like a river of Paradise, more copiously than others carries salutary dogma throughout the world; and, with the eyes of the inner man, we delightedly admire its beaming in the House of the Lord like a star amidst the firmament; we judge it fitting and proper that we should unflaggingly pursue those things through which that studium and its university may continue to flourish in its present state, and be preserved from harm and happily augmented by an unbroken succession of gains.[16]

Although such commendations cost them little, the popes also provided more tangible evidence of their favor in the form of ecclesiastical offices. In the fourteenth century it became customary for the popes to award preferential treatment to the collective petition for benefices (the *rotulus beneficiandorum*) compiled by the University of Paris on behalf of its members. By this time, papal support of the Parisian studium was such that masters at rival institutions like Oxford sought to catch up in one stroke by petitioning the pope for "the same favors." [17]

---

[7] *Chart.*, III, nos. 970-87, pp. 414-42.
[8] *Ibid.*, II, no. 681, p. 143.
[9] *Ibid.*, no. 790, pp. 238-39.
[10] *Ibid.*, no. 888, p. 322.
[11] *Ibid.*, III, no. 1023, p. 485.
[12] *Ibid.*, II, no. 1124, p. 576.
[13] *Ibid.*, no. 1147, pp. 610-14.
[14] *Ibid.*, no. 1176, p. 655.
[15] *Ibid.*, III, no. 1406, pp. 223-27. See also Kibre, *Scholarly Privileges*, pp. 259-60.
[16] *Chart.*, III, no. 1318, p. 142.
[17] *Ibid.*, II, no. 818, p. 269, quoted by Rashdall, I, 555, n. 1. See the whole discussion in Rashdall, I, 555-58 and Kibre, *Scholarly Privileges*, p. 230 *et seq.*

Although the Parisian masters' close cooperation with the popes brought them exceptional benefits, their dependence upon papal patronage also carried risks, for any crisis that affected the papacy could ramify to the university as well. The Great Schism of the Latin Church was to provide an agonizing instance of that possibility. Ironically enough, considering subsequent difficulties, the masters entered the crisis unawares because at first no one outside Rome suspected any irregularity in the election of Urban VI. The professors routinely recognized him as pope in May 1378,[18] and in June sent their traditional inaugural rotulus to Rome.[19] The masters at Paris only began to learn of the irregularities accompanying Urban's election later that summer.[20]

Indeed, the election of Urban VI on April 8, 1378, had not proceeded normally. The Roman populace invaded the conclave to demand a Roman, or at least an Italian, pope.[21] After resorting to such expedients as a mock coronation of Cardinal Tibaldeschi to quiet the mob, the cardinals selected a leading administrator in Gregory XI's curia, the Archbishop of Bari, Bartholomew Prignano. Despite their having passed over all their own number and despite the disorder, they insisted they had elected a true pope. They so notified the crowned heads of Europe and the handful of cardinals who had remained in Avignon. They participated routinely in the coronation of Urban VI and petitioned him for benefices.

Within a few weeks, however, the cardinals regretted their choice. The new pope had decided to reform the cardinal college, a goal the cardinals might not have unswervingly opposed had Urban not initiated his program with such tactless disregard for practices that had become customary at the gorgeous Avignon court. After weeks of recriminations, the cardinals withdrew from Rome to Anagni. There, on August 9, they declared the election of Urban VI void under the terms of the bull, *Ubi periculum majus*, which stated that violence or fear of violence at a conclave invalidates an election, and declared Bartholomew an intruder. On September 20, to replace Urban they elected Robert of Geneva, one of their own number,

---

[18] *Chart.*, III, no. 1605, p. 552.

[19] *Ibid.*, no. 1606, p. 553.

[20] *Ibid.*, no. 1608, pp. 553-55.

[21] Similar disorders occurred in Carpentras during the election of John XXII. G. Mollat, *Les Papes d'Avignon*, 9e ed. (Paris, 1949), pp. 38-40.

who took the name Clement VII. Thus began a schism in the Latin Church that was to last almost forty years.[22]

No account of the impact of the schism on the studium can neglect the position of the French kings Charles V and Charles VI and their entourage. For, in addition to being heavily indebted to the kings for the numerous privileges named above, Parisian scholars felt a growing attachment to the kings of France as defenders of the Church in general and of the university in particular. More concretely, the royal palace was separated from the university only by the River Seine. Consequently, the royal attitude toward the possibility of restoring the papacy to Avignon would be a factor of considerable importance to the professors.

The kings of France had benefited considerably from the uninterrupted line of French popes who ruled in Avignon from 1309 to 1376.[23] Although the majority of these popes were not from the areas of Northern France where devotion to the king was strongest, three-quarters of the cardinals they named held episcopal sees in France and fifteen in the northern provinces of Reims (six), Rouen (three), and Sens (six), as compared to 47 from more southern provinces (including Bourges), out of a total of 81 cardinals elected in the 65-year period.[24] Clement VI (1342-52) himself is an excellent example of a man born in the south who nonetheless held important northern benefices, for he had been Abbot of Fécamp, Bishop of Arras, Archbishop of Sens, and Archbishop of Rouen before his elevation to the cardinalate by Benedict XII.[25] Guy de Boulogne, Giles Aycelin, Jean de Dormans, Etienne de Poissy, and Jean de la Grange were other cardinals closely linked to the King of France.[26] Connections of this sort at the papal curia help explain the favorable treatment received by the Valois rulers. The popes lent them money and

---

[22] N. Valois, *La France et le grand schisme d'occident*, 4 vols. (Paris, 1896-1902), I, 8-83; E. Delaruelle, E.-R. Labande, P. Ourliac, *L'Église au temps du Grand Schisme et de la crise conciliaire (1378-1449)*, vol. XIV of A. Fliche & V. Martin, eds., *Histoire de l'Église*, 2 vols. (Paris, 1962-64), I, 3-17.

[23] At that time, Avignon was not part of France. The town itself was held by the Angevin princes of Naples, deeply involved in Iberian and Italian politics and vassals of the Holy See. It formed an enclave in the Comptat-Venaissin, which belonged to the popes. Mollat, p. 18.

[24] B. Guillemain, *La Cour pontificale d'Avignon (1309-1376)* (Bibliothèque des Écoles Françaises d'Athènes et de Rome, fasc. 101; Paris, 1962), pp. 204-6.

[25] Mollat, p. 84, n. 2.

[26] Guillemain, pp. 197-201. For Jean de la Grange in particular, see Valois, I, 69-70. For Guy de Boulogne, Guillemain, pp. 249-51. See also *ibid.*, p. 194.

allowed them to keep a percentage of ecclesiastical taxes such as the tenths, annates, and caritative subsidies. Tenths levied for the crusade that was in a way the chimerical basis of the Avignon papacy itself [27] were collected by the kings of France and spent on other projects. Charles V in particular was permitted to collect the annates from the whole of France except Languedoc from 1369 to 1377. Besides extending these fiscal courtesies, the Avignon popes supported French foreign policy, most importantly by helping to reserve the hand of the heiress of Flanders for Philip of Burgundy, thus excluding Edmund, son of Edward III of England.[28] Small wonder that Charles V energetically opposed all suggestions that Urban V or Gregory XI return to Rome!

The proximity of the papal court was also important to Louis of Anjou, the king's brother and Lieutenant for Languedoc. Louis was allied by marriage to Gian Galeazzo Visconti, Duke of Milan. He had extensive interests in Provence. In 1375 he bought the Kingdom of Majorca from the *infante* James's sister, Isabella, even though it was claimed by Peter of Aragon. This brother of Charles V had lived in 1374 and 1375 at Avignon. Obviously, a prince with such extensive Mediterranean interests would only reluctantly forego convenient access to the sympathetic popes, who could wield greater influence in southern Europe than any French prince alone.[29]

We have no evidence that after Gregory XI actually restored the papacy to Rome in January 1377, Charles V or any of his house ever proposed to effect the prompt return of the papacy to Avignon. But when Gregory died in March 1378, and news from the conclave that had elected Urban VI began to reach Paris, Charles surely grasped its import. In August he promised money and military aid to guarantee the safety of the dissident cardinals as they weighed the consequences of renouncing Urban.[30] The biggest question was whether to proceed to elect a new pope, and if so, whom. With the Church in this confused situation, on September 11 Charles convened a meeting of his clergy, attended by prelates, canonists, and theologians, to raise the question of what policy he should adopt. At this point Clement VII had not

---

[27] Mollat, p. 16; 397.

[28] *Ibid.*, p. 395.

[29] Mollat, 432; Valois, I, 145-46; F. Lehoux, *Jean de France, Duc de Berri*, 4 vols. (Paris, 1966-68), I, 384, and n. 4; M. de Boüard, *Les Origines des guerres d'Italie: La France et l'Italie au temps du grand schisme d'occident* (Paris, 1936), p. 9.

[30] Valois, I, 97.

yet been elected, and Charles's support of the cardinals was not known in France. The conflict to be resolved was between Urban and his cardinals, not between two popes. The clerics felt that a general council was the only competent authority, but they were divided over who could call it. The pope? The cardinals? Or, in greater conformity with the Gallican tradition begun when Philip IV had tried to discipline Boniface VIII, should the secular princes have the prelates of their territories hold a council to which the cardinals could summon Urban to defend his case? Because of these doubts and their knowledge that the cardinals had at least temporarily accepted Urban, those present at the council advised the king not to take sides, but to await further reports and clarifications.[31] At the first intimation of trouble, therefore, the clergy's first response was to invoke a general council. It was not a solution peculiar to the university.[32]

The king, however, wanted a freer hand for his diplomacy than a council would permit, and he suggested sending royal emissaries to mediate between the conflicting parties.[33] At this juncture the council broke down, with each member suggesting a different person as messenger, questioning whether he should be an Italian, a cleric, or a prince, and what his qualifications should be. Independent intervention was the course chosen by the king, though hardly impartial mediation. In mid-October, before he could have known that the cardinals had

---

[31] "Offizielle Antwortsnote der königlichen Regierung Frankreichs an die Gesandten der Kardinäle zu Anagni, September 1378," Appendix I (hereafter "Antwortsnote"), in F. P. Bliemetzrieder, *Literarische Polemik zu Beginn des Grossen abendländischen Schismas* (Publikationen des Österreichischen Historischen Instituts in Rom), Band I (Wien und Leipzig, 1910), pp. 1-2: "Non videtur ... ad alium iudicem recurrendum nisi ad consilium generale, quod concilium est in hac disceptacione verus iudex. Quis autem haberet in hoc casu concilium congregare? Diverse sentencie super hoc affuerunt. Dicebant aliqui, quod illum, qui erat in possessione papatus. Et sic ipsi concilio causam suam posset submittere. Alii, quod ad dominos cardinales . . . alii, quod principes seculares super hoc concordes in unum quilibet prelatos sue iurisdiccionis sive districtus facerent adunari pro predicto concilio celebrando, ad quod domini cardinales haberent Baren[sem] evocare, et sic ibidem possent proponere contra eum ea que nunc proponunt." Cf. Valois, I, 104.

[32] Recourse to a council had already been suggested, in July, by the three Italian cardinals who were reluctant to abandon Urban VI. Valois, I, 76.

[33] "Antwortsnote," p. 2: "Ad quod communi consilio extitit promulgatum, quod . . . fuerunt multe vie aperte. Primo, quod per dominum nostrum regem mitterentur nuncii Baren[si] et dominis cardinalibus, qui interponerent partes suas ad concordiam inter partes."

elected another pope or who he was—unless he knew their intentions before the election of September 20—Charles V sent two letters, one addressed to the dissidents as a group, the other to Robert of Geneva himself. Only the postelection reply from Clement VII to Charles is known; it is filled with expressions of the deepest gratitude to the French king for his letters, which were "so pleasant and so consoling." His cousin in Paris, Clement wrote, would be "quite particularly our right arm and that of the Holy Church of God." [34] Charles therefore ignored the advice of his clergy and moved toward a goal whose pursuit was predictable even before the council was called. Money for the "food and defense" of the cardinals, when the only source of danger was the still "rightful" pope, was not as neutral an action as these terms disingenuously suggest. Opportunistically, Charles nourished the rift that had developed between Urban and his electors, and he probably approved, if he did not nominate, the cardinal chosen as his replacement. Once installed in office, Clement VII moved his entourage back to Avignon.

After the cardinals elected his cousin, it was the king's responsibility to secure the loyalty of his subjects. To that end he called yet another council of the French clergy. Mindful of the council's hesitancy in September, he selected the delegates more carefully this time, and obtained their unanimous recommendation of adherence to Clement VII.[35] With the kingdom committed, what position would the university take? By the end of the year the king had asked to know its members' decision. On January 8, 1379, they requested that he "not force them to decide so quickly for one or the other of the contenders, since it is difficult for his Daughter to come to agreement in this matter, because she is not yet sufficiently informed concerning the truth and because many members say that it would be better to force both contenders to renounce the papacy and for the university to remain neutral." [36] This desire for neutrality reflects the division in the university, whose membership comprised subjects of all the sovereigns in Europe, many of whom had not yet taken sides or had opposed the action of Charles V. Nonetheless, by May the Faculties

---

[34] Valois, I, 107.

[35] *Ibid.*, 114. For further consequences of the "political" view of the schism and its manipulation by the French "crown", see H. Kaminsky, "The Politics of France's Subtraction of Obedience...", *Proceedings of the American Philosophical Society*, vol. 115, no. 5 (1971), pp. 366-97.

[36] *Chart.*, III, no. 1616, p. 561.

of Canon Law, Medicine, and Theology, as well as the French and
Norman nations, had decided they could individually recognize
Clement and send separate petitions for benefices.[37] The university
had to abandon any effort to send a common rotulus. Charles, however,
insisted:

> in order to remove all schism and division, ... considering the deci-
> sion of the Faculties of Theology, Law, and Medicine and the nations
> of France and Normandy, who make up a majority of your number,
> to support Clement VII, and in order to remove all schism and divi-
> sion in the Holy Church as well as in our kingdom, we request that
> you masters deliberate collectively, together, in your congregation,
> and incline yourselves toward the party of our Holy Father, Pope
> Clement.[38]

In the general congregation called to act upon this letter, the
voting reflected the national origins of the masters in each unit.
Groups whose members were principally French, the Faculties of
Law and Medicine and the French and Norman nations, declared
their adherence to Clement VII. Those whose members were drawn
principally from abroad, the Picard and English nations, urged the
university to maintain its earlier position of neutrality. The Faculty
of Theology also declared for Clement, but only after its members
explicitly stated that their decision was based on the reports available
to them,[39] and that it was not a unanimous but only a majority
decision.[40] The division within the university ran so deep that despite
a tradition that three faculties could bind the whole corporation, in
this case the largest faculty, that of arts, and the most prestigious,
that of theology, being divided, no decision could be taken.[41] By
the end of the month, however, in deference to the royal insistence,

---

[37] The university was divided into four faculties: theology, law, medicine,
and arts, which last, by far the largest, was subdivided into the French, Norman,
Picard, and English or English-German nations. See Denifle's résumé of the data
on the relevant deliberations of these bodies, *Chart.*, III., nos. 1619-20, pp. 562-63.
Cf. his note, p. 561, and Valois, I, 137. For the nation system, see P. Kibre, *The
Nations in the Medieval Universities* (Cambridge, Mass., 1948), 15-28, 65-115.

[38] *Chart.*, III, no. 1623, p. 564.

[39] *Ibid.*, no. 1624, p. 570: "... attentis attestationibus et assercionibus tam
verbothenus quam scriptothenus nobis factis per... dominos cardinales Parisius
presentes... et plures alios fidedignos..."

[40] *Ibid.*: "secundum majorem partem magistrorum tunc Parisius in congre-
gatione super hoc facta presentium..."

[41] *Ibid.*, pp. 570-71.

3

university spokesmen announced their recognition of Clement VII to the king.[42]

Clement and Charles were not the only ones who believed that the best way to avoid schism was to enforce partisanship. Even members of the Faculty of Law were embarrassed by their colleague Ameilh du Breuil, who wanted to debate the facts of the disputed papal election and thus threatened to bring the displeasure of King Charles and Pope Clement upon the faculty. They therefore asked Clement VII to impose silence upon their neutralist colleague.[43]

Charles V's attitude began to change the following year, toward the end of his life. He willingly accepted the dedication of Conrad of Gelnhausen's treatise *Epistola Concordie*, in which a general council was recommended as the only authority capable of ending the schism,[44] and on his deathbed Charles expressed willingness to obey the decision of a general council if one could resolve the question.[45]

This final royal declaration encouraged the university to explore further the implications of convoking a general council to end the schism. Already, two German theologians of the Paris faculty, Henry Langenstein of Hesse and Conrad of Gelnhausen, had recommended this path. Moreover, a general council was the solution most consistent with the university's traditional method of problem-solving, which relied on open discussion. Henry of Hesse held that such freedom characterized not only the University of Paris in particular, but Christianity in general, and he contrasted Christian freedom of debate to the putative authoritarianism of Islam. We can imagine the hope the king's new attitude inspired in the heart of a sincere scholastic with a deep trust in the virtue of dialectic. "Does not the exercise of disputation always detect concealed falsehood and fraud in the end?" Henry asked in the *Epistola Pacis*.[46] Open debate would allow the Picard and English nations and the divided Faculty of Theology

---

[42] Valois, I, 139. Cf. *Chart.*, III, no. 1624, p. 572, n. 31.

[43] *Chart.*, III, no. 1431, p. 249 and Valois, I, 140.

[44] Valois, I, 324-25.

[45] *Ibid.*, 327. He died on September 16, 1380.

[46] Henricus Langenstein de Hesse, *Epistola Pacis*, excerpts in C. E. Du Boulay, *Historia Universitatis Parisiensis*, 6 vols. (Paris, 1665-73), at IV, 577, lines 3-9: "Nunquid disputationis iuge exercitium latentem falsitatem et fraudem detegit ultimate? Nunquid hoc est quare Machometus de his quae suae legis sunt, disputare prohibuit, scutis [lege: sciens] crebrum et diligens disputationis ventilabrum fraudem et falsitatem diu latere non posse, unde maximum est veritatis Christianae legis Iudicium, quod in ea omnia acerrimo disputationis examine iam a mille annis exposita sunt et quotidie exponuntur, et tamen perseverant."

to participate more fully in determining university policy and thus mitigate the effects of the schism upon the supranational studium. In addition, the convocation of a council might enable the university's leaders to play a greater role in actually resolving the schism. To Europe's foremost theologians and leading canonists, a convocation was far superior to leaving so vital a matter in the hands of princes, for whom the resort to force was a constant temptation. And whichever of the two popes was adjudicated the winner, or anyone named in their stead by the council, would have an opportunity to appreciate and later to reward the role played by key supporters among the masters.[47] In short, a council would give the university and its leaders a European status analogous to its advisory function in the capital of the French king.

Enthusiasm for the "way of a council" allowed the university members to take their first collective action for forty months (on January 6, 1379, they had asked for time and neutrality) when, on May 20, 1381, they declared that a general council was the best way to end the schism and committed themselves to work unceasingly for such a convocation.[48]

The hope inspired by Charles V's final declaration blinded them to the already visible signs that the late king's tolerant attitude no longer prevailed in France. Indeed, three days before their own decision, the Bishop of Paris, Aimery of Maignac, announced from the steps of Notre-Dame that "All those who do not believe that the Cardinal of Geneva [Clement VII] is the true pope are heretics and schismatics." [49] Instead of the anticipated peaceable debate, political discourse in Paris had been reduced to an "either-or" proposition.

After the death of Charles V on September 16, 1380, power devolved upon his three brothers, with Louis of Anjou acting as regent for the twelve-year-old Charles VI and John of Berri and Philip of Burgundy directing the royal council and administration. These princes quarreled among themselves and competed for access to crown revenues to support their own, differing interests. Politically, Berri was the simplest of the three. His interests were generally limited to France,

---

[47] Thus d'Ailly and Giles Deschamps were named cardinals by John XXIII on June 6, 1411, two years after the Council of Pisa deposed Gregory XII and Benedict XIII (June 15, 1409). L. Salembier, *Le Cardinal Pierre d'Ailly* (Tourcoing, 1932), pp. 252, 261.

[48] *Chart.*, III, no. 1637, p. 582.

[49] Valois, I, 342.

and were concentrated particularly on the lands of his appanage—Berri, Auvergne, and Poitou—and on his lieutenancy of Languedoc, which made him the king's commander in southern France against the English.[50] Philip of Burgundy's major concern was assuring that nothing interfered with his inheritance of Flanders upon the death of his father-in-law, Louis de Male. Desirous of consolidating his present and expected territories in a column from the Jura to the Channel, his focus was mostly eastward and northward.[51] Louis d'Anjou's interests, like John de Berri's, were concentrated in the south, but, as we have seen, as far south as Milan and Majorca. Louis had been one of Clement VII's earliest backers in the French court. In return Clement had negotiated an arrangement whereby Joanna of Naples, another of his early backers, adopted Louis as her heir, thereby giving Louis a solid opportunity to restore the Angevin kingdom in Italy. As regent and president of the council, Anjou had control of the young king's person, and his decisions were authoritative.

The differences in the princes' interests can be illustrated dramatically. In January 1382 Louis of Anjou surrendered his advantageous position in Paris because Clement VII had urged him to recover Joanna of Naples's lands from the Urbanist claimant to her succession, Charles of Durrazzo. To finance his expedition Anjou had Charles VI grant him substantial sums, which could be raised only by reimposing the indirect taxes on consumables that Charles V had abolished. While Louis was heading southward two things happened. First the northern cities, led by Rouen on February 24 and Paris on March 1, rose in revolt because of the taxes.[52] Second, on May 3, Louis de Male, Count of Flanders, pursued by Philip van Arteweld, leader of the urban rebellion in the Low Countries, appealed to his lord, the King of France, for help.[53] Charles VI stalled, but with Anjou gone, Burgundy, who had led the effort to repress the urban rebellions of northern France, was now in control. He persuaded Berri and Charles that military intervention was necessary to save Flanders. The French victory at Roosebecke on November 27, 1382, advanced the interests of the crown in many respects, but it is certainly worth noting that it also helped to preserve the unity of a territory that Philip had

---

[50] Lehoux, I, 320.
[51] *Ibid.*, II, 68.
[52] Valois, I, 145-94; II, 333-34; Lehoux, II, 58-59.
[53] Lehoux, II, 60.

every expectation of inheriting.[54] The events of 1382 show, therefore, that the crown's resources were being apportioned by whichever uncle was best able to manipulate the king.

The following year, Burgundy prevailed in another debate. In early April the royal council had to decide between answering an urgent call for help from Louis of Anjou in Italy and responding to rumors of an English landing near Calais. Louis's envoys went away empty-handed.[55] Thus, although Louis of Anjou lived until September 1384,[56] his influence in Paris ended with his departure in early 1382. Nonetheless, because Ghent was Urbanist and the campaign to Flanders had become something of a crusade, the young king and the princes around him, who had all participated, were not disposed to retreat from Anjou's hard line in the schism, even though Avignon was less central to their personal interests. Until the court had reason to alter the policy established by Louis of Anjou, the university would have to forego a general council. The masters lacked our advantage of hindsight, however, and to discover how they gradually learned this lesson, we must return to the moment in May 1381 when, having just dedicated themselves to effecting the convocation of a general council, they sent Pierre d'Ailly to tell the brothers of Charles V to what degree the university was in conformity with the late king's desires. On this one occasion the Duke of Anjou tolerated the suggestion of a general council.[57] A conciliar solution implied neutrality between the popes, however, and such a policy threatened Louis's dynastic interests. Therefore by mid-June 1381, a strict adherence to Clement was being enforced in Paris. When Master John Rousse of Abbeville went to reiterate the university's position before the court, Louis refused to let him speak. The following night, on Louis's orders, he was dragged from his bed and thrown into prison. To obtain his release the university masters had to pledge themselves to silence on the subject of the papal election and especially on that of a general council.[58]

The regent's firmness brought the royal court into accord with the policy initiated long before, by Clement VII himself. As early as December 18, 1378, Clement had sent John de Cros, the Cardinal of

---

[54] *Ibid.*, 68-73.
[55] *Ibid.*, 75-76.
[56] *Ibid.*, 115; Valois, I, 360.
[57] Valois, I, 339-41.
[58] *Ibid.*, 341-44.

Limoges, to Paris with extensive powers to "search for any ecclesiastical persons, secular as well as regular, believing Bartholomew to be the Roman pontiff, and to seize his messengers, those receiving his letters and mandates, and those obeying him; to take away the benefices of any persons adhering to the infamous Bartholomew, unless they desist from their adherence; to absolve those who have obtained favors from Bartholomew after they have renounced them," [59] and to restore similar "favors" on the part of the "true" pope. Clement renewed this effort on June 6, 1381, when he ordered the Bishop of Paris, Aimery of Maignac, to strip the benefices from all those in his diocese suspected of adhering to Urban VI. As a concession to the masters, the pope added that if a professor should be deprived of his privileges, the bishop should confer the vacant benefice upon another member of the university.[60]

In a Paris dominated by Louis of Anjou and scrutinized by Aimery of Maignac, the death of Chancellor John de Calore on March 3, 1381, provided the pope a welcome opportunity to place an official of similar convictions in the chancellorship.[61] De Calore had been appointed by Gregory XI and hence was acknowledged by all university members. But those who could not accept the legitimacy of Clement VII would have to reject anyone appointed by him to a position of even nominal authority over the studium. On July 15, 1381, Clement named as Chancellor of Notre-Dame John Blanchard, a close associate of at least five years, and a man on whose zealous loyalty he could depend.[62] A review of Blanchard's career to this point will explain the depth of his attachment to Clement, for even before the disputed election of 1378, Robert of Geneva had served Blanchard as a most opportunely placed patron.

Born in the diocese of Tournai in 1322 or before, Blanchard was a Master of Arts in the Picard nation no later than 1343, when he had already begun to study theology at the Sorbonne under Elias de Corsone.[63] Blanchard was ordained a priest by the time he was named

[59] Valois, I, 346, n. 3.
[60] *Chart.*, III, no. 1638, p. 582.
[61] Note that on May 26, 1381, Clement first appointed Nicholas of St-Saturnin as Chancellor of Notre-Dame, but this cardinal never occupied the position and Clement then turned to Blanchard. *Chart.*, III, no. 1460; Valois, I, 345.
[62] *Chart.*, III, no. 1461.
[63] *Chart.*, II, no. 1165, p. 644 and p. 646, n. 23. His birthdate is inferred from the minimum age for a Master of Arts, twenty-one years. *Chart.*, I, no. 20, p. 78.

canon of St-John the Evangelist at Liége, May 22, 1349.[64] He could have become a Master of Theology by 1357,[65] but he is not mentioned with this title until 1362, when he is also listed as a canon at Notre-Dame of Paris.[66] In the interval between his degrees, John divided his attention between a number of benefices in the Low Countries and service of the Count of Flanders. In 1355, Innocent VI ordered him to surrender the parish church of St-Giles of Wacs, in the diocese of Tournai, before accepting two-fifths of the collegiate rectorship at St-Michael's of Ghent.[67] His first known service of a secular prince came in October 1361, when he was sent by Louis de Male as an ambassador to Joanna of Brabant.[68]

It was probably in Flanders that Blanchard met Guy of Boulogne, son of Mary of Flanders, cousin of Louis de Male, and Cardinal Bishop of Porto, who was heavily engaged during this period in the diplomacy surrounding the marriage of Marguerite, the heiress of Flanders.[69] On February 18, 1363, the cardinal petitioned the newly crowned Urban V, seeking the deanship and a canonry with prebend at the cathedral church, St-Lambert's of Liége, for "his chaplain and tablemate," John Blanchard.[70] At this time, John surrendered his rectorship at St-Michael's of Ghent and his canonry at Notre-Dame of Paris,[71] but he retained until 1378, at least, his post at St-Pharahild's of Ghent and another one at Deynze.[72] One may surmise from this information that, even after earning his doctorate in theology, John organized his career much as before, basing himself in the Low Countries, where he combined an active role at the court of Flanders

---

[64] *Chart.*, II, p. 646, n. 23.

[65] The minimum age was thirty-five years. *Chart.*, I, p. 79.

[66] *Chart.*, II, p. 646, n. 23 and Du Boulay, IV, 606, 9-10.

[67] G. Despy, *Lettres d'Innocent VI* (Analecta Vaticano-Belgica, première série, XVII; Bruxelles, 1953), no. 987, pp. 334-35. This series title will be abbreviated as "AVB," and first series assumed.

[68] F. Quicke, *Les Pays-Bas à la veille de la période bourguignonne* (Paris et Bruxelles, 1947), p. 69, n. 29.

[69] Stephanus Baluzius (Baluze), *Vitae Paparum Avenionensium*, ed. G. Mollat, 4 vols. (Paris, 1914-27), II, 344 and G. Mollat, "Gui de Boulogne," in *Dictionnaire d'histoire et de géographie ecclésiastique* (Paris, 1938), X, 105. See also T. G. Voigtel, *Geneologische Tabellen zur Erläuterung der europäischen Staatengeschichte* (Halle, 1811), Tab. 54.

[70] A. Fierens, *Suppliques d'Urbain V*, AVB, VII (Bruxelles, 1924), no. 652.

[71] *Ibid.*, nos. 651, 653.

[72] K. Hanquet, *Documents relatifs au Grand Schisme*, I: *Suppliques de Clément VII (1378-1379)*, AVB, VIII (Bruxelles, 1924), no. 2.

with the administration of his important benefices in Liége and Ghent.[73]

As Dean of Liége, however, Blanchard's relationship with the rest of the chapter was stormy, eventually producing a protracted lawsuit.[74] The affidavits sworn by the contesting parties yield revealing glimpses of the future Chancellor of Paris. John believed the rest of the chapter to be withholding rights that belonged to him by virtue of his deanship, and he complained that he could not win the slightest acknowledgment of the least privilege with the greatest effort.[75] His resentment of this "insubordination" led him to ill-tempered punitive measures, and then, in defense of his actions, to exaggerated claims of jurisdiction and authority. When accused of appropriating money and movables belonging to canons, he claimed the sole right to assign the cathedral's chapels and the prebends of the chapter's *mensa*. He demanded civil and criminal jurisdiction over canons and chaplains, and claimed the sole right to authorize prolonged absences, to approve the wills of canons and chaplains, and to distribute their movables if they died intestate.[76] The canons then accused John of not performing all the endowed masses for which he had received payment, and of not paying the penalty for failure to execute these obligations.[77] Finally, the canons insisted that Blanchard swear the required oath to observe the chapter's constitution as reformed in 1354 by Innocent VI.[78] Bridling at this "affront," Blanchard submitted the whole quarrel to arbitration.

On September 28, 1368, the mediators decided very heavily in the chapter's favor. They agreed, in essence, that Blanchard had sought to appropriate rights and decisions that traditionally had been exercised by deans and canons jointly. They ordered him to restore all that he had wrongfully taken, and to cease his efforts to enlarge the prerogatives of his office beyond those enjoyed by his predecessors.[79] Although Blanchard had initiated the litigation, he would not

---

[73] For his service to Louis de Male, see C. Tihon, *Lettres de Grégoire XI*, I, AVB, XI (Bruxelles, 1958), p. 277, n. 2.

[74] *Cartulaire de l'Église Saint-Lambert de Liége*, S. Bormans et E. Schoolmeesters, eds., 6 vols. (Bruxelles, 1893-1933), IV, no. 1648.

[75] *Ibid.*, Blanchard's article 9.

[76] *Ibid.*, the chapter's articles 1-7.

[77] *Ibid.*, arts. 16 and 17.

[78] *Ibid.*, Blanchard's art. 8, the chapter's art. 2. For Innocent VI's initiative see *ibid.*, no. 1423, pp. 185-86.

[79] *Ibid.*, pp. 463-69, esp. p. 467.

accept the panel's judgment. He appealed to Urban V and left Liége, even at the risk of sacrificing the revenues from his benefices there.[80] Nonetheless, he could still rely on his prebend at St-Pharahild's of Ghent, and apparently he was still welcome at the court of Louis de Male.

The affair at St-Lambert's conveys an impression of Blanchard as a strongly self-centered man, convinced of his own superiority, and easily persuaded that his personal circumstances justified actions he would condemn in others. The pique and exasperation communicated by the two sides' depositions even through the dry, legal formulations, indicate that this was not a conflict of two reasonable yet differing interpretations of institutional functions, but rather a clash of personality between an offended group of men and a person they considered intolerable. We must conclude, therefore, that Blanchard was by temperament ill-equipped to consider the viewpoints of others and too inflexible to compromise when a dispute arose.

After his humiliation at Liége, it seems that Blanchard concentrated his attention on the court of Flanders, for it was at the request of Louis de Male that in 1371 Gregory XI agreed to let John receive the fruits of the deanship of Liége in absentia for two years.[81] On May 12, 1372, again through the intercession of Cardinal Guy of Boulogne, John received permission to add another prebend to his holdings in Liége.[82] Almost a year later, Louis interceded again on John's behalf for renewal of the two-year license to receive his revenues in absentia. Louis referred to Blanchard as "cappellanus et familiaris et continuus commensalis noster." [83]

Gregory XI then decided to utilize Blanchard's function as a "consiliarius" of the Count of Flanders and, on February 17, 1374, he asked Blanchard to use his good offices to help the papal nuncio, Peter Masuyer, compose a quarrel between the count and the Archbishop of Reims.[84] This task was apparently too much for the un-

---

[80] For evidence that the suit continued as late as 1376 see Tihon, *Lettres de Grégoire XI*, III, AVB, XXV (Bruxelles, 1964), no. 3625, and for even later developments, K. Hanquet and U. Berlière, *Documents relatifs au Grand Schisme*, II: *Lettres de Clément VII (1378-1379)*, AVB, XII (Bruxelles, 1930), nos. 782-83.

[81] Tihon, I, no. 654.

[82] Tihon, *Lettres de Grégoire XI*, II, AVB, XX (Bruxelles, 1961), no. 1598.

[83] *Ibid.*, no. 2104.

[84] *Ibid.*, no. 2510, where Blanchard is called a "consiliarius" of Louis. See also L. Mirot and H. Jassemin, *Lettres secrètes et curiales du Pape Grégoire XI (1370-1378) relatives à la France* ("Bibliothèque des Écoles Françaises d'Athènes et Rome,"

diplomatic Blanchard. Within a year, on February 20, 1375, the pope wrote Louis to reassure him that, despite what certain envious men might say, John had always been a faithful defender of Louis's honor and that never, in the pope's presence, had John spoken ill of the count. Gregory concluded by urging Louis to allow John to re-enter his service.[85] The pope's intervention was not successful. It would seem therefore that Blanchard had been cut adrift in the upper-middle ranks of the late medieval administrative world, for the Cardinal of Boulogne had died on November 25, 1373,[86] and John had not been welcome at the court of Flanders since early 1375. The contrary is true, however, since Blanchard's services were "inherited" by Guy's nephew,[87] Robert, Cardinal of Geneva and future Clement VII. On May 22, 1376, John's new patron petitioned Gregory XI on behalf of his "chaplain and tablemate," for the biennial permission to receive the revenues of his Liége benefices in absentia.[88]

The schism of 1378 could hardly have caused Blanchard a moment's hesitation. Robert of Geneva had not used his uncle's death in 1373 as an excuse to drop the impolitic Blanchard. Instead he supported him consistently through troubles with the Count of Flanders and the chapter of Liége. It may even have been through Robert's intervention that Gregory XI excommunicated Blanchard's opponents at St-Lambert.[89] Blanchard's close relationship to the future Clement VII may also be inferred from his being given precedence in a rotulus submitted by all the "oratores" of the new pope immediately after the election.[90] On the fourth day of his pontificate, November 3, 1378, Clement responded to this petition by reserving John a canonry with prebend at Cambrai, a chapter over which he himself had

---

3ᵉ série, vol. VIII, pt. 1; Paris, 1935), no. 1499. The first notice of Gregory's intervention is dated Nov. 27, 1373, and is addressed to Louis de Male (*ibid.*, no. 1455). Other documents relevant to these negotiations are nos. 1456, 1458, 1497, 1498, and 1527.

[85] Tihon, III, no. 3054.

[86] C. Eubel, *Hierarchia Catholica Medii Aevi*, rev. ed. (Regensberg, 1913), p. 18.

[87] G. Mollat, "Clément VII," *Dictionnaire d'histoire et de géographie ecclésiastique*, XII (Paris, 1953), 1162.

[88] Tihon, III, no. 3625. This document also refers to the lawsuit at Avignon between Blanchard and the Liége chapter, whose prosecution made it impossible for him to remain in that city.

[89] *Cartulaire St-Lambert*, IV, no. 1735.

[90] Hanquet, no. 2.

presided as bishop until Gregory XI made him cardinal.[91] Blanchard, in turn, was prompt in his service of the new pope. In July 1379 John undertook, with two other emissaries, a trip to London to advance Clement's cause before a skeptical English court.[92] In the years that followed, Clement did much to ensure Blanchard's continued adherence. On February 1, 1379, Clement reserved him a canonry with prebend at Tournai.[93] On January 29, 1381, John was given the treasurership of Cambrai as well.[94] Finally, on July 15, 1381, Clement VII named John Blanchard Chancellor of Notre-Dame.[95] By 1381, the cities of Ghent and Liége had turned Urbanist, and Blanchard's benefices there had probably become untenable.[96] But this only served to dramatize Clement's attentive patronage, since the Avignon pope replaced with benefices to the west those that John had lost to the east.[97]

The appointment to the Chancellorship of Paris of so heavily indebted a client of Clement VII as John Blanchard made life in Paris still more difficult for non-Clementine scholars. The threat of jail or the deprivation of benefices was bad enough, but now licenses were to be conferred by a representative of Clement! Nor was aversion to the Clementine chancellor born of ethical considerations alone. Reflecting the mood of his letter to Bishop Aimery, Clement VII had instructed his new chancellor to see that no one suspected of obeying

---

[91] Hanquet et Berlière, no. 24. Robert of Geneva had been Bishop of Cambrai from October 11, 1368, to May 30, 1371 (Eubel, p. 21, 160). John took possession of his canonry at Cambrai on August 16, 1379. (Cambrai, Bibliothèque Municipale, ms. 1046, f. 135ᵛ.) D'Ailly was not directly associated with the Cambrai chapter until May 27, 1391, when he was made archdeacon. A. J. G. Le Glay *Recherches sur l'Église métropolitaine de Cambrai* (Paris, 1825), p. 118. Thus d'Ailly does not seem to have had any contact with Blanchard at Cambrai prior to the conflict between them to be described below.

[92] Valois, I, 243, n. 3.

[93] Hanquet, no. 2321. We know that Blanchard actually obtained this benefice from his own statement to that effect. Du Boulay, IV, 606, 29-32.

[94] U. Berlière, *Suppliques d'Innocent VI*, AVB, V (Bruxelles, 1911), 32, n. l. K. Hanquet, *Documents relatifs au Grand Schisme*, III: *Suppliques et lettres de Clément VII (1379-94)*, AVB, XII (Bruxelles, 1934), no. 236. *Chart.*, III, no. 1461, p. 301, n. 2.

[95] See above, n. 62.

[96] See below, pp. 137-40. On Sept. 17, 1379, Urban VI revoked the excommunications obtained by Blanchard against the Liége chapter. *Cartulaire St-Lambert*, IV, no. 1735. These are also mentioned in Hanquet and Berlière, nos. 782-83. Cf. Valois, I, 276, n. 3.

[97] Blanchard explained the progress this way himself. Du Boulay, IV, 606, 15-21, quoted below, p. 135, n. 87.

Urban VI receive the magisterium.[98] Surely continued residence under so rigidly Clementine a regime would render Urbanists suspect even to their own pope; and Urban had announced the removal from benefices of all Clementines at least as early as April 6, 1380.[99] Starting in the summer of 1381, men whose homelands were Urbanist felt obliged to leave Paris, a migration with severe consequences for the university. Many of these men not only failed to return, but also played important roles in founding, or more solidly establishing, rival universities in Urbanist lands. Thus Henry of Langenstein went to Vienna, Henry Totting of Oyta to Prague, and Conrad of Gelnhausen became the first Chancellor of Heidelberg. Gerald Kalkar, only a Bachelor of Theology, went to Cologne with at least 32 masters of arts, and Marsilius of Inghen, a former rector, went to Heidelberg.[100] Three prominent French scholars went to Rome to support Urban: the doctor of both laws, John Giles; John Rousse of Abbeville, after he got out of prison; and William of Salvarville, a theologian and canon of Notre-Dame, after Clement VII removed him as a schismatic from his canonry.[101] Pierre d'Ailly, the theologian who first proposed a council to the royal court, although a Frenchman and a Clementine, retired from the capital to a canonry at Noyon, after creating a further impression with his biting, pro-council *Epistola Leviathan*.[102] The restlessness within the Faculty of Theology

---

[98] *Chart.*, III, no. 1511, p. 358, art. 45: "Bartholomiste [a Bartholomeo Prignano, Urbano VI] non debebant admitti ad talem gradum, quodque super hoc habebat bullas a domino nostro papa." Valois, I, 345, states that Blanchard was not to grant the license to those suspected of adhering to Urban, but the context from which his quotation is taken makes it clear that the magisterium was intended. The problem focuses on the antecedent of the word *talem*, and since the person in question, John Duchêne, had already been licensed, it must have been the magisterium that was to be withheld. On the other hand, since Alexander IV's *Quasi lignum vitae* (1255), popes had considered the two terms virtually synonymous. For more on Clement's prohibition see below, pp. 106-112.

[99] E. von Ottenthal, *Regulae Cancellariae Apostolicae. Die päpstlichen Kanzleiregeln von Johannes XXII. bis Nikolaus V* (Innsbruck, 1888; reissue, Aalen, 1968), p. 49. Cited in H. Nelis, "La Collation des bénéfices ecclésiastiques en Belgique sous Clement VII (1378-1394)," *Revue d'Histoire Ecclésiastique*, 28 (1932), 47-48.

[100] Valois, I, 366-67. For an extensive study of the Eastern European scholars' exodus from Paris and an original evaluation of its significance, see Zenon Kaluza, " 'Translatio studii,' Kryzys Uniwerytetu Paryskiego w latach 1380-1400 i jego skutki," [" 'Translatio studii,' The Crisis of the University of Paris and its Effects."] *Studia Mediewistyczne* (Wroclaw, Poland), 15 (1974), 71-108.

[101] *Chart.*, III, no. 1446, p. 290n., and no. 1640, p. 583.

[102] *Ibid.*, 358. The invective is published by P. Tschackert, *Peter von Ailly* (Gotha, 1877), App. V. Although d'Ailly attacks opponents of the council with

did not pass unnoticed by Clement VII, who, on October 26, 1381, wrote the theologians saying that he expected only the highest standards of conduct from them and did not want to be disappointed.[103]

After the Faculty of Theology, the body within the university that contained men of the most diverse national backgrounds was probably the English-German nation of the Faculty of Arts, where masters from the British Isles and the countries east of the Rhine were associated. Many of these masters came from countries whose sovereigns adhered to Urban VI. In fact, the only notable exception were the Scots, whose king, Robert II, in alliance with Charles V, had declared for Clement. It is especially fortunate therefore that the English nation's records from this tumultuous period have survived. The *Liber Procuratorum* contains, among other things, the minutes of all the meetings of the nation until May 1383, where there is a gap until 1392.[104] One can therefore follow in detail the various tactics adopted by these men, most of them presumably Urbanists, to maintain normal academic routine under the eye of the new Clementine Chancellor of Notre-Dame.

The Faculty of Arts, we recall, differed from the others in that its bachelors could receive the license either from the Chancellor of Notre-Dame or from that of Ste-Geneviève, also called the Chancellor of Arts because he awarded degrees almost exclusively to candidates from that faculty.[105] When the schism began, the latter chancellor, Josse Ghisil, was an Urbanist, and so the first expedient was simply to receive the license from him. In late 1381, however, in accordance with Clement's letter to Bishop Aimery, Ghisil was removed from office and replaced by a Clementine, whose name is not known; thus this avenue was henceforth closed. In their meeting of November 13, the English masters feigned surprise that a new chancellor should be named even though the old one had fulfilled his duties so well.[106]

Other documents reveal, however, that the façade of innocence was intended to cover a deliberate act of nonrecognition: that is, the English masters were refusing to admit the legitimacy of the new

---

trenchant irony, he does not expound systematically his reasons for favoring it. For his claim to priority in advocating a council before the court, see Tschackert, App. XII, pp. 36-37, and Valois, I, 340-41.

[103] *Chart.*, III, no. 1643, pp. 585-86.

[104] *Auctarium Chartularii Universitatis Parisiensis*, ed. H. Denifle and E. Châtelain (6 vols. to date; Paris, 1937-   ), I, 660. (Hereafter cited as *Auct.*)

[105] See above, p. 13.

[106] *Auct.*, I, 613, 47.

chancellor, just as they denied that of the papal authority behind his appointment. In the Parlement of Paris, the dissidents later denied that Josse Ghisil had been removed from office.[107] Indeed the parlement's record of the complaint brought against them describes the extent to which the masters not only of the English-German nation, but of the Norman and Picard nations too, acted on this conviction. According to the legatine reform of 1366, the Abbot of Ste-Geneviève was to choose four examiners, one from each nation, and a subchancellor, who were to take oaths of office before the whole Faculty of Arts. In an action that evinces a remarkable independence of Avignon, the three nations, whose members had homelands bordering on the Channel and had supplied the greatest number of exiles, set up an alternative examination system. The Urbanists in the English nation elected a subchancellor from among their own members. Then the three dissident nations each elected one examiner, thus constituting a panel that proceeded to administer examinations and recommend bachelors to Josse Ghisil, who licensed them as if he had never been removed from office.[108]

This secession illustrates on a smaller scale the kind of geographical divisions that underlay Gallicanism. The English-German nation was immune to it, but the Picard and Norman nations were inspired by different aspects of the Gallican tradition. The latter two nations, though not Urbanist, were sufficiently independent of a papal authority already weakened by the schism to draw strength from the Gallican tradition of local self-determination, and resisted papal measures they regarded as harmful to the studium. The French nation, with its membership from the Ile-de-France, conformed to the other major theme of Gallicanism and aligned with the king. It is the particularist aspect of Gallicanism that explains why, at first, the Faculty of Arts did not divide simply along French-English lines. After the parlement's adverse decision, however, that configuration was imposed upon them.

The Abbot of Ste-Geneviève could not tolerate so flagrant a disregard of his prerogatives for long; by February 25, he had refused to assign a room for the extralegal examinations.[109] On March 24, the rebellious nations resolved that if the abbot did not cooperate, they

---

[107] *Chart.*, III, no. 1468, p. 309.
[108] *Ibid.*, pp. 305-6. The English nation selected its examiner on Jan. 13. *Auct.*, I, 614, 33.
[109] *Auct.*, I, 615, 35.

would proceed against him in the Parlement of Paris.[110] The plaintiffs
in the trial at the parlement, however, were the Abbot of Ste-Geneviève and the French nation, whose masters were incensed by the
Urbanists' fiction. They complained that the other nations did not
recognize the new Chancellor of Arts and had ignored their nation
in choosing examiners, and that the false subchancellor and examiners
had never sworn the oath of office to the whole faculty.[111] For these
reasons, when finally asked to name an examiner to work under Josse
Ghisil, the French masters refused.

The masters of the other three nations argued that this refusal
constituted an unwarranted impediment to the normal functioning
of the faculty, and sought to have it overruled by the parlement. They
maintained that the French masters should yield because the other
three nations formed a majority of the faculty.[112] This last point is of
special interest since it was only because of an unusual invocation of
majority rule, under pressure from Charles V, that the university had
declared for Clement VII in May 1379.[113] Ironically, the masters of
the French nation now denied that the three others could bind them
and, in a statement redolent with provincial particularism, contended
that the nation was justified in proceeding against the others because
university members have a deeper kind of loyalty to their nation than
to their faculty, or, as they put it, "scholars have been accustomed to
swearing loyalty to their nations earlier than to the faculty." [114] On
July 12, the parlement declared the Abbot of Ste-Geneviève to have
the right to appoint and remove chancellors of arts as he saw fit.[115]

Clement VII did not remain inactive while the masters of the
English nation ignored him. On February 28 of the same year, 1382,
he issued a bull, proclaimed to the Faculty of Arts on April 15, in
which he annulled all the examinations passed and licenses awarded
during the conflict and abrogated the appointments of both old and
new chancellors, subchancellors, and examiners. To replace them,
he delegated John Maubert and Armand Jausserand, from the French
nation, to preside over a special congregation of the arts faculty
called for the purpose.[116] The new examiners were chosen on
April 25.[117]

---

[110] *Ibid.*, 618, 36.   [111] *Chart.*, III, no. 1468, pp. 305-8.
[112] *Ibid.*, p. 307.   [113] See above, pp. 35-6.
[114] *Chart.*, III, no. 1468, p. 308.   [115] *Ibid.*, p. 309.
[116] Valois, I, 346, n. 3, for the text of the bull, and *Chart.*, III, no. 1468, p. 308,
for the delegates' names.
[117] Valois, I, 347.

Clement VII's strong action and the adverse decision of the parlement were sufficient to deprive the English nation of the other two nations' support, but its masters had been preparing to endure the crisis on their own. As early as April 1, they had resolved not to accept as a master any bachelor who had accepted the license from Blanchard. The treasurer would refuse their payments, the proctor would not take their oaths, and the beadles would not summon them to meetings.[118] Then, on the same day as the papal delegates presided over the replacement of the officers at Ste-Geneviève, the masters of the English nation renewed their resolution to acknowledge only Josse Ghisil as Chancellor of Arts and to leave everything unchanged, "as if no bull had come and nothing had been done by the delegates." [119] This decision was taken unanimously except for one master, who did not actually "dissent" but "differed somewhat" and did not "expressly consent," namely Arnold Ghise of Arnhem, whom the papal delegates had just named the new examiner.[120]

We learn only indirectly that the nation actually carried out its threat to exclude any bachelor licensed by Blanchard. Without ever mentioning a previous formal act, the *Liber Procuratorum* relates that, on May 7, Henry Poelman, also of Arnhem, came to a congregation of the nation, although not summoned by the beadle. When the masters asked him three times to leave and referred to the nation's recent resolution, he replied that the nation had "deliberated fatuously." Because of his insistence, the masters were forced to admit that his presence would not obstruct the conduct of their business.[121] In August, after a similar scene in June,[122] the masters finally decided that Henry could attend meetings on a regular basis provided he would swear not to reveal the proceedings.[123] Why this concession was made is not clear. The majority of the nation was not yet Clementine, although the parlement's decision of July 12 must have discouraged many.

Nonetheless, when the question of sending a rotulus beneficiandorum to Clement was raised in the university congregation of October 12, the English nation resumed its recalcitrant posture, with only two masters favoring the action.[124] Still, it was the issue of the rotulus that dramatized the effects of the English nation's

---

[118] *Auct.*, I, 619, 4.
[120] *Ibid.*, 4 and 27.
[122] *Ibid.*, 622, 43.
[124] *Ibid.*, 628, 33.

[119] *Ibid.*, 620, 7.
[121] *Ibid.*
[123] *Ibid.*, 624, 37 - 625, 14.

independence and forced the university to discipline the errant masters. On November 8 two members of the nation, William Trebron and Arnold Ghise, complained to a university congregation that those men licensed at Notre-Dame and denied admission in the English nation would not be listed in the current rotulus.[125] Then, in the nation's independent meeting, William and Arnold conducted what must be described as a separate Clementine caucus, for they invited a master from the French nation to attend, referred to him as proctor, and caused him to count the votes. The real proctor left in protest.[126] The next day, November 9, the Rector of the Faculty of Arts asserted his leadership and summoned the masters of the English nation to appear before a university congregation called for the tenth. At that time, with the full authority of the university behind him, the rector insisted that the nation accept all its members licensed by John Blanchard at Notre-Dame, and admit them to all its acts and prerogatives. He advised the nation to deliberate separately before acting, but warned that if there were opposition, he would proceed as against schismatics and rebels. After their private meeting, the proctor reported that his colleagues did not wish to rebel against the university.[127] On November 16, the masters of the English nation made full submission. Although they were able to avoid the humiliation of actually inscribing the names of the licentiates before the entire assembly, the proctor apologized for rejecting the oaths of the licentiates and the treasurer did the same for refusing their payments.[128]

The efforts of the Clementine masters to ensure that all those licensed by Blanchard were included in the rotulus to be sent to Avignon spelled the end of the English nation's experiment in independence. The collective strength of the university in petitioning for benefices was too important to the other masters to risk compromising it by respecting the Urbanist scruples of a weakening majority in one nation. Once the new Clementines licensed by Blanchard and reluctantly admitted into the nation were received, the plurality probably shifted in favor of outright adherence to Clement. On November 28, the day after the princes of France crushed the "Urbanists" at Roosebecke, the English nation participated

---

[125] *Ibid.*, 630, 17 and 27.
[126] *Ibid.*, 30.
[127] *Ibid.*, 632, 4.
[128] *Ibid.*, 632, 42 - 633, 17.

without incident in a congregation of the faculty called to receive the oaths of office of the new examiners and subchancellor of Ste-Geneviève, who had been appointed under the eyes of Clement VII's delegates.[129] An eloquent testimony to the shift of forces in the nation was the election, with only two dissenting votes, of the old renegade Henry Poelman as proctor on January 13, 1383.[130] Once in office, Poelman sought to have the "fatuous deliberations" of 1381 expunged from the *Liber Procuratorum*.[131] There was some hesitation concerning such an act, but after setting up a committee to consider the question,[132] the nation agreed to censor its own records on February 17.[133]

Meanwhile, with Henry Poelman as proctor, the English nation agreed in the university assembly of February 3 that the corporation should compose a new declaration of fidelity to Clement that would be appended to the collective petition for benefices. Poelman stipulated, however, that the letter should be sealed with the seal of the university and that the English nation's seal should not be used.[134] The nation's ambivalence is further revealed in repeated references to the difficulty of inducing members to register themselves in the rotulus and in the final, forlorn admission that "few men from our nation were enrolled." [135] Most had left Paris. On February 26, 1383, the rotulus and the attached declaration of allegiance were finally sent.[136]

The painful submission of the English nation to the Faculty of Arts, the departure of many theologians, the fear of physical violence or loss of benefices—all these are reflections of the anxiety experienced by university members in the early years of the Great Schism. The price of relative security was adherence to Clement VII and silence on the question of a general council. We have seen how Henry of Langenstein favored recourse to an open forum in which debate guided by reason could ferret out the truth. It is also clear that a council promised a larger role for academics than any other means of ending the schism. The appeal to a general council by university members, therefore, was not merely sentimental. Their conciliarism embraced

---

[129] *Auct.*, I, 637, 12. Valois, I, 364-66, shows the coincidence of military victory in Flanders and repression of civil insurrection in Paris with the submission of the English nation.

[130] *Auct.*, I, 644.

[132] *Ibid.*, 646, 38.

[134] *Ibid.*, 646, 7.

[136] *Chart.*, III, nos. 1650-52.

[131] *Ibid.*, 645, 44.

[133] *Ibid.*, 651, 14.

[135] *Ibid.*, 659, 9.

calculations of corporate interest, political judgments, and theoretical considerations elaborated in response to changes within the Church over the previous century. This is not the place to review the development of these ideas by Thomas Aquinas, John of Paris, William of Ockham, Marsilius of Padua, and the glossers of canon law.[137] It is nonetheless desirable to set forth here the principal theses of conciliarism to provide a standard against which critical thinking about the Church and the role of theologians and the university may be measured. Therefore, I offer the following paraphrase of the earliest comprehensive and most influential exposition of the expediency and legality of the conciliarist solution to the schism, Conrad of Gelnhausen's *Epistola Concordie*.[138] The German theologian's treatise was written at Paris in May 1380 and dedicated to Charles V.[139] Conrad began in a straightforward manner with three arguments to support his principal conclusion: "A general council can and ought to be called ... to remedy the present schism." [140]

1. Councils have been convoked for lesser matters, as we see in both the Old and New Testaments,[141] and therefore one can even more urgently be called in the present case.[142] The present schism is an extremely grave matter of the faith, in that it touches the head of the faith on earth, many heresies are sprouting, and, in the Church, a bicephalous monster (the papacy) is exposed.[143] Each pope preaches that the other is a manifest heretic and that he publicly teaches heretical errors.[144] Just as the four great councils of the early Church were

---

[137] B. Tierney, *Foundations of the Conciliar Theory* (Cambridge, Eng., 1955), pp. 132-219; M. Spinka, *Advocates of Reform* (Philadelphia, 1953), pp. 93-95. See also A. Kneer, *Die Entstehung der konziliaren Theorie* (Rome, 1893); A. Gewirth, *Marsilius of Padua and Medieval Political Philosophy*, vol. I of *Marsilius of Padua, The Defender of Peace* (New York, 1951), 260-302.

[138] Delaruelle, et al., *L'Église au temps du Grand Schisme*, p. 43. Francis Oakley has composed a similar "definition" of conciliarism based on a memorandum written Jan. 1, 1409, by d'Ailly. "The 'Propositiones Utiles' of Pierre d'Ailly: an Epitome of Conciliar Theory," *Church History*, 29 (1960), 398-403. D'Ailly's systematic expositions of conciliarism did not begin until after the turn of the century, and I thought it preferable to summarize a treatise contemporary with the events studied here. Consequently I have turned to Conrad of Gelnhausen. The similarity between the two expositions, however, is quite remarkable.

[139] The treatise was published by F. P. Bliemetzrieder in his *Literarische Polemik*, as App. V, pp. 111-40.

[140] Conrad of Gelnhausen, *Epistola Concordie*, *ibid.*, p. 117, lines 20-22.

[141] *Ibid.*, 117, 37-118, 18.

[142] *Ibid.*, 117, 25-29.

[143] *Ibid.*, 119, 19-21.

[144] *Ibid.*, 119, 21-23.

necessary to restore a uniform faith, so it is necessary to call a general council now.[145]

2. Because the present schism endangers the whole Church, no single person or particular corporation (*universitas*) or college (*collegium*) is competent to resolve it. The popes and the cardinals themselves are spreading schism like a poison that is affecting the heart and very life of the Church.[146] "And therefore all the members are bound to rise up very willingly for the reformation of an injured head, since they know their own health depends upon the safety of that head, and since Holy Church, whose head is concerned here, is the common mother of all Catholics. It is therefore incumbent upon all Christians to suffer with her and resist the things that oppress her, since 'what affects all, should be treated by all, or on behalf of all.' " [147] Consequently, the schism can only be resolved by an entity whose competence is general.

3. The examination and resolution of any questionable situation affecting the Church is to be referred to superior authority. But the Universal Church, of which a general council is representative, is superior to the college of cardinals, whose situation has become a problem. Nor is there any other superior on earth to whom recourse may be had. Therefore, for the examination and resolution of the present schism, appeal must be made to the Universal Church, and that means to a general council.[148] The superiority of the Universal to the Roman church (consisting of pope and cardinals) may be demonstrated as follows. Any church outside of which there is no salvation is superior to that outside of which there can be salvation. But there can be salvation outside the college of pope and cardinals and there cannot be salvation outside the Universal Church. Therefore the Catholic Church, which may be represented by a general council, is superior to the local, Roman church.[149] The same proof may be stated with regard to a church that cannot err and one that can, and historical examples may be adduced to show that popes and cardinals have erred, even at the very beginning of the Church, when Peter and the other Apostles wavered in their faith.[150]

Against the above three arguments, Conrad says, opponents allege that it is impossible for a general council to be called or held without

---

[145] Conrad., 118, 19-24.
[147] *Ibid.*, 120, 40 - 121, 5.
[149] *Ibid.*, 122, 21-26.
[146] *Ibid.*, 120, 12-29.
[148] *Ibid.*, 121, 39 - 122, 7.
[150] *Ibid.*, 124, 1-3.

the authority of the pope. Today, however, papal authority cannot intervene because no one is undisputedly recognized as pope, and if only one of the popes were to convene a general council, the followers of the other would not recognize it.[151] The fallacy in this objection, observes Conrad, lies in the assumption that the law requiring papal convocation of a general council is insurmountable. Conrad claims to overcome this scruple in the light of the three following considerations.

1. The locus of authority in the Church. The Holy Catholic Church is the "congregation of the faithful in the unity of the sacraments." [152] Its faith will never waver. It is a body whose unfailing head is Christ and not the college of pope and cardinals nor any particular college on earth.[153] In the Church there are, therefore, two heads, the one subordinated to the other. The first and principal head is Christ, who infuses the Church with grace, and thus keeps it free of error. The second head, the vicar of the first, is the pope, who can die or be deficient in grace, and of whom the Church can be deprived. But when this happens the body and members live on by divine ordination.[154]

2. Immanent necessity. It is recognized that in times of necessity, acts that are normally illicit may become not only licit, but mandatory. This is explained by the superiority of divine and natural law to human law, as is seen, for example, when the hungry are permitted to take food from those having a surplus.[155] For this reason, the absence of a law permitting the convocation of a general council by anyone other than a pope cannot be permitted to impede its meeting in an emergency.[156] Who would say, for example, that if a city is attacked, its citizens cannot run to its defense without first asking permission from the ruler? And what if he is absent? [157] Such an absurdity shows that a general council may be called even without papal authority in a case of extreme necessity, such as exists today.[158]

3. *Epikeia*, or equity. It sometimes happens that in particular cases the uniform application of the law would cause injustice, harm the public good, and contradict the legislator's intention. In such cases it is expedient to overlook the laws and do what the principle of justice directed toward the common good would indicate. Aristotle

---

[151] *Ibid.*, 127, 4-10.
[152] *Ibid.*, 128, 28-29.
[153] *Ibid.*, 128, 11-18.
[154] *Ibid.*, 129, 10-42.
[155] *Ibid.*, 130, 5-21.
[156] *Ibid.*, 130, 32-36.
[157] *Ibid.*, 130, 37-44, and 131, 6-11.
[158] *Ibid.*, 131, 4-5.

calls the virtue of overcoming these contradictions *epikeia*, or equity, which governs legal justice and is nobler than it, because through equity the legislator's intention is more perfectly fulfilled.[159]

A judge endowed with epikeia would conclude that neither the absence of papal authorization nor the lack of a law anticipating the present schism should be considered an obstacle to calling a general council.[160] Yet the cardinals see the damage done by the schism and fail to call one. The cardinals, as pastors of the people, should seek not their own advantage, but that of Jesus Christ, and they ought to labor for a council even if it cannot technically be called under the strict construction of the law.[161] It is obvious to anyone sensitive to epikeia that the Church in schism fits the case referred to above of a threatened city whose inhabitants are able to take up arms without specific authorization from the prince.[162] Self-defense may also be invoked if it is the prince who oppresses the city, as Aristotle explains in Book V of the *Ethics*: "If a king or prince should wish to waste a city or destroy the unity of citizens, for whose safety and guardianship he is responsible, ... his subjects may, indeed are bound, to resist him powerfully." [163] In the present schism "the same reasoning applies." [164]

For these reasons it is clear that a convention of persons, rightly convoked, representing or acting in the place of the different estates, orders, sexes, and persons of all Christendom can and ought to debate concerning the common good of the Universal Church.[165] Such a council, convoked by reference to epikeia, would meet under the authority of the Church's unfailing head, Jesus Christ, who is able to make good any defect.[166] Moreover, it is very likely that the Holy Spirit would direct its deliberations, because Jesus has said "if two or three of you agree on earth about anything they ask, it will be done for them, ... for I am in the midst of them" (Matt. 18:19-20).[167]

It could be thought, Conrad suggests, that both popes would consent to the convocation of a peacemaking council.[168] Nonetheless, it is "obvious to some that hinderers of so great a good, of whatever

---

[159] Conrad, 132, 8-37. For epikeia see E. Jacob, *Essays in the Conciliar Epoch* (Manchester, 1943), pp. 9 *et seq.* and G. I. Jordan, *The Inner History of the Great Schism of the West* (London, 1930), pp. 45-61.

[160] Conrad, 134, 28-29.

[161] *Ibid.*, 135, 4-12.
[162] *Ibid.*, 137, 6-9.
[163] *Ibid.*, 137, 12-14.
[164] *Ibid.*, 137, 16-17.
[165] *Ibid.*, 131, 45-132, 5.
[166] *Ibid.*, 137, 41-138, 1.
[167] *Ibid.*, 139, 10-13.
[168] *Ibid.*, 138, 19-20.

estate or preeminence, are not proponents of the Fathers' laws, but prevaricators, and that all those having zeal for the law ought to clamor against them ... since the convocation of a general council is extremely necessary for the common good, in which the salvation and utility of each and every believer in Christ is included, and consequently, it is to be preferred to every private convenience or advantage." [169]

Conrad's *Epistola Concordie* shows that the irresponsible behavior of the competing popes and cardinals, their refusal to help end the schism (except by converting or conquering the other side) or to jeopardize their own positions, was seen by some professors at Paris as prolonging the schism. In the face of this obvious threat to the Church, Conrad maintained that representatives of the whole corporate body which is the Church could unite against that threat, even if the pope were the source of that danger. For the real head of the Church is Christ—the pope is only His vicar—and He promised to guide any assembly convoked in His name. The preservation of the Church, therefore, clearly coincides with His intention, and so, even though the laws did not foresee this particular emergency, the body of Christ, the Church Universal, can legitimately exercise both its natural and its divine right of self-preservation. Thus, Conrad concluded, the private advantage of the Roman church, which is determined by pope and cardinals, must be subjected to the will of Christ and the good of the whole Church as determined by a general council.

Conrad's conciliar ideas, therefore, involve perspectives that differ markedly from the main themes of early Gallicanism. Although both viewpoints draw upon corporation theory, Gallicanism emphasizes the distinctness of component parts—French church as opposed to Roman church, secular as opposed to regular clergy, particular dioceses as opposed to Universal Church—whereas conciliarism gives superiority to the whole over any part, whether the papacy or the French church. For the conciliarists, therefore, the representatives of the whole Church, whose primary head is Christ, receive direction immediately from Him and their decisions consequently coincide with the Legislator's intention. The authority that conciliarists assigned to the general council depended fundamentally

---

[169] *Ibid.*, 139, 28-36.

upon its complete representativeness. The popes obviously claimed this universality for themselves, but it was undermined by the schism, and other circumstances were put forward by theorists in which the integrity of the Church would reside only in the collectivity of its members. It is true that in implementing their conciliarist formulas, the fathers of Pisa and Constance used the diocese and the nation (and the university) as districts from which representatives should be sent, but these were clearly subordinated to the whole.

In Gallicanism, by contrast, each constituency had to defend its own independence, hence its willingness to substitute a "sympathetic" lay prince, whose constituency was limited, for popes whose claims to universality were ancient and checked only by logic or determined political opposition. Gallican writers insisted that the pope was essentially one bishop among many, "primus inter pares," at best, whereas conciliarists could concede papal universality precisely because it was subject to the superior authority of the universal Church represented in council. Conciliarism gave a constitutional structure to Gallican particularism. Thus the authority apportioned equally but "anarchically" in early Gallicanism could be delegated to representatives of each particular jurisdiction and recomposed in a general council. The body of the Church could then take action even against the pope, its secondary head, an important part but less than the whole.

Before this was actually accomplished, however, political thought of the kind expressed in Pierre d'Ailly's two treatises against John Blanchard lay in an ill-defined middle ground, drawing, as circumstances tempted, upon both Gallican and conciliar constructions. Moreover, times were bad. In 1381 the masters of the Paris studium had been forced to remain silent on the question of a council in order to obtain John Rousse of Abbeville's release from prison. The princes' attitude toward free debate did not change significantly until 1394, when Clement VII died and was succeeded by Benedict XIII. Charles VI had been suffering since 1392 from the mental debility that would render him politically ineffective, and his uncles, ruling again in his stead, knowing they could not gain the same advantages from Benedict as from Clement VII, relaxed their defense of the pope.[170] Before that change, opportunities for working out the implications

---

[170] Kaminsky, "The Politics," p. 367.

of political theories in real conflict situations, however great or small, were few indeed.[171]

One exception, however, arose from the resentment provoked in the university by Clement VII's recently appointed Chancellor of Paris, John Blanchard. In the pages that follow, Blanchard's conduct in office, the movement against him, and d'Ailly's speeches will be studied in detail. Finally, an effort will be made to assess the significance of the Blanchard affair against the background of the university's internal development, the schism in the Church, and the ideological movements that accompanied both.

---

[171] For one example, see the treatise written around 1390 by an anonymous Master of Theology entitled "Whether the University of Paris is Always and Forever Obliged to Pursue the Union of the Church," in which the author criticizes for negligence all those capable of helping to end the schism but not working toward that goal. The treatise is published under the title "Pro Unione Ecclesiae," by P. Glorieux, ed., in J. Gerson, *Œuvres complètes*, vol. VI (Paris, 1965), no. 253a, pp. 1-21. See also *Chart.*, III, no. 1663, pp. 595-97. Indirectly relevant is the Monzon affair, mentioned in Chapter I, which concerned the assertion of the Dominican Juan de Monzon that the Faculty of Theology did not have the right to discipline him for refusing to retract "heretical" statements made in his vespers (*Chart.*, III, nos. 1557-83). In his prosecution of Monzon, d'Ailly further developed ideas on the role of the theologian that he considered in his speeches against Blanchard. The Monzon affair is being studied in detail in the dissertation of my student Douglass Taber, Jr. D'Ailly's speeches are in Duplessis d'Argentré, *Collectio Judiciorum de Novis Erroribus*, 3 vols. (Lutetiae Parisiorum, 1728-36), I, 66-151. For further university activity at the very end of Clement VII's pontificate, see Valois, II, 406-30. The most important initiative was the poll taken of the university's members that produced the letter of June 6, 1394, written by d'Ailly, Deschamps, and Nicholas of Clamanges expounding the "three ways" to end the schism. *Chart.*, I, no. 1683, pp. 617-24, or, for complete text, Du Boulay, IV, 687-96.

CHAPTER THREE

THE BLANCHARD AFFAIR

The Blanchard affair is the controversy through which, in 1386, the professors at Paris effected the removal from office of Chancellor John Blanchard on the grounds that he had exacted money or gifts and oaths of obedience to himself as a condition of the license to teach. Blanchard provoked the masters by his rigorous efforts to supplement the revenues of his office, systematically demanding payment of the customary but forbidden emoluments from students at different stages of their academic career, but especially upon the conferral of the license.

The most prominent figure in the masters' attack upon the chancellor was the thirty-five-year-old doctor of Theology, Pierre d'Ailly, destined to become one of the most famous of all late-medieval churchmen. D'Ailly was easily identified by a number of contemporaries as the "principal leader" [1] in the Blanchard affair, and even as the one who had "fostered this quarrel." [2] Later on, d'Ailly called himself the "first to begin" treating the theoretical aspects of the affair in scholastic debate and compared himself to "the small ... dog who incites the larger, stronger hounds to hunt." [3] He represented the university in Avignon when documents relevant to the affair were presented to Clement VII,[4] and was its advocate for the suit brought against Blanchard in the Parlement of Paris.[5]

D'Ailly's position as university spokesman in the Blanchard affair was the logical outcome of his outstanding academic career and early activity as a young theological master. Son of a butcher, Colard Marguerite d'Ailly, and his wife Perrine, Pierre d'Ailly was born in

---

[1] *Chartularium Universitatis Parisiensis*, ed. H. Denifle and E. Châtelain; 4 vols. (Paris, 1889-97), III, no. 1521, p. 416, test. vii, super xxii: "caput principale." (Hereafter cited as *Chart.*)

[2] *Ibid.*, p. 412: "Magistri Petrus de Alliaco in theologia et Johannes de Marsonno in artibus fuerunt moti ad nutriendum istam litem."

[3] In his speech "Radix Omnium," edited in the Appendix, p. 198, l. 28-31.

[4] *Chart.*, III, no. 1519, pp. 399-402.

[5] Radix, pp. 198, 32 - 199, 2. "Quia enim ex concordi deliberatione dicte universitatis deputatus fui ad proponendum in Parlamento supra materia fidei." In the parlement, d'Ailly accused Blanchard of heretically defending illicit practices as licit. Thus the affair is a "matter of the faith."

Compiègne around 1350, according to his own testimony.[6] Although he was supported by a scholarship at the prestigious College of Navarre in the University of Paris, possibly from 1363 or 1364, and certainly from 1372,[7] we need not infer that he was poor, because these grants were controlled by the Confessor of the King of France, to whom only those of a certain influence had access.[8] We know that d'Ailly's father held real estate in Compiègne because in 1366 he transferred revenue from four houses there to his son and contrasted this income to that from a field near the city.[9] Thus, d'Ailly came from a prosperous bourgeois background.

One of d'Ailly's earliest teachers was the Navarrist John Caillaudi de Quercu (Duchêne), whose quest for the license and magisterium in theology contributed to the conflict we are about to study.[10] D'Ailly became a bachelor ("determined") in the Faculty of Arts under

---

[6] *Chart.*, III, p. 259, n. 33. L. Salembier, *Le Cardinal Pierre d'Ailly* (Tourcoing, 1932), pp. 15-16.

[7] J. Launoy, *Regii Navarrae Gymnasii Parisiensis Historia* (1677), consulted in Launoy, *Opera Omnia*, 5 tomes in 10 vols. (Cologne, 1731-32), Tome IV, pt.i, p. 335.

[8] Although of a slightly later date (1374), this letter from Charles V to the College of Navarre confirms that the confessor's role as distributor of scholarships was already customary: "Dantes hiis presentibus in mandatis dilecto et fideli Confessori nostro et successoribus suis, qui de nostra licentia bursas predicte domus quando vacant conferre consueverunt" (Paris, Archives Nationales, M. 180, no. 4). The humanist, Nicholas of Clamanges, himself a graduate of Navarre, shows how scholarships were obtained in his letter (after 1412) to the royal confessor, Peter of Cantella, on behalf of an unnamed nephew: "Ut grammaticas illi iuvenculo bursas in memorato collegio, cuius ad te ex officio confessionis cum bursarum collatione dispositio pertinet, mee huius prime petitionis obtentu conferre velis." (Nicolaus de Clamengiis, *Opera Omnia*, ed. I. M. Lydius (Leiden, 1613), Epistola LXII.)

The royal confessor's supervisory role over the College of Navarre emerges even more clearly from the following incident reported by Launoy (p. 328): "Hoc eodum anno [1382], Petrus Nivernensis Episcopus, qui Regi erat a secretis conscientiae, XIX Calend. Februarias, invisit Collegium, et quo potuit sermone et consilio levavit sollicitum et anxium, quod per hebdomadas XXVIII statae pensionis nihil accepisset." Although the evidence is not conclusive, I believe these entries show that by the 1380's, the royal confessor had full power to fill any vacancy in the college and even to name the headmaster. In view of his influence, it would be naive to assume that the electoral procedures set forth in Joanna of Navarre's testament (Launoy, p. 293) were respected any longer. That such a function is consistent with the royal confessor's duties generally appears from F. Lot and R. Fawtier, *Histoire des institutions françaises au Moyen Age*, 3 vols. (Paris, 1957-62), III, 427-28.

[9] L. Salembier, *Petrus de Alliaco* (Latin doctoral thesis presented to the Faculty of Theology at Lille: Lefort, 1886), p. 12, n. 3, and App. I

[10] See below, ch. IV, pp. 106-9.

Duchêne's sponsorship in 1365.[11] He was licensed in arts in April or May 1367, and incepted under William Carnificis, probably in the spring of 1368, three years before reaching the traditional minimum age.[12] When he entered the French nation, William de Marchia, the proctor, levied an initiation fee of eight pounds. This sum was high for the period, exceeded only by that of twelve pounds paid by Reginald of Gaudricuria.[13] In 1372, d'Ailly himself served a three-month term as proctor of his nation.[14] D'Ailly entered the Faculty of Theology in the autumn of 1368, lectured on Peter Lombard's *Sentences* in 1375, received his license in theology on February 15, 1381, and was granted the magisterium in theology on April 11, 1381, when he was four years younger than the minimum age for this honor.[15]

In this early period, d'Ailly benefited from the special regard the popes had always shown the studium and from the patronage of the French kings. The first university rotulus in which d'Ailly would have been entitled, as a Master of Arts, to place his request for a benefice was the "inaugural" roll sent immediately after the accession of Gregory XI, which unfortunately is lost.[16] In response to it, however, the new pope wrote, on January 27, 1371, to the Chancellor of Paris, John de Calore, and referred to Pierre d'Ailly as "a cleric of the diocese of Soissons, Master of Arts, . . . third-year scholar in theology at Paris, and without any ecclesiastical benefice," but holding an

---

[11] C. E. Du Boulay, *Historia Universitatis Parisiensis*, 5 vols. (Paris, 1665-70), IV, 979, and Salembier, *Petrus*, p. 12. For the *determinatio* see *Chart.*, I, no. 201, p. 228, and H. Rashdall, *The Universities of Europe in the Middle Ages*, new ed. by F. M. Powicke and A. B. Emden, 3 vols. (London, 1935), I, 454.

[12] *Chart.*, III, p. 259, n. 33. For the minimum age established in 1215 see *Chart.*, I, no. 20, pp. 78-79.

[13] Du Boulay, IV, 979. Salembier, *Le Cardinal*, p. 31, refers to Du Boulay, but gives the erroneous impression that the sum was paid "pour obtenir ce grade." This sum was instead the fee paid for entrance into the French nation in the Faculty of Arts. D'Ailly was not buying a degree, but paying the graduated initiation fee of a professional organization.

[14] Du Boulay, IV, 979.

[15] *Chart.*, III, p. 259, n. 33. In "L'Œuvre littéraire de Pierre d'Ailly: Remarques et précisions," *Mélanges de Science Religieuse*, 22 (1965), 62-78, Glorieux gives a bibliography of d'Ailly's literary production and meticulously correlates it with his career. For earlier bio-bibliographies of d'Ailly, see Paul Tschackert, *Peter von Ailli* (Gotha, 1877; reissue, Amsterdam, 1968), pp. 348-66; Salembier, *Le Card.*, pp. 288-359, and "Bibliographie des œuvres du Cardinal Pierre d'Ailly, Évêque de Cambrai," *Le Bibliographe Moderne*, 12 (1908), pp. 160-70 (printed separately at Besançon, 1909, in 8⁰, 11 pp).

[16] *Chart.*, III, no. 1368, p. 199, and no. 1364, n. 1, p. 196.

expectative grace to be provided by the Abbess of St-Mary's of Soissons, which d'Ailly had described as "practically worthless." Therefore, Gregory ordered the chancellor to reserve for d'Ailly, in the diocese of Tournai, a benefice worth forty small pounds of Tours, if the cure of souls was involved, or thirty pounds, if not. He also annulled the expectative grace at St-Mary's, but in compensation stated that possession of this benefice (Tournai) was not to preclude the possibility of holding others.[17]

On June 1, 1375, Gregory provided d'Ailly with a canonry at Soissons, perhaps in compensation for the benefice in Tournai, which d'Ailly never obtained. Presumably, it would have been of roughly equal value. In return for the benefice at Soissons, Clement ordered d'Ailly to surrender one of two other benefices that we now hear of for the first time: either the parish church at Sommeuil (probably Sommery),[18] in the diocese of Rouen, worth no more than 27 small pounds of Tours, or the chapel of Stephen Haudry at Paris.[19]

After the Great Schism began with the election of Clement VII, there was real difficulty in the Faculty of Theology and the English nation, in deciding whether a rotulus should be sent to a pope with questionable credentials. In May 1379, however, the French nation entrusted its roll to Pierre d'Ailly, who carried it to Avignon, not only before the university as a whole could compose a list, but even before it could decide the question of Clement's legitimacy, and indeed even before Clement himself had reached Avignon.[20] In this roll, d'Ailly described himself as "subdeacon of Soissons, *bacallarius formatus* in theology, Master of Arts in Paris, and the messenger sent to carry this roll to Your Holiness." He asked for a canonry at Laon. The request was made, he said, in spite of his benefice (*personatum*) at Baisieux,[21] in the diocese of Amiens, and his post in the chapel of Stephen Haudry.[22] Clement sent his answer on November 14, 1379,

---

[17] Archivio Vaticano, Reg. Aven. 178 (note that Denifle cites this volume according to an older system, as Greg. XI, vol. VI), ff. 521ᵛ-522ᵛ.

[18] Sommery, Seine-Inférieure, canton de St-Saëns, arr. de Neufchâtel, 36 km. from Rouen. Adolphe Joanne, *Dictionnaire géographique de la France*, 2ᵉ ed. (Paris, 1869).

[19] Reg. Aven. 198 (Greg. XI, vol. XXVI), f. 156.

[20] *Chart.*, III, p. 340.

[21] Dép. de Somme, canton de Corbie (11 km.), arr. d'Amiens (21 km.).

[22] Reg. Vat. Supplic., Clement VII, an. 1, pars 3 (also cited as: Reg. Suppliche no. vecchio 47, no. nuovo 53), ff. 148ᵛ-149ʳ.

and promised him a canonry of unspecified value at Amiens.[23] I do not know when d'Ailly actually received the Amiens benefice or another canonry at Meaux, mentioned later.

Even in these early years, before becoming a Master of Theology and immediately thereafter, d'Ailly was engaged in a public career of high visibility. A leader of the university faction favoring a general council, he had been first to advocate this solution before the royal court.[24] He also had been a leader in the university's efforts to discipline Hugh Aubriot, the Provost of Paris, who had infringed the privileges of the Alma Mater by denying the rector and other university officers their accustomed places in the funeral cortège that accompanied the body of Charles V to St-Denis. Largely at the university's insistence, Aubriot was condemned to prison on May 17, 1381, despite the support mustered by Louis d'Anjou for the provost and his men.[25] Since d'Ailly first proposed the conciliar solution in the hostile atmosphere of the royal court, shortly after May 20, 1381,[26] this new Master of Theology must have seemed bold indeed to make such a statement just a few days after Aubriot's condemnation. Then, conscious of the fate of John Rousse of Abbeville and the example of the other theologians who had left Paris by the summer of 1381, d'Ailly must have understood the wisdom of withdrawing to a quiet refuge away from the capital.[27] His timely reception into the cathedral chapter of Noyon, on September 14, 1381,[28] suggests the intervention and protection of an influential friend, perhaps one of the dukes [29]

---

[23] Reg. Aven. 217, ff. 110ᵛ-111ʳ.

[24] See above, pp. 39, 46.

[25] The Aubriot problem dragged on until 1383, at least. There are sparse accounts of this dispute, with bibliographies, in *Chart.*, III, no. 1454, p. 293, and no. 1457, p. 298; Valois, I, 336-42, 366. Praise for d'Ailly's energy in pursuit of Aubriot is quoted from Paris, Bibliothèque Nationale (hereafter BN), ms. lat. 15107, by the editors of the *Auctarium Chartularii Universitatis Parisiensis*, 6 vols. to date (Paris, 1937-   ), I, 607, n. 4. The records of the English nation follow the affair until Jan. 4, 1383, when it does not appear to be over. *Ibid.*, I, 638-43. See also Eugène Déprez, "Hugo Aubriot, Praepositus Parisiensis et urbanus praetor, 1367-1381," (Thèse, Université de Paris, 1902); Le Roux de Lincy, "Hughes Aubriot, Prévot de Paris sous Charles V," *Bibliothèque de l'École des Chartes* (5ᵉ série), 1862, pp. 173-213.

[26] N. Valois, *La France et le grand schisme d'occident*, 4 vols. (Paris, 1896-1902), I, 340.

[27] See above, ch. II, p. 46.

[28] Valois, I, 358, n. 4.

[29] In a document dated June 20, 1403, establishing masses to be said at the College of Navarre after his death, d'Ailly specified that prayers were also to be said "specially" for the souls of Charles VI and Louis of Orleans, "his benefactors." Launoy, p. 352. These men were too young to help d'Ailly in 1381, but this text shows he was known personally in the highest circles.

or a royal confessor with institutional links to the College of Navarre. It also seems likely that he could return to Paris only if he had confidence in a highly placed protector. His appointment, in 1384, to the headship of the College of Navarre, controlled by the King's confessor, provides evidence of just such support.[30] That office was worth forty Parisian pounds per annum.[31]

One of d'Ailly's first acts as headmaster, dated September 23, 1384, established a common treasury from which to buy wine for the theologians, the *opus vini pro Collegio Theologorum*.[32] Later he significantly enlarged the college's physical plant, erecting a new building with quarters for twelve bachelors and their servants.[33] Even after leaving the administration of the college, d'Ailly remained a faithful and generous alumnus. In 1403, he set up a fund, later incorporated in his will, which allocated money for increasing students' allowances and teachers' salaries, with any remainder going to the library of each division, the wine cellar, and the chapel.[34]

Far more important, of course, was the intellectual ambiance at the College of Navarre under d'Ailly's direction, when it became the birthplace of French humanism.[35] John Gerson, Nicholas of Clamanges, and John Carlini of Montreuil, three of this movement's pioneers, were all colleagues at Navarre and knew the guidance of Pierre d'Ailly.[36] Other Navarrists were Gerard Machet, John Courte-

[30] *Chart.*, III, p. 259, n. 33.
[31] Students of theology received eight Parisian shillings per week. The rector received double, or sixteen shillings, which works out to forty Parisian pounds per annum or fifty pounds of Tours. Launoy, 293-94.
[32] *Ibid.*, 328-29.
[33] A description of this building can be extracted from the early-eighteenth-century debate on the reform of the college preserved in Paris, B.N., ms. fr. 16869, ff. 52-61, esp. at f. 58. Also see Salembier, *Petrus*, p. 23, n. 2.
[34] Launoy, 353-54.
[35] G. Ouy, "Le Collège de Navarre, berceau de l'humanisme français," in Comité des Travaux historiques et scientifiques, *Actes du 95e congrès national des sociétés savants, Reims, 1970* (Section de philologie et d'histoire, jusqu'à 1610), I, 275-99. See also: *idem.*, "Gerson, émule de Pétrarque," *Romania*, 88 (1967), 175-231, and *idem.*, "La Plus Ancienne Œuvre retrouvée de Jean Gerson," *Romania*, 83 (1962), 433-92. Ezio Ornato, the editor of Jean de Montreuil's letters, in his book, *Jean Muret et ses amis Nicolas de Clamanges et Jean de Montreuil* (Centre de recherches d'histoire et de philologie de la IVe section de l'École Pratique des Hautes Études, V, Hautes Études Médiévales et Modernes, 6; Genève, 1969), pp. 36-37, places the College of Navarre clearly above the rest of the university for its cultivation of literary humanism.
[36] Ornato, *Jean Muret*, p. 157. The origins of French humanism have been studied with great energy and fruitful results since Franco Simone's *Il Rinascimento Francese* (*Biblioteca di Studi Francesi*, Vol. I, 2a ed., Torino, 1965). Gilbert

cuisse, who helped draw up the Cabochian Ordinance, and Giles Deschamps, whose encounter with John Blanchard is described below, and who, with d'Ailly and Nicholas of Clamanges, co-authored the university's famous letter of 1394 describing the three ways of ending the schism, and who, finally, was licensed in theology only three years after d'Ailly but raised to the cardinalate at the same time, in 1411.[37] At the close of the fourteenth century, the College of Navarre enjoyed a prestige equal to that of the Sorbonne.[38]

Although the university was not to send a common rotulus to Clement VII until July 31, 1387, d'Ailly's entry in that document makes it clear that, in the meantime, his pursuit of benefices had not been dependent on university-sponsored initiatives. In that roll, d'Ailly reminded the pope that in 1379 he had requested a canonry at Laon, which had not been granted because, as he here admits, he had failed to acknowledge that he was simultaneously seeking another benefice through the intervention of Charles V.[39] The king had obtained a canonry worth no more than thirty pounds of Tours in the collegiate church of St-Clement's of Compiègne for d'Ailly, who now offered to abandon it in return for Laon. This request was made, d'Ailly said, in spite of his office at Stephen Haudry's chapel, "which I do not hold at present;" his benefice at Baisieux; his prebend at St-Marcel, near Paris, which latter office he had obtained in exchange for his sub-deaconry of Soissons; and the cantorship of Noyon, which he had

---

Ouy and his Équipe de recherche sur l'humanisme français des XIVe et XVe siècles have led the way. The progress of this group's many interconnected studies may be followed in the *Annuaire de l'École Pratique des Hautes Études, IVe Section* (Sciences historiques et philologiques), under the colloquium "Codicologie Latine Médiévale."

[37] For this group of Navarrists, see A. Coville, "Recherches sur Jean Courtecuisse et ses œuvres oratoires," *Bibliothèque de l'École des Chartes*, 65 (1904), 491-529; L. Froger, "Jean Courtecuisse, chanoine du Mans et évêque de Genève," *La Province du Maine*, 13 (1905), 221-27; H. Oberman, *Forerunners of the Reformation* (New York, 1966), 60-62; D. Cecchetti, "Nicholas de Clamanges e Gerard Machet," *Atti della Accademia delle Scienze di Torino*, 100 (1966), 136-93. Remember also that Gerson lived until 1427, and that Nicholas of Clamanges returned to the College of Navarre from at least 1425 until possibly 1434. Gerson, *Opera Omnia*, ed. L. E. Dupin, 6 vols. (Antwerp, 1706), I, xxxix, and cf. *Chart.*, IV, no. 2324, p. 482 and no. 2319, p. 480. For Deschamps, see below, pp. 109-10, and *Chart.*, III, p. 241, n. 4, where Denifle says he attended the College of Harcourt, and *ibid.*, p. 624. Cf. Launoy, IV, I, 337.

[38] For the early history of the Sorbonne, see P. Glorieux, *Aux Origines de la Sorbonne*, 2 vols. (Paris, 1965-66), I, 71-145.

[39] Clement VII had formulated this rule on March 1, 1379. Emil von Ottenthal, *Regulae Cancellariae Apostolica* (Innsbruck, 1888; reissue, Aalen, 1968), p. 105.

acquired only on January 18, 1387 (n. s.).[40] In this rotulus, which reveals a chastened d'Ailly who had learned the price of incomplete disclosure, he did not mention the canonries of Amiens or Meaux. I therefore conclude that he received these offices between July 31, 1387, the date of the roll, and October 7, 1389, the date of the first evidence known to me that they were in his possession.[41]

In consideration of the above requests, grants, promises, and exchanges, we can infer that at the time of the Blanchard affair, the Master of the College of Navarre also enjoyed additional revenues as prebendary of St-Marcel, whose value was not more than thirty to forty small pounds of Tours (assuming that Soissons had been given to replace Tournai and that the exchange of Soissons for St-Marcel was made at no loss to d'Ailly); canon of St-Clement's of Compiègne, valued at thirty pounds of Tours; priest of Baisieux (no value given); and canon of Noyon (no value given). D'Ailly said in the rotulus of 1387 that his total income from all benefices (including the cantorship of Noyon) was no more than one hundred pounds of Tours.[42] This sum was almost certainly less than Blanchard's income. Although the Chancellorship of Paris paid only forty pounds, a significant portion of the thousand pounds that Blanchard said he received from Cambrai and Tournai before the schism must be added since, as will be shown later, the revenues from the canonry and treasurership of Cambrai, at least, were probably coming to him routinely.[43]

Such, then, were the origins of the man who would eventually become Chancellor of Paris (1389), Bishop of Le Puy (1395), Bishop of Cambrai (1396), and Cardinal of San Chrysogono (1411).[44] Not only does d'Ailly's early career suggest that he will go far, it also provides many clues to this future prelate's character. His intellectual gifts are apparent from his rapid advance at the university and from the quality of his early writings. His readiness to acknowledge Clement and bear the rotulus to Avignon shows his ability to make decisions and execute them quickly, even before the public eye, especially in matters involving his own advancement. The absolute confidence of the

---

[40] Reg. Supplic., 73 (Clement VII, an. 9, pars 2), ff. 2(5)ᵛ-3(6)ʳ. For Noyon see Paris, BN, ms. fr. 12032, f. 12ʳ. Salembier, in *Petrus*, p. 22, fails to adjust the year and gives January 13.

[41] *Chart.*, III, no. 1552, pp. 482-83.

[42] Reg. Supplic., 73, f. 2(5)ᵛ.

[43] See below, pp. 140-3. Compare this conclusion to Denifle's description, *Chart.*, III, 340n, and see his overlong list of benefices on p. 447, n. 1.

[44] *Chart.*, III, p. 259, n. 33.

Epistola Diaboli Leviathan, which portrays opponents of a general
council as in league with the Devil, illustrates the righteousness he
always attributed to his own convictions. Like Blanchard, he was
easily able to banish uncertainty from his mind and to consider
opposition from others a sign of their moral inferiority. Unlike
Blanchard, however, d'Ailly could get things done. In fact, his
admission in the rotulus of 1387 shows that, even early in his career,
d'Ailly was not always restrained by the scruples of others. His
ability to cloud the truth with selective omissions or distortions he
carried into the Blanchard affair, where his treatises openly avow a
predatory instinct. There he shows himself capable of mixing mere
logical inventions indiscriminately with the most conscientiously felt
objections. He can confuse the license and the magisterium to attack
Blanchard and distinguish between them to defend university practice.
However, this ruthlessness, only partly restrained by ethical standards,
was not fueled exclusively by self-centered ambition.

D'Ailly was a man who identified easily with institutions—in his case
the College of Navarre, the university, and the Church. True, he
used the university as his gateway into politics and he never lost sight
of the benefits its prestige could bring him, but we must credit
him nonetheless with a deep conviction that the health of the university was important. He similarly enhanced his prestige at the
Council of Pisa and was named a cardinal by a pope of the Pisan line.
Yet despite his ability to profit personally from the occasion, no one
could deny the Church's need for decisive leadership in 1409. Without
looking so far into the future, however, we can see d'Ailly's character
encapsulated in an intriguing episode in the middle of the Blanchard
affair. It adds to our assessment of his effectiveness an appreciation
of his theatrical flair, a capacity for stage-managing frequently found
in men seeking political influence.

The records of the French nation show that on June 8, 1385, John
Trelon of Malincuria, Master of Theology and Subchancellor of
Ste-Geneviève, made a public apology to Pierre d'Ailly for certain
words that might have appeared insulting but that had not been so
intended. We do not know precisely what the offensive words were,
but they occurred after John Trelon had referred to Raoul Glachard,
Dean of the Faculty of Theology, and John Blanchard, Chancellor
of Notre-Dame, as "very important men of the world" (*majores
mundi*). Pierre d'Ailly intervened, apparently to defend the majesty
of the king and pope. In response, John may have implied that

d'Ailly objected only because he wanted to be counted among the *majores mundi*, though, of course we cannot be certain. In his apology Trelon sought to clarify his original statement. He had not been comparing the dean and chancellor to the pope or the king, but to other theologians. He drew his conclusion, he said, from the importance of the theologian's office, which is to cause faith to grow in the hearts of men and, once generated, to defend it. And although their duty is very great, theologians are not great in terms of authority or power. D'Ailly accepted this apology in front of nearly 120 masters![45] Thus the humility of Pierre d'Ailly and the grandeur of king and pope were simultaneously safeguarded.[46]

The College of Navarre's young headmaster was clearly one of the university's outstanding personalities. When he returned to Paris to take over the college, probably in the summer of 1384 (he was acting as head by September 23),[47] only the first signs of a movement to reform the licensing procedures were visible. But the first indication that the venality of academic formalities was becoming a problem did not involve the license. It appears from a complaint made to Clement VII by John de Basilia, the Prior General of the Augustinians, that the beadles of the Faculty of Theology were asking more than the three francs to which they were entitled for participating at the opening of courses on the *Sentences*. In a letter dated June 28, 1384, the pope asked his Chancellor of Paris to investigate.[48] Once raised, however, the subject of fees within the academic process was not so easily dismissed. Even though the Augustinian friars had been the first to complain, the whole university debated the question over the summer and, on October 6, the masters took steps against this abuse.

The first indication known to me that the masters were preparing legal action against the chancellor's exactions appeared on October 6, 1384, when they republished verbatim those phrases from papal privileges that regulated the license, "lest anyone, through ignorance of these [privileges], be able to excuse his wrongdoing."[49] The clauses are then listed.

From Gregory IX's *Parens scientiarum* of 1231, the first resolution states: "The chancellor will exact no oath of obedience or other

---

[45] *Chart.*, III, no. 1499, p. 338.

[46] Trelon and d'Ailly were apparently reconciled, for later in the summer of 1385, d'Ailly referred to Trelon as "trustworthy." *Ibid.*, p. 388, lxx.

[47] This is the date on which he instituted the *opus vini*; Launoy, 328-29.

[48] *Chart.*, III, no. 1485, p. 319.

[49] *Ibid.*, no. 1491, pp. 331-32.

caution from the masters about to be licensed, nor receive any emolument or promise for awarding the license." [50] The second clause comes from Robert of Courzon's Statutes of 1215, providing that "no one should incept who was licensed by the chancellor or by another, if he gave him money, swore him faith, or made with him any other pact." [51]

The third clause comes from the reforms of 1366 imposed by the cardinals delegated by Urban V, John of Blandy and Giles of Montagu, who applied and extended the above prohibitions to the Faculty of Arts, and anticipated a variety of subterfuges that would violate the spirit of the earlier legislation:

> Let those about to be licensed in arts give nothing nor promise that they will give, either themselves or through others, directly or indirectly, to the chancellor or the subchancellor in whose examination they may wish to be licensed, nor to the examining masters, nor to the master under whom they will be licensed, nor to any of the assistants of these or of any of the aforesaid by reason of labor, assigning readings, or whatever reason or occasion touching the examination; let them not give dinners for them, all fraud and interpretation aside. And let the said candidates be held to swear this at the entrance of their examination.[52]

It was no accident that all three passages quoted refer to payments and oaths demanded by chancellors in the past and declared illegal in each piece of legislation. Indeed, the 83 articles of accusation against Blanchard that the masters would submit in May 1385, to be studied in detail in Chapter IV, were to denounce these exactions more insistently than any of the other alleged offenses.

On January 9, 1385, the masters pressed beyond the recapitulation of past regulations and into action with three resolutions aimed, as they said, "at the reform of abuses." [53] The first measure was to reimpose the traditional oath of loyalty to the rector upon all bachelors beginning their teaching functions in any faculty:

> Each bachelor about to be permitted to determine in arts or to lecture in the other faculties should swear in his faculty to observe and defend the honor of the rector and the rector's office, and the statutes, liberties, privileges, and laudable customs of the University of Paris in whatever station to which he may come, and keep the secrets of the university, revealing them to no one.[54]

---

[50] *Chart.*, III, no. 1491, p. 331, quoting from vol. I, no. 79, cited above, p. 15.
[51] *Ibid.*, quoting from vol. I, no. 20, cited above, p. 12.
[52] *Ibid.*, quoting from vol. III, no. 1319, p. 146.
[53] *Ibid.*, no. 1504, pp. 340-41: "ad reformationem abusuum."
[54] *Ibid.*, p. 341.

This oath shows that the abuses the reformers were concerned to eliminate affected students prior to the award of the license.

Indeed the second provision was intended to make it impossible for bachelors to swear an oath of obedience or pay any fee for becoming bachelors or receiving the license. The tactic adopted to end this practice was to prevent bachelors from participating in these transactions by forcing each one to swear that "he has given or promised nothing, will give or promise nothing, before the license, to anyone, for the sake of being permitted to determine or to lecture, or even for the license, or upon receipt of the *signetum* [a notice that the license will be awarded], under any pretext, all fraud removed."[55] This oath was to be at the center of the controversy between the chancellor and the reformers because it made it impossible for any bachelor to accede to demands made of him by the chancellor, and regarded by the latter as traditional and licit,[56] without violating the oath imposed by the university.

In confronting the chancellor, the masters took one other initiative, that of claiming the right to rank the candidates seeking the license in the three superior faculties according to their own judgment: "In the Faculties of Theology, Law, and Medicine, the masters of the said faculties ... should deliberate among themselves and decide concerning the bachelors and their competence, and concerning the order of license or of rank, according to the method which will seem expedient to each faculty."[57] And this is to be done "before the opening of the examination of the Chancellor of the Church of Paris or the summoning and depositions of the masters."[58] The chancellor considered it his prerogative to rank the candidates.[59] He clearly feared that if he permitted the masters to list the bachelors in order, he would be reduced merely to executing the decisions of the individual faculties. Thus the investigation into the faith and morals (as distinct from the knowledge) of the candidate, assigned to him by *Parens scientiarum*, would be rendered superfluous and opportunities for extortion lost.

In Paris, therefore, the initiative for reform was made public on January 9, 1385, but we do not know exactly when the masters first complained formally of the chancellor's alleged abuses to

---

[55] *Ibid.*
[56] *Ibid.*, no. 1520, arts. 2, 13-15.
[57] *Ibid.*, no. 1504, p. 341.
[58] *Ibid.*
[59] *Ibid.*, no. 1520, p. 404, art. 7.

Clement VII.[60] The earliest papal response already refers to prior legal actions.[61] The papal letter ordering Peter of Montagu, the Cardinal of Laon, to investigate the university's charge of abuses in "assigning rank and awarding the license" by Blanchard and his officials, is dated February 8, 1385.[62] In this document it appears that Clement VII was desirous of avoiding a formal legal procedure,[63] yet by April 14 the university had formally empowered its representatives.[64]

In accord with his papal commission, on April 15 the Cardinal of Laon summoned Blanchard, Pierre Plaoul the subchancellor, and the four examiners, as well as the rector and other deputies or proctors of the university, to testify before him.[65] On May 25 the university's syndics presented the masters' list of 83 articles of accusation against the chancellor, thus obtaining a considerable psychological advantage over him.[66] In fact, the chancellor's situation was gloomy indeed. During April and May, Blanchard had been unable to find a legal representative. His difficulty is easily understood, for most of the qualified lawyers of Paris had, as students, taken the oath of lifelong loyalty to the rector of the University, and hence could not accept a case against the corporation.[67] Even when the Cardinal of Laon ordered three men, Odardus de Molinis, Ralph de Ulmonte, and

---

[60] Du Boulay, *Historia*, IV, 785, says that Blanchard appealed, but in the transcripts of the proceedings before the Parlement of Paris, the University's representatives acknowledge that they took the initiative: "[Ceulz de l'Université] dient que le Chancelier a fait plusieurs abus par convenances et autrement. Et affin qu'il en fust puny, ils ont baillé une supplication au Pape... et le Pape a commis la cause à deux Cardinaux, pour sçavoir la verité des faits." *Ibid.*, IV, 611, lines 13-11 bot.
The first complaint might have been contained in the lost rotulus of 1383, see *Chart.*, III, no. 1474.

[61] *Chart.*, III, no. 1505, pp. 341-42. Clement refers to a previous commission of three cardinals, whose report was insufficient to allow him to come to a decision; hence the present order (p. 342). Denifle also points out that on Oct. 20, 1384, the university published an earlier version of the masters' claim to have sole right of ranking the candidates in order (*ibid.*, no. 1504, p. 341, n. 2).

[62] *Ibid.*, no. 1505, p. 342.

[63] *Ibid.*: "Committimus et mandamus quatinus... summarie simpliciter ac sine strepitu et figura judicii de premissis etiam extrajudicialiter auctoritate apostolica diligentius te informes."

[64] *Ibid.*, no. 1507, pp. 343-45.

[65] *Ibid.*, no. 1509, pp. 346-47.

[66] *Ibid.*, no. 1510, p. 348.

[67] *Ibid.*, p. 348, "Relatio historiae." Blanchard's party needed extra time to prepare its case "cum nullum reperiant, qui eorum causam postulare et prosequi vellet contra universitatem predictam, eo quia de sacramento universitatis se fore asserunt excusantes."

John de Bournazel, to serve as Blanchard's representatives, they said that "as sworn men of the university, they could not be the chancellor's advocates." [68] The cardinal then released them from their oaths,[69] but none of them complied.[70] Finally, on May 25, when the university's agents presented their articles of accusation, Blanchard had to appear in person, alone, to complain that he had found no counsel and that his defense would be deficient, "since he did not know how to express himself very well." [71]

Despite his handicap, the chancellor legally challenged the university in two ways. First, he asked the Cardinal of Laon to dismiss the case against him because the masters, he asserted, had violated one of the principal rules governing legal investigations, that the parties to the dispute should undertake no new measures until the final judgment had been rendered. In fact, not all the actions of which he complained had been instituted since the commission was established. In particular, Blanchard objected that the three superior Faculties, of Theology, Law, and Medicine, had imposed upon all degree-recipients in each faculty an oath to observe the new university statutes. He was referring to the oaths imposed on bachelors by the statute of January 9, 1385, whose implications have been discussed. Blanchard was especially disturbed by the policy of the Faculty of Arts. Not content with the injuries inflicted by the other faculties, "but heaping evil upon evil," he lamented, "the Rector of the University with the Faculty of Arts refuses to let any bachelor licensed in the examination at Notre-Dame [i.e. by Blanchard's examiners] pay the usual payments or swear the usual oaths." [72] Blanchard's complaints notwithstanding, the two prohibitions had been enacted at the same time for all faculties: no payments and no oaths. He represented the situation more accurately in his testimony before the Parlement of Paris, where without

---

[68] *Ibid.*, Maii 17: "Universitas in advocatos et consiliarios mag. Petrum Forteti, decanum Nivernens., et mag. Guillelmum de Marchia per distributionem recepit, cancellarius vero Odardum de Molinis, Radulphum de Ulmonte et priorem Carnotens. [Johannem de Bornasello seu Bournazel]; quibus replicantibus ipsos ut juratos Universitatis non posse esse advocatos cancellarii, cardinalis obtinuit ut a juramento solverentur."

[69] *Ibid.*

[70] Blanchard's counsellor was John de Valle. *Chart.*, III, nos. 1517 and 1520.

[71] *Ibid.*, no. 1510, p. 348: "Et dictus cancellarius tradidit et presentavit eidem domino quandam supplicacionem suam, in qua dicebat quod ipse partem intentionis sue [imminueret], cum nesciret sic bene verbo exprimere, et dubitaret in loquendo deficere."

[72] *Ibid.*, no. 1512, p. 366.

distinguishing between faculties he said, "the masters made the bachelors swear they would not send anything to the chancellor." [73]

The only action mentioned by Blanchard that might be considered an initiative undertaken after the investigation had begun was the masters' decision to exert pressure on his supporters. In particular, they prevented Fleming du Martroy, a Bachelor of Theology under Blanchard's sponsorship, who was also one of his examiners in arts, from conducting his lectures in the Faculty of Arts. When he refused to obey this order and appealed to the pope, they expelled him from the university. Thus, on the grounds that no new initiatives should be taken *lite pendente*, and because fear of reprisals had deprived him not only of legal counsel, but even of the advice of his friends, Blanchard argued that the case should either be dropped or transferred to the Holy See. The cardinals refused this petition, apparently accepting the reply of the university syndics to the effect that such a motion was valid only in a formal trial, whereas this was merely an extrajudicial investigation. [74]

Blanchard also used a second argument in his appeal to the Cardinal of Laon. He accused the masters of violating the oath never to contravene in any way the rights of the chancellorship sworn to him and his predecessors by those receiving the license. [75] In effect he was trying to use the licentiate's oath to the chancellor in the same way the masters were using the oath to the rector. The masters would later remind the chancellor that he had once sworn the oath of obedience to the rector, just as Blanchard now reminded the masters of their oath to him. Although the controversy over these two oaths served to embitter the conflict, the professors knew the chancellor's interpretation of their oath would never stand up. They had already cited *Parens scientiarum*, which explicitly states that the only oath a bachelor about to be licensed can swear to the chancellor is to "provide faithful testimony concerning bachelors" to be licensed in the future. The Cardinal of Laon was unmoved by Blanchard's petition.

Blanchard never overcame the obstacles that hindered him in May,

---

[73] Du Boulay, IV, 607, 36: "Les Maistres on fait jurer les Bacheliers qui ne bailleront rien au Chancelier"; or again, *ibid.*, 608, 4-6: "Ce ne fut le premier [serment] que les Maistres ont fait aux Bacheliers à licentier de rien payer au Chancelier."

[74] *Chart.*, III, no. 1512, p. 366. A vivid account of another example of pressure exerted against Blanchard's friends is given by Bonitus Litelli, *ibid.*, no. 1521, test. 2, pp. 412-13.

[75] *Ibid.*, no. 1512, p. 366.

1385. They limited his effectiveness throughout the investigation. In a process of this sort, each side was responsible for composing its own deposition and producing witnesses willing to vouch for the truthfulness of its individual articles.[76] The university was able to muster 72 witnesses, who were examined from July to October.[77] By September, even though the Cardinal of Laon had summoned 185 witnesses whom Blanchard had said were "necessary to prove his case," [78] the chancellor found only fifteen men willing to testify on his behalf, seven of whom had also testified for the university.[79] The articles of accusation, Blanchard's deposition, and the testimony gathered by the cardinal's commission—altogether a considerable body of information—will be analyzed in detail in the following chapter.[80] Here, let us simply note that Blanchard was undismayed by the massive evidence compiled against him. Indeed, he resolutely insisted that the university's reforming decrees constituted a usurpation of his rights as chancellor, and refused to change any of his practices. His obstinacy provoked the Faculty of Theology, on July 7, to threaten him with a boycott, that is to order all masters, bachelors, students, and beadles to avoid the chancellor, his company, his classes, and his ceremonies, if he should continue to violate the university's resolutions regarding the license.[81] Not needing much evidence to be convinced of the chancellor's stubbornness, the masters soon took disciplinary action against those closest to him, namely his subchancellor, Pierre Plaoul, and his examiners, Willian Gorren, Fleming du Martroy, John Hokelem, and Nicolas of Vaudemonte. "In contempt of the chancellor and his office, and under the pretext of pretended abuses" runs Blanchard's complaint, the masters consider all these men excluded from the consortium and community of the university congregation." [82]

---

[76] Thus the university submitted its articles of accusation "ad finem quod super contentis in dictis articulis vobis placeat vos informare etiam extrajudicialiter, et testes, quos dicti procuratores seu eorum quilibet dictorum rectoris et universitatis duxerint producendos, super dictis articulis, recipere, et eorum juramenta et ipsos examinari facere." *Ibid.*, no. 1511, p. 349.

Blanchard's representative, John de Valle, requested the Cardinal of Laon to "examinare... vel facere examinari testes per eum [Blanchard] aut ipsius nomine super premissis articulis producendos." *Ibid.*, no. 1520, pp. 410-11.

[77] *Ibid.*, no. 1513.

[78] *Ibid.*, no. 1518, p. 396: "Asserit [eos] necessarios ad probandum intentionem suam."

[79] *Ibid.*, no. 1521.

[80] *Ibid.*, nos. 1511, 1513, 1520, 1521.

[81] *Ibid.*, no. 1514, p. 390.

[82] *Ibid.*, no. 1516, p. 395.

By autumn 1385 the chancellor was finally able to obtain a hearing at Avignon.[83] It must have been on this occasion that, in accord with Clement VII's original order, transcripts of the testimony taken in Paris were presented to the curia by the investigating cardinals. One such transcript exists today in the Vatican Archives as Collectus 440. It is our principal source of information on the cardinal's investigation.[84] Since the university's witnesses were still testifying in October,[85] the hearing in Avignon could not have been earlier. Pierre d'Ailly represented the masters and spoke before the pope on the theme "Domine vim patior".[86] His speech must date from October or November 1385. It must also have been at this time that Blanchard submitted a list of articles outlining his position for the pope.[87] Thus ended the Cardinal of Laon's investigation of the university masters' complaints.

With the completion of the dreary investigative process, the university community expectantly awaited the pope's decision. The tension broke as the conflict reached a surprising climax and a new legal process was initiated. During the Christmas ordinary term, from the resumption of classes on October 1 to Christmas, the chancellor traditionally conducted his examination of the candidates named by the masters of the three higher faculties; within three months of the request for the degree, he was to send *signeta* notifying acceptable bachelors that they would be licensed. In the autumn of 1385, however, in accord with their resolution of the preceding January 9, the masters of the Faculty of Theology themselves ranked the bachelors and sent to the chancellor the names of their recommended candidates

---

[83] *Ibid.*, no. 1517.

[84] Denifle devoted eighty pages of the *Chart.* to Arch. Vat. Collect. 440, which he published nearly in its entirety. The manuscript contains copies of official correspondence concerning the investigation, documents and depositions presented by the opposing parties, and a transcript of the 83 witnesses' testimony.

[85] *Chart.*, III, no. 1513, p. 368.

[86] This speech does not receive a detailed examination in this book because it is superceded by the two speeches that d'Ailly gave the following February. They are studied at length in Chapters V and VI and edited in the Appendix. In "Domine Vim Patior" d'Ailly used his papal audience more to show off his learning (note the reference to Petrarch, p. 400) and rhetorical skills than to deal with specific facts or arguments. The essential material from this discourse is mentioned here in its due place. For the rest see Denifle's edition in *Chart.*, III, no. 1519, pp. 399-402. The transcription is accurate; the omitted material is of no consequence. Note that Paris, B.N., ms. lat. 3122, f. 61 contains the marginal notation, "coram papa propositio."

[87] *Ibid.*, no. 1520.

listed in order. Outraged by this "usurpation" of what he considered his right to rank the candidates at his own discretion, in a flamboyant gesture of resentment, Blanchard tore up the list.[88] Furthermore, because the university had imposed an oath on the bachelors not to send their "gifts," he in turn refused to send the signeta [89] until the bachelors were released from their oaths.[90] Summoned to explain his actions before an assembly of masters, he refused to talk.[91] The university then appealed to the Parlement of Paris, where the case was heard on February 5 and 6, 1386.[92] On February 12, the judges asked the two parties to write additional briefs. They promised to consult the Cardinal of Laon before taking final action, but so far as is known, they never issued a verdict.[93]

D'Ailly was the university's spokesman at the Parlement,[94] and his two speeches against the chancellor, "Radix Omnium" and "Super Omnia," were outgrowths of this suit. The former comprised a

---

[88] Du Boulay, IV, 608, 25-34: "Et à ce que ceux de l'Université ont fait proposer que le Chancelier a desiré la scedule qui luy fust presentée de par les Maistres en Theologie pour les Bacheliers à licentier. Respond le Chancelier et dit qu'il n'a rien fait au contempt de l'Université de des Maistres, mais pource que ladite scedule n'estoit pas en bonne forme, mais estoit contre les droits de la Chancelerie, il la desira; car le Chancelier assigne les lieux aux Bacheliers selon sa conscience, et par la derniere scedule, les Maistres assignoient les lieux, et disoient la scedule telle premiere, telle seconde, et entreprenoient les Maistres, ce que compete à l'Office du Chancelier, et pour ce a desiré ladite scedule pour garder son droit."

[89] *Ibid.*, 3-7: "Quant au delay d'envoyer le signet du Chancelier aux Bacheliers à licentier, dont ceux de l'Université se sont complains, dit le Chancelier que ce ne fut le premier [serment] que les Maistres ont fait faire aux Bacheliers à licentier de rien payer au Chancelier, et que les Bacheliers fussent demeurez en la liberté qu'ils estoient auparavant le serment, le Chancelier n'eust pas differé a envoyer son signet." Cf. p. 607, lines 35-39.

[90] *Ibid.*, 608, lines 40-41: "Et si c'est que les Bacheliers à licentier seroient relaxez de leur serment, il envoyra ses signets."

[91] *Ibid.*, lines 34-37: "A ce que dient ceux de l'Université, que quand le Chancelier fut interrogé en l'Université, pourquoy il avoit desiré ladite scedule, il répondit qu'il n'estoit pas là venu pour répondre *de quolibet*...."

[92] The transcript of the hearing is given in *ibid.*, 606-14. The growth of the parlement's *de facto* jurisdiction over ecclesiastical matters of this sort is traced in Lot and Fawtier, *Histoire des institutions*, II, 455-59.

[93] Du Boulay, 614, 13-19: "Finablement parties oüyes au long en repliquant et dupliquant, Appointé est que les Parties escriront par maniere de memoire, et verra la Cour la Complainte, les Bulles et aultres lettres de Ceux de l'Université, et commettra aucuns de la Cour pour parler au Cardinal de Laon du Procés de Cour de Rome, et mettront lesdites Parties devers la Cour, tout ce dont ils se vouloient ayder en cette matiere, et escriront lesdites Parties à toutes leurs fins, Playdoyez; Et tout considéré, la Cour fera droit.

[94] See above, p. 60, n. 5.

systematic presentation of d'Ailly's arguments followed by a point for point rebuttal of Blanchard's position. It was delivered at the College of Navarre between the court sessions of February 5 and 6.[95] The latter, in form an open disputation, was a thorough review of each argument in "Radix Omnium" with further efforts to resolve objections raised by Blanchard's partisans to each of d'Ailly's earlier statements.[96] It may have been intended for the second stage of the court's deliberations. If so, then it must postdate February 12.

What is the evidence for so precise a dating of the earlier speech? "Radix Omnium" is divided into two parts. The first expounds d'Ailly's view of the issues, the second refutes Blanchard. In stating some of his opponent's arguments, d'Ailly paraphrases and nearly quotes statements made by Blanchard in the Parlement of Paris on February 5.[97] Moreover, the transcript for February 6 shows that d'Ailly, acting as the university's advocate, paraphrased "Radix Omnium" when he said "It seems that what the Chancellor wills to have is simoniacal and to say the contrary is heretical." [98] Furthermore, in "Radix Omnium," he implies that the hearing is not yet over when he explains that he is speaking "for practice," and adds "in case it *might* be necessary to declare and maintain certain things on this matter." [99] If the process had been completed and all his testimony delivered, d'Ailly would not have used the subjunctive in referring to what he might say. Therefore, since in "Radix Omnium" d'Ailly quotes the proceedings of February 5 and implies that they are not yet over, and since, furthermore, he would restate the thesis of "Radix Omnium" in court on February 6, I conclude that "Radix

---

[95] Paris, Bibliothèque de l'Arsenal, ms. 520, f. 74: "Declaratio determinata per Petrum de Alliaco in scholis Navarre." Cf. Paris, BN, ms. lat. 3122, f. 51v: "Questio determinata per eundem in scholis Navarre, in materia symonie." The dating will be discussed below.

[96] "Super Omnia," edited below, in Appendix, p. 237, l. 4-8: "Intendo prout promisi, veritatem, quam in quadam questione alias declaravi, pluribus rationibus tunc contra me factis et quibusdam aliis impugnare, et easdem pro posse solvere. Ac eciam non solum ipsis sed aliis nunc faciendis...aliqualiter respondere..."

[97] For the textual comparison, see below, pp. 124-6. Again in "Radix Omnium," p. 228, l. 25-7, d'Ailly refers to Blanchard's testimony of Feb. 5. Du Boulay, IV, 608, 6-7.

[98] *Ibid.*, 613, 53-54: "Ce que le Chancelier veut avoir *est simoniacum*; et dire le contraire *est hereticum*." Cf. *ibid.*, lines 24-25.

[99] Radix, p. 199, l. 2-5: "... in casu quo oporteret declarare et sustinere [in Parlamento] quedam in hac materia....Ideo expediens iudicavi ad exercitium et eruditionem meam, questionem inferius proponendam, scholastice pertractare."

Omnium" was delivered between the court sessions of February 5 and February 6. D'Ailly must have been working at a frenetic pace during the trial if he represented the university in court on two successive days and delivered "Radix Omnium" some time in between.

When the Parlement of Paris failed to reach a conclusion in the spring of 1386, attention turned to Clement VII, who took his final action in the case on September 28 of that year. There was no verdict. Blanchard was not condemned. The consequences were less severe than the punishment for selling the license prescribed in the provision *Quoniam ecclesia* in canon law, deprivation of all benefices.[100] Realizing that Blanchard would no longer be tolerated by the Parisian masters, Clement, on September 28, 1386, conferred the chancellorship upon an alumnus of the College of Navarre, a long-time follower of the Avignon faction, but still only a Bachelor of Theology, John de Guignicourt.[101] On the same day, Clement made Blanchard the Archdeacon of Ghent, which was still Urbanist, and treasurer of the chapter at Reims, which was Clementine.[102] Given Blanchard's new offices, we need not regard Clement's reference, in appointing Guignicourt, to the vacancy created "by the free resignation of John Blanchard" as laden with irony.[103]

The masters' dissatisfaction with Clement's decision was manifest. On December 16, 1386, they sent a messenger to Cambrai, where Blanchard still held the treasurership and a canonry with prebend,[104]

---

[100] *Corpus Juris Canonici*, X. 5, 5, 1; ed. E. Friedberg, 2 vols. (Leipzig, 1879), II, 768-69.

[101] *Chart.*, III, no. 1527, pp. 424-25. For Guignicourt's affiliation with the College of Navarre, see Launoy, p. 334. Guignicourt had been one of the dissident cardinals' messengers during the summer of 1378, bearing their news to Charles V. Valois, I, 96, 101. He was as devoted to Clement as Blanchard.

[102] H. Nelis, *Documents relatifs au Grand Schisme*, III: *Suppliques et Lettres de Clement VII (1379-94)*, AVB, XIII (Bruxelles, 1934), no. 1203. In 1386 Ghent was a strongly Urbanist city. In this appointment Clement was anticipating future advances. See below, pp. 138-40. The treasurership in Reims should have been tenable.

[103] *Chart.*, III, no. 1527, pp. 424-25: "Cum itaque postmodum cancellaria ecclesie Parisiensis per liberam resignationem dilecti filii Johannis Blancart ipsius ecclesie cancellarii de illa, quam tunc temporis obtinebat..." Denifle has found a reference to Blanchard living out his years as a canon at Laon or Thérouanne, bitterly complaining about his "expulsion" from the chancellorship (*ibid.*, no. 1522, p. 420n.), but this suggestion is outweighed by the documents cited below, in notes 104 and 113-116.

[104] Blanchard's positions at Tournai, Cambrai, and Ghent were reassigned only on June 4, 8, and 16, 1393, respectively, "per obitum extra Romanam curiam Johannis Blanchardi." See Nelis, *Documents*, AVB, XIII, nos. 2360-2362, 2364, and 2376.

to demand that he appear before their assembly within twenty days or suffer exclusion from the "privileges, franchises, and liberties" of the university.[105] Not surprisingly, no such appearance is recorded.[106]

When Blanchard's successor as chancellor, John de Guignicourt, continued to demand the same oaths and promises as Blanchard, the masters again complained to the pope, who in 1389 forbade the exaction of an oath, a payment, or a promise to swear or pay. This time he explicitly condemned the use of signeta to extort "gifts" and, the auction of academic ranks, and disallowed the chancellor's labor in administering the degree as an excuse for receiving money.[107] With Guignicourt persisting in the old pattern, Clement made no objection to changing chancellors again. On October 7, 1389, he allowed Guignicourt and Pierre d'Ailly to exchange benefices. D'Ailly gave up his canonries at Amiens and Meaux in return for the chancellorship.[108] Thus the former representative of the indignant masters was given the opportunity to eliminate by his own actions the abuses he had contested so long. Clement VII facilitated d'Ailly's task by allowing him to add newly vacant benefices to that of the chancellorship until the revenues of that office were augmented to a total of one hundred pounds of Tours.[109] (Of course this did not mean that d'Ailly could not hold other benefices, only that the chancellorship would be worth more.) Blanchard, by contrast, had testified in the Parlement that the chancellorship was worth a maximum of forty pounds per annum.[110] He did not specify whether these were pounds of Paris or of Tours,[111] but even if they were pounds of Paris, the

---

[105] *Chart.*, III, no. 1532, p. 440 and n. 3.

[106] The masters did not give up. On July 27, 1387, they empowered a long list of professors to proceed against Blanchard on the university's behalf. P. Doncœur, "La Condemnation de Jean de Monzon par Pierre d'Orgement," *Revue des Questions Historiques*, 82 (1909), 181. I am indebted to Douglass Taber for this reference.

[107] *Chart.*, III, nos. 1550 and 1555. See especially no. 1555, p. 484: "... ordinamus quod decetero aliquis bacallarius studii predicti in aliqua facultate licentiandus in receptione signeti ab eodem cancellario aut alias per se vel alium nullatenus det, tradat aut presentet, vel se daturum promittat aliquod munum eidem cancellario aut ejus officiariis seu familiaribus quocunque titulo ratione licentie hujusmodi aut loci in ea habendi sive occasione laboris aut quovis alio exquisito colore...."

[108] *Ibid.*, p. 340, and nos. 1552 and 1553.

[109] *Ibid.*, no. 1556, pp. 485-86.

[110] Du Boulay, IV, 606, 22-33.

[111] Innocent VI's letter appointing Grimerius Bonifacii chancellor in 1360-62 mentions a maximum annual revenue of 25 pounds of Paris (*Chart.*, III, no. 1259, p. 77); hence the sum was not always expressed in terms of any one currency.

sum would equal only fifty pounds of Tours, one-half the revenue subsequently allowed d'Ailly.[112]

If, in increasing the revenues of the chancellorship, Clement showed understanding for the burdens and temptations of the office, he also continued to show considerable solicitude for the man who formerly had occupied it. Clement's concern for Blanchard's welfare continued to manifest itself until the ex-chancellor's death. On March 11, 1390, Blanchard was given a pension of two hundred gold francs a year in return for resigning the treasurership at Reims.[113] Then, on December 14, 1390, John was again called "familiaris pape" when Clement VII named the Abbott of St-Martin's of Tournai and the deans of Tournai and St. Peter's of Lille his legal representatives for one more try at Blanchard's old lawsuit in Liége! [114] On September 25, 1391, still calling John "familiaris noster," Clement appointed Blanchard provost and canon with prebend at St-Omer,[115] but from a papal tax collector's entry in the thirteenth year of Clement's pontificate (October 31, 1390-October 30, 1391), we learn that John Blanchard died before he could take possession of these new benefices.[116]

The foregoing account of the Blanchard affair leaves an important question unanswered. If, as Blanchard maintained, the donation of money or gifts as part of the licensing process had been tolerated for so long that it could seriously be defended as customary, why did the professors choose this particular time to oppose it? For an answer we must turn to the university's articles of accusation and the testimony they elicited, to gain a picture of Blanchard's administration and his conduct as Chancellor of Paris.

---

[112] These calculations are based on the ratio of four pounds of Paris to five pounds of Tours. Because both men supplemented the revenues of the chancellorship with outside income, the papal limits on the chancellorship do not indicate the two chancellors' relative fortunes.

[113] Nelis, *Documents*, no. 1767, p. 672.

[114] *Ibid.*, no. 1898, pp. 694-95.

[115] *Ibid.*, no. 1917, p. 342.

[116] U. Berlière, *Les Collectories pontificales dans les anciennes diocèses de Cambrai, Thérouanne et Tournai au XIV*e*s*, AVB, X (1929), 583.

CHAPTER FOUR

THE ACCUSATIONS

The 83 articles of accusation against Blanchard are unevenly distributed among five categories.[1] (1) In the Faculty of Arts, the chancellor has rigidly systematized the exaction of fees from candidates for the license (arts. 11-23), and is aided in this by the subchancellor (arts. 58-80). (2) Together with his notary, he has corruptly administered the university's five-year privilege (art. 81). (3) In the Faculty of Theology, he has extorted money, goods, or both from those about to read the *Sentences* and from candidates for the license by delaying their progress unduly and withholding their notice of promotion, the signetum, until payment has been received (arts. 25-39, 41-45, 47-48, 50-53). (4) In the Faculty of Theology, he has not consulted all the masters about the qualifications of candidates as required by *Parens scientiarum* and has ranked the candidates in an order different from that determined by the faculty (art. 55).[2] (5) By threats, promises, and other means, he has forced bachelors to abandon their own masters and to incept under him in the Faculty of Theology (art. 54).

The individual articles are sometimes quite detailed, but because accusations are biased by their very nature and because these 83 were composed with considerable attention to their rhetorical effect, they must be assessed in the light of statements made by the 65 witnesses who testified for the university, the eight who spoke for Blanchard, and the seven who gave depositions for both sides. Among those who endorsed the university's articles were some men like Nicholas Decani and Siger Baert, Blanchard's assistants (*familiares*), and Stephen Boussard, his notary, who had direct knowledge of his practices.[3] Yet it is not always possible to accept their testimony at face value, because these men would have had an interest in coloring their accounts of their former patron's behavior in order to detach themselves from him and thus escape eventual sanctions. Still other

---

[1] *Chartularium Universitatis Parisiensis*, ed. H. Denifle & E. Châtelain, 4 vols. (Paris, 1889-97), III, no. 1511, pp. 349-65. (Hereafter cited as *Chart.*) Articles 1-9 reiterate the masters' recent legislation of late 1384 and early 1385, reaffirming earlier regulations concerning the license.

[2] In the Faculty of Medicine he has abused his authority as specified here in points 3 and 4.

[3] *Chart.*, III, no. 1513, witnesses (test.) 34, 52, 53, and 51, respectively.

witnesses, like the former masters of "stolen" bachelors or the licentiates who paid for their degrees, may have been nursing a grudge that could distort their testimony severely. Another group were those who testified [4] to the traditional nature of the chancellor's procedures, the maliciousness of his attackers, and his personal integrity and widespread good reputation.[5] The fifteen men in this group were on the whole much more independent of the prosecution than the previously mentioned witnesses, though their accounts may be biased by their partiality for the chancellor. Seven of these men, however, also testified on the university's behalf; these seven came closest to a neutral position.

In the evaluation that follows, testimony from witnesses in all these groups as well as information from the articles of accusation themselves will be used. The general position of each witness will be identified, but no effort will be made to analyze fully the personal bias of each one. Our goal is not a judicial verdict on the chancellor, but an understanding of his administration and the motivation for the attempt to reform it. To this end biased testimony may be useful, provided it is understood as such and properly interpreted.

The articles concerning the Faculty of Arts are arranged chronologically to produce the impression that Blanchard and his subchancellor, Pierre Plaoul, had gradually built an efficient system of fee-exaction. In his first year as chancellor, according to article 11, Blanchard took sixteen francs from John de Augia, who was to be the Flemish nation's examiner. When Fleming du Martroy succeeded John, the sixteen francs were returned, but the price of the office was now twenty francs (art. 12). Nicholas de Vaudemonte paid fifty francs when he was named examiner for the French nation (art. 12).

The next ten articles itemize methodically the sums given to Blanchard's assistants for themselves and for the chancellor by the bachelors being examined.

In the first examination or hearing (*auditio*) of the first year of Blanchard's administration, 1381-82, twelve bachelors collected six francs, of which they gave one franc for the chancellor's assistants and the remaining five for the subchancellor "so that they might be passed more quickly" (art. 13). In the second examination that year, eighteen bachelors collected two francs, which they gave to the chancellor's

---

[4] *Ibid.*, no. 1521, pp. 412-20.
[5] *Ibid.*, no. 1520, pp. 402-11.

assistants in the chancellor's name and in the end for him, so that they might be passed more quickly (art. 14). In the third examination of the first year, 24 bachelors collected four francs; one franc for the assistants, and three for the chancellor (art. 15). In the fourth examination, 27 bachelors each gave two *solidi* of Paris to the chancellor's assistants, so that they would be passed more quickly (art. 16).[6]

In the second examination of the second year, sixteen bachelors gave twelve francs, of which two went to Siger Baert and William Rolins, the chancellor's assistants, and five to the chancellor himself, "for which gift the chancellor graciously thanked the bachelors as they left the examination room" (art. 17). In the third examination of that year, nineteen bachelors collected ten francs, which they gave to Baert and Rolins. When the assistants said the bachelors would not receive a very quick decision, they gave four francs more. And, concerning this gift, the assistants said to the bachelors as they left the examination room that the chancellor thanked them, thus accepting and ratifying the abuse (art. 18). In the fourth examination, 21 bachelors collected fifteen francs, of which ten were given to the assistants for the chancellor so that they might have a faster decision (art. 19).

In the first examination of the third year, twelve bachelors collected twelve francs, of which six were for the chancellor and three apiece for the assistants (art. 20). In the second examination that year, twenty bachelors collected twenty francs, of which ten were for the chancellor. "And, since one of the students in the examination was said to have taken a rose from the chancellor's garden, and the lord chancellor himself was greatly angered by this, ... the students of that examination had two very beautiful rose garlands worth one franc bought and presented to the chancellor, who received them with joy. In addition, the students of that examination, as they left the hall, gave two gold francs to his assistants with the chancellor's knowledge" (art. 21).

---

[6] During the reigns of Charles V and Charles VI, until March 11, 1385, the gold franc was legally fixed at twenty silver solidi (sous or shillings) of Tours (s.t.), each in turn worth twelve denarii (deniers or pence) of Tours (d.t.) French kings also minted another series of silver coins "of Paris," based on the ratio of twelve denarii (d.p.) to one solidus (s.p.). The silver coins of Paris and Tours were fixed at a rate of four s.p. to five s.t. Thus twenty s.t. and sixteen s.p. would both buy one (gold) franc. (E. Fournial, *Histoire monétaire de l'occident médiévale*, Paris, 1970, pp. 119-24). In the present example, the contribution of the 27 bachelors who each gave two s.p. was 54s.p., or 67s. 6d.t., or 3 fr. 7s. 6d.t. The transactions described in the articles of accusation were made before the currency change of 1385. See note 48 below.

In the third examination of the year, twenty bachelors were included by Arnaldus de Trajecto, who lived with John Hokelem, examiner for the English nation, and some of his colleagues, to give something to the chancellor "so that they might be pleasing to the chancellor and for a faster decision" (art. 22).

Although the degree in arts was awarded by the authority of either the Chancellor of Ste-Geneviève or the Chancellor of Notre Dame,[7] the latter did not administer examinations in person. This task was delegated to the subchancellor Plaoul, who controlled entrance to the examinations and was accused by the masters of using his position to extort payments in money and in kind from the candidates (art. 58). They allege that he received, on a collective basis, six francs from the bachelors of the first examination of the first year; five francs from those of the second examination and five francs from those of the fourth examination of the second year; and in the third year, four francs from those of the first examination, ten from those of the second, and eight from those of the third (art. 60). Despite this shadow over his early career, Plaoul eventually emerged as a prominent university spokesman and major Gallican theorist at the Paris council of 1398,[8] but in the first two years of Blanchard's administration he received more from the groups of bachelors being examined than the chancellor did (see Table I).

Table I shows that as time passed, each candidate's contribution to the collective payments quadrupled from an average of approximately four solidi of Tours in the first year to one franc, so that

---

[7] See above, p. 13.

[8] With Simon de Cramaud, Pierre Leroy, and Giles Deschamps, Plaoul was a major advocate of the subtraction of obedience from Clement VII's successor, Benedict XIII, in 1398. By 1407, these radicals had attracted moderate allies like d'Ailly, Gerson, and Fillastre in efforts to force Benedict XIII into a simultaneous resignation with his Roman counterpart Gregory XII. (E. Delaruelle, E.-R. Labande, P. Ourliac, *L'Église au temps du Grand Schisme*, vol. XIV of A. Fliche & V. Martin, eds., *Histoire de l'Église*, 2 vols., Paris, 1962-64, I, 100-101, 130.) These men later became influential leaders at the Council of Pisa, which deposed Gregory and Benedict.

Plaoul was born in 1353 in the diocese of Liége, and was a Master of Arts and Bachelor of Theology at the Sorbonne by 1385. After Blanchard's departure in 1386, Plaoul attracted the patronage of Pierre Ameilh, Cardinal of Embrun, who probably helped him obtain a canonry at St-Omer by 1388. Plaoul became a Master of Theology in 1393, and was made Bishop of Senlis on October 2, 1409, by Alexander V, only three months after the pope's election at Pisa. (*Chart.*, III, p. 347, n. 2; p. 418, test. xii; p. 482; p. 501). He died on April 11, 1415. U. Chevalier, *Repertoire des sources historiques du moyen âge, Bio-Bibliographie*, 2 vols. Paris, 1907, col. 3774.

Table I
Collective Payments in Arts Examinations

article [a]	witness [b]	examination	year	bachelors	total collected	amount (in s.t.) per bachelor	francs to assistants	francs to chancellor	% to chancellor	francs to sub-chancellor
13	22	1	1	12	6 fr	10 s	1 fr	0	0	5 fr[c]
14	—	2	1	18	2 fr	2 s	—	2	100	—
15	12	3	1	24	4 fr	3 s 4d	1	3	75	—
16	48	4	1	27	3 fr 7s. 6d.	2 s 6d.	3 fr 7s. 6d.	0	0	—
—	—	1	2	—	—	—	—	—	—	—
17	—	2	2	16	12 fr	15 s	2	5	41	5
18	61	3	2	19	14 fr	14 s 9d	4	10	71	—
19	18	4	2	21	15 fr	14 s 3d	—	10	67	5
20	58, 46[a]	1	3	12	12 fr	20 s	2	6	50	4
21	36[e]	2	3	20	23 fr	23 s	2	11	48	10
28	59[f]	3	3	20	20 fr	20 s	2	10	50	8

a From *Chart.*, III, no. 1511.

b From *ibid.*, no. 1513.

c Witness 22 says one-half franc from each bachelor for subchancellor.

d Witness 46 confirms fact of giving in examination of third year, but his sums vary from those who describe individual cases, so I have preferred the latter.

e Witness 36 confirms two francs to assistants.

f Witness 27 was present but reverses distribution; article 22 wrongly gives ten francs to assistants; witness 59 was present.

the chancellor's half of the collection more than doubled. Threats of a slower decision (art. 18) and such pretenses as damage to the chancellor's garden (art. 21) were used to increase the amounts. Friends of the chancellor's assistants or examiners also encouraged candidates to give and thus create a favorable impression on the chancellor (art. 22). The sale of office to examiners, an increased take from his assistants, and the threat of red tape were also listed by Blanchard's accusors to substantiate their account of his exploitation.

In addition, bachelors were induced to make individual payments to the subchancellor, usually to gain admittance to an earlier examination. Plaoul was able to extract bribes of four francs from Roland Ramier, 10 solidi of Paris from Thomas le Mauge, four francs from Robert de Barris, four francs from Jacob de Celatis on behalf of one friend and ten francs on behalf of Peter de Burgondia, four francs from Henry de Palma, four francs from John de Novavilla, and ten francs from Nicholas Robaut (art. 61). Master Henry of Univilla gave him a half-ell of cloth worth three francs for John de Campo, and four francs for Robert de Barris, both his students, "to procure their license" (art. 64).⁹ "For the same reason," Simon Ourardi gave a half-ell of cloth at the suggestion of the examiner, Fleming du Martroy (art. 65).

For admission to the examination, a speedy decision, and award of the license, candidates offered banquets for Plaoul and other Blanchard assistants. The most spectacular of these was sponsored by Richard Railardi, who, during his examination period, arranged a cruise down the Seine and served two lavish meals at Boulogne for the subchancellor, along with examiners Fleming and John de Hokelem (art. 68).

The sums spent on these parties give a general indication of the real value of the money changing hands in the university. Nicholas de Rivo paid about two francs for a meal to which Plaoul and three examiners were invited (art. 70). Robert Tessardi paid three francs for a banquet for Plaoul and three associates (art. 71). Peter de Burgondia paid two francs for a meal for the subchancellor and some of his associates (art. 74). Peter Valleti gave a meal for the subchancellor and four of his colleagues that cost three francs (art. 75). If we assume that the bachelor was himself present at the meal, we can deduce from

---

⁹ It is unclear whether the four francs that Henry of Univilla paid on behalf of Robert de Barris are the same as those mentioned in article 61 as paid directly by Robert himself.

these figures that two or three francs would feed five or six people at a banquet sumptuous enough to constitute a gracious bribe and certainly not so frugal as to risk offending the subchancellor. Others spent even more (arts 76 and 77).

Occasionally, the subchancellor's schemes went awry. Henry Ludenschede promised him sixteen francs and gave collateral. When he was licensed, he paid the money and asked for the return of his pledge. Plaoul refused. Henry organized an ambush, had Plaoul beaten, and thus obtained restitution. "And because of this almost the whole university and its neighbors were scandalized" (art. 63). Thomas de Borvilla used his books as a deposit in anticipation of a twenty-franc payment, but, once he received the license, he refused to pay, and got his books back by threatening Plaoul with another beating (art. 62).[10]

Even if some hardy bachelors resisted Plaoul with force, institutional pressures led the majority to accede to the increasingly systematized routine of payments. Moreover, as the articles of accusation asserted, those who did not pay, even if worthy, would not be licensed.

> Two noble brothers, the youths Walter and William de Momalia, although they were worthy of being licensed in arts, nonetheless, because they did not give the chancellor fur-trimmed clothes, spices, or jewels in the manner of nobles, and even though he was several times offered twenty francs on their behalf, they still were not licensed, but were rejected, because they did not give enough (art. 23).

Gifts from bachelors in arts may not have been extracted as methodically as the articles of accusation imply, but the testimony suggests that there was indeed a system. William Gorren, who testified that all 37 of Blanchard's assertions in his own defense were true,[11] nonetheless confirmed some of the university's charges, specifically those concerning the sums paid in the examinations of Blanchard's third year and the payment made by Flemming de Martroy for John de Augia's resignation as examiner and Nicholas de Vaudemonte's payment for that office.[12]

The best account of the chancellor's administration of arts examinations at Notre-Dame was provided by his former assistant,

---

[10] See also *Chart.*, III, no. 1513, p. 382, test. xlviii.
[11] *Ibid.*, no. 1521, test. xiv, p. 419.
[12] *Ibid.*, no. 1513, p. 381, test. xlvi.

Nicholas Decani, who answered as follows to a question about article 15:

> In the time of his service, no examination would take place in which something was not given to the chancellor and his assistants. When an assistant received the money, he would carry it to the chancellor, who would take from it what he wanted, and send the rest to be distributed among the assistants as he ordered, not equally.[13]

Asked how many assistants there were, he said that there were usually five, and sometimes six, who all participated, but unequally, in the distribution of the aforesaid money. And the names of the assistants who were there in his time are these, viz., Colardus de Leon, a squire from the diocese of Liége, William Rolins, clerk, and Siger Baert, a relative, both from Ghent, the said witness, and the cook, who was frequently changed.[14]

Siger Baert in his turn testified that he knew nothing about articles 10-21, concerning the examinations in arts, but that, as stated in article 22, it was true that the bachelors in the third examination of the third year "gave to him and to William Rolin, his colleague, two francs and something more, concerning which quantity he did not remember [15] to be divided among the other assistants for the "courtesy and services" they had rendered. Asked who distributed it, he answered to this and other questions that he did not remember. "Asked why they gave to them rather than to the others, he said it was because they had rendered greater services than the others." [16]

Decani, Rolin, and Baert were understandably vague about the types of pressure applied to encourage donations. Apart from the force of institutionalized tradition, money was useful to gain entrance to the examinations and a high rank among the candidates.[17] These payments would be negotiated individually. Once the group of candidates for a given examination was constituted, its members could be pressured to make a collective payment because they would subsequently be treated as a group and none would be licensed until each had been examined and ranked. The money they gave "to be passed more quickly" was to ensure that this process took no more than about

---

[13] *Ibid.*, p. 377, test. xxxiv, super xv.

[14] *Ibid.*, pp. 377-78, super xvii.

[15] Article 22 specifies ten francs for the assistants, but Arnardus de Trajacto (no. 1513, test. xxvii) agrees with Siger.

[16] *Ibid.*, no. 1513, p. 384, test. liii.

[17] *Ibid.*, no. 1511, arts. 58 and 68, and no. 1513, p. 382, test. xlviii.

three weeks.[18] To speed the procedure, bachelors with more money were willing to contribute on behalf of those with none.[19]

A final factor that helped persuade candidates to pay for the degree in arts from the Chancellor of Notre-Dame was the uncertain authority of the Clementine Chancellor of Ste-Geneviève, which was not effectively established until April 1382 at the earliest.[20] The articles of accusation, which deal only with the first three years of Blanchard's administration, mention by name only five men who turned to Ste-Geneviève as a means of escaping Blanchard's venal examination system, as compared to the 189 who entered examinations at Notre-Dame. Furthermore, the first three refugees apparently were from the heavily Urbanist English-German nation: John de Nassa, student of John de Austria,[21] Drago Roleg,[22] and John Evelin.[23] Peter Reguordi and William de Blesis also renounced their intention of being licensed at Notre-Dame and instead received their degrees from the Chancellor of Ste-Geneviève.[24] Thus, the schism all but cut off an escape route for refugees from the Île de la Cité that had functioned effectively since the beginning of the university. This feeling of being trapped on the island, or at least relatively less free than in the past, was heightened by the rising cost of the degree in arts under Blanchard.

Two reasons account for the increased cost of the license. The first is that with the accession of Blanchard, the sums collected were distributed to more officials. The second is that in the early years of Blanchard's rule, Ste-Geneviève was not a viable competitor. With regard to the first reason, Simon Freron, fifty-eight years old, Master of Theology for thirty years, Headmaster of the College of Navarre from 1362 to 1372, and subchancellor for eight years during the tenure of John of Acyaco (1349-60), although sympathetic to Blanchard, nonetheless made it clear that the licensing procedure in arts was simpler in his day. He said that "when he was licensed in arts, he and his colleagues together gave something to the assistants for their services, but he did not remember how much. Asked if it were customary for the artists to give something to the chancellor or subchancellor, he replied he never saw anything given to the chan-

---

[18] *Chart.*, III, no. 1513, p. 371, test. xii; p. 385, test. lix.
[19] *Ibid.*, p. 373, test. xviii.
[20] See above, p. 49.
[21] *Chart.*, III, no. 1513, p. 373, test. xvi.
[22] *Ibid.*, p. 374, test. xx.
[23] *Ibid.*, no. 1511, p. 326, art. 67.
[24] *Ibid.*, art. 78.

cellor or subchancellor, nor did he receive anything himself in the period when he was subchancellor." [25] Thus, the practice of giving to both chancellor and subchancellor was a more recent development.

By the time of Chancellor John de Calore (1370-81), payments were made to the subchancellor but not to the chancellor, according to John de Guignicourt, who had been Calore's subchancellor for two years and who testified for both sides. When he held the office, the money was given after the subchancellor and the four examiners had agreed on who should pass and in what rank. Then, he said, after the signetum was sent to those who would receive the degree, "the bachelors were well accustomed by their own agreement, arrived at in a common meeting, to give two or three francs for wine or spices to the subchancellor for the labor of conferring the signeta." [26]

Pierre Plaoul, whose exactions as subchancellor have been discussed above, said that when he was licensed in arts under Calore, "he gave ... together with others of the same examination, viz. to the chancellor's assistants." [27] "Assistants" can include the subchancellor, but it certainly excludes the chancellor. Plaoul's testimony is naturally suspect in this hearing, but on this point he was speaking of personal experience, and his statement is corroborated by that of John de Guignicourt. Furthermore, the contrast between Calore's and Blanchard's administrations implied by these two witnesses suggests that Blanchard took a share in revenues that previous chancellors had left in their assistants' hands.

As the number of officials dividing the revenues increased, pressure must have mounted to augment the contributions. John Luqueti, a Master of Arts and Bachelor of Theology living at the Sorbonne who testified for both sides, attested to this trend when he stressed the traditional nature of the giving; he had "always heard it said ... of the artists ... that they give only two solidi for each one about to be licensed." [28] This customary payment contrasts significantly with the sums received by Blanchard and his officials after his first year in office.

For Bachelors of Arts, therefore, Blanchard's chancellorship represented a significant departure from past practices. He had venalized the administration of the arts examination at Notre-Dame by

[25] *Ibid.*, no. 1521, p. 414, test. iii, super xv.
[26] *Ibid.*, no. 1513, p. 380-81, test. xliii, super x.
[27] *Ibid.*, no. 1521, p. 419, test. xii, super xv.
[28] *Ibid.*, p. 418, test. xi, super xv.

selling the office of examiner, and by taking so large a cut from his
assistants that the sums they demanded in return for "services"
increased markedly between his first and third years. Furthermore,
he at least tolerated a subchancellor who, though not as adept as his
master, had effectively increased the cost of the license for many. As
more officials received a share of the candidates' presents, and as the
schism and its ramifications at Ste-Geneviève all but eliminated an
alternative source, the price of the license in arts from Notre-Dame
inevitably rose.

Before moving to the grievances affecting the Faculty of Theology
alone, we shall consider one which attracted little attention from the
Cardinal of Laon's investigators, but which confirms the impression of
Blanchard that emerges from the above account of his administration.
According to article 81, the chancellor is the *ex officio* judge and
conservator of the university's five-year privilege, awarded in 1219
only to the Faculty of Theology, extended in 1330 to the whole
university, and renewed in 1334.[29] Under the provisions of this papal
grant, clerics actively studying at Paris could receive the revenues of
their benefices *in absentia* for up to five years. When the active status
of a student or teacher was challenged, he could receive verification
from the chancellor after his continuous presence had been confirmed
by his faculty. Article 81 charged that Blanchard and his notary had
turned their capacity to certify a scholar's active status into a means of
personal enrichment. Presumably this means that instead of being
satisfied with a small tip for drawing up the necessary documents,
they had begun to demand systematically a more substantial sum.
Although little evidence was offered on this largely neglected charge,
two witnesses who had acted as Blanchard's notaries testified that he
demanded a percentage of the revenues generated by this modest
service.[30]

During the first year of Blanchard's chancellorship Adam de S.
Amando became his notary, but he resisted pressures to share revenues

[29] *Chart.*, I, no. 32, p. 91; II, no. 908, p. 340, and no. 1068, p. 537.

[30] Pearl Kibre, in *Scholarly Privileges in the Middle Ages* (Cambridge, Mass.,
1962) takes the recommendations of the two cardinal legates in 1366 (*Chart.*,
III, no. 1319, p. 146) as the basis of her account (p. 231) of how this privilege
was administered, but she omits mention of the "executor," whom article 81
identifies as the chancellor. After the proper petitions had been made and oaths
sworn, the process of documentation was not complete until the whole file had
been presented to the "executor" of the privilege, or his delegate, who could
issue the final certificate of residence ("petita citatio concedatur").

with the chancellor. One day, Blanchard asked him to prepare a room for a hearing. Adam spent twelve francs fulfilling this assignment, but Blanchard refused to repay him. When challenged, Blanchard told his notary that the profits of his office were greater than the sum he had expended. In Adam's interpretation, this was the chancellor's method of taking his cut.[31]

The next notary to the chancellor was Stephen Boussardi, who, according to Adam, divided his revenues equally between himself on the one hand and the chancellor and his assistants on the other.[32] As Boussardi related his experience, it was understood from the beginning that the chancellor would get a share, but the exact percentage was not specified. After a year Blanchard asked to be paid, and Stephen gave him ten francs. The next request came only six months later, and the notary was reluctant to give him anything because the office had yielded very little in the interval. Finally, because he was unwilling to pay, Stephen left the office.[33]

The complaint about the five-year privilege reinforces the general picture of the way Blanchard operated. The two notaries describe the chancellor's efforts to capitalize on a regular source of income, originally conceived of as gifts or gratuities, increase it, and take a large share. This mentality had already been at work in the days of Calore, who was perhaps the first to allow his subchancellor to receive gifts, but who personally refrained from taking them from bachelors in arts. Blanchard systematically demanded a share for himself and his assistants whenever he saw money coming in.

The most frequently made accusation in the Faculty of Theology concerned the exaction of money prior to awarding academic honors. Two occasions in scholars' careers lent themselves to such demands. From those whose earlier training was not at Paris, a case especially frequent among the religious, the chancellor could demand money before granting permission to lecture on the *Sentences*, because this constituted a special award of bachelor status. From those whose earlier training had been at Paris and who had acceded to bachelorship within the faculty, the chancellor could receive payments either for the license itself (through direct negotiation) or as a "gift" sent upon receipt of the signetum. The practice had become so common that the

---

[31] *Chart.*, III, no. 1513, p. 371, test. xiii.
[32] *Ibid.*
[33] *Ibid.*, p. 383, test. i.

term "signetum" was sometimes applied to the payment rather than the chancellor's notice.[34] Of the 23 payments listed under this heading, four are for permission to read the *Sentences* (arts. 26, 28, 29, 42), thirteen are given to the bearer of the signetum (arts. 30-39, 41, 43, 50), and six concern direct negotiations with the chancellor over the sum to be paid (arts. 44, 45, 47, 48, 51, 52).[35]

The most colorful of these cases tells us a great deal about the way Blanchard worked. Richly described in the documents, the case can stand for many others. William de Roseriis, a Dominican, had been delegated by his chapter general to read the *Sentences* at Paris and had a papal letter confirming this assignment. The university's article 26 states that Blanchard withheld his authorization in order to have lawyers in Paris verify that the documents were valid. To remove this unwarranted hindrance, William gave Blanchard twenty gold francs and a measure (*cauda*) of Beaune wine worth fifteen francs. The chancellor received these gifts, but nonetheless gave priority to a less competent Dominican who had given the chancellor sixty francs.[36] When questioned about the wine by the Faculty of Theology, Blanchard "did not blush" to admit he had received it and likewise acknowledged it before the whole university.[37]

This accusation is confirmed in some detail by Andrew de Gyaco, a bachelor in canon law, who had acted as Friar William's go-between with Blanchard.[38] Andrew said that William had previously taught the Bible at Paris for two years (1376-78), but because he had been sick, he was not able to continue directly to the *Sentences* as authorized by his order in 1378 and 1380. After these successive delays, Friar William obtained papal letters authorizing his reinstatement into the

---

[34] See *Chart.*, III, no. 1511, arts. 40-49, esp. art. 40, where we find the expression "dare unum bonum signetum de xl francis." The two usages appear together in the statement "dedit cancellario . . . centum leones auri in una bursa in signeto et pro signeto." *Ibid.*, no. 1521, p. 412.

[35] One payment that does not fall into these categories was made by Philip de Goutulis, a Carmelite, who had been absent from Paris for four years and, according to accusatory article 53 (*ibid.*, no. 1511, p. 359), was made to pay twenty francs before the chancellor would discuss his case. Under questioning, Philip acknowledged a gift of "nineteen or twenty francs" for the signetum, but made no reference to his earlier interview or any payment to obtain it. (*Ibid.*, no. 1513, p. 379, test. xxxix, super liii, and see below, p. 97.)

[36] *Ibid.*, no. 1511, art. 26.

[37] *Ibid.*, art. 27.

[38] *Ibid.*, no. 1513, p. 372, test. xv. I supplement Andrew's account with details from Denifle's notes, *ibid.*, p. 229 and p. 230, n. 5.

academic routine by teaching during the summer term of 1383. Andrew presented the letters to the chancellor in the spring. At first Blanchard stalled by repeatedly asking Andrew to come back in a few days for an answer. Then Andrew got "great lords" to accompany him and he even obtained letters on Friar William's behalf from the King and the Duke of Burgundy urging the chancellor to decide. Blanchard "always answered pleasantly, but did nothing." Finally, a short while before lectures were to begin, the chancellor said to some friends of William that he had heard rumors that William had been leading an evil life and that an investigation into his morals was necessary. Andrew obtained 31 witnesses who testified to William's good character, and still the case did not advance.[39] Then Andrew took aside one of the chancellor's assistants, Nicholas Decani, bought him a drink, gave him a franc, and asked his advice. The next day, Nicholas advised giving wine to the chancellor. Andrew then took ten francs in a purse to the chancellor in his hall; the chancellor counted the coins, put them back in the purse, and commented that William would not get off that easy. Andrew left with nothing accomplished. Two or three days later, on the advice of his friends, Friar William himself went to the chancellor and gave him twenty more francs. Andrew did not see the money being handed over, he said, but the next day, June 23, Friar William's case was approved.

Over the summer, Friar William lectured on the first two books of the *Sentences*. In the autumn, he petitioned Clement for permission to finish the last two books after Christmas. Clement granted this request and enjoined Blanchard to admit the Dominican to read "in the term of ordinary study," which would end on June 29, 1384. When Andrew presented Friar William's letters to Blanchard, the chancellor waited a few days and said that he would not grant his permission unless he received a cauda of wine from Friar William. Andrew promised, bought, and presented the wine, which cost fifteen francs. On August 19, 1384, Clement ordered Blanchard to license William, whose teaching obligations had now been met, but the friar was still a bachelor at the time the articles of accusation were drawn up and investigated (spring and summer 1385), and was not licensed until two years later.

Many witnesses confirmed Friar William's story,[40] the most in-

---

[39] Giles, Beadle of the Faculty of Theology, said that as far as he knew, this charge had never been cleared. *Ibid.*, no. 1513, test. vi, pp. 369-70, super xxvi.

[40] *Ibid.*, test. vi, xxi, xxx, xlii, lii.

teresting of them being Nicholas Decani, the assistant of the chancellor
who advised Friar William to give wine, and whose testimony
illustrates Blanchard's routine.[41] Nicholas had been a boarder in
Blanchard's house for two years, paying him twenty francs annually.[42]
Although speaking of Friar William, Nicholas Decani gave the clear
impression that this case was not exceptional. He was an eyewitness
to the gift-giving and saw it *frequentissime*, though he did not see the
actual transfer of goods "because the chancellor did not wish any of
his assistants to be present at such matters." Gifts included wine,
chickens, partridges, rabbits, cheese, and other foods brought on
behalf of advanced students, whom he declined to name. He saw
luncheons and dinners given for the chancellor both by bachelors
being admitted to lecture on the *Sentences* and by those being licensed.
Moreover, he heard several times from trustworthy candidates that
they gave the chancellor money, silver vessels, and other valuable
items so that they would be approved more quickly to read the
Sentences or receive the license, and so that they would be ranked
higher among the graduates. As proof, Nicholas referred to precious
objects he had seen in the chancellor's possession, which must have
been gifts because Blanchard could not have bought them without
Nicholas's knowing. Further establishing his strategic place in the
chancellor's household, Nicholas Decani recalled the day during the
previous jubilee (licensing time) when Friar Nicholas de Costa,
O.F.M., arrived in the company of a Lombard merchant. Decani
opened the door for them and asked what they wanted "and then
Friar Nicholas said that he had had sixty francs carried by the merchant
to the chancellor." Decani ushered the merchant into the chancellor's
study, where he left them alone. Friar Nicholas de Costa was licensed
soon thereafter.[43]

William Rolins, another of Blanchard's assistants, substantiated
the story of Friar William de Roseriis, testifying that "the chancellor
received the cauda of wine, it was placed in his cellar, drunk in his

[41] *Chart.*, III, test. xxxiv, p. 377.

[42] I do not know whether work as an assistant was part of the rent, or, as in
the case of Simon Freron (*ibid.*, no. 1521, p. 412, test. iii, super xiv), it was a
method of anticipating an eventual payment for the license in service rather than
cash.

[43] Nicholas de Costa was licensed in 1383[4] (Paris, BN, ms. lat. 12850, "Ordo
licenciatorum," f. 80). His use of a moneylender is also mentioned in the university's article 47, *Chart.*, III, no. 1511, p. 358.

house, and the witness himself drank it many times." [44] The numerous long delays imposed upon Friar William explain why "impediments" and "vexations" or the purpose of giving "to be passed more quickly" are so often mentioned as excuses for giving in the Faculty of Theology.[45] Many were there who paid Blanchard to avoid the hindrances he could place in their way, or who, once ensnared like William de Roseriis, could only buy their way out.

In contrast, such obstacles did not impede those who gave happily in return for the chancellor's "courtesy." This is surely the explanation for the Carmelite Philip de Goutulis, who had been away from Paris for just as long as Friar William, but who reportedly paid twenty francs for a conference with the chancellor to dispose of this irregularity,[46] who admitted paying nineteen or twenty francs for the signetum, and who "would have sent more if he had more because of the courtesy the chancellor had done him." [47] Friar John Ade, O.P., states of his own case that he gave sixteen francs to the chancellor and four to his assistants explaining his calculations as follows: "That each [bachelor] about to be licensed should give ten current florins for the signetum is an old custom, but because he was anticipated by the chancellor [two years] before the accustomed time for his magisterium [sic], in thanks he gave the chancellor six francs above the aforesaid ten, on account of this courtesy." [48]

Although many paid for avoidance of, or extrication from, the bureaucratic gauntlet erected by John Blanchard, there was no fixed price for advancement to the license in theology. Blanchard's partisans upheld a statement saying that it was traditional in the Faculty of Theology to give the chancellor "ten francs or more, as much as pleases the bachelor about to be licensed, and according as it seems fitting to the liberality of his spirit, the potency of his wealth, and

---

[44] *Ibid.*, no. 1513, p. 384, test. lii, super xxvi.

[45] *Ibid.*, no. 1511, arts. 26, 28, 41, 50.

[46] *Ibid.*, art. 53.

[47] *Ibid.*, no. 1513, p. 379, test. xxxix, super lii.

[48] *Ibid.*, p. 387, test. lxix. Note the interchangeability of the terms florin and franc. Throughout the Blanchard affair, references to money seem to apply to the gold coinage of the mid-fourteenth century, whether florins, leos, agnels (moutones), or francs. No attention is paid to fluctuations in their value. For this coinage see J. Lafaurie, *Les monnaies de rois de France de Hughes Capet à Louis XII* (Paris et Bâle, 1951), I, 67-68; A. Dieudonné, "La Monnaie royal depuis la réforme de Charles V jusqu'à la restauration monétaire par Charles VII," *Bibliothèque de l'École des Chartes*, 72 (1911), 473-82.

the demands of his station." [49] The sums were paid in secret,[50] but the articles of accusation are corroborated by testimony that shows how rare it was for a payment to be much less than eighteen or twenty francs. The Carmelites made a rule that no one was to give gifts totaling more than twenty francs.[51]

The cases of higher payments or actual bargaining can be explained as Blanchard's exploiting special circumstances, such as an absence from the studium or an agreement to disregard the university's residence requirement. Friar William de Roseriis, whose case we studied above, had to overcome absences caused by illness, and it cost him 35 francs to be licensed alone, not with his fellow candidates during a jubilee, presumably so that he could leave to take possession of his see.[52] Similarly, Bernard Calveti believed himself to be under pressure from his order to receive his degree before a certain time, and so paid eighty francs to be licensed out of jubilee.[53] Some men, by a special papal arrangement to be described shortly, received the license after being approved by only three or four masters. Half of those licensed after summary examinations gave very high gifts, the other half made more usual payments. Adam d'Ay paid 42 francs, Nicholas de Costa sent 40 or 60 through a moneylender, and Peter de Candia, the future Alexander V, paid 80 francs.[54] These higher sums do not appear to be out-and-out bribes, because other beneficiaries of this procedure gave much less: John de Attignaco, 22 francs; Matthew Silvestris, 23; and John Mericy, 14.[55] Yves Lamederii, who

---

[49] *Chart.*, III, no. 1520, p. 405, art. 14.

[50] *Ibid.*, no. 1521, p. 417, test. viii, super xiv and p. 418, test. xi.

[51] *Ibid.*, test. iv. Cf. test. v.

[52] *Ibid.*, no. 1511, p. 359, art. 51 and p. 365, n. 34.

[53] *Ibid.*, p. 357, art. 43.

[54] For Adam d'Ay see *ibid.*, arts. 31, 55, and no. 1513, test. 42. For Nicholas de Costa see *ibid.*, art. 47, and no. 1513, p. 377, test. xxxiv, which sources disagree on the sum, as they do on de Costa's first name. There is a Nicholas de Costa, O.F.M., and a William de Costa, from Cluny, both mentioned as having been approved by only four masters (*ibid.*, no. 1511, art. 55). The Cluniac was not licensed until 1386(7), so Decani's testimony must refer to Nicholas, whose order and degree are both identified correctly in his account. Denifle, too, corrects this error in *ibid.*, p. 662, *corrigendum ad* p. 377. The date of Nicholas's license is given on p. 365, n. 42. For Peter de Candia see *ibid.*, no. 1511, art. 52 and no. 1463.

[55] For John de Attignaco see *ibid.*, no. 1511, arts. 36, 55, and no. 1513, test. xlii. For Matthew Silvestris see no. 1511, arts. 38, 55. The identity of the Augustinian mentioned in article 55 is Denifle's reasonable guess based on the fact that Paris, BN, lat. 12850, the "Ordo Licenciatorum," f. 80ʳ, lists him as the lower of two Augustinians and the fifteenth of sixteen licentiates for his year (*ibid.*, p. 365, n. 41). For John Mericy see *ibid.*, no. 1511, art. 39, and no. 1450.

also benefited from the smaller review panel, was opposed by other masters. He promised Blanchard one hundred francs, but paid only a first installment, received the license, and never paid the rest.[56]

In sum, when a candidate was not rushed and could satisfy the university requirements, he would give the chancellor approximately twenty francs.[57] If a candidate's progress departed in any way from the routine, a special situation arose, and petitions to Blanchard cost time and money. Once a technicality had to be overlooked, the chancellor could be pitiless, as the following article (48) shows:

> In order to be admitted to the license [in Theology], Master Raymond Augeri, an Augustinian, presented twelve francs, which [the chancellor] refused, because he would be granting it two years early. And afterwards Raymond drew from his purse nine other francs, out of which he presented eight to the chancellor, which twelve plus eight francs the chancellor then accepted. Then the chancellor, seeing the one franc remaining, sought it by saying these words: "That one too, that one too!" And although the master said to him that he would be left without money, the chancellor added that that didn't matter, because one was so little anyway.[58]

The variation in individual cases makes it difficult to tell just how much Blanchard exacted for the license in theology. Some payments cannot be averaged in. For example, two bachelors paid only fractions of what they promised. The payment of Nicholas de Costa cannot be calculated because the sum is recorded as xl francs in one place and lx in another. We cannot be sure whether Philip de Goutulis made one or two payments of twenty francs. Despite these troublesome cases, one can derive certain conclusions from the available evidence, itemized in Table II. In contrast to his treatment of artists, Blanchard did not increase his exactions from the theologians as time went on. Instead, the amounts varied with the circumstances. Candidates requiring special consideration paid as much as the chancellor could get, from forty to one hundred francs, whereas candidates progressing routinely paid approximately twenty.

[56] *Ibid.*, no. 1511, arts. 44, 55.

[57] Two who proceeded routinely and made unusually small payments were: John de Condeto, who read the *Sentences* in 1381-82, was licensed in 1383(4), and gave fifteen francs (*ibid.*, no. 1511, art. 35, and p. 365, n. 12 and Paris, BN, lat. 12850. f. 80[r]); and Christian de Altaripa, who read the *Sentences* in 1380-81, gave sixteen francs, and was licensed in 1383(4) (*Chart.*, III, no. 1511, art. 33, and no. 1445, p. 289). Table II below shows, however, that twenty francs is roughly the median for the lowest cluster of payments.

[58] Some ambiguity exists also in the Latin: "Cancellarius subiunxit, quod non erat curandus, quia modicum erat de uno" (*ibid.*, no. 1511, p. 358, art. 48).

Table II

Sums Paid for Signetum or License in Theology under John Blanchard

Year	Licentiate	Sum	Article	Special Circumstances
1381(2)	P. Gracilis, Aug.	20 fr.	37	licensed out of jubilee
—	B. Calveti, Carm.	80	43	later Pope Alexander V; approved by only four masters [a]
—	P. de Candia, O.F.M.	80	52	
1382(3)	Y. Lamedarii, Carm.	60	44	promised 100 fr.; approved by only four masters [b]
—	J. Ade, O.P.	20	32	
—	N. Valle, O.P.	10	50	
1383(4)	A. Tardi, O.F.M.	18	30	
—	A. d'Ay, O.F.M.	42	31, 55	approved by only four masters
—	C. de Altaripa, Aug.	16	33	
—	Gull. Episcopus	20	34	
—	J. de Condeto, Carm.	18	35	
—	J. de Attignaco, O.F.M.	22	36, 55	approved by only four masters
—	M. Silvestris, Aug.	23	38, 55	approved by only four masters
—	J. Mericy, O.P.	14	39	approved by only three or four masters [c]
—	B. de Boscarello, O.P.	25	41	
—	Nic. de Costa, O.F.M.	40 or 60	47	xl or lx francs brought by moneylender; approved by only three or four masters [a] "That one too!"
—	R. Augeri, Aug.	21	48	incepted under Blanchard; accused of adhering to Urban V
—	E. de Campis (Deschamps)	104	49	paid for signetum and conference too?
—	P. de Gottulis, Carm.	20+20?	53	promised much more after long absence from Paris
[1385]	J. de Quercu (Duchéne)	12	45	licensed alone, out of jubilee; elected Bishop of Venice
—	H. le Barbu	100	51	

Notes: [a] *Chart.*, III, no. 1463. [b] *Ibid.*, no. 1423. [c] *Ibid.*, no. 1450. [a] *Ibid.*, no. 1440.

Even more difficult is comparing Blanchard's receipts to those of his predecessors. The chancellor's defenders provide some information on this point because they were concerned to show that the payments were traditional. Thus, John de Basilia, the General of the Augustinians, cited a Master Honofrius, of his order, who gave at least fifty francs to John de Calore, Blanchard's predecessor; and Master Francis de Perusio, O.F.M., who gave thirty francs to Grimerius Bonifacii, John de Calore's predecessor; and Jacob de Elbaco, a Cistercian, who gave seventy francs to Calore, which latter gift John de Basilia carried personally. Basilia related a rumor that the one hundred leos that Leoninus de Padua, another Augustinian, sent to the chancellor of his time, whom he thought was Robert de Bardis, were returned out of friendship.[59] John de Guignicourt mentioned lending one friend ten francs to send the chancellor for the signetum, but knew another had sent fifty.[60] Other witnesses simply related the amounts they themselves had paid, and these sums are either ten or twelve francs.[61] These data are simply insufficient to permit a comparison of average payments, though it appears that the ten-to-twelve-franc price range of his predecessors was roughly half Blanchard's preferred gift of eighteen to twenty-five francs. In both periods, of course, exceptional payments spiraled upward.

The higher payment made in unusual circumstances raises an important question. If the chancellor demanded greater sums from those who had bypassed regulations, were the authors of the accusations complaining because the rules had been violated, or because the price was so high? The answer may be found in the curious way the accusatory articles are phrased, for they frequently indicate that some university rule has been broken. The articles would not have mentioned the faults of candidates if the only objection were the demand for money. Indeed, rhetorically it would have been preferable to portray all the bachelors as innocent. The irregularities were specified precisely to point out that the chancellor should have refused or delayed these men, and to object to his licensing them only for money.

It is in this context that we must understand the next category of the masters' grievances. The chancellor abused his office, they said, "by admitting the unworthy, concerning whom the masters of the Faculty of Theology have not given depositions or heard a word

---

[59] *Chart.*, III, no. 1521, p. 412, test. i.
[60] *Ibid.*, p. 417, test. ix, super xiiii.
[61] *Ibid.*, no. 1521, test. viii, x, and no. 1513, test. ix.

about them in the faculty, and by juggling the ranks, placing the unworthy ahead of the worthy, contrary to the votes and deliberations of the masters of the Faculty of Theology and against the privilege that he swore to observe." [62] This category actually contains two related but distinct complaints. The chancellor licensed men not approved by the masters, and he disregarded the rank assigned the candidates by the masters in order to include his own men or those sponsored by the pope among the licentiates, all ranked in an order determined by him. The significance of ordering the graduates was that rank was understood to be indicative of academic excellence, and it determined precedence in subsequent ceremonies and examinations. Also, because the university's Register of Licentiates listed the graduates in the order in which they were licensed, a man's rank was a matter of permanent record.

The question of ranking candidates seems to be a new issue within the university, for there is no legislation about it prior to the Blanchard affair, and neither party cites any precedents. Although the masters claimed the right to order their candidates in their memo of January 9, 1385,[63] in their accusatory article 55, drafted later in the same year, they referred to ranking as a custom that was in their possession "ora lmost." [64] The only Blanchard supporter who addressed this question was John de Basilia, who stated that he had never "seen nor heard that the masters could assign the places of those about to be licensed, rather, only the chancellor [could do this]." [65]

That a spontaneously developed practice like ranking should provoke contradiction between already opposed groups is hardly a cause for wonder. More surprising is the apparent ignorance even in Blanchard's camp of the broadest authorizations for the chancellor's freedom to award the license without the faculty's approval. Even John Golin, who testified only for Blanchard, conceded that he had never "seen that [the chancellor] could license anyone without the indication (*vocatione*) of the masters." [66] Stephen Gaudeti said the chancellor "cannot omit the depositions of the masters," whom he must follow as concerns the candidates' knowledge, but who can be overruled in matters of reputation.[67] Only John de Basilia seems to

---

[62] *Chart.*, III, no. 1511, art. 25. The privilege is *Parens scientiarum*.

[63] See above, p. 70, and *Chart.*, III, no. 1504, p. 341.

[64] *Ibid.*, no. 1511, art. 55.

[65] *Ibid.*, no. 1521, p. 412, test. i, super iii.

[66] *Ibid.*, p. 414, test. iv., super. vi.

[67] *Ibid.*, p. 416, test. viii, super vii.

have understood that *Parens scientiarum* was not the only text regulating this practice. Although unaware of the ancient origins of the licentia bullata, he related that Blanchard's predecessor Calore had told him that "by virtue of a certain apostolic bull, [the chancellor] could license in theology without having to depend upon the masters in theology." [68] Although Basilia indicates no specific source, he could have cited *Quasi lignum vitae* or *Servus crucis*, which latter permits the chancellor to license worthy men of his own choosing, or the tradition initiated by Honorius III in 1218, when he ordered the chancellor to license a candidate approved by three masters.[69] Except that the number of masters specified had risen to four, as we shall see, this was precisely the arrangement under which Blanchard was operating.

The masters' article 55 accused Blanchard of having licensed two Franciscans (Adam d'Ay and John d'Attigny), an Augustinian (Matthew Silvestris), Nicholas de Costa, O.F.M., and William de Costa, Clun., without questioning each member of the faculty as stipulated in *Parens scientiarum*.[70] In two of these cases, however, the allegations seem insufficiently supported by the evidence. First, the Register of Licentiates shows William de Costa as licensed only in 1386(7), after the Blanchard affair.[71] Second, a papal letter dated December 27, 1379, states that before coming to Paris, Nicholas de Costa O.F.M., had already read the *Sentences* at Cambridge and was on the verge of receiving the license there, but could no longer travel to England because of the war between Charles V and Edward III. Consequently, Clement wrote Calore, then the chancellor, ordering him to permit Nicholas to teach the *Sentences* during the next summer (1380). With the course completed and after examination by three or four masters, the chancellor was to award the magisterium and the license to Nicholas.[72]

In the light of Clement's letter, it would seem that the masters' anger at not all being consulted on Nicholas de Costa's competence should have been directed not at the chancellor, but with greater justice, at the pope himself, and that the problem derived not from

[68] *Ibid.*, p. 412, test. i, super iii.

[69] See above, p. 11.

[70] The names of Adam and John are supplied by Herveus Sulven, *Chart.*, III, no. 1513, p. 380, test. xlii. For the identity of the Augustinian, see above, n. 55.

[71] Paris, BN, lat. 12850, f. 80ᵛ and *Chart.*, III, p. 365, n. 42.

[72] *Chart.*, III, no. 1440, pp. 286-87.

chancellorial self-aggrandizement, but from the papal conception of
the magisterium. Clement and Blanchard employed the summary
procedure to speed the advancement of other scholars, not mentioned
in article 55, such as John Mericy, O. P., Ivo Lamederii, Carm., and
Peter de Candia, O. F. M., the future Alexander V,[73] and it is possible
that similar papal directives may lie behind the other cases mentioned
in article 55. That Blanchard did, in fact, carry out small-scale examinations involving only three or four masters is suggested by Simon
Freron, one of Blanchard's closest adherents, who, when questioned
about article 55, replied that "he did not know whether [Blanchard]
licensed the aforesaid bachelors or others without or against the will
of the other masters because the votes and depositions of the masters
were accustomed to be sought separately, in such a way that each
remained ignorant of the vote of the other." [74] Freron obviously was
one of the three or four doctors Blanchard consulted. Others might
have been John Golin, Stephen Gaudeti, and Jacob Juvenis, who
were all witnesses only for Blanchard and who, at sixty, sixty-eight,
and sixty years of age, constituted with Blanchard (then at least
sixty-three), and Freron (fifty-eight) the faculty's Old Guard.[75]
Blanchard's use of them as examiners would also explain how they
could have stated so innocently that the chancellor cannot license
without consulting the masters when Blanchard was being accused of
doing precisely that.

    Blanchard's licensing of at least some men without taking depositions
from all the masters, therefore, was authorized by letters from Clement
VII in accordance with long-standing precedent. The chancellor
was operating within a reasonable interpretation of his rights. The
bulls sending some scholars to him specified that the approval of
only four masters was needed. The addition to the list of licentiates
of the men thus approved inevitably impinged upon the ranking
devised by the professors. Both sides could legitimately claim the
right to rank candidates since the conflict over this practice had not
been resolved, though it would seem that papal authority was on the
side of the chancellor. One danger for the university in Blanchard's
ability to administer certain cases out of sight of the full faculty was
the discretion it gave him in determining not only their rank, but also,

---

[73] See *Chart.*, III, nos. 1450, 1423, and 1463.
[74] *Ibid.*, no. 1513, test. ix, p. 371, super xlvi (lege: xlv).
[75] *Ibid.*, no. 1521, test. iii, iv, viii, xv.

as we have seen, their academic progress, so that he could charge money for preferential treatment. Because more money was changing hands even in routine cases than previously, masters contemplating the overall situation could not help feeling that under Blanchard, money bought not just swift passage through red tape, but even rank, and in some cases the degree itself. Questioned why some were licensed without depositions from all the masters, Herveus Sulven said "he believed it was on account of money." [76] John Ade, who testified for both sides, felt "the chancellor often placed those ahead who ought to have been placed behind and vice versa." [77] Given what we know about Blanchard's acquisitiveness, one is hardly shocked to read the Franciscan Arnald Grelli's version of the logical conclusion on the matter of ranking: "The chancellor had often preferred insufficient candidates to more sufficient ones . . . according as they gave him more or less in payments." [78] Although a summary procedure had been authorized by the pope, Blanchard's opponents considered his practices so corrupt they could not imagine any explanation for his behavior except extortion and bribery.

The last category of complaints, contained in articles 25 and 54, accused Blanchard of forcing students to abandon their chosen masters and accept him as their sponsor. The reason for doing this was so that Blanchard would be entitled to the traditional gifts given by the student to his master upon receipt of the license and of the magisterium, and even afterward. In the articles drawn up in his own defense, Blanchard claimed that it was customary for some bachelors to send the chancellor, or his assistants, or both, cloth or hides from which to make clothes.[79] Freron, Blanchard's associate, said more precisely that "licentiates, when they incept or are made masters *under the chancellor* are accustomed to doing [this] . . .; otherwise he does not remember having seen it." [80]

Six men are mentioned whom Blanchard attempted to attract to himself. Article 40 relates that John Solacii had been presented for the license by Stephen de Calvomonte, but Blanchard refused him on the grounds that Solacii had studied under John de Calore, and, therefore, he should study with him since a chancellor should have

---

[76] *Ibid.*, no. 1513, p. 380, test. xlii.
[77] *Ibid.*, test. lxix, p. 388.
[78] *Ibid.*, test. xxxvi, p. 379, lines 5-7. For similar statements, see also test. lxvii.
[79] *Ibid.*, no. 1520, p. 405, art. xvi.
[80] *Ibid.*, no. 1521, p. 414, test. iii, super. xv i.

his predecessors' students. When Solacii demurred and declined to pay a "compromise" sum of forty francs, Blanchard denied him the license. Unfortunately, Solacii did not testify in the Cardinal of Laon's hearing, and when Master Stephen testified he did not mention this incident, which therefore cannot be confirmed. Nor can the "theft" of William Trebron be corroborated since he did not testify and his former master is not named. Henry Herout substantiated Blanchard's use of pressure to attract his former student, William Gorren,[81] although Gorren, who testified for both sides, did not mention the subject.[82] The three remaining men will be discussed together not only because Blanchard's pressuring them to accept his sponsorship can be verified, but also because their stories show an interesting connection between the university's domestic scandal and the broader crisis of the schism.

The first case is that of John Caillaudi de Quercu, or Duchêne. John had been a Master of Arts at least as early as 1359, when he was elected Proctor of the French nation,[83] and he was one of Pierre d'Ailly's first teachers.[84] In 1362, he was enrolled in theology at the College of Navarre,[85] but he left Paris without the theological license in 1369 to teach arts at Montpellier.[86] There followed a long absence from Paris which persuaded some masters that Duchêne had not fulfilled the university's residence requirement of four years between reading the *Sentences* and receiving the license.[87] To get around this problem, Duchêne negotiated with Blanchard; the two men agreed that in return for first place among the licentiates, John would incept under the chancellor and give him and his assistants generous gifts of clothing and money.[88] The chancellor fulfilled his promise and licensed John in first place, but John gave the messenger bearing the signetum only twelve francs for the chancellor.[89] Double-crossed, Blanchard did all he could to prevent Duchêne from receiving the

[81] *Chart.*, III, no. 1513, p. 370, test. vii.

[82] *Ibid.*, pp. 381-82, test. xlvi; and no. 1521, p. 419, test. xiv.

[83] *Ibid.*, p. 92, n. 8.

[84] C. E. Du Boulay, *Historia Universitatis Parisiensis*, 5 vols. (Paris, 1665-70), IV, 979.

[85] J. Launoy, *Regii Navarrae Gymnasii Parisiensis Historia* (1677), in *idem*, *Opera Omnia*, 5 tomes in 10 vols. (Cologne, 1731-32), tome 4, part i, p. 334.

[86] *Chart.*, III, p. 92, n. 8.

[87] *Ibid.*, no. 1319, p. 144, and see below, p. 108 and notes 101, 102.

[88] One hundred francs, according to John Thome, O.P., *ibid.*, no. 1513, test. xli, p. 380.

[89] *Ibid.*, no. 1511, pp. 357-58.

magisterium. He refused to arrange an appointment for Duchêne's vespers.[90] When called upon to explain, Blanchard was in a spot. He could not admit that Duchêne had not qualified for the license in the first place, because he was the one who had conferred it. He could not denounce the licentiate for breach of contract, because that would make him a party to bribery. Finally, the chancellor based his refusal to advance Duchêne upon the pretense that Duchêne was an Urbanist and that Clement VII had specified that no partisans or suspected partisans of Urban be admitted to so high an honor.[91] To surmount this impediment, Duchêne had recourse to influential friends, and finally the Bishops of Lodève and Geneva forced the chancellor to relent and allow an assistant to preside over the necessary ceremonies. In the end, John paid nothing more and was still made a master.[92] Duchêne must have received the license in 1385.[93]

Simon Freron had been Duchêne's sponsor before the deal with Blanchard and was the master under whom the licentiate finally incepted.[94] Freron testified for both sides and even while serving as a university witness, defended the chancellor's practices as traditional.[95] His deposition was generally damaging to the university, but he also confirmed the fact that Blanchard had denounced Duchêne as a

---

[90] *Ibid.*, no. 1513, test. 30, p. 376. This is confirmed by John de Guignicourt (*ibid.*, test. xliii, p. 381).

[91] *Ibid.*, no. 1511, art. 45, p. 358: "Et quia promissum non implevit, idem cancellarius ne magistraretur quantum potuit impedivit, sumpta occasione, quod Bartholomiste non debebant admitti ad talem gradum quo[d]que super hoc habebat bullas a domino nostro papa." Note that in reference to this passage, N. Valois, *La France et le grand schisme d'occident*, 4 vols. (Paris, 1896-1902), I, 345, states that Blanchard was not to grant the *license* to those suspected of adhering to Urban, but the context makes it clear that the magisterium was intended: "ne magistraretur." Some confusion might arise from the expression "ad talem gradum," but since Duchêne had already been licensed, it must be the magisterium that was to be withheld.

[92] *Chart.*, III, no. 1511, art. 45, p. 358. John of Guignicourt specified that the chancellor did not personally preside over the examinations. *Ibid.*, no. 1513, p. 381, test. xliii.

[93] Note that Denifle assigns the license to Duchêne in 1381 (*Chart.*, III, 92, n. 8) citing the Register of Licentiates (Paris, BN, ms. lat. 12850, "Ordo Licentiatorum in Sacratissima Theologiae Facultate," f. 80ʳ), but my reading does not confirm that, nor do I see Duchêne's name in the other manuscript of the register, ms. lat. 5657a. Both these manuscripts have a lacuna for the years 1385 and 1386; therefore I conclude that Duchêne was licensed in one of the unrecorded years, but obviously before the date of this process.

[94] *Chart.*, III, no. 1513, test. ix, super lxvi (lege: lxv), p. 371.

[95] *Ibid.*, no. 1513, test. 9, super xxv, p. 370. See also his testimony for Blanchard, *ibid.*, no. 1521, test iii, p. 413.

schismatic. Freron said that "the chancellor had raised a certain objection with Master John," implying that he was an Urbanist; and he reported that "the chancellor had a papal order, which he showed in writing, that he should admit no one suspected [of being an Urbanist] to the license of his magisterium."⁹⁶ Unlike the other masters, Freron accepted Blanchard's claim that Duchêne had attended a meeting in Germany called on behalf of Urban VI.⁹⁷ No one else who spoke of the Duchêne case mentioned the mysterious meeting in Germany.⁹⁸ Giles, the Beadle of the Faculty of Theology, denied that Duchêne, whom he knew, was an Urbanist, and attributed Blanchard's accusation to Duchêne's refusal to pay up.⁹⁹ The Franciscan Arnaldus Grelli considered Duchêne the only one he knew who had managed to avoid paying the chancellor.¹⁰⁰ Most masters saw the accusation that Duchêne was an Urbanist as a pretext.

According to university regulations, Duchêne should not have been awarded the license for several years. As Giles, the beadle, explained, Duchêne had not fulfilled the university's residence requirement,¹⁰¹ and, at the Parlement of Paris, d'Ailly called him "an unworthy bachelor." ¹⁰² That is, d'Ailly cited Duchêne as an example of Blanchard's licensing unqualified candidates. Yet this technicality is precisely the reason why Duchêne bargained with Blanchard in the first place. Even if Blanchard's charge of Urbanist sympathies was fabricated, as seems likely, Blanchard was nonetheless able to halt Duchêne's progress until he had been cleared of the accusation. On

---

⁹⁶ *Ibid.*, no. 1513, test. ix, super xlvi (lege: xlv), p. 371: "Et est verum etiam quod dictus cancellarius debatum aliquod fecit dicto magistro Johanni, ... et ipse cancellarius habebat mandatum apostolicum, quod per litteras ostendebat, quod nullum admitteret suspectum ad licenciam sui magisterii."

⁹⁷ *Ibid.*: "...quia dicebatur ipsum fuisse in quadam congregacione in Alamen-[nia] ex parte Bartholomei [Prignano, Urbani VI] facta."

⁹⁸ Those who mention this case are Giles, Beadle of the Faculty of Theology, *Chart.*, III, p. 369; Stephen de Calvomonte, p. 374; John Kaerloret, p. 376; Arnaldus Grelli, p. 379; John Thome, p. 380; and John de Guignicourt, p. 381.

⁹⁹ *Ibid.*, test. vi, super xlv, p. 369.

¹⁰⁰ *Ibid.*, test. xxxvii, p. 379.

¹⁰¹ *Ibid.*, test. vi, super xlv, p. 369.

¹⁰² Du Boulay, IV, 612, 28-32: "Au premier Iubilé du Chancelier il advint que un Bachelier indigne fut preferé és Vesperies. Le Chancelier volt empeschier le Licentié, si il n'avoit robes et argent, et le convient faire cesser par les Evesques de Genéve et de Lodéve." There are some curious discrepancies in this account. Blanchard's first jubilee (licensing occasion) was in 1382, yet Duchêne was licensed in 1385. In 1382, first place was given to Joannes a Synerea of the Sorbonne (Paris, BN, lat. 12850, f. 80ʳ) and we know that Duchêne was licensed in first place. D'Ailly said nothing about Blanchard's claim Duchêne was an Urbanist.

the authority of Clement VII, in other words, the chancellor could impose the criterion of political loyalty upon a licentiate seeking the magisterium. Whatever his motives, political loyalty was the principle he invoked. Clement VII's order not to promote Urbanists was an accepted fact.

The second example of an effort by Blanchard to obtain another master's student also involves a reference to suspected Urbanism. It concerns Giles Deschamps, who in 1394 was to be a joint author, with d'Ailly and Nicholas of Clamanges, of the university's letter expounding three possible solutions to the schism.[103] Deschamps was d'Ailly's successor, in 1389, as Headmaster of Navarre,[104] and was very active in the Gallican councils of the late 1390's and in the abortive effort of 1407 to induce the two popes to meet at Savona. He was named Bishop of Coutances in 1408, and cardinal in 1411. He died in 1413.[105] Born in the diocese of Rouen, he was educated at Paris in the College of Harcourt, and began his theological studies in 1371. In 1373 he lectured on the Bible, and in 1377 began Peter Lombard's *Sentences*.[106] As the time for Deschamps's license approached, however, Blanchard intervened and, in the manner recorded in the masters' article 49, said to him:

> Your adherence to the antipope Bartholomew has been noted, and since, in the next jubilee, you will have completed your term and fulfilled your requirements, on which account you rightly ought to be licensed, and yet you do not wish to obtain the license under me, whom you know to be canonically appointed to the chancellorship by the most holy lord, our Pope Clement, I therefore advise you, in order to clear yourself of this reputation, not to initiate the pursuit of the magisterium under any master of your [Norman] nation.[107]

---

[103] *Chart.*, III, no. 1683, pp. 617-24 and 624n.

[104] Launoy, 338.

[105] A. des Mazis, "Giles Deschamps," in *Dictionnaire d'histoire et de géographie ecclésiastique*, ed. A. Baudrillart, XIV (Paris, 1960), cols. 331-34.

[106] *Chart.*, III, p. 241, n. 4.

[107] *Ibid.*, no. 1511, art. 49, p. 358: "Item et quod magister Egidius de Campis, magister in artibus et in theologia, cui quando erat baccallarius in proximo licentiandus, cancellarius dixit hec verba vel similia: 'Vos estis notatus de adherendo Bartholomeo antipape; et quia in anno jubileo proxime preterito compleveratis tempus vestrum et feceratis facta vestra, propter quod merito debebatis licenciari, et noluistis sub me (quem sciebatis ad officium cancellarie a sanctissimo domino nostro papa Clemente fore canonice institutum) gradum licencie obtinere: quare consulo, quod non incipiatis ad magisterium sub aliquo magistro nacionis vestre ad purgandum notam predictam.'"

There is no solid evidence, in any record known to me, that Deschamps was personally an Urbanist—nothing even comparable to Duchêne's meeting in Germany. Conceivably, one could find a basis for suspicion in Deschamps's Norman origins. The Archbishop of Rouen, Philip d'Alençon, though a cousin of Charles V, was a steadfast supporter of Urban VI and made a cardinal by the Roman pope.[108] As a subdeacon in Rouen from at least 1379, Deschamps was certainly under the archbishop's authority.[109] Still, Philip d'Alençon's Urbanism has very convincingly been shown to be a personal, spiteful matter, resulting from the prelate's resentment of the way Charles V handled a quarrel between himself and the Bailiff of Rouen in 1374, and need not have involved anyone else.[110] At the same time, the Norman nation had joined the revolt of the English nation until April 1382, and several Normans had left Paris for Rome—actions that could not have been quickly forgotten by Blanchard, against whom they were largely directed.[111]

Yet those who knew Deschamps's story did not think the question of papal allegiance was at its core. Richard, the Abbot of the Parisian monastery of St-Magloire, confirmed the gist of the story reported in article 49, but his version makes Blanchard's allusion to Deschamps's Urbanism seem very artificial. Abbot Richard heard the chancellor say to Giles that "unless he would incept under him, he would report to the curia that [Giles] adhered to Bartholomew [Prignano, Urban VI]." [112] This incident was also referred to by Henry Heroult, the master from whom Blanchard "stole" Deschamps,[113] and by John Thome,[114] but they refer to it only as an example of Blanchard's pressuring bachelors to incept under him, without mentioning any particular threat. Well-founded or ill-founded, the accusation, or the threat of eventually being accused, sufficiently alarmed Deschamps that he chose Blanchard as his sponsor and paid him 24 francs for expenses and eighty francs to buy clothes.[115] As a result, Deschamps was licensed in first place in 1383(4).[116]

---

[108] Valois, I, 118.

[109] *Chart.*, III, no. 1433, p. 264.

[110] L. Mirot and E. Déprez, "Un conflit de juridiction sous Charles V. L'affaire de Philippe d'Alençon, archevêque de Rouen," *Le Moyen Age* (1897), pp. 129-74.

[111] See above, p. 46.

[112] *Chart.*, III, no. 1513, test. lxviii, p. 387.

[113] *Ibid.*, test. viii, p. 370.

[114] *Ibid.*, test. xl, p. 380.

[115] *Ibid.*, no. 1511, art. 49, pp. 358-59.

[116] Paris, BN, lat. 12850, f. 80r. *Chart.*, III, 241, n. 4.

It is not altogether clear whether Blanchard truly believed that Duchêne and Deschamps were Urbanists. Only such Blanchard sympathizers as Simon Freron took the accusation against Duchêne at face value, and Abbot Richard's testimony gives the impression that Blanchard simply used the threat of denunciation as a pressure tactic without suggesting there was any factual basis for the accusation. It is clear, however, that the scholars believed the accusation alone would prevent their being promoted, and that the scholarly community in general was stymied by this tactic.

One man the chancellor may indeed have sincerely believed to be Urbanist was the first of the three men he had forced to accept him as sponsor, John of Florence. In the statement of John's former master, Baldwin Agni, one of those who testified on both sides, we read, "the chancellor told the Servite [John] and the witness and other members and bachelors of the Faculty of Theology that he would not promote the Servite unless he would incept under him, asserting that by a custom and statute of the Servite order, Servites had to incept under the chancellor." [117] In fact, however, the published statutes of the Servites contain no such provision.[118] A second witness, John Kaerloret, reported the chancellor's use of yet another argument, namely, that John of Florence had been a student of the previous chancellor, Calore, and therefore, with the death of his master, should choose the new chancellor, as it were, *ex officio*.[119] But, Kaerloret objected, this argument runs directly counter to university practice, for "there is a strictly observed custom in the faculty that bachelors whose masters have died or left can choose anyone they want from among the regents." [120] Baldwin Agni, John's real master, also objected to Blanchard's procedure, but "he dissimulated lest the Servite be cheated of his license." [121] Despite the objections of the masters,

---

[117] *Ibid.*, no. 1513, test. xlv, p. 381.

[118] *Annalium Sacri Ordinis Fratrum Servorum Beatae Mariae Virginis*, 2ᵈ ed. by Arcangelo Giani, 3 tom. (Lucae, 1719-25). I have checked the following passages relating to the Servite college at Paris: I, pp. 181, 216, 241, 258, 290-91, 301, 315, and 333. Denifle has published a typical example of these regulations in *Chart.*, III, no. 1278, p. 104. The practice referred to by Blanchard may have originated in the Parisian college itself, but that is not what he said.

[119] *Chart.*, III, no. 1513, test. xxx, p. 376. We have already heard this argument used in connection with John Solacii, above, pp. 105-6.

[120] *Chart.*, III, no. 1513, test. xxx, p. 376.

[121] *Ibid.*, test. xlv, p. 381.

John was licensed under Blanchard in 1381(2).[122] Blanchard was then officially John's sponsor, and as chancellor could have conferred the magisterium upon him, yet he did not do so. As far as I know, John of Florence was never made a Master of Theology at Paris.[123]

One might conclude that by delaying his inception indefinitely, Blanchard was punishing the Servite for resisting his will, were it not for a papal letter that invites a more intriguing explanation. On November 21, 1387, Clement VII permitted John, whom he still addressed as Bachelor in Theology, to switch from the Servite order to the Benedictines so that he might be open in his adherence to Clement, for there were no Servite houses in regions obeying Clement.[124] As a member of an order whose houses were located only in Urbanist countries, and as an Italian, John's loyalties may indeed have seemed questionable. If they did, it means that John could have been a victim of Clement VII's order that no suspected Urbanist receive the magisterium. One way for the chancellor to prevent this would have been to compel John to become his student and then abandon him. Whether or not this was in fact Blanchard's motivation, the plight of the Florentine must have lent credibility to the chancellor's threats and helped induce Duchêne and Deschamps to abandon their chosen masters rather than risk the fate of the Servite. Yet the evidence for Blanchard's belief in John of Florence's Urbanism is only circumstantial. None of the witnesses who refer to John mention the Servite's political affiliations as an issue. Nor did Blanchard accuse him of loyalty to Rome, an accusation he made readily in the case of Duchêne and Deschamps, and one that was very common in the climate fostered by the schism. The information concerning John of Florence is simply too sparse for us to conclude that Blanchard excluded him from the magisterium for reasons related to the schism.

The cases of Duchêne, Deschamps, and John of Florence tell us a good deal about Blanchard's conduct in the chancellorship. These three are the men most likely to be "suspected of adhering to Bartholomew," yet there is no clear evidence that Blanchard took any measures to enforce Clement VII's order that Urbanists not receive

---

[122] Denifle erroneously gives the date of John the Servite's license as 1381 in *Chart.*, III, 365, n. 40, but corrects himself *ibid.*, no. 1544, n. The information comes from the "Register of Licentiates," Paris, BN, lat. 12850, ff. 79v-80v.

[123] John of Florence is called a master in article 54 (*Chart.*, III, no. 1511, p. 359), but this must refer to his status in the Faculty of Arts.

[124] *Chart.*, III, no. 1544, p. 466.

the magisterium. At the same time, it is apparent that Clement had in fact issued that order and that he wanted uniform adherence within the University of Paris. Thus there existed two sources of interference with the normal functioning of the studium: the pecuniary exactions of the chancellor, and the pope's desire to prevent the promotion of suspected schismatics. The first influenced the daily lives of students and teachers, the second merely pervaded the atmosphere as a potential source of authoritative intervention. Blanchard exhibited no more alacrity in enforcing Clement's order on promoting Urbanists than he had in granting members of the religious orders permission, at papal request, to read the *Sentences*. But the cases of Duchêne and Deschamps show that Blanchard had no scruples about using the schism to force bachelors to do his will or pay him.

The university's 83 articles of accusation themselves provide enough information to explain why offenses tolerated in previous chancellors were opposed in Blanchard. The most apparent reason is money. In the first three years of his tenure, he raised the standard expenses associated with the license in arts by a factor of ten, and in the Faculty of Theology he doubled them. His tactics left no doubt about his ultimate purpose. Even in an area where his action was sanctioned by papal authority, that of licensing designated theologians after review by only three or four masters, the other professors were convinced that his motive was simple bribery. And when Blanchard was not stuffing his coffers with coins from previously untapped sources—e.g., gratuities given his assistants in the arts examination —he was staunchly countering university efforts to extend the corporation's control—as, for example, over the ranking of candidates.

Resentment of Blanchard's personality is apparent in the articles. I believe this explains the inclusion of such colorful direct quotations as "that one too, that one too," when one coin remained in a candidate's purse (art. 48), or his sarcastic "That friar wanted to give 25 francs; let 25 years go by before he becomes a master" (art. 31). Certain phrasing evinces the masters' conviction that Blanchard's administrative pronouncements were capricious and arbitrary. When John Duchêne was not permitted to advance to his vespers, it was for the "assumed excuse" that Urbanists ought not to be promoted to so high a degree (art. 45). Thus, the masters were offended not just by the chancellor's monetary exactions, but also by his resolute opposition to any expansion of their rights and by his arrogant, abrasive manner.

Naturally, the articles of accusation must be considered critically. To this end I have given greatest weight to evidence from men who testified for both sides, and to those rare occasions when a partisan of one side would concede a point to the other. This assessment has shown the masters' accusations were fully substantiated with respect to the exaction of money for degrees, but exaggerated as concerns their exclusive right to examine and rank candidates for the licence.

Greatly heightened monetary demands from a recently appointed official with an overbearing manner could provoke reform in many contexts, but in a Parisian studium recently purged of some of its most prominent theologians, the newcomer clearly exacerbated an already difficult situation. Although the articles of accusation eschew a moralizing tone in favor of a legal style, they are for the most part arranged in a roughly chronological order that gives the distinct impression of matters becoming progressively more difficult as Blanchard gradually implemented his program. The core of the affair, therefore, lies in the conflict between the masters and the chancellor and the bitterness occasioned by Blanchard's systematic exploitation of every prerogative still available to his largely honorific office.

CHAPTER FIVE

BLANCHARD'S DEFENSE

Although he was hampered in preparing his defense, John Blanchard was not silenced by the movement that produced the articles of accusation. Nonetheless, to the best of my knowledge, only one systematic presentation of Blanchard's position has survived—the deposition compiled by John de Valle and submitted to the Cardinal of Laon for use in questioning the chancellor's witnesses.[1] Blanchard's defense was not, however, limited to this document. He also testified in the Parlement of Paris, and some details may be gleaned from the records of that forum.[2] Furthermore, in his speeches against the chancellor, Pierre d'Ailly introduced arguments attributed to Blanchard or his party in order to rebut them. Some of these, it will be shown, came from the letter Blanchard sent to Avignon to accompany the transcripts of the testimony before the Cardinal of Laon. From all these sources, therefore, Blanchard's position can be reconstructed.

Blanchard's response took two very different tacks. On the one hand, he tried to discredit his opponents by attributing malign motives to them. On the other hand, he maintained that his actions were legitimate and produced evidence to support this claim. Blanchard's efforts to stigmatize his attackers will be treated first, and then his defense proper.

In his testimony at the Parlement of Paris, Blanchard suggested that the whole affair was sparked by disgruntled candidates for the license who received a lower rank than they wanted.[3] Although the problem of ranking was certainly a major issue in the conflict, given the entire range of complaints against the chancellor, it seems most unlikely that this one matter outweighed all the others, especially the monetary grievances.

In a more serious effort to portray the masters' reform as a cover for some secret cause, Blanchard or his partisans apparently insinuated

---

[1] *Chartularium Universitatis Parisiensis*, ed. H. Denifle & E. Châtelain, 4 vols. (Paris, 1889-97), III, no. 1520, pp. 402-11. (Hereafter cited as *Chart.*)

[2] The proceedings are published in C. E. Du Boulay, *Historia Universitatis Parisiensis*, 6 vols. (Paris, 1665-73), IV, 606-14.

[3] Du Boulay, IV, 614, lines 10-12: "Et font faire ceste complainte aucuns singuliers indignez de ce qu'ils n'ont pas eu si bons lieux en la license qu'[ils] vouloient."

that the suit was really a politically inspired move by crypto-Urbanists. We know of this tactic only indirectly, through d'Ailly, and although he did not always report Blanchard's ideas fairly, he would not have mentioned this rumor in Avignon were it not actually current either there or in Paris.[4] In his speech "Domine Vim Patior," made before Clement VII in October or November 1385, when the pope received the testimony gathered by the Cardinal of Laon, d'Ailly felt it necessary to counter his opponent's suggestion that "certain men of the university oppose us by reason of the schism (*occasione scismatis*), and therefore they apply this persecution." [5] So direct an allusion to Blanchard's allegation surely reminded all those present of the difficulty with which the university's declaration in favor of Clement VII, not unanimous until 1383, was extracted. Blanchard's implication that Urbanists were still lurking in the studium, where they were engaged in covert persecution of Clement's loyal officials, had to be persuasively refuted. D'Ailly prefaced his mention of Blanchard's contention with a long reiteration of the university's allegiance to Clement:

> Surely, most Holy Father, your frequently mentioned Daughter [the University of Paris], obedient and subject to Your Holiness, truthfully and unanimously acknowledges you to be not only her Father, but her Lord, and not just any Lord, but the supreme and universal Head of the Church. And although Terence says, "There are as many opinions as there are men," nevertheless, even though they are individuals from remote and distant nations, all the members of the aforementioned university now come together and are peacefully united in this one opinion. . . . And this is sufficiently clear from the fact that she published her holy and just declaration of adherence [to Your Holiness] throughout the different parts of the world.[6]

D'Ailly supported this declaration of loyalty by referring to the university's delegates to the Lille council of September 1384, who counseled Philip the Bold and the clergy of Flanders on the merits of unifying the Flemish territories in acceptance of Clement VII: "And, what is of more recent memory, she delegated her own special

---

[4] On d'Ailly's fairness in this regard, see below, pp. 125-6.

[5] *Chart.*, III, no. 1519, p. 400: ". . . [A]dversarius Filie Vestre et ipsius complices . . . ass[ev]erant quosdam de Universitate predicta eis occasione scismatis latenter adversari et hanc ideo persecucionem inferre. . ."

[6] *Ibid.*, pp. 399-400.

messengers and solemn emissaries to calm the schism in Flanders." [7] Finally, the orator reminded Clement that d'Ailly's very presence as a representative of the university at the papal court seeking help in implementing a reform constituted an open act of recognition: "But what is greater than all these things and to the perpetual memory of your name, she now wishes, under the authority of Your Holiness, to be reformed generally in all her privileges and statutes, and to this end she arrays herself with all her strength." [8] It was only within this elaborately reassuring context that d'Ailly felt it safe to allude to the rumor of Urbanist sympathies in the studium.

Although any responsible spokesman for the university would have to be deeply concerned about the reputation of his institution at the papal court, our earlier investigation shows that after 1383, there was little indication of secret Urbanist activity within the studium. The Urbanist theologians had left in the second half of 1381, and during the winter of 1382-83, the English nation had been brought to accept the university's pro-Avignon orientation. With this accomplished, the university as a whole drew up a new declaration of fidelity to Clement VII, which was sent to him along with a petition for benefices on February 26, 1383.

The only cases that could possibly be invoked in support of Blanchard's contention were those of John Duchêne and Giles Deschamps, whose progress Blanchard had blocked on the grounds of their Urbanist sympathies. We have seen, however, that the chancellor's accusations were contrived. If there was any Urbanism lurking in the university at the time these men were licensed, it was in the imagination of the chancellor, when he found it expedient. John of Florence might be an exception, but he was licensed in 1381(2), before the date in question, and there is no record that anyone opposed his advancement for political reasons. All in all, we may safely conclude that however dangerous the insinuations of the Blanchard party might have been for the university's reputation and for this particular suit, they had no basis in fact.

Blanchard's third effort to discredit his opponents was the most

---

[7] *Ibid.*, p. 400. Details on this legation may be found in H. Nelis, "La Collation des bénéfices ecclésiastiques en Belgique sous Clément VII (1378-1394)," *Revue d'Histoire Ecclésiastique*, 28 (1932), 61, and N. Valois, *La France et le grand schisme d'occident*, 4 vols. (Paris, 1896-1902), II, 257, which correct Denifle, *Chart.*, III, no. 1653, pp. 591-92.

[8] *Chart.*, III, no. 1519, p. 400.

legitimate. In the deposition submitted to the Cardinal of Laon's commission by Blanchard's advocate, John de Valle, Blanchard asserted that the alleged "abuses" were really the chancellor's legitimate prerogatives. The whole suit should be dismissed summarily, he said, because it was dishonestly fabricated by envious, proud, and selfish men, who were moved by a desire to avenge themselves of an insult they suffered when the chancellor innocently allowed himself to be seated before the rector. According to Blanchard, the whole investigation into the sale of licenses and the ranking of candidates was a pretext to punish him for inadvertently having slighted the honor of the rector, the Faculty of Arts, and the university.[9]

The incident in question occurred in June 1384, at the inception-celebration for the Franciscan Adam d'Ay, a new Master of Theology.[10] After dinner, Blanchard explained, the guests moved from the table to a hall where wine and spices were to be served. Then, "not by any presumption of his own or any other sinister motive, but because of the arrangements of the seats . . . he was placed first and the above-mentioned Rector of the University second." Though seated in the more honorable place, the chancellor refused to be served before the rector, yet the latter took umbrage and ordered the chancellor to appear before the Faculty of Arts to answer for his action. When the general congregation was called, the chancellor refused to attend, saying he had to prepare for academic exercises the next day. For his failure to appear, Blanchard was declared contumacious.

A few days later, the rector cited him again to appear, and this time, though not obliged to do so, he complied.[11] There he was forced to listen to an extremely hostile speech by Peter Bidaud, whom he had

---

[9] *Chart.*, III, no. 1521, arts. 23-25, 31-37, esp. art. 23, p. 406: "Omnes articuli pro parte sua adversa in hac causa . . . sunt mendose confecti ex appetitu vindicte occasione indignacionis per aliquos concepte contra eum ex causa prioritatis sedis . . . aut ex invidia aliquorum et appetitu vane glorie, una cum affectu propriorum commodi et honoris, vel alio quovis sinistro motivo..." See also art. 25, with reference to the chancellor and the rector and the question: "quis illorum esset major," which is interpreted, "sicut hec que modo vertitur causa inter universitatem studii et cancellarium ecclesie Parisiensis radicitus habuit ortum."

[10] Note that Adam received his license two years earlier than university regulations permitted, and that he was one of those approved by only four masters. See above, p. 103.

[11] On this immunity see Blanchard's deposition, *Chart.*, III, no. 1520, pp. 407-8, arts. xxv-xxix; *Chart.*, I, no. 528; and P. Kibre, *Scholarly Privileges in the Middle Ages* (Cambridge, Mass., 1962), pp. 123-25. It seems strange that Blanchard made no more of this precedent, but no further mention of it appears in this process.

recently licensed in canon law. In the manner of an academic lecture, Bidaud argued that anyone who disobeys an order of his superior should be (1) considered a heretic; (2) cut off from the company of those over whom his superior has authority, like a sick sheep who might infect the flock; (3) deprived of all his benefices if he is an ecclesiastic; (4) declared ineligible for any other benefice; and (5) decapitated(!). Bidaud then concluded that the chancellor had disobeyed the order of his superior, the rector, and therefore all these penalties should apply. The faculty then approved these propositions. Despite the hostility and insults heaped upon him, and notwithstanding the noises made by the multitude who did not want to hear him out, the chancellor then humbly and reverently excused himself for having taken the wrong seat and for not having attended the first congregation to which he was called. Thus, he placated the anger that had been stirred up against him.[12]

Blanchard's banquet theory failed to divert the cardinal's commission from its investigation, but centuries later it won the adherence of Heinrich Denifle, editor of the monumental *Chartularium Universitatis Parisiensis*,[13] who in turn convinced Hastings Rashdall[14] and Astrik Gabriel.[15] Denifle's acceptance of Blanchard's plea is partly explained

---

[12] *Chart.*, III, no. 1520, arts. xxxi-xxxvi, pp. 408-10. Others reported the substance of Bidaud's speech more objectively. John Luqueti confirmed only "that the said Master ... maintained that anyone who disobeys an order ... of his superior ought to be considered a heretic" (*ibid.*, no. 1521, p. 418, test. xi, super xxxvii). Nothing here about decapitation. Note also that Pierre Plaoul and John de Hokelen insisted that the elder members of the faculty opposed Bidaud's conclusions (*ibid.*, tests. xii & xiii).

[13] Despite differences with Denifle's overall interpretation of the Blanchard affair, I gladly acknowledge my indebtedness to a number of the insights tucked into his introduction to the relevant documents, which he grouped together as nos. 1504-22, pp. 340-420, of *Chart.*, III. As one example among many, he deserves the credit for recognizing the generational conflict underlying the reform.

[14] H. Rashdall, *The Universities of Europe in the Middle Ages*, new ed. by F. M. Powicke and A. B. Emden, 3 vols. (London, 1936), I, 401 n.: "It is clear that the suit was promoted by the Faculty of Arts—largely at the instigation of d'Ailly who (as Denifle suggests) wanted the chancellorship himself, in consequence of a renewal of the dispute with the rector for precedence at the inception-banquet, and that the chancellor's irregularities might otherwise have been winked at."

[15] A. Gabriel, "The Conflict between the Chancellor and the University of Masters and Students at Paris during the Middle Ages," in *Die Auseinandersetzungen an der Pariser Universität im XIII. Jahrhundert*, ed. A. Zimmerman (Miscellanea Mediaevalia, X, 1976), pp. 106-54, esp. pp. 119-36. Canon Gabriel considers the quarrel a matter of precedence, having its origin in the banquet incident, and he reinforces Denifle's antipathy for d'Ailly. He gives no consideration to the price of the license or to Blanchard's own less than lovely record and personality.

by the former's pronounced antipathy to Pierre d'Ailly, whom he denounces at length for hypocrisy, greed, ambition, and cunning.[16] Denifle cites two relatively impartial witnesses (who were, however, closer to Blanchard than to his opponent) who named d'Ailly as the man who shaped the resentment over the banquet incident and mobilized the dissident artists against the chancellor. John Ade, O.P., the man who had distinguished himself for the "courtesy" he had shown the chancellor in gratitude for receiving his degree two years early,[17] nonetheless showed some impartiality when, in testifying for the university, he admitted that the chancellor sometimes licensed candidates because they had paid him court.[18] In testifying on Blanchard's deposition, Ade affirmed the chancellor's good reputation, which, he said, had been widespread until he had been defamed by his persecuters. When asked who they were, he replied, "as far as he is able to tell, they are the artists and Master Pierre d'Ailly, who is the principal leader in this." [19] He further stated that the controversy "began because of a certain debate between the rector and the chancellor over seating priority." [20]

A second witness who considered d'Ailly the artists' leader in exploiting the banquet incident was Bonitus Litelli, O.P., who, though more clearly a partisan of Blanchard (he testified only on his deposition), nonetheless deserves a hearing because of his efforts to moderate the conflict and the abuse he suffered as a result.[21] In

---

[16] *Chart.*, III, p. 340. The examples of Denifle's hostility toward d'Ailly are numerous. Where Blanchard complained in his deposition that the case had been fabricated by men moved "by a desire for glory," Denifle comments in his notes, "Pierre d'Ailly is certainly intended." (*Chart.*, III, no. 1520, art. xxiii, pp. 406, 411, n. 10.) Denifle attributes the university's articles of accusation to d'Ailly, because they seem to have been composed with a uniform viewpoint (non semel maleficii magnitudinem adaugendo aut indicium commutando) and in a highly prejudicial manner (omnia promiscue miscentur, non distinguendo, sitne aliquid de antiqua consuetudine necnon, ex curialitate, vel ex pactu). *Chart.*, III, no. 1511, p. 349, intro.

[17] See above, p. 97.

[18] *Chart.*, III, no. 1513, pp. 387-88, test. lxix, super lv.

[19] *Ibid.*, no. 1521, p. 416, test. vii, super xxii: "Interrogatus qui sunt persequentes, dixit quod quantum potest percipere, sunt artiste et magister Petrus de Ailliaco, qui est in hoc caput principale."

[20] *Ibid.*, super xxiii: "[Discensio] incepit pro quodam debato prioritatis sedis inter rectorum et cancellarium...."

[21] On two occasions Litelli's colleagues expressed their annoyance with him. "Laxaverunt se ad graves injurias verbales contra dictum deponentem" and "Dum semel examinaretur per deputatos universitatis in dicta causa super qui-

Litelli's opinion, the suit had been propelled principally by d'Ailly and John de Marsono, who had been rector when the university published its first warnings about money for the license, October 6, 1384.[22] He also told the cardinal's investigators that

> he believes the existing controversy between the university and the chancellor arose out of the annoyance of the then rector at the fact that the chancellor preceded him in sitting at a certain luncheon and the following supper, because he had never heard any mention of the matter of the suit before then. Moreover he believes that, out of a desire for vengeance and their resentment of the chancellor, certain men of the university stirred up the present suit, which he believes never would have arisen without the above annoyance.[23]

Yet we cannot attribute the whole affair to d'Ailly. Even if he had organized the university's suit against the chancellor single-handedly, and even if his behavior seems highly objectionable to some, we must not lose sight of the things Blanchard did that predictably turned masters and students against him.

An additional qualification emerges from the relatively impartial testimony of John Luqueti. Denifle calls Luqueti a friend of the opposing side,[24] which means a friend of d'Ailly, and in fact both men had been associated with the College of Navarre, where Luqueti was licensed in arts in 1374.[25] Since then, like Blanchard, he had been connected with the Sorbonne, [26] but he remained on friendly terms

---

busdam articulis factis contra dictum cancellarium, aliqui ex deputatis multum sibi indignabantur, quia non respondebat ad mentem eorum." *Ibid.*, test. ii, pp. 412-13.

[22] *Chart.*, III, p. 412: "Magistri Petrus de Alliaco in theologia et Johannes de Marsono in artibus fuerunt moti ad nutriendum istam litem" (cited by Denifle, *ibid.*, p. 340). For John de Marsono, see *ibid.*, no. 1491, p. 331, and p. 420, n. 9, where Denifle points out this connection.

[23] *Ibid.*, no. 1521, test. ii, p. 412.

[24] *Ibid.*, p. 340.

[25] *Ibid.*, p. 259, n. 41. D'Ailly had begun his study of theology there only a few years earlier.

[26] *Ibid.* There are undertones of a rivalry between the Sorbonne and the College of Navarre in the Blanchard affair, but there is no strict division along this line. The most important exception is Simon Freron, who was a Navarre alumnus and its Head from 1372 to 1382, but who clearly was not an opponent of Blanchard (see above, pp. 107-8). Luqueti, slightly partial to Blanchard but still called a "friend" by d'Ailly, was an alumnus of Navarre, residing in the Sorbonne (*ibid.*, no. 1513, p. 388, test. lxx, super lviii et lix). D' Ailly himself had lived at the Sorbonne for a while (*ibid.*, super lxiii: "in domo Sarbone, in qua dictus testis pro tunc morabatur").

with d'Ailly.[27] Luqueti's views were not extreme and he testified for both sides. As a witness for the university, he supported some of the accusations only with qualifications. He was careful to point out that some gifts were customary, and he even ventured to defend Blanchard to the extent of saying that the gifts were given in return for "trouble and labor." [28] On the other hand, as a witness for Blanchard, when asked about the university's articles of accusation, he said

> he had not seen the articles . . . for which reason he would not know how to state the truth [about them], except that he believed firmly, that some men had ordered them to be drawn up out of a desire for revenge and vainglory. Asked for the names of those whom he believed thus to have ordered them, he answered that he did not remember, but he believed firmly that they are artists, although few. *Nevertheless, he believes that the majority of the university believes that they have done well.*[29]

A former rector himself,[30] Luqueti had been at the ill-fated banquet and later testified that he "saw that in the distribution of spices, the chancellor was first, which surprised him." [31] This implies that Luqueti believed the rector should have had precedence. Indeed, Luqueti explicitly affirmed his belief that the rector "was not moved or inflamed against the chancellor for any unjust reason," but, by implication, for a genuine grievance.[32] Even so, he said, Lawrence Quilleti, the rector, might not have done anything had the other artists not insisted. Shortly afterward Luqueti "saw and heard that certain artists were criticizing the rector because he had allowed the chancellor to sit first. The rector said that it was not by his will that the chancellor was first to sit in the first seat, and that by right the first seat ought to be his." [33] But it was "by some others" that the rector "was asked to call a congregation of the Faculty of Arts." [34] Although some of the artists took counsel together to provoke a quarrel with Blanchard, this collusion was not, at least not yet, aimed at bringing him to court for selling the license, but only at summoning him to be

---

[27] Luqueti was one of those from whom d'Ailly heard the story about Duchêne. D'Ailly referred to him as "amicus meus in aula Sarbone." *Ibid.*, p. 388, lxx.

[28] *Ibid.*, no. 1513, test. xliiii, p. 381.

[29] *Ibid.*, no. 1521, p. 418, test. xi, super xxiii.

[30] *Ibid.*, no. 1474, p. 312.

[31] *Ibid.*, no. 1521, test. xi, super xxxi, p. 418.

[32] *Ibid.*

[33] *Ibid.*

[34] *Ibid.*

disciplined by the Faculty of Arts. After Blanchard failed to appear at the artists' first assembly, it was clear that he meant to challenge the jurisdiction of the faculty and the precedence of the university's acknowledged head.[35] He was thus declared contumacious, and by this time matters had changed so that even Blanchard's eventual apology had no effect. Legal action against the chancellor began the following autumn, and the articles of accusation were submitted to the Cardinal of Laon in May 1385. If this view is correct, Luqueti properly distinguished between the citation to appear before the arts faculty, clearly originating in the banquet incident, and the articles of accusation, which, though drawn up by a few artists, nonetheless had the support of the majority of university members. Luqueti's nuanced reconstruction indicates that not even all those who were well disposed to Blanchard accepted his view of the banquet incident. Yet we must grant the importance of the quarrel over precedence even if we deny the exaggerated interpretation given it by Blanchard's partisans.

That the banquet incident was not the masters' sole reason for attacking Blanchard may be inferred from his defending himself on other grounds as well. Blanchard took great pains to show that his actions flowed naturally from a complex background of legal precedents, venerable traditions, and institutional practices. As we proceed from Blanchard's counterattack to his defense proper, the reader should bear in mind that so far our sources for Blanchard's position—his deposition for the Cardinal of Laon and his testimony in the Parlement of Paris—emanate directly from Blanchard or his counsel and must be considered an accurate reflection of the chancellor's position. Of more doubtful accuracy are the arguments attributed to Blanchard by Pierre d'Ailly, who cited them only to refute them. In the second half of his speech "Radix Omnium" the young theologian answered what he called the "fraudulent cavils" of his opponent,[36] and in "Super Omnia" d'Ailly replied to further objections that were not necessarily part of Blanchard's own defense, but which might reasonably have been raised on his behalf.[37]

---

[35] *Ibid.*, no. 1520, arts. xxv-xxx, pp. 407-8.

[36] "Radix Omnium," edited below, in Appendix, p. 214, l. 10-11.

[37] "Super Omnia," edited below, in Appendix, p. 236, l. 4-8. There is reason to question whether these objections were actually taken from the floor in a live debate with partisans of Blanchard. They may have been proposed as questions by d'Ailly's students in an exercise, or he may simply have compiled them from pro-Blanchard documents.

Before we can supplement Blanchard's depositions with material introduced by d'Ailly, we must ascertain how accurately he reported his opponent's arguments. Fortunately we are able to compare d'Ailly's reconstruction of Blanchard's reasoning against Blanchard's deposition to the pope and his testimony before the Parlement of Paris. A first test is provided by d'Ailly's treatment of one of Blanchard's main contentions as quoted from the document that d'Ailly calls the "Articles Presented . . . to the Lord Pope." [38] This is the letter Blanchard sent to accompany the testimony compiled by the Cardinal of Laon. It is a later recension of the document already known to us as the deposition drawn up by John de Valle. The following textual comparison will show that the document known to d'Ailly could have differed from that known to us only in minor details. In the text to be examined, d'Ailly is restating Blanchard's contention that the bachelor's payments are not made for the license, but as an expression of joy upon receipt of the signetum. D'Ailly's résumé is too concise to allow the presentation of parallel texts. Instead, I have italicized those of d'Ailly's words which correspond etymologically (that is, in the Latin they vary only in inflection) to those used in Blanchard's deposition, and I follow them with the number assigned by Denifle to the article from which they are taken. D'Ailly relates that one of the reasons advanced by Blanchard in his "Articles Presented . . . to the Lord Pope" for giving money to the chancellor is that

> the bachelors *about to be licensed*, having received those *notices* which *at Paris are commonly called signeta* (12), and by means of which they are *made sure* and certain *of obtaining the license* (14), and without the chancellor or any other asking for anything [cf. without any intervention whatsoever (17)], the individual bachelors *of the Faculties of Theology, Canon Law, and Medicine* (12), *as a sign of virtuous recognition and* joyful *congratulation*, by their own *free and* wholly *spontaneous will* (17), *were accustomed* (18), *through the messengers* (13) who brought them the *signeta* (13), to send *little gifts* (18) of money or other goods, as much and of such a nature as *it might seem expedient* (14) to them in the freedom of their grace, *to the chancellor* (18), whom, he afterward licenses, without bearing any grudge against those who sent only a little.[39]

---

[38] Radix, p. 214, l. 16-17.

[39] Radix, p. 214, l. 16-28: "Ponit in Articulis per eum Domino Pape in Romana Curia presentatis, scilicet quod Bachalarii *licentiandi* receptis *cedulis* illis, que *Parisius communiter signeta vocantur* (12), et per quas *de* eorum *licencia obtinenda securi redduntur* et certificati, (14), Cancellario a dictis Bachalariis, nec per se, nec per alium quidquam petente [cf. absque . . . intervencione quacunque

Thus, d'Ailly's account of Blanchard's first argument is a collage of phrases from five different articles, pasted side by side in a single tortuous sentence. The verbal similarity of d'Ailly's paraphrase to Blanchard's deposition is sufficiently close to establish the derivation of Blanchard's covering letter from the deposition drawn up by John de Valle.

With this near-identity established, the fairness of d'Ailly's paraphrase may be assessed. D'Ailly's account of Blanchard's statement varies from the deposition in three details, all at the end, two of which are minor, one major. First, Blanchard never specified that the "gifts" could be made either in money or in kind. D'Ailly's addition makes the bachelors' "spontaneous reaction" seem considerably more formal, more like the terms of a contract. Second, d'Ailly's interpolation of the statement that the chancellor received the gifts "without bearing any grudge against those who sent only a little" added an ironic note that probably drew a laugh. The third divergence from the deposition is more serious. Blanchard nowhere stated that the payments were to be made *before* the award of the license. The implication that the chancellor was intentionally concealing this detail lest he give the impression that payment was a condition of the license should be considered d'Ailly's own, and not a reflection of Blanchard's position.

A second example will conclude our consideration of d'Ailly's reliability in presenting Blanchard's views. In his testimony before the Parlement of Paris on February 5, 1386, Blanchard maintained that money was given not for the license, but to repay him for his labor and expenses. First, to establish the very close relation between d'Ailly's version and Blanchard's original testimony, I present the two in parallel columns below. To make the French conform to the Latin syntax, I have moved to first position a phrase that was in the middle of Blanchard's original sentence.

---

(17)], singuli Bachalarii, scilicet *trium Facultatum* (13) *Theologie, Decretorum, et Medicine* (12), *in signum virtuose recognitionis et* gaudiose *congratulationis* de ipsorum *libera et* mere *spontanea voluntate* (17) *consueverint Cancellario* (18) *per nuntios* qui eis dicta *signeta* (13) portaverunt remittere, sive in pecuniis, aut aliis enceniis, aliqua *munuscula* (18), tanta et talia sicut eorum gratuite libertati *expedire videtur* (14), quos postea licentiat, nullum super eo quod parum misit calumniando."

The numbers in parentheses correspond to the articles in *Chart.*, III, no. 1520, pp. 404-6, from which the italicized words or phrases were taken.

d'Ailly	*Blanchard*
Bachalarii in theologia licentiandi	De chacun Bachelier [à] licentier en Theologie
ex laudabili consuetudine et	
usu hactenus observatis	en usant du Droit de ses predecesseurs et du sien
debent et tenentur sibi dare et mittere	il est en possession et saisine de recevoir
post dictam receptionem signetorum	apres la commission du signet
et ante licentiam	
ad minus decem francos auri et ultra liberum est.	dix francs du meins par especial de ceux qui ont dequoy.[40]
Et hoc dicit esse	
sibi licitum recipere	Et est chose raisonnable et recevable
ratione sui laboris quem habet occasione dicte licentie conferende. [41]	que celuy qui a pein, ait profit.[42]

D'Ailly has distorted Blanchard's case in two particulars. First, he did not quote the clearest statement of the argument. In another, adjacent passage, Blanchard does not merely say that the money is compensation for his labor, but also explicitly *denies* that money is sent "to obtain the license." [43] By excluding that denial, d'Ailly deprived his opponent's argument of much of its force. Second, d'Ailly again added the detail that the bachelors must send the gift "before the license." D'Ailly's reliability as a reporter of Blanchard's ideas, therefore, is not total. On the other hand, his interpolations, while intolerable in a historian, are not so grossly misleading as to disqualify him as a source. The first two variations mentioned above were purely rhetorical. The repeated insistence upon the exaction of the gift before the conferral of the license, although an interpolation, is historically justifiable. In short, d'Ailly's paraphrase of Blanchard's ideas is not entirely scrupulous, but with a critical understanding of his role in the affair, one can use the information he provides to help reconstruct Blanchard's position.

Our review of the available sources completed, we are now in a position to recreate the theoretical framework within which Blanchard

---

[40] Du Boulay, IV, 607, 27-29.
[41] Radix, pp. 214, 30-215, 5.
[42] Du Boulay, IV, 607, 11-12.
[43] *Ibid.*, lines 7-9: "Est ... ledit Chancelier en possession et saisine d'avoir de chacun bachelier au moins onze francs, et pour ce qu'il a envoyé à chacun son signet *pro poena, labore et expensa*, non pas *pro licentia obtinenda*...."

elaborated his defense. In the deposition submitted to the Cardinal of Laon's commission in July 1385, Blanchard indicated the line of reasoning he was to pursue throughout the affair. Rather than deny that he received money or ranked candidates, he claimed that these practices were not abuses, but prerogatives of his office either specifically granted in papal letters or established by immemorial custom.

The chancellor began by reviewing those rights he claimed by virtue of papal privileges. Among these was the right to examine the candidates for the license presented by the masters of the individual faculties (except for those in arts, who may be presented to and examined by the Chancellor of Ste-Geneviève).[44] The chancellor's "examination" is to be a veritable investigation of the candidate's "morals, knowledge, and eloquence, as well as his sense of purpose and potential for progress." Testimony is to be taken from "all the masters of the candidate's faculty present in Paris as well as from other honest and literate men from whom the truth may be known." When the inquiry is finished, "in the light of what in good faith seems decent and expedient, the chancellor may grant or deny the license according to his own conscience." Curiously enough, the papal document that thus describes the process of licensing, interpreted by Blanchard as his "right," is *Parens scientiarum* (or its rescript of 1237),[45] the same one upon which the masters founded their arguments.

More important, in Blanchard's view, were the consequences of his affirmative decision. The chancellor considered his award of the license to be absolutely binding upon the university. To begin with, as he explained in article eight of his deposition, his license was universally considered valid: "Those licensed by the chancellor are recognized and have been accustomed to be recognized as licensed by the rector and all the officials, masters (regent and nonregent), bachelors and students, individually and collectively, of our Alma Mater, the University of Paris." [46] But Blanchard went much further, trespassing over the boundary between the license and the magisterium when he continued: "And, [the licentiates] are freely admitted to all magisterial activities *and to the magisterium* of that faculty in which they were . . . licensed . . . *without any contradiction whatsoever*." [47] More precisely, the masters were to accept into their association not

---

[44] *Chart.*, III, no. 1520, arts. i-v, vii, pp. 403-4.
[45] *Ibid.*, p. 411, n. 1.
[46] *Ibid.*, art. viii, p. 404.
[47] *Ibid.*

just those who were licensed in first place (*primi*), but even the runners-up (*etiam sequentes*), indeed, by implication, all who were licensed.

The implications of this phrasing, which disregards the distinction between the license and the magisterium, are crucial to an understanding of the masters' efforts at reform. In his eighth article, Blanchard was reaffirming the implications of the papal position on the magisterium upheld since Alexander IV's *Quasi lignum vitae*, (1255), and he consequently regarded as a natural inference the statement that the masters must award the magisterium to anyone licensed by the chancellor. The reforming masters, however, were trying to move in the opposite direction by attacking Blanchard's practice of granting the license to men designated by the pope after examination by only three or four masters, that is, from their point of view, without consulting all of them. The reformers really were confronting papal authority on this question: just as Clement VII was the source of Blanchard's use of the summary examination, so papal authority also underlay his assertion that licentiates are expected to receive the magisterium. Clement VII's use of this authority is most apparent in his letter to John de Calore of March 17, 1380, ordering the chancellor to allow Christian de Altaripa to read the *Sentences*, and "after he has completed his lectures, provided that he has been found worthy and sufficient by your diligent examination and that of other masters of the studium in the same faculty, . . . you should award to Christian the honor of the magisterium and the license to teach." [48]

As if to underline the papal authority behind article eight, in his eleventh article Blanchard paraphrased Innocent IV's letter in support of the friars, in which the pope ordered a then (1250) recalcitrant chancellor to award the license "not only to those presented by the Faculty of Theology and who request it, . . . but even to those, especially the religious, who are not presented and do not request it, if in good faith they are seen to be well-suited to it in his [the chancellor's]

---

[48] *Chart.*, III, no. 1445, p. 289. For other examples of Clement VII's use of "honor magisterii" and "licentia docendi" as virtually synonymous, see *ibid.*, nos. 1440, 1448, 1455, and 1480. Note that the cases in which Clement ordered Blanchard to grant the "licentiam seu magisterium" and those in which the chancellor was directed to use the summary examination procedure were not necessarily the same. The articles of accusation object only to the summary examination procedure, but the attitude behind the practice to which they objected is plainly visible in Blanchard's articles 8 and 11. See above, p. 11.

conscience." [49] Thus the chancellor has the right not only to license those who seek that honor, but even the obligation to license those who do not, provided they are worthy. In addition, following Blanchard's logic (and Innocent IV's), the individual faculties would be compelled to accept all these licentiates as masters. How ironic that Blanchard should invoke precisely this precedent! Over a century before, Innocent IV had used the chancellor's declining powers as a lever to keep the university open to mendicants, then despised by chancellor and masters alike. Now Blanchard is claiming as a privilege the very bull with which Innocent had applied pressure on his predecessor. Nonetheless, Blanchard's allusion to this authority, the papal conception of the magisterium, makes it clear that if the masters wished to oppose his view, they would also have to contest papal influence over the studium. We have seen that Blanchard was relying upon papal authority when he asserted his right to rank the candidates for the license.[50] This claim was only alluded to in the deposition of July 1385, when he averred that the university was obliged to accept "not just those who were licensed in first place, but even the runners-up" into their association. By the next winter, however, this issue had become a leading point of contention. Consequently Blanchard's position was more boldly expressed in the parlement: "The chancellor assigns ranks to the bachelors according to his conscience." [51]

Blanchard's deposition did not end, however, with his claim to compel award of the magisterium to all whom he licensed. Instead, after claiming the right to rank candidates, he began to move gradually from those rights he enjoyed by specific papal mandate toward those he claimed on the basis of custom. Clearly in the latter category is the receipt of a gift from those about to be licensed. Never denying that he received gifts, the chancellor took refuge in tradition. He defended the gifts by a patient explanation of the customary practices associated with the award of the license "for so long that no one remembers when they were initiated." [52]

Blanchard explained the custom attacked by the masters as follows. After the examination, on the day before the successful candidates are

---

[49] *Ibid.*, no. 1520, art. xi, p. 404. Cf. *Chart.*, I, no. 191, p. 219, and above, p. 17.

[50] Above, p. 101-4.

[51] Du Boulay, IV, 608, 30-31: "Car le Chancelier assigne les lieux aux bacheliers selon sa conscience...."

[52] *Chart.*, III, no. 1520, art. 1, p. 403.

to receive their licenses, the chancellors have been accustomed to sending them a certain announcement, called a signetum, sealed with the seal of the chancellery.[53] The bachelors customarily receive the signeta with great joy and reverence, and serve the chancellor's messengers wine and spices. This celebration over, each recipient of the signetum, certain now that he will be licensed on the next day, was accustomed to send the chancellor a gift of money that varied according to the faculty. Those in medicine sent two francs; those in canon law, one franc; those in theology, whether secular or regular, were accusomed to send a purse of ten gold coins worth at least ten francs or more; as much as the bachelor might desire, according to the liberality of his soul, the potency of his wealth, and the demands of his station. A smaller gift of up to four or more florins was usually given to the chancellor's servants. For each hearing in chambers [*audicione camere*], since they were certain of obtaining the license, those in arts as well were accustomed to give to the chancellor's assistants more or less money for the labor undertaken and the services performed during the examination. Some even sent clothes for the chancellor and his staff.[54]

The chancellor took great pains to insist that the bachelors gave these gifts "with a free and spontaneous will, without any exaction whatsoever, and without the tacit or express intervention of any antecedent, connected, or concomitant pact."[55] Or again, and this time with a passing reference to the university's accusation that rank was assigned according to the size of the gift, Blanchard maintained that the gifts were given

> without any intervening or previous agreement whatever on the award of the license, or the assigning of rank, or on any other thing done for them by the chancellor; but only as a sign of virtuous congratulation over the danger they have escaped and the honor they have received; and as a sign of the honor, reverence, favor, and good will that they feel toward the chancellor; and even as a thankful recognition of the labor that the chancellor has undertaken on their behalf, before they had attained the degree of master.[56]

Therefore, he maintained, the students give out of their joy and gratitude for the efforts expended in their behalf by the chancellor.

[53] *Chart.*, III, no. 1520, art. xi, pp. 404-5.
[54] *Ibid.*, arts. xiii-xvii *passim*, p. 405.
[55] *Ibid.*, art. xiii, p. 405.
[56] *Ibid.*, art. xvii, p. 406.

Blanchard's second argument, therefore, was that the gifts were given not as a price for the license, but as compensation for his efforts in overseeing the process of licensing. His description of the labor involved sheds considerable light on the implementation of the licensing procedures mandated by *Parens scientiarum*. First, the chancellor must question all the masters who know the bachelor concerning his life, letters, and intellectual promise. Apparently the masters came to testify one by one in the chancellor's quarters. Since most of them were men with important benefices, Blanchard felt compelled to receive them suitably and entertain them with wine and sweetmeats, which entailed considerable effort and expense.[57] The deposition of each master then had to be registered by the chancellor, personally.[58] Second, the chancellor had to interview each of the bachelors for information concerning their life and learning.[59] Having formed his opinion, the chancellor must maintain it steadfastly in the face of outside pressure. The chancellor was obligated in principle to prefer the worthy to the unworthy, but this was extremely difficult when students were of high lineage or presented letters of recommendation from great lords and ladies.[60] The chancellor must also take an active role in the actual licensing ceremony, at the bishop's hall. He must deliver a sermon in praise of learning and the masters,[61] and then take part in an extemporaneous disputation.[62] Further, he must send the

---

[57] Du Boulay, IV, 606, 32-36: "Dit que les maistres en Theologie, quand ils sont faits maistres, iurent faire une bonne relation des bacheliers à licentier, et iure chacun maistre à part *de moribus et scientia*, et chacun bachelier à licentier. Et en ce il convient que le Chancelier dépende, et qu'il donne vin et espices. Car les maistres qu'il interroge [qui l'interrogent, Du Boulay] sont de grand estat..."

[58] *Ibid.*, 38-40: "Et enregistre le Chancelier la deposition d'un chacun maistre et ne souffriroit pas que son clerc l'enregistrast."

[59] *Ibid.*, 41-43: "Et encore s'informe et est tenu interroger les bacheliers à licentier et aussi les maistres *super scientia et moribus*, de ceux qui sont à licentier..." Blanchard's statement is ambiguous. It is not clear whether he simply examined each bachelor or whether they were asked to testify about one another.

[60] *Ibid.*, 43-47: "Est tenu en conscience preferer les dignes aux indignes. Dit que quand aucun bachelier à licentier appete avoir bon lieu et honneste, s'il est de bon lignage, ou s'il a lettres de grands seigneurs ou de grandes dames, il est en tres grand' perplexité, consideré son serment. Et neantmoins il l'a tousiours gardé."

[61] *Ibid.*, 48-50: "Dit que quand on doit faire les licentiez, le Chancelier doit faire un serment, et en icelle recommander la science et les maistres, et en a peine."

[62] *Ibid.*, 51-53: "Doit aller dans la salle de l'Evesque, quand on fait les licentiez, et arguer et faire ce qu'il appartient au maistre et au Chancelier. Et tout ce *ex improviso*, et en ce grand charge a."

berets to those licensed and pronounce certain ceremonial formulas.[63]
Blanchard concluded that he received little remuneration for such
great "trouble" and "perplexity." [64] It was therefore fitting that he
should receive a traditional compensatory gift from the graduating
bachelors.

In his first speech, "Radix Omnium," d'Ailly attempted to ridicule
these two arguments—that the gifts were given freely and that they
were compensation for labor—by saying that they were contradictory,
in that wages paid for labor are owed, not given freely.[65] D'Ailly's
argument reveals something about the level on which the debate was
conducted. Clearly the two reasons invoked by Blanchard may be
complementary, and are not necessarily incompatible. At the same time,
one may agree with d'Ailly that few students would give out of sheer
gratitude if there were no sense of obligation toward the chancellor,
or better yet, an institutionalized means of pressuring candidates to
give—for example, retaining the license until after the gift was
received.

Blanchard's reply does not challenge the theologian's method of
reasoning, but instead attacks his conclusion by asserting that it is in
fact possible for a thing to be both owed and freely given. For example,
Blanchard argues, sustenance is fairly (*ex debita justitia*) owed to
preachers by the people to whom they preach. Furthermore, Augustine
in *De Opere Monachorum* says: "The Lord decreed that those who live
by the Gospel may eat free bread supplied by those to whom they
preach free grace." [66] This bread, then, "although it is owed to them,
nevertheless is free and freely given. Consequently something exists
which is freely given and yet owed." [67]

Having thus dealt with d'Ailly's charge of self-contradiction,
Blanchard nonetheless preferred not to insist upon the element of joy
in the candidates' giving, but instead concentrated on adducing
reasons why it was legitimate for him to receive in return for his labor.
For example, the above argument from Augustine stated that the
necessities of life are owed to preachers. There can be no doubt that

---

[63] Du Boulay, IV, 606, 50-51: "Et avec ce doit bailler les birrets aux licentiez et
dire certaines paroles formelles."

[64] *Ibid.*, 47-48: "Et n'est emoulument tres grand pour telle peine et telle per-
plexite."

[65] Radix, pp. 216, 26 - 217, 2.

[66] J. P. Migne, *Patrologiae cursus completus*. Series latina (221 vols.; Paris, 1864-
68), 40, 555.

[67] Super, pp. 259, 60 - 260, 5.

this was true even in the time of the Apostles, says Blanchard, because Christ told them "The worker is worthy of his hire." [68] On this basis, Paul confirmed the same practice, asking "Who serves at his own expense?" [69] The chancellor interpreted these authorities as implying that material goods can be owed for the labor of performing a spiritual act. And since the office of preaching is no less spiritual than the office of licensing, the chancellor should be able to receive for the labor of performing his office. [70]

The Apostles' practice of receiving for the labor of preaching was prefigured by the Old Testament prophets, continues Blanchard, and since the use of prophecy is no less spiritual than that of licensing, the chancellor may receive *temporalia* for his labor. The same analogy holds for the priests of both the Synagogue and the Church, who received "annual revenues and temporal payments" in return for their spiritual services. If this was accepted under the Old Law, *a fortiori* it should be licit for the chancellor to receive a price for his ministry. In more general terms, it is licit to rent out one's work or skill, even in spiritual matters, as do teachers for teaching, and lawyers for advice and defense: so in the same way, the chancellor may receive a price for his work in licensing. [71]

Blanchard then shifted from Scriptural authority to institutions within the contemporary Church, and he focused first upon the universities. At the University of Toulouse, he said, the Archdeacon confers the license to teach theology as part of his office and receives a fee of twelve francs, although he had received twenty francs until a compromise was reached in papal court. Now this sum is more than what the Chancellor of the University of Paris receives, even though at Toulouse the Archdeacon neither personally confers the license nor argues in disputations. In other universities, he claimed, gifts are also given by bachelors about to be licensed. [72]

Developing this point further, Blanchard displayed the only touch of humor in his entire testimony. Conceding that the chancellor licenses on behalf of the pope, Blanchard granted that neither he nor the pope should charge money for sending licentiates out to labor as

---

[68] Luke 10:7.

[69] I Cor. 9:7.

[70] Radix, p. 215, l. 14-32. The interpretation of the license as a spiritual benefit is a cornerstone of d'Ailly's prosecution and will be examined in Chapter VI.

[71] Radix, p. 216, l. 2-19.

[72] Super, p. 274, l. 13-24.

preachers to the faithful. But, alluding to the university's practice of soliciting benefices for its graduates and teachers, he argued that the pope, and therefore the chancellor, would certainly be justified in demanding compensation from those who entreat and beseech him for benefices even when it is inconvenient and the Church has no need of them.[73]

Nor is the award of the license the only university occasion on which gifts are bestowed, continued Blanchard. Masters receive gifts of clothing when their bachelors are made masters, and these clothes are usually worth more than what the chancellor asks.[74] Even earlier in their academic careers, students are asked to give.[75] At Paris and Orleans, students are asked to contribute to a collection for those who lecture "ordinarily, in the morning." [76] At Paris in canon law and at Orleans in both laws, the bachelors make payments to their masters; and when they want to become masters themselves, they are obliged to pay yet other fees.[77] According to canon law, the maximum one can spend on one's magisterium is 3,000 *gros tournois*; and John Andraea says this does not include the expense of the private examination.[78] What are the gifts sought by the Chancellor of Paris in comparison to a sum like that!

Finally, Blanchard cites an example whose relevance d'Ailly had to concede; namely, that canon law permits a bishop to charge for consecrating a church or performing a visitation.[79] This example is extremely important because, in his report of Blanchard's argument, even d'Ailly recognized that in return for performing a task to which he is bound *ex officio*, the bishop is paid a fee over and above the income of his benefice, which normally is considered adequate compensation for performing all the acts connected with it.[80] D'Ailly limited the application of this example somewhat by reminding his

---

[73] Super, pp. 266, 33 - 267, 6.

[74] Super, p. 277, l. 27-34.

[75] Du Boulay, IV, 607, 13, 19.

[76] *Ibid.*, 12-14.

[77] *Ibid.*, 21-23.

[78] *Ibid.*, 15-18. *Constitutiones Clementis Pape Quinti*, una cum apparatu domini Joannis Andree (Venetiis: Thomas de Blavis de Alexandria, 1489), supra 5, 1, 2, ad verbum *doctoratum*: "expensas privati examinis non videtur includeri." Firenze, Bib. Naz., Incunabulo D. 7. 34, fol. seg. h^v a.

[79] X. 5, 3, 10; ed. Friedberg, II, 751 (for consecration) and Gratian, C.10 q.3 c.9; ed. Friedberg, I, 625-26 (for visitation) quoted in "Super Omnia," p. 269, l. 1-3.

[80] Super, p. 268, l. 28-32.

audience that if the congregation cannot afford to pay a fee, the bishop is obligated to perform the act at his own expense,[81] yet the theologian could not dispose of the law permitting the practice. In fact, when Blanchard cited Gaufredo da Trani's comment to the effect that the fee is not actually for the visitation or consecration, but for the labor of the journey,[82] d'Ailly could only cite Bernard of Parma and Hostiensis and reply that the charge is licit not because of the bishop's labor, but because it is permitted by law.[83]

If one were to take Blanchard's argument further than d'Ailly did, the conclusion would run like this: If a bishop may licitly exact additional fees for acts which he is obligated by his office to perform, and for which he is compensated by his benefice; then the chancellor, although he has a benefice, may still exact a fee for the labor of licensing the bachelors.[84] Furthermore, the chancellor's case would seem to be even clearer than the bishop's because the chancellor's benefice remunerates him for an office that did not originally include administering the license to teach.[85]

The gratifying example of a legal supplement to the revenues of an ecclesiastical office lay at the core of the third principal argument Blanchard used in his defense. He stated that even if the chancellorship had been given to him expressly for awarding the license, it did not yield enough to support him properly, and therefore he could licitly exact fees to supplement his income.[86] To the parlement, Blanchard portrayed himself as caught between two sets of extenuating circumstances. First, he claimed that before the schism he had enjoyed an annual revenue of 1,000 to 1,500 pounds, but because of his adherence to Clement VII he had lost that income. For this reason, he said, the pope gave him the Chancellorship of Paris, which yields, however, only forty pounds per annum.[87] At the same time, he also explained his financial difficulties as a result of the mandatory residence requirement of the chancellorship, which forced him to vacate his other

---

[81] Super, p. 269, l. 21-23.   [82] Super, p. 269, l. 17-19.
[83] Super, p. 269, l. 19-21.   [84] Cf. Super, p. 269, l. 3-7.
[85] Super, p. 275, l. 25-28.   [86] Super, p. 275, l. 27-30.
[87] Du Boulay, IV, 606, 15-23: "Dit qu'il est de belle nativité, et devant le Scisme de l'Eglise, il estoit bien et grandement Beneficié de mil à mil et cinq cents livres de rente, et si tost que le Scisme fut en l'Eglise, il adherdit à la partie de Nostre S. Pere Clement, et perdit ce qu'il avoit lors, et dist qu'il est Maistre en Theologie, et seroit grand' pitie qu'il demeurast sans Benefice, pour ce que le Pape a donné en conferé au Chancelier la Chancelerie, cuidant estre de grand profit. A dit qu'il a grand charge à cause de son Benefice, et ne valent pas les rentes ordinaires plus de 40 livres de rente par an."

benefices and thus to sacrifice the considerable fruits of his canonries at Cambrai and Tournai.[88]

The second explanation may be dealt with first. Apparently Blanchard still held his canonries at Tournai and Cambrai, but there is no reason to believe he could not receive their revenues. The residence requirement attached to the Parisian chancellorship does not state that the position must be held to the exclusion of others, only that its holder must be in residence.[89] Furthermore, we have seen that with the support first of Guy de Boulogne and later of Robert of Geneva (Clement VII), Blanchard had received the revenues of the deanship of Liége for some years after he left that city. Admittedly, I have not found any petition to Clement VII asking for permission to receive Cambrai- and Tournai-based revenues in absentia, but it seems unlikely that Clement, Blanchard's long-standing patron, who provided Blanchard with the benefices in Tournai and Cambrai in the first place, would have insisted that he sacrifice their fruits in order to assume the Chancellorship of Paris. Moreover, when the surrender of a previously held prebend was necessary for the receipt of another, that condition was explicitly stated in the letter of provision, as can be seen in Urban V's letter appointing Blanchard to the Deanship of Liége in 1363.[90] Yet Clement VII's conferral of the Parisian Chancellorship upon Blanchard contains no such demand.[91] It seems fair to conclude, then, that Blanchard was not in fact deprived of his revenues from Tournai and Cambrai because of his required residence in Paris.

---

[88] *Ibid.*, 29-32: "Dit que le Chancelier doit faire sa residence sur son Benefice, et par consequent ne peut demeurer sur ses aultres Benefices, et en cecy perd les fruits de ses aultres Benefices; qui sont bien anotables, car il est Chanoine à Cambray et de Tournay." On the basis of this statement, Louis Salembier considered Tournai and Cambrai Blanchard's only benefices before becoming Chancellor of Paris. *Le Cardinal Pierre d'Ailly* (Tourcoing, 1932), p. 68. Denifle provides considerable information on Blanchard's finances, especially at *Chart.*, II, p. 644 and p. 646, n. 23, but he did not compare his data to Blanchard's testimony at the parlement. In fact, his only reference to the suit in the royal court is intended to show to what lengths the upstarts at the university would go to persecute their chancellor (*ibid.*, III, no. 1522, p. 420).

[89] *Chart.*, I, no. 6, p. 65.

[90] A. Fierens and C. Tihon, *Lettres d'Urbain V*, I, Analecta Vaticano-Belgica (AVB) IX; Bruxelles, 1928, no. 651, p. 239: "Johanni Blankardi cui eadem die de canonicatu et prebenda ecclesie Leodiensis provisum extitit, confertur decanatus in dicta ecclesia Leodiensi, per resignationem Guidonis, episcopi Portuensis, vacans ... [Et] Personatus de Donza sine cura, tertiam partem ecclesie S. Michaelis Gandensis ... dimittere tenebitur."

[91] *Chart.*, III, no. 1461.

It is possible, of course, that these revenues had been cut off as a result of the schism. Blanchard mentioned that crisis as one cause of his relative poverty, though he did not specify the particular losses it caused him. To recapitulate, in 1378 his benefices consisted of the deanship combined with a canonry and prebend at Liége, and a canonry with prebend at St-Pharahild's of Ghent. Early in the schism, Clement VII awarded him first a canonry with prebend at Tournai, and later a canonry with prebend, and then the treasurership of Cambrai.[92] A look at how the schism affected those cities will permit us to estimate its effect on Blanchard's financial situation.

Clustered around the Low Countries, Blanchard's benefices were in a territory dramatically affected by the Great Schism. Here loyalties were determined by no single factor. The area was divided between the political forces of German Emperor and French King, Flemish and French language, French and English economic ties; for each town, court, or region, a different consideration might be decisive.[93] Furthermore, even if a city declared for one pope, its walls never excluded all partisans of the other, even though the crisis was marked by frequent purges. Nor were outlying districts always in conformity with the center. The diversity was such that each pope had to contend with "schismatics" even in dioceses whose bishops were loyal to him.[94] Such circumstances make it extremely difficult to establish whether or not Blanchard received income from a particular benefice. We must assume that his revenues from places loyal to Rome ceased, and, conversely, that income from Clementine areas continued.

Although he represented himself as a victim of the schism's mutual excommunications and purges, Blanchard did not mention Liége and Ghent by name when he told the parlement of his lost benefices. This is especially surprising in the case of Liége, where he had con-ducted extensive litigation and which the schism clearly forced him to abandon. The see of Liége became vacant on July 1, 1378. Urban VI

---

[92] See above, pp. 41-45.

[93] H. Nelis, "La Collation," pp. 35-36. For other studies on Flanders in this period see: F. Bliemetzrieder, "Flandern und der grosse abendländische Schisma," *Studien und Mitteilungen aus dem Benediktinerordern*, 28 (1906), 625-33; G. van Assel-donck, "De Nederlanden en het Western Schisma (tot 1398)," Diss. (Nijmegen, 1955).

[94] J. Favier speaks of a certain Jaques Garrel, who, in 1385, was named a subcollector by Clement VII for "les parties schismatiques des diocèses de Tour-nai, Cambrai, Thérouanne, Arras, Liége et Utrecht." *Les Finances Pontificales à l'époque du grand schisme d'occident* (Bibliothèque des Écoles Françaises d'Athènes et de Rome, fasc. 211; Paris, 1966), p. 717. Cf. Valois, II, 260.

appointed Arnold van Hoorn, then Bishop of Utrecht, perhaps as early as September. Clement VII confirmed Eustache Persand de Rochefort on November 8.[95] The issue was resolved by force of arms on February 11, 1379, when the allies of Arnold defeated the allies of Eustache.[96] In May, Clement VII's envoy, Guy de Malesset, Cardinal of Poitiers, ostensibly traveling to secure Flemish obedience to Avignon, did not dare to approach the city.[97] On May 11, the clergy officially recognized Urban VI, an act of "disobedience" for which they were excommunicated by Clement VII. As dean of the cathedral chapter, Blanchard was obviously opposed to this Urbanist trend, but he had not resided in Liége, where his conflict with the canons had been so bitter, since at least 1371. Blanchard was certainly no more welcome at Liége after his pope had excommunicated the clergy of the city than he had been before, and therefore, on May 19, 1379, Clement thoughtfully renewed John's authorization to receive his Liége-based revenues in absentia.[98] Shortly thereafter, on September 13, 1379, Urban VI, from his side, began to reverse the measures that Blanchard had obtained from Gregory XI in his suit against the Liége chapter, first by separating the deanship of St-Lambert from the prebend that Gregory XI had added to it, and second, by revoking Gregory's excommunication of that chapter for mistreating its dean.[99] It is questionable whether Blanchard had received any money from Liége since the mid-1370s, unlikely that he did so after the victory of Bishop Arnold, and clearly impossible after August 1, 1382, when the chapter removed him, as a schismatic, from the deanship.[100] Liége remained firm in its obedience to Rome until at least 1391, when, with Cologne, the city served as headquarters for Boniface IX's nuncio, Guglielmo della Vigna, who administered the "schismatic" or Clementine sees of Thérouanne and Tournai.[101]

The other city whose adherence to Urban cost Blanchard his benefice, and which consequently would have served as a perfect

---

[95] K. Hanquet, *Documents relatifs au Grand Schisme*, I: *Suppliques de Clement VII (1378-1379)*, AVB, VIII (Bruxelles, 1924), no. 2, pp. xxi-xxix.

[96] Valois, I, 273-276; F. Quicke, *Les Pays-Bas a la veille de la periode bourguignonne* (Paris et Bruxelles, 1947), 370-73; Nelis, pp. 57-58.

[97] *Ibid.*

[98] K. Hanquet and U. Berlière, *Documents relatifs au Grand Schisme*, II: *Lettres de Clement VII (1378-1379)*, AVB, XII (Bruxelles, 1930), nos. 782-83.

[99] *Cartulaire de l'Église Saint-Lambert de Liége*, S. Bormans et E. Schoolmeesters, eds., 6 vols. (Bruxelles, 1893-1933), IV, nos. 1734-35.

[100] Nelis, p. 53.

[101] Valois, II, 262, n. 3, and 263.

example in his testimony before the Parlement, was Ghent, the most active center of Roman loyalty and of revolution in Flanders. In December 1378, the clergy of Flanders met in Ghent to elaborate a response to the crisis in the Church. They decided to support Urban VI provisionally, and to await further advice from the University of Bologna and other sources of information closer to the scene of the elections in Italy. On June 1, 1379, they met again. With the backing of Louis de Male, Count of Flanders, an Urbanist himself, they definitively endorsed the Roman pope.[102] Although nominally subject to the Bishop of Tournai,[103] the Ghent clergy was dissatisfied with the incumbent, Pierre d'Aussay, who had been appointed by Clement VII on May 18, 1379. Consequently, when on May 15, 1380, Urban named Jan van West, who had been expelled from the deanship of Tournai for his leanings toward Rome, d'Aussay's authority was reduced principally to the episcopal city itself.[104] Jan established himself in Ghent and ran a shadow diocese of Tournai from there. A native of Ghent, Jan supported the burghers of that city in the revolt against the Count of Flanders they began in October 1379. The bonds between the rebellious citizens and "their" bishop were such that Ghent's Urbanism was unshakable. After Charles VI of France, Louis de Male, and his eventual successor, Philip the Bold of Burgundy, united to quell momentarily the rebellion of Ghent at the Battle of Roosebecke on November 27, 1382, the city was brutally sacked. The campaign bore some resemblance to a crusade, but the residents of Ghent remained steadfast in their allegiance to Rome.[105] Even during the negotiations that ended the rebellion on December 18, 1385, Philip, the new Count of Flanders, knew better than to make conversion to Avignon a condition of peace.[106] Evidence of Ghent's continued loyalty to Rome can be found as late as 1393.[107] It is certainly not

---

[102] G. Meersseman, "Les Dominicans flamands et le Grand Schisme sous le généralat de Raymond de Capoue," *Archivum Fratrum Praedicatorum*, VI (1936), 117-19.

[103] G. Piot, "Les Limites et les subdivisions de l'ancien diocèse de Tournai," *Annales de la Société d'Emulation de Bruges*, 3e ser., V (1870), 184, 214.

[104] Valois, I, 261. For Ghent, see also: U. Berlière, "Jean de West, Évêque urbaniste de Tournai," *Bulletin de la Commission Royale d'Histoire* 73 (Bruxelles, 1904), 351-88; and Napoleon de Pauw, "L'adhésion du clergé de Flandre au Pape Urbain VI et les évêques urbanistes de Gand." *ibid.*, pp. 671-702.

[105] Richard Vaughan, *Philip the Bold* (Cambridge, Mass., 1962), pp. 19-32, and Quicke, pp. 297-355, 376.

[106] Nelis, p. 43; Quicke, pp. 376-378; Vaughan, pp. 37-38.

[107] Valois, II, 263, 266.

coincidental, then, that the last reference I have found to Blanchard as Canon of St-Pharahild occurs in 1378.[108]

Why did Blanchard withhold the names of Liége and Ghent, the two cities in which he had lost his benefices because of the schism, when he was presenting reverses of this type as an extenuating circumstance, and when greater precision in the matter could only have strengthened his case? Possibly he did not want the embarrassing circumstances of his departure from Liége to become known. Whatever the reason, his reticence resulted in an outright inversion of the true situation, for the benefices he mentioned in Tournai and Cambrai were very likely producing their revenues quite regularly, as a survey of the situation in those cities will show.[109]

The episcopal city of the diocese of Tournai represented the Clementine pole that opposed the Urbanist center of Ghent. Located in the French-speaking part of Flanders, Tournai originally accepted Pierre d'Aussay, confirmed by Clement VII in May 1379. But after the clergy of Ghent elected its Urbanist anti-bishop, the cathedral city was isolated in its obedience to Clement.[110] Unlike Ypres and Bruges, Tournai did not participate in the rebellion led by the burghers of Ghent, yet after the Battle of Roosebecke, Charles VI sanctioned a purge of the Urbanists in Tournai that was vividly described by Froissart and labeled as "tyranny" by the author of the *Chronique de Tournai*.[111] The desire of the French knights to receive fines from residents accused of Urbanism hardly proves that the city had been Urbanist before the purge, but Valois implies that this mistreatment drove it to the Roman side. He cites the case of a certain Nicholas Cokel, who, on January 4, 1386, complained to Clement VII that he

---

[108] Hanquet, no. 2, and Hanquet and Berlière, no. 24. These two documents also contain the last mention of Blanchard's benefice at Deynze in the Diocese of Tournai.

[109] Perhaps this "inversion" could be explained as an extraordinary lapse on Blanchard's part. He might erroneously have named Tournai and Cambrai instead of Liége and Ghent. Or a similar slip might have been made by the secretary at the parlement who transcribed the proceedings. Even if Blanchard had no intention to deceive, his argument that he had lost revenues because of his required residence in Paris is certainly illogical.

[110] Valois, I, 253-61.

[111] Jean Froissart, *Œuvres*, ed. K. de Lettenhove, 25 vols. in 26 (Bruxelles, 1867-77), X, 189-91. "Chronique des Pays-Bas, de France, d'Angleterre et de Tournai," in *Corpus Chronicorum Flandriae*, ed. J. J. de Smet, III (Bruxelles, 1856), 279. Quicke commits an obvious slip (p. 378), when he says the Count of Saint-Pol conducted a purge of Clementines. Valois, I, 362-63.

could not obtain the revenues of a canonry at Tournai that had just been provided him.[112]

Against this conclusion, however, other evidence must be weighed. Beginning with Jan van West himself, in 1379, until the case of Nicholas Cokel, only Urbanists were deprived of benefices in Tournai proper.[113] Furthermore, it is important to remember that, even though Jan van West was based in Ghent, his title was "Bishop of Tournai," and the same is true of his successor in Ghent, Willem van Coudenberghe, who is referred to as Bishop-elect of Tournai on March 18, 1385. But William was driven out of Flanders, lived mostly in England and Italy, and does not seem ever to have been received in Tournai.[114] Clement's statement of 1392, addressed to the faithful bishops of Arras, Tournai, and Therouanne, welcoming their errant subjects back to the fold, and crediting Philip of Burgundy for his cooperation in the conversion of the populace, refers generally to "the lands and domains especially of Flanders and Artois," rather than to any particular city.[115] We may safely conclude, therefore, that the cathedral city and its immediate environs constituted the only Clementine fulcrum in the diocese of Tournai, and that this center was isolated from the neighboring Clementine dioceses of Arras and Therouanne by Louis de Male. After the accession in February 1384 of Philip of Burgundy, whose attitude was much more tolerant, the sharpness of this isolation was relaxed.[116] Clementinism, therefore, was strong in Tournai from the beginning of the schism, and became stronger as Philip of Burgundy gradually brought the rest of Flanders around after his accession in 1384. There seems to be no reason why Blanchard would have been deprived of revenues from Tournai between his appointment in February 1379 and his suit in Paris seven years later. Clement continued to regard Blanchard as the holder of his office in Tournai until John's death in 1391, for it was not until June 4, 1393,

---

[112] Valois, II, 260.

[113] Nelis, (pp. 50-51), does not mention Cokel. His list shows some Clementines deprived of offices, but outside the immediate area of Tournai. The Urbanists were Guy Parent (April 15, 1380) and Jacob de Vinea (February 8, 1382).

[114] E. Perroy, "Un Évêque urbaniste protégé de l'Angleterre, Guillaume de Coudenberghe, Évêque de Tournai et de Bâle," *Revue d'Histoire Ecclésiastique*, 26 (1930), 106; de Pauw, pp. 683-84.

[115] Valois, II, 269, n. 2.

[116] *Ibid.*, pp. 234-71. Valois here conducts a painstaking study of Philip's attitude toward the schism. Cf. Quicke, pp. 384-85.

that he named a replacement "per obitum Johannis Blanchardi."[117]

In Cambrai the situation was analogous to that in Tournai. Clement VII had personal ties in Cambrai, because as Robert of Geneva he had been bishop of that city from October 11, 1368, to May 30, 1371.[118] Thus his confirmation of the new bishop, Jan Tserclaes, on November 5, 1378, was accepted routinely in Cambrai, and the clergy there even agreed to pay expenses for an emissary from the Avignon cardinals.[119] Cambrai was an imperial city, however, and consequently might have been expected to follow the Emperor in obeying Urban. On March 11, 1381, Urban named Arnold van Hoorn, the Bishop of Liége to the see of Cambrai. This action reduced Jan Tserclaes's authority to the southern, French-speaking part of the diocese, while the Flemish part looked to Liége for leadership.[120] When Arnold died in 1389, Urban named John of Bavaria his successor at both Liége and Cambrai, although it was understood that he was merely to "administer" the western diocese.[121] The failure of the Urbanist bishops of Cambrai to reside there is partially explained by their being simultaneously bishops of Liége, a powerful center of Roman influence, and hence the importance of their absence as an indication of Clementine strength in Cambrai should not be exaggerated.

That the cathedral city remained solidly Clementine may be inferred more securely from the welcome it extended to Clement's wandering nuncio, the Cardinal of Poitiers, who finally took refuge there from the wave of Urbanism that had driven him westward across the Low Countries. He arrived at Cambrai on June 6, 1379, about the same time as Blanchard, who had been at the mercy of the same political currents.[122] Moreover, two Urbanist canons, Louis and Nicholas de Baschio, were expelled from the Cambrai chapter on August 24, 1381, and May 3, 1382, whereas I know of no Clementines who were excluded.[123] The Cardinal of Poitiers continued to use Cambrai as his base of operations until February 1382,[124] and it was apparently from Cambrai that he sent Blanchard and John of Chamberlhac to represent Clement's cause in England in July 1379. Blanchard was formally received as Canon of Cambrai on August 16, 1379, and it

---

[117] H. Nelis, *Documents relatifs au Grand Schisme*. III, *Suppliques et lettres de Clement VII* (1379-1394), AVB, XIII (Bruxelles, 1934), nos. 2360-61.

[118] Conrad Eubel, *Hierarchia Catholica Medii Aevi*, ed. altera (Regensberg, 1913), pp. 21, 160.

[119] Valois, I, 254, n. 1.   [120] Hanquet, p, xvii.

[121] *Ibid.*   [122] Valois, I, 259.

[123] Nelis, "La Collation," pp. 50-54.   [124] Valois I, 259.

may have been through his association with the nuncio that John was named Treasurer of Cambrai on January 29, 1381. A few months later, July 15, 1381, Blanchard was made Chancellor of Paris, where he went to reside. It seems clear, nonetheless, that Blanchard preserved his interests in Cambrai, because on December 16, 1386, after he had left Paris in disgrace, it was to Cambrai that the university masters sent a messenger to find him.[125] Furthermore, as at Tournai, it was not until 1393 that Clement filled John's posts at Cambrai.[126]

To conclude this digression in pursuit of a fuller understanding of Blanchard's finances than he offered the parlement, the political circumstances in the Low Countries during the period 1378-86 suggest that it had indeed been impossible for Blanchard to receive any money from Liége or Ghent; but, even though his losses there might have been cited as evidence of sacrifices in the Clementine cause, he never mentioned these cities by name. His revenues from Tournai and Cambrai were probably unaffected by the schism, yet Blanchard claimed he could not touch them because of his obligation to live in Paris. To his first point, weakened by his failure to mention the cities involved, Blanchard added the second, although a non sequitur, as another extenuating circumstance forcing him to take special measures to increase his income. Because the revenues from his benefices were insufficient to support him properly, Blanchard argued, it was licit for him to increase his income by receiving gifts, as it was licit for a bishop to charge a fee for the visitation of a church, even though theoretically the bishop could live on the proceeds of his office.[127] This was one of a series of analogies Blanchard drew to show that elsewhere in the Church, practices were followed that paralleled his own receipt of considerations in kind or in money at the time the license was awarded.

So far, Blanchard had referred principally to his receipt of material goods: clothing, wine, money. As he based his arguments more and more upon custom, however, he also began to refer to another benefit, the oath of loyalty to the chancellor's office, that had been strenuously opposed by the masters.[128] This oath was crucial to Blanchard, because, once sworn, it could bind those who had taken it to respect all the other rights he claimed. Blanchard described the

---

[125] See above, pp. 79-80.
[126] Nelis, *Documents*, no. 2364, p. 766.
[127] See above, pp. 134-5.
[128] See above, pp. 69-74.

oath as early as July 1385, in his deposition to the Cardinal of Laon: "Each and every master of the Parisian studium, even if he is or was rector ... (excepting only those who were licensed in arts at Ste-Geneviève ...), at the time when he was licensed, swore to uphold the rights, privileges, usages, and customs of the chancellor and the chancellorship of the Church of Paris." [129] The systematic refusal of the candidates to swear this oath remained at the center of the dispute even as late as the hearing in the parlement, where Blanchard again stressed his right to receive it.[130] The implication was that by forcing the bachelors not to swear the oath of reverence to the chancellor, the masters were violating that very oath. Yet Blanchard's right to receive this oath lay only in custom. Consequently the more he insisted on his right to receive this oath, the more he invoked the sanction of custom.

Returning then to his strategy of defense by analogy, the chancellor claimed that in some places there are customs according to which a sacrament is not given, or some other spiritual act is not performed, unless money is paid or an oath is sworn. Treating money first, he said that in some places, priests do not administer the sacraments unless their parishioners first give them money, and bishops do not ordain without having received money.[131] In other places, he claimed, an excommunicate must pay money and swear an oath to obey the commands of the Church or of the judge before he may be absolved.[132] In England there is the custom that the Eucharist is not administered until the parishioners have sworn to pay their tithes for that year. It would be absurd to say that all who conform to these traditions are simonists, and therefore, he concluded, "the custom of a place or of a country makes that method of exacting licit." Blanchard contended that the same reasoning applied in his case, for the chancellor has had the "laudable custom of exacting an oath of this sort for so long that there is no memory to the contrary." [133]

Introducing a more formal argument, Blanchard continued with the example of the tithe, which is owed to priests on the basis of divine law as stated in Numbers 18:21, but in certain places, which he does not name, the tithe is not paid. "Now it would be absurd to conclude,"

---

[129] *Chart.*, III, no. 1520, art. ii, p. 403.
[130] Du Boulay, IV, 607, 30-40.
[131] Super, p. 287, l. 1-3.
[132] Super, p. 281, l. 1-6.
[133] Super, p. 287, l. 4-12.

he argued, "that all in those places who do not pay are in mortal sin, and consequently the custom of the place or of the country excuses them." [134] Where an exemption from paying the tithe is involved, there is also an exemption from the provisions of Scripture; therefore, Blanchard concluded: "If custom may be established against divine law, how much more readily against human law." And consequently the chancellor has licitly acquired the custom of receiving payments and oaths. [135]

D'Ailly replied to this argument by referring to canon law and stating that if practices such as those alluded to by the chancellor or his partisans do in fact exist, they must be considered abuses rather than custom. [136] There is no value in following d'Ailly's references to canon law on these points. More important was his reassertion of the force of the university's privileges against this attack, which is more appropriately treated with the exposition of d'Ailly's thesis in the following chapter. Nonetheless, it is important to see how d'Ailly handled the reference to the tithe, which even he considered exceptional.

D'Ailly argued that the tithe was not established by divine law in the sense alleged by Blanchard. He referred to Thomas Aquinas, who said that the precept to pay the tithe was partly moral and partly judicial. Thus it would accord with natural, rather than divine, law. The moral part is this: For those who manage the divine cult for the welfare of the people, the people manage the necessities of life, as natural reason dictates. The judicial part is this: Although "introduced by divine institution," the provisions of the Old Law must be interpreted figuratively under the Law of Grace. Hence the decision on the amount of the tithe does not derive any longer from the authority of divine law, but only from that of "those who establish the law" or of "the established Church." Thus if no canon of the Church prevents it, local or national custom may even determine that another fraction of one's income, say, a fourth or a third, is to be paid. But it does not follow from this that custom may be secured against divine law. [137]

Once the chancellor shifted his emphasis to the oath he sought from

---

[134] Super, p. 287, l. 15-18.
[135] Super, p. 287, l. 18-20.
[136] Super, p. 287, l. 32-34.
[137] Super, p. 292, l. 4-27. Thomas Aquinas, *Summa Theologica* II II, Q. 87, art. 1.

the bachelors, he was obliged to introduce new examples of analogous exactions. First he cited the oath exacted by the popes from bishops about to be consecrated and from archbishops about to receive the pallium. If such an oath is licitly exchanged for episcopal consecration, he argued, it is against neither divine nor natural law and hence may also be exacted for the theological license.[138] Then Blanchard turned to the University of Paris for an example of oath-taking. The masters of the university, he said, were being inconsistent in criticizing him for requiring an oath before granting the license when the university, through the rector, and the individual faculties all required oaths before allowing a bachelor to read either the *Sentences* or the Bible or allowing a licentiate to become a master.[139]

Similarly, Blanchard continued, no one is admitted to membership in cathedral churches or other ecclesiastical corporations unless he has previously paid certain customary fees and sworn certain oaths of loyalty (*juramenta obsequiosa*) to maintain the privileges, keep the secrets, and observe the statutes of the organization. "Therefore, *a simili*, either all such churches [are] simoniacal, which is absurd, or the chancellor is not guilty of simony for exacting in the same way." [140]

Blanchard's best argument from custom, however, lay not in situations analogous to his own, but in the practices of earlier Chancellors of Paris, and especially of his immediate predecessor, John de Calore.[141] We have seen that witnesses called by both sides in the Cardinal of Laon's investigation agreed that Blanchard's exactions, even if considered abuses, were nonetheless traditional. The best way to measure the force of this argument is to analyze closely d'Ailly's maneuvers in "Super Omnia" to circumvent it.

To be sure, d'Ailly conceded that bachelors in the past had given to the chancellor.[142] The theologian's tactic, however, was to smother this concession in a blanket of distinctions that would obscure the chancellor's fundamental point. In the first place, not all the bachelors gave, "for I know," d'Ailly claimed, "that some, even in the time of *this* chancellor, and previously, gave nothing.[143] Some gave "of their

---

[138] Super, p. 251, l. 3-9.
[139] Super, p. 280, l. 8-27.
[140] Super, p. 280, l. 28-34.
[141] Super, pp. 260, l. 29 - 261, 2; cf. Du Boulay, IV, 607, 25-27.
[142] Super, p. 261, l. 5: "Licet multi dederint..."
[143] Super, p. 261, l. 3-5.

own free will." [144] In other cases, despite the external appearance of simony, some who gave had clear consciences and honest "or at least not corrupt" intentions.[145] Still others may have given out of ignorance.[146] Although ignorance of common law and especially divine law does not excuse, ignorance of a private law such as the privilege *Servus crucis* can excuse, as long as the ignorance is sincere and not assumed.[147] A further distinction, if not an inconsistency, is implicit here. In his earlier speech, "Radix Omnium," d'Ailly had said that the university's other great privilege, *Parens scientiarum*, which forbids *exacting* money for the license, should be considered common law so that, consequently, violations of it would be punishable by secular authority.[148] Here, he classifies *Servus crucis*, which forbids *giving* money for the license, as a privilege, or private law, so that he can excuse from simony those who were ignorant of it.

Continuing his list of categories of bachelors who may have given without committing simony, d'Ailly mentioned those who paid "to ward off persecution" (*ad redimendam vexationem suam*). This contingency is foreseen in canon law,[149] which expressly permits such a payment when it is made to effect release of a right unjustly withheld.[150] Furthermore, among those who give, some know they have the knowledge to teach and some know they do not. If the latter give in order to receive the license, they are guilty of simony. If, knowing that in any case they are worthy of the license, the former give in order to receive a higher rank, they are guilty not of simony, but of ambition. Although they may have sinned, they are still legitimately licensed.[151]

Having completed his catalogue of excuses for those who gave to Blanchard's predecessors, d'Ailly rejects any similarity in the case of Blanchard, because he *exacts* his gifts and the oath and thus is openly

---

[144] Super, p. 261, l. 7.
[145] Super, p. 261, l. 12-17.
[146] Super, p. 261, l. 18-25.
[147] Super, p. 264, l. 25-27.
[148] Radix, pp. 211, l. 28-212, 3, discussed below, p. 173.
[149] X. 5, 3, 28; ed. Friedberg, II, 758-59.
[150] Super, pp. 261, l. 26-262, 2.
[151] Super, pp. 262, l. 30-263, 11. Here d'Ailly draws on Thomas Aquinas (Quodlibet III, Quaestio IV, art. 9), who said that is it possible for a man to know with certainty whether he has the knowledge to teach. If he does, it is not presumptuous for him to seek the doctorate. By contrast, one cannot know whether one has the charity necessary to be a pontiff, hence it is evil to seek a pontificate. Quoted at p. 262, l. 13-26.

simoniacal, and those who give participate in his simony and are simoniacs just as he is.[152] One may legitimately ask, it seems to me, why the tolerance d'Ailly showed earlier givers should not be extended to those licensed by Blanchard. It is also unclear why those who gave to Blanchard should not be understood to have given "ad redimendam vexationem suam," especially since d'Ailly has consistently, and in this very passage, claimed that Blanchard *demands* a payment and does not award the license until he has received it.[153]

Further weighting the balance in favor of Calore, d'Ailly proceeded to treat as sincere certain legal dodges employed by Blanchard's predecessor. Unlike Blanchard, d'Ailly claimed, Calore did not demand payments from bachelors, but received only what was freely offered. To circumvent abuses by his subordinates, d'Ailly said, Calore used to force those who were to deliver the signeta to swear not to use them to extort payments. According to d'Ailly, the preceding chancellor further instructed his messengers to refuse any gift the first time it was offered. "I know," claimed the theologian, "that some money freely given to him was sent back." [154]

Blanchard retorted that if what d'Ailly said about Calore were true, that he accepted even freely given gifts, then Calore would be guilty of violating the privilege *Parens scientiarum* which states that the chancellor may receive nothing for conceding the license.[155] If these practices do not condemn my predecessors, challenged Blanchard (pretending that the payments made to him were voluntary), then why must *I* defend them? Invoking an astonishing double standard, d'Ailly used for Calore an excuse that Blanchard had claimed for himself: namely, that the privilege prohibits exacting money but not receiving what is freely given.[156] Undeterred, Blanchard pointed out that the privilege *Servus crucis* says: "Let no one licensed by the chancellor or by another incept if money was given." In defense of Calore, d'Ailly replied, again in the style of Blanchard, that this only forbids the bachelors from giving, but not the chancellor from receiving, at least not expressly. Moreover, d'Ailly continued, this provision does not forbid all gifts to the chancellor. If a bachelor does not intend to incept,

---

[152] Super, p. 263, l. 21-26.
[153] See above, p. 146, and Super p. 263, l. 23-26. "Illi qui sibi sic exigenti darent . . . [non] possent redemptionem vexationis excusari."
[154] Super, p. 263, l. 27-35.
[155] Super, pp. 263, 36 - 264, 1; see above, p. 15.
[156] Super, p. 264, l. 1-6.

a freely given gift would be licit.[157] This fine distinction, applicable in only a minority of cases and still contrary to *Parens scientiarum*, was less valid as a defense of Calore than as an implied criticism of Blanchard. What is in fact permitted, said d'Ailly, is a free gift after the license and after inception and not in money,[158] because from money arises the appearance of evil.[159]

Blanchard's defense of his exactions of oaths and payments for the license were no less disingenuous than d'Ailly's defense of Calore for the same thing. The exactions of oaths and money were not, however, the only practices for which Blanchard was under attack. He was also accused of forcing bachelors to incept under him, and in response to challenges on this question, he referred to papal orders not to advance schismatics. Even though there is no evidence that he ever tried to enforce the substance of Clement's order, and even though he invoked this authority only to facilitate the enlargement of his own clientele, all those who had testified on article 45 concerning Duchêne, as well as others who knew the story, understood the strength of Blanchard's position on this point. Moreover, there were other aspects of the chancellor's position that the pope could be expected to support, notably the licentia bullata with its summary examination procedure, and the consistent disregard of the masters' distinction between the license and the magisterium. In planning an attack on Blanchard, therefore, despite his apparent corruption, d'Ailly had to take into account the pope's interest in maintaining the chancellor's strategic position as an agent of papal power within the Parisian studium.

---

[157] Super, p. 264, l. 9-17.
[158] Super, p. 265, l. 13-15, 22-30.
[159] Super, p. 266, l. 2-9.

CHAPTER SIX

D'AILLY'S PROSECUTION

The preceding study of Blanchard's defense has shown that however objectionable his fiscal exactions and personal conduct may have been, there were aspects of his administration which accorded with the papal view of the magisterium and for which Clement VII's support could be predicted. Accordingly, d'Ailly steered a deliberate course in his prosecution. He avoided reference to summary examinations and the maneuvers to attract students, and instead emphasized Blanchard's exactions of oaths and gifts. For this reason he selected the sin of greed as the theme of his first speech, a choice the Dutch historian Johan Huizinga considered typical of the exaggerated abstraction debasing late medieval discourse. "A systematic idealism, which grasps at the relationship between things according to their supposedly essential qualities, leads to rigidity and to a sterile tendency to classify." [1] In this harsh judgment, Huizinga failed to appreciate the strategic advantages of d'Ailly's approach, which allowed him to cast the university in the role of an ecclesiastical corporation threatened by the perversion, through greed, of one who should contribute to its welfare. [2]

The theme of greed related directly to the sin of simony, the illicit exchange of a spiritual for a material good. D'Ailly maintained that because of his greed, Blanchard withheld the spiritual benefit of the license to teach theology until he had received a payment and an oath of loyalty, both classified as material benefits. It will be seen that d'Ailly's principal thesis contains a parallel but implicit argument that would also apply to Clement VII's order to halt the progress of Urbanists. The description of the license as spiritual provides the basis of both arguments, which may be restated thus: no private, temporal advantage, neither the monetary needs of the chancellor nor the political interests of the pope, can be allowed to diminish the spiritual benefits that flow to the whole Church when the license to teach theology is freely granted to men judged worthy by the Faculty

---

[1] J. Huizinga, *Le Déclin du Moyen age* (Paris, 1961), p. 262.

[2] *Chartularium Universitatis Parisiensis*, ed. H. Denifle and E. Châtelain, 4 vols. (Paris, 1889-97), vol. III, no. 1519. (Hereafter cited as *Chart.*)

of Theology at Paris. In this way d'Ailly employed the contrast between the welfare of private parties and that of the whole Church, a basic theme of conciliarism. He also drew upon the early Gallican tendency to view the Church as a congeries of corporations, each with its own rights to defend. Thus he proposed redefining the ecclesiological status of teachers of theology in a way that would limit outside authority, whether of pope or chancellor, over the university and the license. He emphasized *Parens scientiarum*, the papal document that attributes the greatest role to the body of regent masters in determining who should be licensed to counter the papal view of the magisterium elaborated in *Quasi lignum vitae* and afterwards. Further, he claimed a direct relationship between the welfare of the Church and that of the university, hoping thus to elevate the status of theologians within the ecclesiastical hierarchy. Ostensibly straightforward demonstrations that Blanchard's demands of oaths and money were illicit, the two speeches we are about to study constitute extensive reviews of the nature of the license and its correct administration construed very heavily in favor of the university masters.

The first speech, "Radix Omnium," was delivered on February 5 or 6, 1386, at the College of Navarre. The second, "Super Omnia," was delivered after February 12; it has the form of an open disputation, with d'Ailly responding to objections concerning each part of the earlier speech.[3] The first speech, therefore, exhibits a more systematic organization. In form a scholastic *quaestio*, it constituted a review of the arguments d'Ailly was making and planned to make in the judicial proceedings.[4] In the following presentation, the general organization of "Radix Omnium" will be followed, with material from the second speech introduced as appropriate.

"Cupidity is the root of all evils," announced d'Ailly as he opened his attack on Blanchard. It is indeed the most serious of crimes, because the thirst for wealth is a perturbation of the mind that leads to errors in the faith.[5] The danger to orthodoxy is magnified, he said, when this evil appears in an ecclesiastical person, especially one in a high position and, more serious yet, associated with the University of Paris; for now "this awful root [cupidity] has so perilously spread forth its shoots that it has occupied deceitfully not just country fields,

---

[3] See above, ch. III, p. 78.
[4] "Radix Omnium," edited below, in Appendix, pp. 198, 31 - 199, 5.
[5] Radix, p. 197, l. 1-20.

but precisely that purest field of knowledge, the venerable corporation of the University of Paris, and has tried to entangle its ripest fruits." [6]

D'Ailly located the germ of this weedlike invasion in a "certain person," clearly Blanchard, who has been driven by avarice to turn freely bestowed gifts of knowledge and liberal degrees of learning into venal things.[7] D'Ailly never paused to support his accusation with evidence. Instead, he applied St. Paul's rule that avarice leads to errors in the faith and attacked Blanchard as a heretic on the grounds that, in defending his licensing procedures, the chancellor had violated Catholic truth.[8] Therefore the theologian attacked the chancellor not for simony or extortion, but for heretically maintaining that illicit practices are licit.

D'Ailly's allusion to the faith appears to have been a bold initiative. It seems that the other members of the Faculty of Theology were unwilling to attack Blanchard on doctrinal grounds. In his preface, d'Ailly admits that the university had "often" resolved that masters should treat the affair in scholastic exercises,[9] yet in February 1386, he was the first to do so, though the affair had been brewing since late 1384.[10] Therefore, the prosecution of Blanchard as a heretic was the result of d'Ailly's personal initiative. The young theologian openly assumed the role of "principal leader," [11] not only by becoming the university's spokesman, but even by comparing himself to "the small hound who incites the larger and stronger dogs to hunt." [12] From the very beginning of the speech, we recognize the strength of d'Ailly's identification with the prosecution of Blanchard and his efforts to further his own career by assuming the role of university champion.

With the scent of heresy in the air, d'Ailly began to analyze Blanchard's "error." He expressed the scholastic *quaestio* as follows: "Is it heretical to say that it is licit to give or receive money for the license to teach?" [13] This question was then divided into two parts: the first,

---

6 Radix, p. 198, l. 12-16.

7 Radix, p. 198, l. 17-19.

8 Radix, p. 198, l. 19-22.

9 Radix, p. 198. l. 27-28: "[Mater mea universitas,] ... pluries concorditer deliberavit quod magistri de hac materia tractarent in actibus scholasticis."

10 Radix, p. 198, l. 28-29: "Ego autem, licet omnium minimus, prius incepi."

11 See above, p. 60.

12 Radix, p. 198, l. 29-31: "... ut, juxta similitudinem Orosii in Prologo De Ormesta (Historia) Mundi ad Augustinum, 'parvus canis venaticius majores ac potentiores canes excitet ad venandum.' "

13 Radix, p. 199, l. 17-18.

an affirmative answer to the question, the second, a reply to the arguments of the opposing side. D'Ailly constructed his presentation around three "principal conclusions," which he listed at the beginning: "(1) To give or receive money for the license to teach theology is simony in the strict sense; (2) it is against natural and divine law; (3) to say that it is licit thus to give or to receive is heretical." [14]

Beginning with a definition of simony, d'Ailly related that the sin was named after Simon Magus, who according to Acts 8:19 offered money to the Apostles for the power of conferring the Holy Spirit. Peter refused the offer and chastised Simon for believing that a gift of God could be had for money. D'Ailly emphasized that although Simon was prevented from buying the power he sought, he did not thereby avoid sin, because simony is "a sin of the will." [15] For this reason, he defined simony as "the will to buy or sell anything spiritual or connected to the spiritual." [16] And those things are spiritual "by which the Holy Spirit is received, or given, or by which it is indicated as received or given. [For example, the Holy Spirit] is possessed by virtue, it is given by the sacrament, and it is indicated as present in one who has the power to prophesy or to perform miracles." [17] A complementary definition of "spiritual" introduces the trenchant concept of gratuity, whose cutting edge d'Ailly wielded effectively throughout his speeches: "All that may be considered spiritual which . . . is a free, supernatural gift of God—that is, which cannot be obtained by natural means." [18] Buying or selling is defined as "any contract that is not gratuitous," [19] and thus simony can be redefined in terms of the second definition, as "the will to buy or sell any gratuitous gift of God." [20] According to d'Ailly, this definition alone suffices to explain why simony is illicit. A spiritual thing has three essential characteristics: its source is God, it cannot be obtained by man's own efforts, and

---

[14] Radix, p. 200, l. 13-23. D'Ailly's biographers generally have been content to leave their treatment of the Blanchard affair with the quotation of these three conclusions, as does Louis Salembier, *Le Cardinal Pierre d'Ailly* (Tourcoing, 1932), pp. 68-72. P. Tschackert, *Peter von Ailly* (Gotha, 1877), pp. 67-68, gives a more profound, but equally brief résumé.

[15] Radix, p. 201, l. 21-22.

[16] Radix, pp. 200, 33 - 201, l. As d'Ailly acknowledges, this definition is taken from Raymond of Peñafort and Thomas Aquinas. The references accompany the relevant passages in the Appendix.

[17] Radix, pp. 202, 30 - 203, 2.

[18] Radix, p. 203, l. 5-9.

[19] Radix, p. 202, l. 19-20.

[20] Radix, p. 203, l. 24-25.

yet it was freely given. It would be wrong to sell such a thing, because no price can be put on that which is given by God, and because what was received freely should be given freely.[21]

Although the above definitions deal with buying and selling, it must not be imagined that simony is committed only when money is exchanged for spiritual things. Indeed, the definition of simony includes anything that can be measured by or compared with money. Therefore, "if spiritual gifts are given principally to obtain services, flattery, intervention with great lords, the favor of men, or anything of that sort, it would strictly be simony." [22] Thus Gregory the Great distinguished between three kinds of gifts that might be considered payments for spiritual things: "a gift by the hand, like money; a favor, like the performance of a service not owed; and a gift by the tongue, like praise." [23] The extension of the definition of simony to include material benefits other than the simple gain of money clearly covers the oaths of loyalty exacted by Blanchard, but how broadly will d'Ailly interpret Gregory's statement? Later we shall discuss whether d'Ailly thought Clement's insistence on uniform political loyalty from licentiates could also be condemned as simony.

Having defined simony, d'Ailly had to prove that Blanchard's practices were simoniacal. He did not simply say that buying or selling the theological license is simony, but instead developed his argument in stages, moving in turn through each of the following subordinate propositions:

1. "Theology is a spiritual gift of God.
2. "The teaching or preaching of theology is spiritual.
3. "The license, power, or authority to teach or preach theology is spiritual.
4. "The power to grant this license is spiritual."[24]

To prove that theology is a gift of God, d'Ailly drew upon a discussion by William of Auxerre, who distinguished between those gifts which affect the will and those which affect the intellect. William considered theology a spiritual gift that "illuminates the intellect and is possessed through knowledge." [25] Citing a theologian's opinion, however, was not sufficient. D'Ailly turned also to I Corinthians 12:8,

---

[21] Radix, pp. 204, 8 - 205, 6.
[22] Radix, p. 205, l. 10-18.
[23] Radix, p. 205, l. 18-22.
[24] Radix, p. 207, l. 7-14.
[25] Radix, p. 207, l. 21-22.

where the gifts of the Spirit are listed: the word of wisdom, the word of knowledge, faith, the power to heal, the power to work miracles, the power to prophesy, and others; among which, according to d'Ailly, Paul intentionally gave first place to theology or "the word of wisdom." [26] But further interpretation was needed to establish the identity of Paul's "word of wisdom" with theology. D'Ailly might have cited the *Glossa Interlinearis*, where the phrase "sermo sapientiae" is interpreted to mean the ability to convey understanding of divine things to others, but the word "theology" is not used.[27] To establish the middle term of his syllogism, he turned instead to Aristotle: "Theology is properly called wisdom, because wisdom concerns divine things." [28] Hence theology is wisdom, wisdom is a gift of the Spirit, and therefore theology is a free gift of God.

D'Ailly eventually did turn to the *Glossa Interlinearis* because his opponent seized upon the reference to Aristotle and argued that the wisdom referred to by Aristotle is one of the five intellectual habits, and these are natural. Therefore theology is not a gift of God and there is no reason why it could not be taught by a non-Christian, and, further, no reason why it could not be sold.[29]

Replying to the first conclusion, d'Ailly stated that a non-Christian could only learn and expound theology if this be taken rather broadly, as discourse concerning the "sense of Scripture," with explanation and proof of one dictum by another.[30] Taken more strictly, however, the teaching of theology implies a belief in the truths of Scripture, and this comes only from faith, which is a gift of God.[31] Furthermore the Scriptures themselves were obtained by supernatural revelation. Thus any discourse upon them, whether by a believer or a nonbeliever, is ultimately dependent upon revelation and may therefore be called spiritual.[32] But the dual nature of theology need not prevent its being considered spiritual, for the sacraments present the same distinction. Just as the sacraments are corporal and natural as regards the material with which they are performed, but are spiritual and supernatural be-

---

[26] Radix, p. 207, l. 28-31.
[27] *Biblia Sacra cum Glossis*, 6 vols. (Venetiis, 1603), VI, 304-5, *ad verb.* "sermo": "Non solum sapientia, id est de divinis intelligentia et scientia de humanis, sed earum sermo, ut aliis possint eloqui."
[28] Radix, p. 207, l. 31-33.
[29] "Super Omnia," edited below, in Appendix, p. 238, l. 19-25.
[30] Super, p. 239, l. 10-16.
[31] Super, p. 239, l. 6-13.
[32] Super, p. 240, l. 1-8.

cause they confer sacramental grace and were divinely instituted; so teaching and preaching theology, although corporal acts, are also spiritual and supernatural, because they are related to the divinely inspired sacred Scriptures.[33]

In his rebuttal of the second conclusion, that theology is natural, d'Ailly returned to the *Glossa Ordinaria* on I Corinthians,[34] which refers to Augustine's *De Trinitate*, where wisdom is defined as the "cognition of divine things." [35] D'Ailly then proceeded to explain how Augustine divided the faculty of reason into a lower reason devoted to science, and a higher reason devoted to wisdom or the understanding and contemplation of the divine. Thus the object of the higher reason is also the object of theology. Knowledge of divine things is itself divided, however, between those truths which may be known by purely natural, human reason, as in Aristotle, and those which are revealed supernaturally. But truths revealed by divine influence are spiritual, as was shown in the preceding argument; therefore no payment can be demanded for teaching or preaching them.[36] Furthermore, since both Augustine and Aristotle agree that divine things are the object of both wisdom and theology, "theology" may also be understood for "wisdom" in that famous prohibition of Proverbs 23:23: "Do not sell wisdom." Hence the sale of theology is forbidden in both the New Testament (story of Simon Magus) and the Old.[37]

To prove that the chancellor engaged in simony, d'Ailly was content to show that the subject matter of only one university faculty is spiritual and cannot licitly be made venal. He did not attempt to show that knowledge of arts, law, or medicine was also spiritual. But it clearly served the theologian's purpose from a rhetorical, if not a logical, point of view to associate the other fields of knowledge as far as possible with theology. Thus he concluded this part of his proof with the statement that "to buy or sell any science whatsoever is simoniacal, but depending on the nature of the science, it is greater or lesser simony." [38] As for theology itself, d'Ailly had no doubt that it is

---

[33] Super, p. 240, l. 13-19.

[34] *Biblia Sacra cum Glossis*, VI, 304-5, *ad* I Cor., 12:8.

[35] Augustinus, *De Trinitate*, Lib. 12, cap. 15; P. L. 42, 1012: "Ad sapientiam pertineat aeternarum rerum cognitio intellectualis." Quoted in Super, p. 240, l. 27-28.

[36] Super, pp. 240, 29 - 241, 14.

[37] Radix, p. 207, l. 31-33.

[38] Radix, p. 207, l. 22-24.

a spiritual gift of God and that it would be simony to buy or sell it.[39]

D'Ailly's treatment of his first major proposition, that theology is spiritual, has important consequences for his idea of the university. His approach suggests that he conceived of the university as being in an intermediary position between God and man. In the Faculty of Theology, at least, the university dispenses the divine gift of theological knowledge, which is received efficaciously by those who have received the grace and are so disposed. His analogy between the sacraments and theological teaching is eloquent testimony to his implied belief that, like the priest, the doctor of theology bestows a good which perfects those who have been properly prepared by God. Such a theory views the university as a church in microcosm. Accordingly, the two institutions are seen as sharing the same function, that of developing for those in attendance a divine disposition already granted, which in the case of the university is the construction of theological science on the foundation of faith. In the same way, Church and university, both unique institutions, share a similar ecumenical character and authority. In the next part of his argument, d'Ailly will further develop this parallel between the Church and the university by a conscious assimilation of teaching and preaching.

Having shown the spiritual nature of theology, d'Ailly moved to his second major proposition, that not only theology itself, but even its teaching or preaching is spiritual.[40] For the remainder of his presentation, d'Ailly recognized that teaching and preaching are distinct Church functions, but for tactical purposes insisted that they were essentially the same. With one exception the Biblical texts he quoted refer only to preaching, but, without citing any authority or precedent for doing so or explicitly stating what he was doing, he treated them as applying equally to teaching. Although the implied comparison is not original with d'Ailly, he gradually extended the metaphor to posit an institutional parallel between the offices of preacher and teacher.[41]

---

[39] Radix, pp. 207, 31-208, 2. For the history of this notion see Gaines Post, Kimon Giocarinis, and Richard Kay, "The Medieval Heritage of a Humanistic Ideal: 'Scientia Donum Dei est, unde Vendi non Potest,' " *Traditio* XI (1955), 195-234.

[40] Radix, p. 208, l. 3-4.

[41] This assimilation is not original with d'Ailly, yet his development of it seems unusually systematic. For example, in the phrase "ut mittat operarios in messem suam" (Matt. 9:37), the *Glossa Interlinearis* explains "operarios" as "praedicatores," whereas Nicholas of Lyra glosses "operarii," from the preceding verse, as "doctores et praedicatores verbi," and "operarios" as "praedicatores ad erudiendum populum." *Biblia Sacra cum Glossis* V, 185-86. The use of the word

To a very large extent, of course, preaching *is* teaching, especially in the context of the apostolic or primitive Church, where both functions could be personally exercised or directly supervised by the priest or bishop. In the Latin Church of the twelfth century, however, the introduction of the *scholasticus*, schoolmaster, or chancellor into the cathedral clergy effected a clear division of labor, and further developments such as the emancipation of university teachers from the bishop and his chancellor and the introduction of the mendicant colleges carried this specialization even further.

In view of this extensive institutional evolution and the divergent testimony of the Scriptural texts, d'Ailly's relentless insistence on the close association between teaching and preaching is surprising. He asserted that they shared a common origin, namely, Christ's sending out of the Apostles, an act that, as we shall see, he likened to the licensing of theological masters. On a general, ecclesiological level, his comparison elevated the role of the theological professor in the Church to a status more nearly equal to that of the bishops, since teachers, too, thus become successors of the Apostles. On the acade-

---

"erudire," however, also serves to compare preachers to teachers because this function was traditionally attributed to the masters at Paris, as we learn from Nicholas IV's letter of 1292, in which he delights in the word and its etymology. "By the study of letters," he says, "viri efficiuntur scientiis eruditi" and "rudes erudiuntur." Therefore he grants the *ius ubique docendi* to all those licensed at Paris, in order that graduates "ubique possint omnes erudire." (*Chart.*, II, no. 578.) On the other hand, when Dist. 21, cap. 2 of Gratian's *Decretum* quotes the corresponding passage in Luke (10:24), Johannes Theutonicus interprets "operarios" as "doctores." *Decretum Gratiani cum glossis Bartholomei Brixiensis* (Venetiis, 1496), f. 17ʳb.

The literature on this question is extensive. See: M. Peuchemaurd, "Le Prêtre, ministre de la parole...," *Recherches de Théologie Ancienne et Médiévale (RTAM)*, 29 (1962), pp. 52-76, and *Idem*, "Mission canonique et prédication: Le Prêtre ministre de la parole dans la querelle entre Mendiants et Séculiers au XIIIᵉ siècle," *RTAM* 30 (1963), 122-44; 251-76. R. Guelley, "La Place des théologiens dans l'Église et la société médiévale," dans *Miscellanea historica in honorem Alberti de Meyer*, 1 (Louvain, 1946), 571-89. J. Leclercq, "Le Magistère du prédicateur au XIIIᵉ siècle," *Archives d'Histoire Doctrinale et Littéraire du Moyen Age*, 21 (1946), 104-47. G. Le Bras, "Velut Splendor Firmamenti: Le Docteur dans le droit de l'Église médiévale," dans *Melanges offerts à Étienne Gilson* (Toronto & Paris, 1959), 373-88.

D'Ailly himself developed his views on the authority of the theological doctor within the Church in his speeches against the Dominican Juan Monzon, who denied the Faculty of Theology the right to censure his teaching. (Duplessis d'Argentré, *Collectio Judiciorum de novis erroribus*, 2 vols.; Paris, 1736, vol. I, pt. 2, pp. 75-129.) The views of Gerson and d'Ailly on the role of the theologian within the Church are the subject of Douglass Taber's dissertation for Stanford University (in progress).

mic level, d'Ailly exploited his parallel thoroughly. First he invoked it
to imply that both teaching and preaching are spiritual because both
were specifically enjoined by Christ. Second, he used it to claim that
the office of the chancellor is spiritual, because the act of licensing is
done in imitation of Christ, who, in sending the Apostles on their
mission, "licensed" them to "teach all nations." [42] D'Ailly's rhetoric
is intended to evoke memories of Christ and Paul teaching and preaching, but his reasoning, both fairly and unfairly, imposes the standard
of apostolic simplicity upon an administrator fulfilling an office that
had undergone a complex and extensive evolution over almost two
centuries.

With this sketch of the general direction of d'Ailly's position in
mind, we return to a more detailed consideration of the way he used
his arguments against the chancellor. It will be recalled that d'Ailly's
opponent had previously claimed that theology is a natural intellectual
habit, and consequently not spiritual. Because theology is not spiritual,
"whoever knows theology should be permitted to preach and teach
[it] without any special authorization," let alone a spiritual one.
Because preaching and teaching are natural works of mercy, the
argument continues, anyone knowing how to teach or preach should
be allowed to do so. Thus a large number of preachers and teachers
might be obtained, to the marked benefit of the faithful.[43]

In reply, d'Ailly quoted Romans 10:15, "How shall they preach
unless they be sent?" and then denied that anyone can teach or preach
publicly unless he has been specially "sent" or "licensed." [44] After
introducing this parallel, he described his idea of mission more fully.
Those who are sent may be sent directly by God, like Moses or John
the Baptist, who proved their mission by performing miracles or showing that their coming had been prophesied. Without proof, those who
say they are sent by God are not to be believed, because heretics say the
same thing. Others are sent by God through human agency, as Moses
sent Joshua, or St. Paul sent the disciples he had specially tested. Then
there are those who are sent by God through the Church, and among
them some are instituted ordinarily, such as the bishops, who are sent
in place of the Apostles, and the parish priests, who are successors
of the 72 disciples. After these two orders were established, the

---

[42] Radix, p. 209, l. 5-8.
[43] Super, p. 241, l. 19-27.
[44] Super, p. 242, l. 22-27.

archdeacons and archpriests were added as *opitulationes*, or those who bring help to their superiors. Further, there are those who are sent extraordinarily by the bishops to help them in their dioceses. Finally, there are those who are sent extraordinarily by the pope, and it is in this way that those who are licensed in theology are sent. But because the cure of souls is the highest of the arts, the office of preaching should not be confided indiscriminately to just anyone, but only to those tested and found suitable for such important work.[45] Having a great number of preachers is not advantageous to the Church, therefore, unless they are all qualified, duly instituted, and approved.[46] Those who preach publicly without this approval, who are not sent by God directly or by God through man, usurp the position of those who are sent—that is, the prelates and the priests.[47]

D'Ailly here invokes the same principles that had earlier informed the seculars' arguments against the introduction of new preachers, the mendicants. He returned to an early Gallican notion in defending the proper function of each order within the ecclesiastical hierarchy against intrusion from the outside. Nor is the similarity in argumentation an accident. D'Ailly's explanation of the orders of the Church—with the bishops succeeding the Apostles and the priests the disciples, later to be supplemented by the opitulationes or archdeacons and archpriests—which concludes with the statement that the addition of preachers who did not fit one of these categories would usurp the functions of those already established, comes directly from William of St-Amour's *Collectiones Catholicae et Canonicae Scripturae*.[48] But his statement that the license in theology may be an example of the special kind of mission that depends directly on papal authority, that "those who are licensed in theology by apostolic authority are sent by [the pope] in this way," is an interpolation into the text he is quoting. His remark may be more a grudging concession to the legality of the licentia bullata than a description of the status of all those licensed

---

[45] Super, pp. 243, 5 - 244, 26.

[46] Super, p. 245, l. 1-16.

[47] Super, p. 246, l. 7-10.

[48] Distinctio 1 (Guillaume de St-Amour, *Opera*, Constance, 1632, pp. 144-46), quoted in Y. M.-J. Congar, "Aspects ecclésiologiques de la quérelle entre mendiants et séculiers...," *Archives d'Histoire Doctrinale et Littéraire du Moyen Age*, 28 (1961), 54, n. 34a. Although both passages contain mostly phrases quoted from authorities and there is little room for variation in phrasing, the similarity is established by the sequence of citations.

in theology (though the latter interpretation could also be defended), but it certainly raised the question of where theological doctors fit within the ecclesiastical hierarchy, and that is the problem d'Ailly addressed next.

Once again he invoked Christ's charge to the Apostles. In sending forth the Twelve over the world, Christ listed the spiritual acts they were to perform. First among them, commented d'Ailly, was the "teaching and preaching of theological wisdom, when He said to the Apostles: 'Go therefore and preach.' " [49] Again proving the same point twice, once by citing Scriptural authority and then by citing theological opinion, d'Ailly turned to William of Auxerre, who stated flatly that "Preaching is spiritual and also connected to the spiritual. It is spiritual because the Holy Spirit is given through it. It is connected to the spiritual, that is to the order [of priesthood], because preaching pertains to the priests, or at least to those ordained." [50] William's inclusion of people who may be ordained for preaching but are not simply priests is ambiguous. Written in the early thirteenth century, his vague formulation may reflect an awareness of the unresolved debates concerning the preaching activities of the newly organized mendicant orders or even the still-evolving teaching activities in the universities. Whatever William's intention, d'Ailly adopted this expression and interpreted it as follows: "And I understand 'ordained' to mean not only those ordained in Holy Orders, but also those in the hierarchical order, that is [the order] of those sent and approved to preach by apostolic authority on behalf of the Universal Church, according to the saying of the Apostle, 'How shall they preach unless they be sent?' " [51] D'Ailly's purpose in broadening the definition of "those ordained" so explicitly was to include not the mendicants, but rather the teaching activities of theological masters. Thus theological masters must be included in the hierarchical order of those who are sent. Moreover, if theologians

---

[49] Radix, p. 208, l. 3-9.

[50] Radix, p. 208, l. 22-25: "Predicatio est spiritualis, et etiam annexa spirituali; quia scilicet per eam datur Spiritus Sanctus; et est annexa spirituali, scilicet ordini, quia sacerdotum est predicare, vel ad minus ordinatorum..." Cf. Guiliermus Altissiodorensis, *Summa Aurea in Quattuor Libros Sententiarum* (Paris, 1500), Lib. 3, tract. 21, cap. 2, f. 226vb.

[51] Radix, p. 208, l. 25-29: "... quod intelligo non solum de ordinatis in Ordine Sacro, sed etiam in ordine hierarchico, id est missorum et approbatorum ad predicandum authoritate apostolica, pro universali Ecclesia, iuxta illud Apostoli: 'Quomodo predicabunt nisi mittantur?' "

were sent, then their authorization to teach is a spiritual power. Once more d'Ailly substitutes theological masters into the formula applied only to preachers in the Bible, the canons, and the glosses: "And therefore it appears that a mission of this sort to preach, which is nothing other than the license to teach, is a spiritual power." [52]

The first three points of d'Ailly's quaestio establish a syllogism that can be reconstructed as follows: the license to teach theology is spiritual; the chancellor sells the license to teach theology; therefore the chancellor exchanges a spiritual good for money and is guilty of simony. The fourth point concerns not the license itself, but the power to confer it. To show that the power to confer the license is spiritual, d'Ailly drew once again upon the parallel he claimed between sending preachers and licensing teachers, by asserting that in sending the Apostles, Christ *licensed* them. Because the power to license teachers was exercised personally by Christ, when he "licensed" the Apostles, saying "Go teach all nations," that power is spiritual and cannot licitly be made venal. [53] This parallel also implies that the power to confer the license is a power that can be granted only by Christ or his vicar, the pope. Thus, D'Ailly maintained that the power to grant the license was transmitted by a kind of apostolic succession: the Apostles "received from Christ not only the license or power to teach and preach" (point three), "but they even received for themselves and their successors the power to license others to teach theology and to preach" (point four). [54] He interpreted the successors of the Apostles as "the pope and his delegates for this purpose." [55] The bishops are the pope's delegates for preaching and the chancellor for licensing. Thus d'Ailly's fourth point brought the pope into his general study of the license, and he, too, must avoid simony. "Christ taught [the Apostles] and their successors, namely the pope and his delegates for this purpose, that they could not sell the spiritual power [to confer the license], but as they had received it freely, so they were obliged to give it freely. And therefore it is clear that to give or receive money for [this power] is simony in the strict sense." [56]

D'Ailly stopped this line of reasoning here without recapitulating his first principal conclusion. If one follows the logic of his argument

---

[52] Radix, p. 208, l. 29-31.
[53] Radix, p. 209, l. 5-8.
[54] Radix, p. 209, l. 10-14.
[55] Radix, p. 209, l. 14-15.
[56] Radix, p. 209, l. 15-18.

to its end, however, d'Ailly will be seen to have proved far more than his stated goal, that it is simony in the strict sense to give or receive money for the license to teach theology.[57] The conclusion to which I believe his four points lead may be expressed as follows: Just as it is simony to give or receive money for the license to teach theology (points 1-3), so it is also simony to give or receive money for the power to confer the license to teach theology (point 4). In fourteenth-century practice the chancellor could receive money for the license, but only the pope could receive anything for the power to confer it. Thus there would have been no need to add point four unless some statement about the pope was intended. The nature of that statement can only be inferred if one remembers Gregory the Great's admonition that simony can be committed for benefits other than money. Thus it would be simony for either chancellor or pope to receive any temporal gain in return for the license itself or the power to confer it. Naturally, in the political climate that had prevailed in Paris since 1381, d'Ailly could not spell out the conclusion to which his logic was tending. Yet d'Ailly had known, ever since Blanchard had produced Clement's written order in defense of his handling of John Duchêne's candidacy, that when Clement VII awarded Blanchard the power to grant the license, he had in fact imposed upon his chancellor the condition that promotion be denied to Urbanists. In d'Ailly's terms, therefore, Clement could be considered guilty of exchanging the spiritual power to grant the license for the material or temporal advantage of consolidating his political base within the Church.

Although d'Ailly never accused Clement VII of simony, he had certainly formulated the principles on which such an accusation could be constructed. In connection with Blanchard's withholding the signetum from bachelors who had pledged not to pay or swear him an oath of obedience, d'Ailly declared: "It is simony in the strict sense . . . to impede the work of charity, that is, the work of teaching and preaching, primarily on account of temporal advantage." [58] According to this wording, it would be simony for the pope to impose any condition or exact any service redounding to his political benefit in return for conferring the power to license in theology. By adding his fourth point, d'Ailly brought the pope into his discussion and

---

[57] Radix, p. 200, l. 19-21.
[58] Radix, p. 231, l. 3-7: "Est proprie simoniacum . . . propter commodum temporale principaliter impedire opera caritatis, scilicet opera doctrine et predicationis."

introduced premises—derived from early Gallicanism and conciliar-ism—that evince a very independent stance toward the papacy, and that historically were invoked in accusing popes of disregarding the rights of corporate entities or of putting their private advantage above the general welfare of the Church.

In the above arguments, d'Ailly leaned heavily on the contrast between the spiritual nature of the license and the material character of money, and also on the text, "Freely you have received, therefore freely give." Blanchard met this line of attack with the claim that he was not charging for the license itself, but seeking compensation for his labor in administering it. Moreover, he asserted, Scripture clearly authorizes the practice. In I Corinthians 16:1-2, Paul ordered the faithful of Corinth to take a collection before he arrived, and in Luke 10:7, after Christ authorized the Apostles to receive the neces-sities of life from those to whom they preached, He explained, "the laborer is worthy of his hire." [59]

D'Ailly was thus compelled to admit that the Apostles had licitly received, but he immediately added: "more properly speaking [they received] not for their labor . . . but for the necessities of life, lest they be forced to abandon the Word of God to occupy themselves with the procurement of necessities." [60] Only "in an emergency," then, could the chancellor licitly receive.[61] In any event, he ought not to do it in a way that could bring scandal to the faith; better yet, he should follow the example of St. Paul, who, "although by divine law had the right to receive from those to whom he preached, nevertheless said, 'but we have not used this power, lest we give some offense to Christ's Gospel.' " [62]

Perhaps Paul's forbearance was too much to expect of a modern Parisian chancellor. Yet d'Ailly perceived an important incongruity in Blanchard's argument. "He might be able to receive from the people to whom the licentiates will preach and to whom he sent them to preach or teach," the theologian conceded, "but not from those whom he sent." [63] To explain this distinction, d'Ailly elaborated an example of a man, easily identifiable as the pope, who sends workers into his field that contains the Lord's flock, to which Christ referred when He

[59] Radix, p. 215, l. 14-20.
[60] Radix, p. 233, l. 15-22.
[61] Radix, p. 234, l. 1-3.
[62] Radix, pp. 229, 26 - 230, 2.
[63] Radix, p. 234, l. 1-6.

told Peter, "Tend my sheep." The sheep are too many for the pope to tend himself, so he "licenses and sends" others to help. On the basis of natural reason alone, d'Ailly argued, it would be absurd to say that such a man, who sends others out to do his work, should receive any payment for the labor of sending them. On the contrary, that man would be obliged to pay those he has sent. Therefore it follows that for licensing some men in theology, "which is nothing other than *sending* them to tend the flock ... committed to him," the pope or the chancellor, who is the pope's delegate in this, should not only not receive or exact anything for the labor of "sending or licensing" them, but rather ought to remunerate them for the labor they do.[64]

In applying this general argument to the special circumstances of the Church, d'Ailly employed the same rhetorical device we have seen in the passage from William of St-Amour referred to above. William had argued that because the pope was the vicar of Christ, he was bound to govern the Church according to Christ's example. Therefore, because the twelve Apostles and 72 disciples whom Christ sent out charged with the cure of souls were men whom He knew and had personally chosen, so the pope was bound to send as ministers only those who had been duly proven and tested.[65] For d'Ailly, the argument based on the example just described is confirmed by the example of Christ, whose vicar the pope is, and whom the pope is bound to imitate in this. "Now, when Christ *licensed* the Apostles, He said, 'Go and preach,' and He received or exacted nothing from them for the labor of licensing, but gave entirely freely and taught them to give freely, even as concerns their labor."[66]

Thus d'Ailly constructed his reply to the use of "the laborer is worthy of his hire" to include the pope. If the pope governs in imitation of Christ, whose representative he is, and Christ freely gave

---

[64] Radix, pp. 218,11 - 219,10.

[65] *Collectiones Catholicae et Canonicae Scripturae*, Dist. 1, in *Opera*, p. 146: "Cum Dominus Iesus Christus (cuius [Papa] est vicarius generalis et propter quod debet eum in suo regimine imitari, tanquam eius generalis Minister...) dum esset in carne mortali, non nisi certas personas a se electas, conversatione expertas, et in suo disciplinatu probatas, miserit ad praedictum regimen animarum: videlicet duodecim apostolos ... et septuaginta duos discipulos...." (Quoted in Congar, p. 55, n. 34a). This passage is also discussed above, ch. I, pp. 20-21.

[66] Radix, p. 219, l. 14-19: "Nam Christus, quando licenciavit Apostolos dicens: 'Euntes predicate,' etc., Matt. 10, 7, pro labore licenciandi nichil ab eis recepit aut exegit, sed omnino gratis dedit. Et eam gratis dare docuit, eciam quoad labore...."

the power to license to the Apostles, then the pope should also confer the power to license freely. Nor can the pope be considered a worker who must be compensated for his labor, for Christ licensed freely. Therefore the pope himself could not charge for his labor even if he granted the license in person. How then could the pope's delegate, the chancellor, do so? [67]

D'Ailly's assimilation of teaching to preaching is the key to his theory of the license and the place of the university in the Church. That fundamental comparison allows him to substitute the verb "license" for the verb "send" in some Scriptural passages that are critical to his argument. On the one hand, if it can be said that Christ "licensed" the Apostles, then popes and chancellors can be judged by very high standards indeed, and certainly they cannot benefit materially from the performance of this office, for Christ enjoined giving freely. On the other hand, if teachers are "sent," then like priests and bishops, they must be remunerated for their labor.

Not all of d'Ailly's arguments were so elaborate. Does the chancellor claim authorization to charge money for the labor of licensing by quoting "The laborer is worthy of his hire"? "This is expressly conceded to *preachers* by divine law," replied d'Ailly, "but not to the chancellor; in fact it is denied," in *Parens scientiarum* as well as other places.[68]

With the abuse of licensing procedures established as simony, d'Ailly terminated his sketch of a theory of the university. He considered that institution a microcosm of the Church within the Church, one responsible for a special office, that of imparting theological knowledge and thereby developing God's freely given gift of faith, a function analogous to the Church's distribution of the sacraments. Just as it would be simony to impede the flow of grace channeled through the Church by withholding a sacrament for money, so it would be illicit to interrupt the free flow of spiritual knowledge through the university for temporal considerations. Like those of the Church, the university's ministers received their mandate directly from Christ and at the same time. And, because the teachers help Christ's vicar, the pope, to fulfill his mission of caring for the flock, they are to be remunerated for their labor, just like those other shepherds, the priests. An extremely important aspect of the metaphor to which we shall now turn

---

[67] Radix, p. 218, l. 4-11.
[68] Radix, p. 233, l. 27-30.

is its implicit exclusion of the chancellor from the university. Receiving in return for labor is permitted to *preachers*, not to those who send them. Thus the chancellor is compared not to one who labors in the field or tends the flock, but to a kind of foreman, who sends out workers on behalf of the pope, and who is clearly distinguished from the body of laborers.

Monetary exactions were not the only ones prohibited in the papal regulations concerning the University of Paris and the legislation on simony. Also forbidden were oaths, or what Gregory the Great called "munus ab obsequio." [69] Thus d'Ailly's argument that Blanchard's practices were simoniacal had to include the dispute over the two different oaths that had emerged as issues: the oath of obedience or reverence demanded by Blanchard, [70] and the oath required of bachelors by the university to the effect that they would neither pay the chancellor money nor swear him the oath of obedience. [71] D'Ailly was concerned to show that the oath of obedience extracted by the chancellor before awarding the license was a case of withholding a spiritual service until receiving a temporal benefit. When Blanchard countered with the assertion that the university's oaths were essentially the same, d'Ailly had to distinguish between the license and the magisterium. He argued that the university's oaths were necessary to its proper functioning as a corporate body, whereas the chancellor does not belong to that body and consequently had no claim to the loyalty of its members, least of all on the grounds of granting the license, an act that must be performed gratis. Therefore, he claimed, the oath demanded by the chancellor lacked a proper rationale.

In the administration of oaths connected to spiritual things, d'Ailly said, basing himself upon Raymond of Peñafort, there are three criteria for determining whether the sin of simony has been avoided. The first is whether the oath is given before or after the administration of the spiritual thing and whether it is exacted by a superior or not. [72] Raymond of Peñafort, Bernard of Parma, Hostiensis, and the Archdeacon Guido de Baysio are all cited as agreeing that "the chancellor cannot, without simony, exact a caution in the form of an oath before promoting the bachelors, even supposing that he were their superior, or that the oath was not contrary to common law,

---

[69] See above, p. 154.
[70] See above, p. 74.
[71] See above, p. 71.
[72] Super, p. 282, l. 26-28.

or to a special privilege, exceptions which, in this case, are all inapplicable." [73] Nonetheless, other canonists had argued that a superior might be able to exact such oaths even before the performance of the spiritual service. Thus d'Ailly had to show why the chancellor should not be considered a superior of university members.

The second criterion is whether the oath is connected to the spiritual thing for which it is exacted. For example, the chancellor licitly asks those whom he is about to license to swear that they will testify honestly about the qualifications of future candidates. Such a promise is connected to the honor of the license. Although it would be more honestly exacted after conferral of the license than before, even if it is exacted before, there is no appearance of simony because it is not in the interest of the person who exacts it, but of the whole community (*respublica*).[74]

The third criterion is whether the oath is *obsequiosum*, that is, to the personal advantage of the one who exacts it. For example, the oath that the chancellor demands from the bachelors requiring that they "preserve the honor, rights, liberties, and customs of the chancellor and his office" is *obsequiosum* and cannot be made a condition for the performance of a spiritual act, whether before or after the performance of that act.[75] Therefore, d'Ailly concluded, the chancellor's insistence upon an oath of reverence is simoniacal.

Blanchard replied that if the oath he demanded was simoniacal, then so were the oaths demanded by the university and its faculties on various occasions.[76] For example, bachelors who have been licensed are made to pay certain fees and swear oaths to honor the rector, to guard university secrets, and to observe its privileges before being admitted to the corporation of masters (i.e., before receiving the magisterium).[77] More recently, the university has instituted the oath restraining the bachelors from yielding to the chancellor's demands.[78] The nature of the university's practice is especially clear in the Faculty of Theology, Blanchard maintained, where bachelors being

---

[73] Super, p. 284, l. 1-6.
[74] Super, p. 284, l. 7-19.
[75] Super, pp. 284, 20 - 285, 1.
[76] Super, p. 280, l. 8-10.
[77] Super, p. 280, l. 21-23.
[78] C. E. Du Boulay, *Historia Universitatis Parisiensis*, 6 vols. (Paris, 1665-73), IV, 607: "Les maistres ont fait jurer les bacheliers qui ne bailleront rien au Chancelier...et pour ce a differé [le Chancelier] à envoyer les signets...."

admitted to teach the Bible or the *Sentences* are made to swear an oath.[79] Since anyone who does not swear these oaths will be prevented from teaching theology, the cases of the chancellor and the faculty would seem to be "wholly similar." [80]

The dissimilarities, d'Ailly replied, are numerous. First of all, the license and the magisterium are quite different. The chancellor's license to teach theology is a spiritual power or authority, but the magisterium, even in theology, is less spiritual than the license ("non est, ultra licentiam predictam, aliqua auctoritas spiritualis") for it is only a kind of civil or political honorary degree. The argument is clarified by the following analogy. The magisterium is to the license as the wedding is to the sacrament of matrimony. Although the sacrament is spiritual, the wedding is only a ceremony to commemorate the sacrament. Even if the university or any faculty were to sell the magisterium, therefore, it would be guilty of extortion or corruption, but not of simony.[81]

D'Ailly later compensated for this disappointing description of the difference between the magisterium and the license. He was forced to deal with the issue in more fundamental terms by Blanchard's contention in the parlement that he was a member of the University of Paris.[82] If he were a member, his granting of the license would indicate a position of some superiority within the corporation, and he would surely claim headship. In this position, his demands of oaths and payments could be much more easily defended, and the distinction between the license and magisterium would be weakened considerably. The university's advocate in the parlement immediately rebutted Blanchard's affirmation: "He is not a member of the university as chancellor, but only as Master of Arts,"[83] and thus clearly subject to the rector by virtue of the oath he swore long ago.

D'Ailly elaborated on the university's position by developing the notion of the university as a corporation, and, following the oldest traditions of Roman law, as an imitation of a republic or, to use d'Ailly's conventional image, a political body. His position on this

[79] Super, p. 280, l. 18-21.
[80] Super, p. 280, l. 21-27.
[81] Super, p. 281, l. 7-25.
[82] Du Boulay, IV, 609, lines 10-11: "Et dit le Chancelier qu'il est un des nobles membres de l'Université."
[83] *Ibid.*, lines 51-52: "Comme Chancelier, il n'est pas membre de l'Université, mais comme Maistre en Arts...."

topic provides the best evidence in the two speeches of d'Ailly's awareness that his ideas derived from formal corporation theory. His statement stands apart from the rest of his text by virtue of its compact logic, technical terminology, and incisiveness. Here we glimpse the Pierre d'Ailly made famous by his theological teaching and later by his advocacy of the conciliar cause. In this paragraph he unites the themes we have previously attributed separately to Gallicanism and conciliarism, and foreshadows those developments from 1398 on which increasingly blur the distinction between the two. Here the Roman law-based corporate particularism of William of St-Amour and the Aristotelian naturalism that Conrad of Gelnhausen attributed to political bodies form a mutually reinforcing synthesis.

The chancellor, d'Ailly maintained, is not a member of the university, not its superior in any way, and not in a position to demand these exactions for the following reasons. The university, with the rector at its head, or any individual faculty, has a certain internal coherence or "political order," by virtue of which it can receive from its members anything useful or expedient for its preservation as a community.[84] "For obviously any rightly ordered and established community can impose, receive, and exact reasonable obligations, either of money or of oaths, as its situation demands, from those whom it admits into its consortium, as from those who are its subjects." [85] The University of Paris was specifically given the liberty thus to regulate itself, and this privilege explicitly mentions the corporation's right to define the obligations of its members: to receive gifts, demand

---

[84] Super, p. 281, l. 26-31: "Rector, Universitas, et Facultas quelibet, respectu suorum bachalariorum, et generaliter respectu omnium suorum suppositorum, habet quemdam politicum ordinem et ordinatam superioritatem, ratione cuius potest recipere et exigere a suis suppositis illa que sunt utilia et expedientia ad conservationem et tuitionem sue politice communitatis."

[85] Super, p. 281, l. 31-35: "Nam quelibet rite ordinata et approbata communitas, ab illis quos in suum consortium admittit, potest, secundum sui status, exigentiam, onera racionabilia sive pecuniarum sive juramentorum, sicut suis subiectis imponere, recipere, et exigere. [Sic] arguitur capitulo primo, De Jurejurando, Liber Sextus [Decretalium], 2, 11, 1; ed. Friedberg, II, 1003-4. D'Ailly's reference here is somewhat obscure. The canon Contingit in nonnullis, which he cites, admits a parallel between oaths imposed on entering canons and those on new podestà, rectors, or officials in cities, fortresses, or administrative districts. Noting that civil officials swear to many conditions that are illicit or contrary to the liberty of the Church, Nicholas III forbids churchmen to swear to them. The canon accepts only tacitly the Aristotelian belief in the natural legitimacy of such political organizations. D'Ailly's statement is much less qualified.

contributions, and exact oaths.[86] Like any body, natural or political, the university has the right to nourish itself by means of contributions from its members. The university's exactions from its bachelors are not for the bachelor's degree itself, d'Ailly asserted, but for the conservation and protection of the institution, and consequently they are licit.[87] Moreover, the university's right to exact these oaths flows naturally from its status as a corporation, whereas the chancellor has no right to demand oaths at all because, as chancellor, he does not partake of the university's "political order." [88] "If he did, there would be many . . . heads in the university, which would be monstrous."[89] Therefore, the right to grant the license (even as a papal delegate) implies no authority over either bachelors or masters, and hence the chancellor cannot exact obligations of this sort from them.[90] These differences between the oaths and payments received by the university and those received by the chancellor show that those of the former are licit and those of the latter are not. Since Blanchard is not entitled to the oath he exacts as a condition prior to the conferral of the license, he is guilty of simony. Moreover, because he violates the oath of office in which he swore to award the license in accord with the privilege *Parens scientiarum*, he is also guilty of perjury.[91]

D'Ailly's second principal conclusion, that the practices he attributed to Blanchard violated natural and divine law, is, like the first, theoretically applicable to the pope. Because divine and natural law are above the human law of the pope, this argument seems to establish one more reason why Clement's prohibition against advancing Urbanists was illicit. Yet to take an implicit theme and make it the covert purpose of d'Ailly's speeches would be wrong. Natural and divine law are introduced not to implicate the pope, but to answer Blanchard's contention that his licensing procedures conformed to immemorial custom. Custom cannot stand against natural and divine law; if these prohibit his practices, they must be abandoned.[92]

---

[86] Super, p. 282, l. 12-15: "Universitas predicta, ad premissa onera exigenda habet privilegium, scilicet de collectis, vel contributionibus levandis, et certis juramentis exigendis. Cancellarius autem non." If d'Ailly is referring here to the Statutes of Robert of Courzon, the authorization is actually much narrower than he suggests. Cf. *Chart.*, I, no. 20, pp. 78-79.

[87] Super, p. 282, l. 1-3.

[88] Super, p. 282, l. 5-7.

[89] Super, p. 282, l. 7-8.

[90] Super, p. 282, l. 8-11.

[91] Radix, p. 231, l. 7-11 and Super, p. 288, l. 21-29.

[92] These passages on divine and natural law in the treatises against Blanchard are discussed by F. Oakley, *The Political Thought of Pierre d'Ailly* (New Haven, Conn., 1964), pp. 174-77.

The sale of the license to teach theology, d'Ailly said, is against natural and divine law because it is simony. Simony is against natural and divine law, therefore the consequence holds.[93] Recognizing his tautology, d'Ailly quickly conceded: "That it is against divine law is well enough known, but that it is against natural law may be proved specially." [94] To do so, d'Ailly referred to Numbers, Chapter 22, which relates the story of the pagan soothsayer Balaam, whom God condemned for accepting gifts in return for his prophecy. Those who, like Balaam, knew neither the Old Testament nor the New were considered by medieval theologians to live under the law of nature, that is, without grace. And since to accept gifts for prophecy is to receive temporal in return for spiritual goods, d'Ailly concluded that the law of nature condemns simony.[95]

In the next paragraph, d'Ailly confused his presentation by trying to do too many things at once. His scholastic training impelled him to give at least an offhand definition of natural law, while, at the same time, his predatory instinct seized the opportunity to compare Blanchard unfavorably to Balaam:

> This vice might fittingly have been named "balaamia" after Balaam himself, its first perpetrator, but it was named after Simon because, in the New Testament, Christ more clearly expressed why it is a crime when he said, "Freely you have received, freely give." Therefore those who live under the New Law sin more against this, but nevertheless, the reason to which Christ refers here ought naturally to have been impressed under the hearts of all men, both under the Law of Moses and the Law of Nature.[96]

Thus Christ's saying, "Freely you have received, freely give," is a natural law precept that has received divine confirmation. And although Balaam is considered guilty of contravening it as natural law, because it is inscribed in the hearts of all men, Blanchard's crime is more serious because he has violated the divine law, expressed by Christ himself. D'Ailly adds yet another reason why Blanchard sins more seriously than Balaam. Whereas the latter had sold the power to prophesy, the chancellor was selling the gift of theological wisdom, which is even more spiritual because when Paul enumerated the

---

[93] Radix, p. 209, l. 25-30.
[94] Radix, p. 209, l. 30-31.
[95] Radix, p. 210, l. 1-8.
[96] Radix, p. 210, l. 8-15.

spiritual and gratuitous gifts, he gave theological wisdom (*sermo sapientie*) precedence over the gift of prophecy.[97]

Because simony violates both natural and divine law, those guilty of it can be judged and punished by a secular prince.[98] D'Ailly explained that the university's privilege *Parens scientiarum*, insofar as it forbids the exchange of temporal things for the license in theology, is not strictly speaking a privilege, that is, a private law applying only to the University of Paris and exempting it from the "common law" regulating the rest of the Church; but is itself a provision of the common law, not just human, but natural and divine.[99] Therefore the violators of *Parens scientiarum* are transgressors of natural law and can be tried and punished by a secular court like the Parlement of Paris.[100] Since *Parens scientiarum* is natural law, it cannot be abrogated by custom, for "custom establishes no precedent against natural or divine law." [101] As if this were not enough, d'Ailly further observed that the custom to which the chancellor referred is specifically anathematized in the decretal *Quanto Gallicana*, where taking exactions for the license is called a "Gallican custom" and described as "depraved." [102] And, according to Vincent of Spain's gloss, it was precisely this practice of the Chancellor of Paris, who was accustomed to exact a mark from every teacher, that inspired the condemnation.[103]

---

[97] Radix, p. 210, l. 16-30. See above, p. 155, for identification of theology with the "sermo sapientie."

[98] Radix, p. 211, l. 13-27.

[99] Radix, pp. 211, 28 - 212, 3.

[100] Blanchard apparently agreed that the Parlement of Paris was the proper forum for this contest, but for another reason. In his testimony there, he claimed that he was "in saisine" of the right to receive eleven francs from each bachelor about to be licensed in theology. ("Les predecesseurs du Chancelier et le Chancelier ont usé et ont esté, et est encore ledit Chancelier en possession et saisine, d'avoir de chacun Bachelier au moins onze francs." Du Boulay, IV, 607, lines 6-8.) By the late fourteenth century, cases like this were heard in secular courts on the grounds that rights to peaceful possession should be guaranteed by the crown. See F. Lot and R. Fawtier, *Histoire des institutions Francaises au moyen age*, II (Paris, 1958), 457-58.

[101] Radix, p. 212, l. 4-7.

[102] Radix, p. 212, l. 7-11.

[103] Radix, p. 222, l. 2-5: "Hoc autem capitulum factum fuit contra Cancellarium Parisiensem, qui a quolibet docente marcam unam exigebat, ut dicit glossa Vincentii in antiqua compilatione." Cf. Bernard of Parma in *Gregorii Papae IX Libri V Decretalium cum Glossis* (Romae, 1582), col. 1651: "Cap. 3 eodum titulo in Prima Compilatione et post Concilium Lateranense sub Alex. III par. 2, cap. 18. Hoc capitulo, ut ait Vincentius, fuit impetratum contra Cancellarium Parisiensum, qui marcham unam a quolibet docente exigebat." Gaines Post also noted Vincent's comment on this letter but he cites *Chart.*, I, Pars Introd. no. 4,

To this point, d'Ailly has established the first two of his principal conclusions: to exchange money (or to exact a self-serving oath) for the theological license is simony, and it violates natural and divine law. The third and final conclusion can be disposed of quickly. Here d'Ailly contended that to defend as licit the exchange of money for the license in theology is heretical. With this thesis, d'Ailly returned to the theme of his preface, where he maintained that he was speaking against an error in the faith.[104] To move from the subject of sin to that of heresy, he distinguished between committing and excusing the crime. The act itself is not heresy, but sin.[105] On the other hand, it is heretical to say that a sin is not a sin. Therefore to assert pertinaciously that selling the license to teach is licit is to err in the faith.[106] The same distinction is valid in Simon Magus. In wishing to buy a spiritual benefit for a temporal price, he erred not only in the will, but in the intellect as well, for he necessarily supposed that "a gift of God could be possessed for money" (Acts 8:20). Such a judgment is heretical, and all who follow Simon in this opinion are to be considered heretics.[107] Of Blanchard, d'Ailly stated that if the chancellor were to assert pertinaciously that his actions were licit, he should be considered a heretic, for such an assertion would necessarily involve the defense of many crimes: simony, extortion, cupidity, exaction, and perjury.[108] But "above all," said d'Ailly, and here he moved to a level of generality that, as we have seen, could also include the pope's order to exclude Urbanists from promotion, to defend these actions one would have to assert that "it is licit to impede works of mercy and charity, namely teaching and preaching." [109]

Two separate trends have been identified in this account of d'Ailly's prosecution of John Blanchard: the theologian's handling of Blan-

---

where finally reference is made to ms. Vat. lat. 1377. Post, "Alexander III, the *Licentia Docendi*, and the Rise of the Universities," in *Anniversary Essays in Mediaeval History by Students of Charles Homer Haskins* (Boston and New York, 1929), p. 260, n. 22.

[104] See above, p. 153; Radix, p. 212, l. 13-15.

[105] Radix, p. 213, l. 5-12.

[106] Radix, pp. 212, 31 - 213, 4.

[107] Radix, pp. 213, 28 - 214, 3. Cf. d'Ailly's earlier reference (Radix, p. 209, l. 22-23) to the Glossa Ordinaria, where simony is considered a heresy, *Biblia Sacra cum Glossis*, in Mat. 10, 7, *ad verb.* "Gratis accepistis." Thomas Aquinas (II, II, q. 100, art. 1), also calls simony a heresy.

[108] Radix, p. 232, l. 13-19.

[109] Radix, p. 232, l. 19-21: "... et insuper esset approbare quod licitum esset impedire opera misericordie et caritatis, scilicet doctrine et predicationis."

chard's abuses as Chancellor of Paris and his use of the affair to pursue independent goals. In the prosecution proper, he accused Blanchard of simony, which he defined as the exchange of a spiritual for a material benefit. The license to teach theology was then shown to be spiritual because of its connection with the truths of the faith and because licensing was an act performed in direct imitation of Christ. D'Ailly classified as simony Blanchard's practice of withholding the license or signetum until money had been paid or promised and an oath of loyalty to the chancellor sworn. Although exactions of this sort had already been condemned in *Quanto Gallicana* and *Parens scientiarum*, and were demonstrably contrary to divine and natural law, Blanchard insisted on defending his abuses as licit, and d'Ailly argued that his tenacity in defense of error rendered him suspect of heresy.

No résumé of d'Ailly's speeches that focuses exclusively on the prosecution can do justice to the theologian's intentions. Much of what he said concerns Blanchard's administration only indirectly, and tends rather to exploit the opportunity the scandal provided to reassess the nature of the license, the university's status within the Church, and related topics. The crisis gave d'Ailly an occasion to air his concept of the apostolic origin and divine mission of theologians in a forum that ensured wide publicity, thus furthering his own reputation and that of his faculty. With his teaching-preaching parallel, he interpreted the established orders of the Church in a way that made teaching a function distinct from the preaching of prelates and priests, and, in saying that Christ "licensed" the Apostles, he invoked an idea of the theologian's place in the Church that compelled immediate comparison to the bishops. Similarly, he explained why theologians should be remunerated for their labor in teaching.

Even as d'Ailly exalted the status of theological professors within the hierarchy, his view of the Church itself called for a reduction of papal authority, as compared, for example, to that implicit in *Quasi lignum vitae*. In Gallican fashion, d'Ailly defended the liberty of his own corporation while restricting the centralizing force of the papacy in theory. *Parens scientiarum* was the document he advanced against the papal view of the magisterium, for it attributed a large role to the professors of each faculty. Nor should that privilege apply to the university alone, like a mere private law. Rather, because it prohibits the exchange of spiritual for material goods, and thus outlaws simony, it should be considered *ius commune* and apply to the whole Church. Not even the pope would then be exempted from its terms, which are consonant with divine and natural law, standards that the pontiff may not violate. Thus the pope's role is seen to be clearly subjected to the law, to Christ's example, and to the welfare of the whole Church, which in turn benefits greatly when professors at Paris are free to teach and choose teachers according to their own best judgment.

Thus the Blanchard affair gave d'Ailly a rare opportunity to discuss openly questions of reform and ecclesiology that had been smothered by the French court's rule of silence. Although the calling of a Church council could not be debated, the critical perspectives of Gallicanism were incubating. The prosecution of John Blanchard shows how they were working beneath the surface.

CONCLUSION

The Parisian chancellor's custom of charging for the license to teach dates back at least to 1172, when Alexander III prohibited that "Gallican" practice as "depraved." The abuse was tolerated even after his order in part because the number and amount of the exactions were limited by custom. Thus the earlier payments were "exacted" by the force of institutionalized tradition, and previous chancellors had been content to accept these revenues as a regular, and regulated, perquisite of their office.

Under Blanchard the situation changed. He demanded more money than his predecessors and also sought new ways to profit from his position. The fees exacted from candidates in the Faculty of Arts were higher and more systematically levied than before, and, although the evidence here is less conclusive, it appears that theologians too were made to pay higher fees than previously. Even those granted papal permission to read the *Sentences* or receive the licentia bullata complained that Blanchard invented difficulties and extorted payments for overlooking them. That members of the religious orders cooperated in compiling the accusations against Blanchard and in testifying against him significantly undercuts his charge that only d'Ailly and disgruntled artists opposed him. Ostensibly a papal delegate for licensing, Blanchard proved himself as independent of papal authority as he did of academic traditions and routines. Blanchard's behavior, as described with substantial accuracy in the articles of accusation, must be considered foremost among the various influences that led the masters to undertake reform. Some of the prerogatives claimed by the chancellor were in fact supported by papal privileges, but this is not sufficient to alter our basic conclusion.

Although Blanchard's fiscal offenses alone were enough to stimulate protest, the resentment they provoked was surely intensified by his peremptory manner, his unconcealed delight in taking students' last coins, and the arbitrary explanations he gave for adverse administrative judgments. One might be tempted to consider his efforts as an unusually intensive pursuit of self-interest were it not that in the end, his very single-mindedness was his undoing. Except for his apology to the Faculty of Arts, made under extreme duress after the banquet incident, not one sign of compromise, not one concession, is cited even by his partisans. As at Liége, Blanchard's personality was certainly a factor.

His systematic or even compulsive contentiousness forced him into conflict with the masters on almost every question. He opposed privileges they valued and sought to extend the prerogatives of his own office at their expense. He claimed to "inherit" *ex officio* the bachelors of masters who left Paris or died. He threatened to denounce bachelors as schismatics unless they incepted under him, he opposed the masters' ranking of candidates, and he advanced the unauthorized oath of obedience to the chancellor as superseding the legitimate one sworn to the rector. In short, Blanchard pursued his self-aggrandizement in an obsessive, consistently tactless manner. He collided directly with the masters, who understandably opposed his systematic efforts to fill his coffers at the expense of their students and to expand the prerogatives of his office in opposition to rights they deemed essential to their corporation.

At the same time these problems were festering within the studium, the university was suffering the consequences of the schism in the Church at large. Silence on the subject of a general council imposed by royal order was not the only sacrifice the schism demanded. The factionalism it naturally produced took a terrible toll within the school. Many notable theologians had left by the end of 1381, and the Faculty of Arts had been torn apart until early 1383. During the period the university was undergoing these trials, Blanchard raised the fees for the license in arts from approxmately 3 solidi, 6 denarii of Tours per bachelor to approximately 15 solidi. Furthermore, fewer candidates could avoid the exactions of the Chancellor of Notre-Dame by seeking the license at Ste-Geneviève, because of the latter's uncertain legitimacy during the same period. It could hardly have escaped notice that all these developments followed hard upon the arrival of Blanchard.

Another constraint upon the masters that coincided with Blanchard's tenure was Clement VII's order that no Urbanists should be promoted. Even though Blanchard made no effort to enforce the order as the pope intended, he used it to force bachelors to incept under him. The very arbitrariness of his administration, the unpredictability with which he resorted to the Urbanist smear, undoubtedly contributed to the insecurity already felt by men hampered by pressures from the royal court and threats of removal from benefices should their loyalty to Avignon be questioned. If the fate of John Rousse was reserved for prominent spokesmen, the example of John the Servite, whether his progress was blocked for reasons connected to the schism or not, put all on notice that failure to cooperate with Blanchard could bring serious consequences.

The banquet incident occurred against this background of schism-related tension, Blanchard's capricious administration, and his increasing pecuniary exactions. None of these circumstances can be explained away by the banquet incident however the chancellor exaggerated it. Still, it is clear that his *faux pas* played a role in releasing the hostility accumulated against him and the frustration built up by the general course of events in the French capital. This complex of pressures upon the studium was hardly simplified by the events of 1384. June of that year was the date of the fateful celebration, but it also marked the end of Blanchard's third year in office, a year during which he had raised the price of the license in arts more than 30 percent over the previous year, to the round sum of one gold franc. Giles Deschamps, one of the bachelors Blanchard "stole" by threatening denunciation as a schismatic, was also licensed that spring. All these circumstances contributed to the appearance, on October 6 of that year, of the university's first reference to a reform of licensing procedures.

In the 1380's, challenges to precedence such as Blanchard's behavior at the banquet were not initiated without forethought, and we need look no further than the university's pursuit of Hugh Aubriot, who had claimed precedence over the rector in the funeral cortège of Charles V, to realize how zealously the corporation of masters defended its honorary rights. Moreover, Blanchard's behavior at the banquet was not a unique challenge to the university. His exaction of an oath to rival that of the rector, his opposition to the masters' ranking the bachelors, and his use of the chancellor's office to "steal" bachelors are all of a piece with an attempt to claim priority over the rector. Blanchard's bid for precedence at the banquet moved the masters to action not only because it came when it did, but also because it so nakedly fit the model of an aggressive chancellor and because that act, unlike his other initiatives, directly collided with an institutionally fostered symbol of autonomy, built up by more than a century of university opposition to control by chancellors. When he took the rector's seat in June 1384, Blanchard opened himself to the most rigorous opposition the university could muster and therefore to retribution for *all* his offenses as Chancellor of Paris.

Just as a whole range of factors contributed to the masters' protest against the chancellor, so Pierre d'Ailly's prosecution involves intellectual currents broader than those relevant to the chancellor alone. One could not discuss a major corporation that propagates doctrine without bringing up a number of ecclesiological questions. More particularly, d'Ailly could not treat the flow of grace achieved by the communication of theological knowledge, so vital to his characterization of the license as spiritual, without reference to the pope.

As we have seen, d'Ailly's fourth point—that the power to confer the license cannot be sold without simony—contains an implicit criticism of Clement VII. Yet the nature of his judgment requires careful analysis. It is tempting to consider the Blanchard affair a forerunner of the kind of opposition to the papacy that appeared in the Parisian councils of the late 1390's, or even Pisa and Constance. But "Radix Omnium" and "Super Omnia," although implicitly critical of papal authority, are not properly a part of conciliarist literature. There is no appeal to a council, no argument for the superiority of council to pontiff, no invocation of epikeia. On the other hand, many of the premises used by Conrad of Gelnhausen in the *Epistola Concordie* are also fundamental to d'Ailly's exposition: the superiority of natural and divine to human law, the self-evident right of a constituted body to preserve itself, and the injustice of a superior who prefers his personal advantage to the interests of those whose well-being is entrusted to him. Certainly d'Ailly was not the only one reflecting upon these ideas. Indeed the principles advanced by Aristotle and reiterated by Thomas Aquinas—that a superior ought to serve the interests of his subjects, and that when he works to their detriment by the abuse of his authority, he may be strenuously resisted—seem to have inspired the conduct of the cardinals who withdrew from Urban VI.[1]

The professors' opposition to Blanchard implies acceptance of the same principles. D'Ailly's explanation, however, draws upon two distinct lines of argument, showing an ambivalence that is of considerable historical importance. On the one hand, he depicted the university as a corporation wholly integrated within the Church because, among other reasons, its welfare benefited the whole Church. For this line of argument he drew upon a conciliar ecclesiology.

---

[1] The constitutional significance of the cardinal's actions in 1378 is explained by Walter Ullmann, *The Origins of the Great Schism* (London, 1948), pp. 170-90.

According to this view, the pope's authority was limited like that of any corporation head, and the chancellor was his delegate. Thus the chancellor could do nothing against the university that the pope himself could not do. On the other hand, d'Ailly also depicted the university as a privileged corporation, distinguished from the rest of the Church by its special function and its proximity to the French crown. To this theme he adapted Gallican ideas. Thus he claimed a strong autonomy for the university by distinguishing sharply between the license and the magisterium and by defining the chancellor as an outsider. In accord with this view, to defend itself the university needed only its prior privileges and bylaws and access to the royal courts, where the corporation's rights could be maintained. Thus Pierre d'Ailly's speeches subtly echo the theoretical conciliarism urged by Conrad of Gelnhausen, which could not be acted upon or even debated after 1381, while at the same time they explore some of the Gallican positions later to win endorsement from the French court.

When Clement VII died in 1394, only the Roman pope, Boniface IX, remained, and the schism could have ended then had the Avignon cardinals refrained from electing a new pontiff. But Boniface himself had been elected by Roman cardinals who had been unable to restrain themselves in a similar situation. Who could expect more of their Avignon counterparts? Besides, there was a difference. Before entering the conclave, each of Clement's cardinals swore an oath that if elected pope, he would do anything necessary to end the schism, even resign. The man they chose, Pedro de Luna, Benedict XIII, had recently been in Paris, where he had advocated resignation or the *via cessionis*, as it was called, before the university and the royal court. From the papal throne, however, his perspectives changed, and despite more and more urgent reminders, he showed less and less interest in stepping down. The court and studium were incensed by his stalling.

One measure he took to withstand their resentment was to assure himself of the loyal counsel of the Chancellor of Paris, Pierre d'Ailly, whom he named Bishop of Le Puy in 1395 and transferred to the wealthy see of Cambrai in 1396. Although d'Ailly continued to favor the pope's voluntary resignation, he was not in a position to support methods of forcing the via cessionis upon Benedict. The King of France, Charles VI, was not personally a significant factor in the maneuvers now aimed at Benedict because, although he had attained his majority in 1388, he was only intermittently sane after

1392. "Royal" policy was therefore therefore usually made by his uncles, the Dukes John of Berry and Philip of Burgundy, or exceptionally by his brother, Louis of Orléans, when the king was well or the uncles away. Orléans, who continued the policy pursued by Louis of Anjou until his death in 1384, favored the Avignon papacy because it furthered his interests in Italy. The Dukes of Berry and Burgundy, by contrast, favored an orientation that would strengthen their hand in northern France. Philip especially had an interest in Church union because, as we have seen, his subjects were divided in their obedience between Rome and Avignon. His diplomatic and economic ties with Urbanist England were also undercut by continuation of the schism. By 1398, Benedict's stalling and the pressure of other interests brought the dukes' patience to an end, and, in the name of the king, they called a council of the French clergy to vote a radical measure, the subtraction of obedience from Benedict XIII.[2] It is in the debates of the Paris Council of 1398 that a reflection of the Blanchard affair appears.

Naturally I do not mean to claim a causal relationship. The expulsion of Blanchard was an internal university matter. But after the imposition of silence by the court in 1381 and the other pressures to which the studium was subjected through 1383, the Blanchard affair provided the first opportunity for action of any kind. Another occasion was the condemnation of Juan de Monzon (1387-89) for challenging the authority of the Faculty of Theology. In 1390 an anonymous master wrote a treatise condemning those who had the power to terminate the schism but were failing to do so. In 1394 the university conducted a poll of its members that produced three suggestions for ending the schism, with the via cessionis the strong favorite, and this program was energetically pursued by university

---

[2] In the following discussion I have drawn upon Howard Kaminsky's two articles, "The Politics of France's Subtraction of Obedience from Pope Benedict XIII, 27 July, 1398," *Proceedings of the American Philosophical Society*, 115, no. 5 (1971), pp. 366-97, and "Cession, Subtraction, Deposition: Simon de Cramaud's Formulation of the French Solution to the Schism," *Studia Gratiana*, XV (1972), 297-317. The pages devoted to "Les Débuts du Gallicanisme" in E. Delaruelle, E. R. Labande, and P. Ourliac, *L'Église au temps du Grand Schisme et de la crise conciliaire* (1387-1449), vol. XIV of A. Fliche et V. Martin, eds., *Histoire de l'Église*, 2 vols. (Paris, 1962-64), I, 329-44, are exceptionally valuable. Ourliac observes that Gallicanism takes a new turn under Benedict XIII (p. 329), and that Gallicanism and conciliarism were not fused until 1406, when Gerson in *De modis uniendi* wrote that the Gallican Church recognized the superiority of a general council over its own decisions (p. 338).

representatives traveling all over Europe. When the dukes and the masters saw that their interests coincided, the decision was made to elicit the approval of the French clergy as a whole for the subtraction of obedience.

There are three ties between the Blanchard affair and the Paris council. First is the prominence in both of Giles Deschamps and Pierre Plaoul, although in 1398 they were both on the same side. Second is the issue of resisting an abuser of authority. Third is the marked similarity of the intellectual framework within which the problems were debated.

The absence of Pierre d'Ailly from the Parisian scene of 1398 enhances the importance of these similarities. If he had been there, one would naturally have expected him to draw on his usual frame of reference. The use by others of ideas that d'Ailly had employed earlier dramatizes the success with which he exploited the Blanchard affair to apply to a practical problem a body of thought that had been developing among canonists and theologians for over a century. Every time they were adapted and applied successfully, they gained attractiveness and force. Thus, without attributing originality to d'Ailly for the ideas he employed in opposing Blanchard, we can nonetheless appreciate his role as an intermediary, using, adapting, and transmitting them to the future.[3]

While it could hardly be argued that Deschamps and Plaoul did not know how the Blanchard affair had been handled, d'Ailly was not the only source of the ideas they were to use. They had the support of colleagues such as Pierre LeRoy and Simon de Cramaud, who were drawing on the same traditions as d'Ailly. Even more important is the fact that those who opposed the subtraction of obedience were using many of the same intellectual referents.

Giles Deschamps argued for subtraction in terms sufficiently general that his experience with Blanchard and Benedict XIII could be seen as analogous: "When a prelate is a scandal for his people and there is no hope that the scandal can be removed as long as he remains over them, he is not to be supported in his office." [4] In a situation like this, one source of relief is the secular ruler, because "it pertains

---

[3] For a lengthier discussion see F. Oakley, *The Political Thought of Pierre d'Ailly* (New Haven, Conn., 1964), 198-231, where d'Ailly's influence is traced to 1688.

[4] Speech of Giles Deschamps, July 1, 1398, in J. D. Mansi, *Sacrorum Conciliorum Nova et Amplissima Collectio*, 26 (Paris, 1903; reissue, Graz, 1961), col. 874.

to the king to provide and preserve the peace of the Church, for his own lies in it also." [5] Thus the clergy can meet with the King of France to end the schism and the University of Paris can sue its chancellor in the royal parlement. Deschamps argued that help may be sought from the king even against a pope, since without recourse to the king the pope's domination of his subjects could become excessive. Thus "it pertains to the king to provide that the Church of his realm be subjected to the pope only as it is fitting, within the limits of reason and as reason dictates . . . [And] therefore the prince ought to provide that [the Church of his kingdom] not be dominated too much." [6] But even if the harmful wielder of authority is not as exalted a person as the pope, the king is a useful refuge, "because there is no one who can harm the Church as much as a pernicious prelate. . . . And thus subjects are urged not to obey unless they ought to, lest they encourage evil rulers in their malice and stubbornness. From all of which it appears that the authority of a king to extirpate schism and preserve the peace of the Church derives from divine, natural, canon, and civil law." [7] The king, therefore, may be used as a shield by the Church at times when ecclesiastical government is characterized by scandal or overbearing rule.

Deschamps' Gallican argument has the defect of implying that the Church has no remedy within itself for a scandalous pope. In fact that situation can never arise, Deschamps argued, quoting William of Ockham, because once a pope becomes a heretic or a schismatic, he automatically falls outside the Church and loses his papal dignity:

> If it should . . . appear that the pope is heretical or schismatic, he ought not to be obeyed, but should be considered a non-pope, even without a [formal] declaration. And the reason for this is that he is now outside the Church and the communion of the faithful, for the pope and the members form one body, of which the pope is the head. If, therefore, the pope is outside the Church, he is no longer pope, but thereby rightly loses his papal office. And Ockham says this in his Dialogue.[8]

As the orator invoked the organic metaphor of head and members, he returned to the familiar realm of corporation theory. But, Pierre Ravat, an opponent of subtraction who used the same metaphor,

---

[5] Mansi, 26, 872.

[6] Ibid.

[7] Ibid.

[8] Ibid., 875. Nor did this idea originate with Ockham. See V. Martin, Les Origines du Gallicanisme, 2 vols. (Paris, 1939), II, 17.

objected that in a corporation as in any body, natural or legal, all the members are expected to contribute, according to their function, to the health of the whole organism. If some members stop obeying the head, why should the label of schismatic not be placed upon the disobedient ones? [9]

Deschamps replied by switching metaphors, from the unity of the body to the responsibility of the shepherd for his flock. Before quoting him, however, the utility of these metaphors even in the modest crisis presented by the Blanchard affair should be recalled. D'Ailly had defined the university as a corporation with a right to tax its members and receive oaths of obedience from them.[10] He used the flock image to compare professors to pastors who are sent to preach, the chancellor to a foreman who authorizes them to do so, and the pope to a superior shepherd, whose labor the professors are ultimately doing.[11] With all discounts made for the drastic differences in the importance and nature of their situations, d'Ailly and Deschamps, in invoking the same metaphors, are employing the same rhetorical paradigms, the same figurative frames of reference, the same models of justification for opposition to superior authority. This, then, is how Deschamps treated the image of the flock:

> If the pope divides himself from the people, he sins in schism more than if the people were to divide themselves from him. And this is proved because . . . the pope is principally ordained to tend his sheep, [or] his subjects, and to unite them to one another in charity and to Christ, their true head and shepherd. And this is what it means to tend a flock. Therefore, if, against the condition and essence of his office, he does not bring them together and unify them, but disperses them and divides them from himself and even from each other, he sins more than the people in dividing themselves from him, because the sheep are not bound to gather him in, but vice versa.[12]

The vice versa opposition at the end of this passage is identical to the one used by d'Ailly when he stated that the man responsible for tending the flock should not charge the workers a fee for the labor of sending them to the fields, but rather is obliged to pay them for the work they are doing on his behalf. The point is different, but the model and structure of the arguments match.

---

[9] Cf. Mansi, 26, 843.
[10] Super, p. 281, l. 26-35 and above, pp. 170-1.
[11] Radix, pp. 218, 11 - 219, 4 and above, pp. 164-5.
[12] Mansi, 26, 875.

From Deschamp's synthesis of corporation theory and Gallicanism, the following conclusion may be drawn. Under certain conditions, when the pope harms his flock, the Church may deny him obedience (since he is no longer pope), and turn for refuge to the secular prince. In the context of 1398, this means that the French, or Gallican, Church would turn to the King of France.

Naturally such radical propositions were not accepted by all. Yet opponents of the Gallican idea argued within the same frame of reference. In commenting on the subtraction of obedience decreed by the council of 1398, Elie de Lestrange, Pierre d'Ailly's successor as Bishop of Le Puy, argued that the council's decision was meaningless because it was a decision of the Gallican Church, the clergy and King of France working as a body. Yet no such body exists, he claimed, and the action taken there is no more than a resolution passed by a number of individuals working together:

> For what is called "Gallican" is not a collective entity that could constitute a corporation or other body. And even if all the prelates and clerks of this kingdom were together, they would be many men as individuals and not as a whole. And the reason is that just as a material body cannot exist without a head, neither can an artificial one, for art imitates nature. And since all [prelates or clerics] in France do not, as Frenchmen or because of being in France, have any head specifically distinct from the head common to all the churches, which is the Roman church and its pontiff, . . . it is impossible for them to constitute a body; and so they cannot make statutes.[13]

Lestrange's argument is that French clerics or non-French ecclesiastics residing in France remain essentially churchmen and not Frenchmen. And although the King of France might be the head of the collective entity constituted by his kingdom, the clerics within it are members of the ecclesiastical corporation, the one Church, whose head is the Roman Church with its pope. Thus the French clergy cannot join

---

[13] *Allegaciones...Helie de Letrangiis*, Paris, B.N., ms. lat. 1475, f. 62ᵛ: "Et quod dicitur gallicana non est aliquod collegium, ut [ms: aut] universitatem vel aliud corpus constituat; etsi omnes prelati et clerici huius regni essent simul, essent plures ut singuli et non ut universi. Racio: quia sicut corpus materiale non potest esse sine capite, ita nec corpus... artis, quia ars imitatur naturam etc. Et cum omnes infra terminos Galliarum constituti ut tales non habeant aliquod caput ut Gallici vel infra Galliam constituti, quia Gallia non habet certum capud distinctum specifice a capite communi omnium ecclesiarum, quod est ecclesia Romana et eius pontifex, ... impossibile est quod ipsi faciant aliquod corpus; et ita nichil possunt statuere." Quoted by Kaminsky, "The Politics," p. 379, n. 67. My translation.

with the king to make binding legislation, because that would be an unnatural union of the members of one body with the head of another.

Even opponents of subtraction, therefore, were deriving their arguments from the same conceptual bases as its advocates. This intellectual framework was also used by d'Ailly in his speeches against Blanchard. It will be recalled that d'Ailly had argued that Blanchard could not take exactions from members of the university because the chancellor was not a part of its political order. The head of the university was the rector, and if the chancellor were to try to function as its head, he would impose a second head on the same body, and that would be monstrous!

The Blanchard affair gave d'Ailly the opportunity to extol the authority of the university at the expense not just of Clement VII, but, theoretically at least, of any pope, whose authority to regulate the studium would be limited by all the restrictions deriving from conciliar and Gallican ecclesiology. D'Ailly's use of the premises developed in fourteenth-century, critical, reformist political thought by William of Ockham, John of Paris, Marsilius of Padua, and certain leading canonists illustrates the degree to which the conduct of popes and cardinals in the schism had tainted the authority of the curia. Intellectuals were thereby encouraged to re-analyze the nature of the Church and recognize the desirability of corrective measures from elements outside of immediate papal circles. In his prosecution of Blanchard, therefore, d'Ailly participated in, and contributed to, the formation of a climate and the articulation of a vocabulary within which, and by means of which, an ideology for Church reform could be advanced.

The theoretical speculations for which the Blanchard affair was one occasion, as well as the recommended redistribution of authority among the component parts of the Church implicit in d'Ailly's speeches, emerged reinforced in both precision and political backing at the Council of Constance. In that revolutionary assembly, the suffrage was extended beyond cardinals and bishops to include professors of theology and canon law.[14] On the model of university constitutions, votes were not counted one to a delegate, but one to each of the four regions from which they were sent, the "Gallican,"

---

[14] N. Valois, *La France et le grand schisme d'occident*, 4 vols. (Paris, 1896-1902), IV, 270.

Italian, English, and German "nations." [15] Thus constituted, the representatives of the Church Universal removed three popes from office. The Council of Constance shows how quickly the universities, those privileged corporations, claimed and exploited their new share of the apostolic authority ineffectively wielded by the popes, whose right to its exclusive use had been cast into question by their sacrifice of the common good in favor of maintaining unchallenged personal rule during the Great Schism. D'Ailly's speeches against Blanchard were early explorations of the role theologians and their universities could potentially play within the Church.

---

[15] Delaruelle, *et al.*, I, 173-74.

APPENDIX

PIERRE D'AILLY'S SPEECHES AGAINST THE CHANCELLOR

A. Radix Omnium

Pierre d'Ailly's "Radix Omnium Malorum est Cupiditas" was published under the title "Tractatus I adversus Cancellarium Parisiensem" in 1706 by L. E. Dupin in Gerson's *Opera* (6 vols., Antwerp), I, cols. 723-44 (*siglum* d). In his edition Dupin used both the manuscripts that I know to contain the treatise: namely Paris, Bibliothèque Nationale, ms. lat. 3122, ff. 51-60ᵛ (*siglum* N) and Paris, Bibliothèque de l'Arsenal, ms. 520, ff. 74-86 (*siglum* A). Both manuscripts belonged in the Middle Ages to the College of Navarre. N is written in a clear chancellery cursive and appears to date from approximately 1400. A is an autograph copy, written out by d'Ailly himself in 1410-11.[1]

A's autograph status is derived from its relationship to Vatican Reginensis, ms. lat. 689B (formerly 689A), ff. 334-53, which has been identified as a notebook (now bound in a miscellaneous collection) into which d'Ailly occasionally copied texts of importance during the last 26 years of his life.[2] The notebook shows a remarkable stylistic development, whose stages can be measured by determining the earliest possible date at which successive texts could have been entered. The script of Arsenal 520 fits stylistically between texts in the notebook on f. 347 (copied after 1410)[3] and ff. 350ᵛ-53ᵛ (copied

---

[1] Alan E. Bernstein, "Pierre d'Ailly, John Blanchard and the 'licentia docendi' in the Fourteenth-Century University of Paris," (Diss., Columbia University, 1972), App. II, pp. 260-69, where the demonstration is worked out in detail. In his review of C. Samaran and R. Marichal, *Catalogue des manuscrits en écriture latine portant des indications de date, de lieu ou de copiste*, I (Paris, 1959), Gilbert Ouy asserted that Arsenal 520 is an autograph of Pierre d'Ailly, as well as Mazarine 934, Mazarine 935, and Cambrai 940 (*Bulletin des bibliothèques de France*, 1960, pp. 387-88). It should be noted that the descriptions of Arsenal 520 and Mazarine 934 and 935 in Samaran and Marichal (at pp. 269 and 398) warn against taking the signatures of d'Ailly that occur in these codices as evidence of their autograph character, but the demonstration may be made independently of this circumstantial evidence. I have endeavored to deal with this hesitation on pp. 270-72 of the dissertation.

[2] G. Ouy, *Le Recueil épistolaire autographe de Pierre d'Ailly et les notes d'Italie de Jean de Montreuil*. Umbrae Codicum Occidentalium, IX (Amsterdam. 1966), pp. v-xvi.

[3] Cf. f. 345ᵛ, which contains a text dated by d'Ailly as follows: "Apud tarasconem, xᵃ januarii Anni m°cccc°viiij° per me P. Episcopum Cameracensem, facta est sequens cedula." The date is 1410, n.s.

after June 18, 1414).[4] This four-year margin is reduced, however, by the reference to d'Ailly on f. 176 of Arsenal 520 as only Bishop of Cambrai, which means the manuscript antedates his elevation to the cardinalate in 1411. Thus Pierre d'Ailly copied Arsenal 520 in 1410 or 1411.

D'Ailly's autograph was followed by Dupin in most cases, since he resolved conflicting readings in favor of A 57 times and in favor of N only nineteen. Yet, despite the autograph character of A, its text is frequently shaky, for d'Ailly made many slips and was sometimes so elliptical that one must refer to N for clear readings. Like Dupin, therefore, I have followed A wherever possible, but have used N freely as a control, drawing on it whenever d'Ailly's errors or omissions made his autograph incomprehensible or excessively difficult.

The need for so eclectic an approach to an autograph should be illustrated in detail. In the two tables below, I present instances of superior readings first in one, then in the other manuscript. In both cases the preferable readings are in the right hand column.

Table I

Superior Readings in N

Readings in *A*	Readings in *N*
que damnat symonie vicium tanquam *licitum*, p. 199, l. 27.	que damnat symonie vicium tanquam *illicitum*
Symonia ostenditur *ens* illicita, p. 204, l. 9.	Symonia ostenditur *esse* illicita.
. . . qui [benivolentiam] venderet, vel illam nisi *precepto* pretio retraheret . . ., p. 205, l. 5.	. . . qui [benivolentiam] venderet, vel illam nisi *recepto* pretio retraheret. . . .
Potestas licenciandi in theologia est potestas spiritualis, que *potest* ex hoc [ ] in novo testamento hanc potestatem exercuit, p. 209, l. 5-7.	Potestas licenciandi in theologia est potestas spiritualis, que *patet* ex hoc, *quia Christus* in novo testamento hanc potestatem exercuit.
'ut mittat operarios in messem suam.' Idest *ad* predicatores, ad congregandum Ecclesiam. p. 218, l. 20-21.	'ut mittat operarios in messem suam.' Id est predicatores, ad congregandum Ecclesiam.
Laborat cancellarius pro *licencia* bacalarii non admissi sicut bacalarii licenciati. p. 226, l. 9-10.	Laborat cancellarius pro *examine* bachalarii non admissi sicut bachalarii licenciati.
Ideo *non* conceditur actio illi qui proponit in appreciatione alicuius rei se esse deceptum ultra medium justi precii. p. 227, l. 6-8.	Ideo *enim* conceditur actio illi qui proponit in appreciacione alicuius re se esse deceptum ultra medium justi precii.

[4] F. 353ᵛ: "Explicit epistola ad dominum papam iohannem xxiij. A Domino P. Cardinali Cameracensi. Data Basilee. Anno 1414. mense junii, die 18."

Table II

Superior Readings in A

Readings in N	*Readings in A*
Avaritia, quamvis in singulis sit detestabilis, singulariter tamen in *ecclesiasticis* viris. p. 198, 1. 1-2.	Avaritia, quamvis in singulis sit detestabilis, singulariter tamen in *declaratis viris.*
Peccatum *Symonie* fuit peccatum voluntatis. p. 201, 1. 22.	Peccatum *Symonis* fuit peccatum voluntatis.
Papa potest [ ] vicium symonie. p. 205, 1. 25.	Papa potest committere vicium symonie.
Cancellarius... non habet potius *ius* quam papa, cuius ipse est commissarius. p. 218, 1. 10.	Cancellarius... non habet potius quam papa, cuius ipse est commissarius.
Tenetur... premium reddere. p. 219, 1. 1.	Tenetur... premium *ei* reddere.
Pro licencia docendi *nullo* precium exigat. p. 222, 1. 11.	Pro licencia docendi *nullus* precium exigat.
Judei in Tholosa dixisse *creduntur* quod rabi fidei nostre fiunt per pecuniam. p. 229, 1. 12-14.	Judei in Tholosa dixisse *traduntur* quod rabi fidei nostre fiunt per pecuniam.
Ut peccandi tollatur occasio, et presumptio male *suspiciendi...* p. 230, 1. 25-26.	Ut peccandi tollatur occasio, et presumptio male *suscipiendi...*
Si eis vite necessaria *denegarent* que eis debentur... p. 234, 1. 14.	Si eis vite necessaria *denegarentur* que eis debentur...

The occurrence of superior readings in both manuscripts indicates that neither was copied from the other.

Further comparison of the two texts shows that in many instances the scribe of A tried to tighten the presentation by eliminating redundancies and favored elliptical expressions over fuller alternatives. A few examples follow. The words appearing in N omitted from A are enclosed in square brackets:

Ex qua conclusione et [ex] eius probatione (p. 210, 1. 31)
potestas [cancellarii] vel officium cancellarii (p. 215, 1. 15)
aut pro predicatione seu [pro] labore (p. 220, 1. 10-11)
Tercia conclusio [est] quod esto quod cancellarius pro labore suo exigere posset (p. 227, 1. 9-10)
quia, [ex] eo quod bacalarii fecerunt (p. 227, 1. 11-12)
In hiis omnibus [casibus] sollicite cavendum est (p. 229, 1. 4-5)

These are not random, involuntary errors, but the result of conscious effort. In fact, some changes go in the opposite direction, with just a word being added to clarify the exposition. In the following examples, the bracketed words were added in A:

> Quia [scilicet] per eam datur Spiritus Sanctus. (p. 208, l. 23)
> Ex quo [tertio] sequitur (p. 213, l. 13)

These cases, too, reflect an editorial effort. Although some of the changes do not seem for the better, they nonetheless illustrate both the fact and the extent of the variation. Some of the superfluous changes are listed below. The bracketed words are omitted in A:

> secundum [Sanctum] Thomam (p. 202, l. 4-5)
> pro aliqua [re] spirituali (p. 206, l. 3)
> et pro ista conclusione [est] expresse Durandus (p. 221, l. 10-11)
> Hoc idem [probatur] principaliter ex iure humano (p. 221, l. 14)
> Intentio iurium est prohibere non solum exigere pro licentia, sed [etiam]
>   pro labore (p. 221, l. 16-17)

The differences between A and N specified in these lists reflect divergent views of how the finished text should be presented. The scribe of N preferred a fuller, more explicit argumentation. D'Ailly sought a more concise, elliptical expression, emphasizing the subdivision of his treatise into component parts. This difference reinforces the inference that neither scribe copied from the other's text, but that both were working from a now lost exemplar, probably in the form of a rough draft or outline, probably also in d'Ailly's hand. This would explain the divergence in the two scribes' approach to introductory clauses like "Tertia conclusio [est] quod . . ." when the exemplar might only have had a numeral three. There is no mistake in either A or N that could not be explained as easily by a misreading of a common exemplar as by a misreading of the other surviving manuscript. The conjectural common exemplar would also explain those instances in which both A and N are wrong, especially in the misquotations of Scripture or the canon law citation "servitus indebite impensa."

The reader may well ask how an author copying his own text could produce a faultier version than another scribe. There is no easy answer; attempts to reconstruct the psychological state of the scribe at the moment of transcription are of dubious value. Certain observations, however, may sketch an approach to an answer. First, there is no need to assume that the inferential exemplar was in the author's handwriting. Admittedly, that is the most likely case, but it could have been based on the notes of a listener. Second, the paleographical evidence points to a date of execution for A of 1410-11, or at least 24 years after the delivery of the oration. Third, copying is mechanical work requiring patience and training. Although d'Ailly was a fine calligrapher, he did not have the hours and hours of practical exposure to the craft that would instill accuracy. It is clearly possible that an amateur scribe-author could produce a less accurate copy, even of his own text, than a skilled professional, though we should disregard changes made by the author less willingly than those made by a scribe.

Although Dupin correctly gave preference to A, my decisions in cases of conflicting readings in the two manuscripts were not always the same. Furthermore, there are shortcomings in his edition that are more than differences in judgment. Most important is his departure from the consensus of the manuscripts 165 times. His changes produce a better reading only twelve times, of which six are provided by the canonical text of Scripture. Dupin regularly transcribed "quare" as "igitur." He rarely handled a reference to canon law correctly, so that "i. q. iii. *Non solum*" emerges on one occasion as "id est *quasi in non solum*" (p. 199, l. 25). He was unable to identify "Ray." as Raymund of Peñafort or "Altiss." as Guillelmus Altissiodorensis (William of Auxerre).

B. Super Omnia

Dupin also published d'Ailly's second treatise, "Super Omnia Vincit Veritas," under the title "Tractatus II adversus Cancellarium Parisiensem," in Gerson's *Opera*, I, cols. 745-78. In his edition he used the autograph manuscript, Paris, Arsenal, ms. 520, ff. 86^v-105^v, which is the only one I know to contain the work. Publication of a unique manuscript is difficult, and I suspect that "Super Omnia" was transcribed for Dupin by a far more competent assistant than was the case in "Radix Omnium." In some instances I have followed Dupin's departures from the manuscript, but all changes are recorded.

C. The Edition

Because it is autograph, I have followed A in matters of spelling and word order and, in conflicting readings, whenever sense allowed. For the reason discussed above, however, it was necessary to control A with N, and I have chosen readings from N to clarify passages that are unintelligible or nearly so in A. It has seemed unwise to adhere so rigidly to A that the reader would be seriously inconvenienced, especially when contemporary alternatives are available.

All such choices are reflected in the apparatus. Dupin's departures from the consensus of the manuscripts have not been noted unless they are particularly suggestive, but his choice between variants is indicated. In "Super Omnia" I have treated Dupin's text as that of an inferior manuscript, and significant departures from Dupin are also recorded. Minor differences between A and N in spelling or word order are not identified. I have capitalized and punctuated according to my own judgment and modernized the use of "u" and "v." References to Dupin's edition are on the interior margins.

In the apparatus I have used the following abbreviations: *om* for *omisit*, *del* for *delevit*, *add* for *addidit*, *it* for *iteravit*, *in ras* for *in rasura* (partly erased or written over an erasure), and *interl* for *interlinearis*. *Corr ex* indicates a correction made by writing the preferred word directly upon the rejected one without erasing or deleting. The rejected word is the one out of which the correction emerges. Square brackets enclose words or letters omitted from all versions, but judged necessary by me. Because the variation between readings is usually so slight, I have not always felt it necessary to repeat the lemma in the apparatus. Unless there is indication to the contrary, the lemma is always the one word preceding the superscript letter referring to the apparatus.

When Pierre d'Ailly quoted another author, he rarely did so with exactly the words that appear in printed editions. Except for special instances, I have not distinguished between words that actually appear in an edition and words that do not, for such a refinement seems otiose unless we know precisely which manuscripts d'Ailly consulted. I have therefore used quotation marks when, according to my judgment, it was the author's intention to quote and the reader would be hindered by the lack of appropriate punctuation. Paraphrases do not have quotation marks, although closely quoted passages within them may be identified. Whenever possible, I have indicated the source of both quotations and paraphrases in the footnotes. In "Super Omnia" d'Ailly refers frequently to William of Rennes's gloss on Raymund of Peñafort's *Summa de Poenitentia*.[5] These quotations are usually linked with references to Raymund; thus, unless otherwise specified, William's words may be found in the same place as Raymund's.

---

[5] See below, p. 261 and note 88.

"RADIX OMNIUM MALORUM EST CUPIDITAS"

Sicut dicit Apostolus prime ad Timotheum, sexto capitulo [10], "Radix omnium malorum est cupiditas, quam quidam appetentes erraverunt a ᵃ fide et inseruerunt se doloribus multis." In quibus verbis crimen cupiditatis gravissimum ostenditur, specialiter propter tria, nam eius radix est malorum productiva, est erroris 5 inductiva, et doloris impressiva.

723, 11   Primo ergo, cupiditas, quantum ad affectum ᵇ, est productiva malorum culpabilium, quia sicut caritas est mater omnium virtutum, sic cupiditas omnium viciorum, et ᶜ sicut radix fomentum prestat omnibus partibus arboris, sic diviciarum cupiditas singulis 10 peccatis. Ideo premittit quod "radix omnium malorum est cupiditas."

723, 18   Secundo, cupiditas, quantum ad intellectum, est inductiva erroris infidelium quia enim "abyssus abyssum invocat," [1] hinc fit ut abyssus cupiditatis quosdam trahat in abyssum infidelitatis. 15 Hoc autem ideo contingit quia, ut ait Ambrosius super Lucam, "furor cupiditatis ita mentem animumque perturbat ut compos sui esse non possit," [2] propter quod dicit Apostolus quod "quidam cupiditatem appetentes," id est, ex cupiditate divitias amantes, "erraverunt a fide." [3]   20

723, 27   Tertio, cupiditas, quantum ad effectum, est impressiva doloris penalium, nam totus cupiditatis effectus nichil aliud est quam labor, timor, et dolor, eo quod divitie cum labore acquiruntur, cum timore custodiuntur, cum dolore relinquuntur, et plerumque in dolorum pene perpetue convertuntur. Unde, propter hoc, de 25 cupidis subdit Apostolus quod "inseruerunt se doloribus multis."

723, 35   Licet autem ista latius possent declarari, quia tamen satis clara sunt ᵈ, ad alia declaranda festinat intentio, ideo ex premissis hoc

---

ᵃ a: *text Vulg* N *om* A
ᵇ effectum Ad

ᶜ et *it* A
ᵈ et (*post* sunt) *add* N

---

[1] Ps. 41, 8.
[2] Cf. S. Ambrosius Mediolanensis, *Expositio Evangelii Secundum Lucam*, VI, 31, ed. C. Schenkel in C. S. E. L. XXXII (Vindobonae, 1902), p. 244, 12-18.
[3] I Tim. 6, 10.

ad presens notasse sufficiat quod cupiditas et avaritia, quamvis in
singulis sit detestabilis, singulariter tamen in declaratis ᵉ viris;
nam sicut ibidem ait glosa, "Nichil tam asperum tamque per-
niciosum quam si vir ecclesiasticus, maxime qui sublimem tenet
5 locum, divitiis studeat, quia non solum sibi ipsi sed ceteris
hominibus obest ᶠ." ⁴

Hec ergo Reverendi Patres et Domini, ideo vestris reverentiis 723, 45
proposui, quia licet ab antiquissimis temporibus radix cupiditatis
longe lateque pululaverit, propter quod olim per prophetam
10 dictum est ,"a minori usque ad maiorem omnes avaritie stu/dent 724
et a propheta usque ad sacerdotem cuncti faciunt dolum." Jeremie
6, 8. Nunc tamen, proch dolor, hiis diebus novissimis, hec radix
pessima palmites suos tam periculose diffudit, ut non solum
rurales agros, sed eciam agrum scientie purgatissimum, ipsum
15 scilicet venerabile ᵍ Universitatis Parisiensis Collegium, fraudulen-
ter occupaverit ipsiusque fructus uberrimos impedire nisa sit.
Nam quidam, ut fama refert, in ea per cupiditatem erravit a fide,
qui per avaritiam non solum gratuita scientie dona et scientiarum
gradus liberrimos pecunia venales effecit, sed eciam, ut suum
20 excuset errorem, contra fidei veritatem quosdam iniustos huius
avaritie ʰ et venalitatis modos tanquam licitos et honestos approbare
conatur. Huic itaque erronee opinioni occurrendum fore existimavi A f. 74ᵛ
/ et ideo presens opus licet meis inproportionatum viribus assumere
dignum duxi.

25   Ad hoc autem triplex me ⁱ ratio impulit: primo, zelus veritatis 724, 18
et confutatio predicti erroris; secundo, obedientia matris mee
universitatis que pluries concorditer deliberaverit quod magistri
de hac materia tractarent in actibus scolasticis. Ego autem licet
omnium minimus prius incepi ut, iuxta similitudinem Orosii in
30 Prologo de Ormesta Mondi ad Augustinum, parvus canis venaticius
maiores ac potentiores canes excitet ad venandum.⁵ Tercio, causa
exercicii et proprie eruditionis, quia enim ex concordi deliberatione

---

ᵉ ecclesiasticis N   ʰ modos (*post* avaritie) *del* N
ᶠ obest *ex* abest *corr* A   ⁱ me *it* N
ᵍ venale d

---

⁴ *Biblia Sacra cum Glossis*, 6 vols. (Venetiis, 1588), G. O., I Tim. 6, 10 *ad verb.*
"Haec fuge."
⁵ Cf. Paulus Orosius, *Historiarum Adversum Paganos Libri VII*, ed. Carolus
Zangemeister, in *Corpus Scriptorum Ecclesiasticorum Latinorum*, vol. V (Vindobonae, 1882), pp. 1-2.

dicte universitatis, deputatus fui ad proponendum in Parlamento
super materia fidei, in casu quo oporteret declarare et sustinere
quedam in hac materia, ex parte dicte universitatis proposita. Ideo
N f. 51ᵛ expediens iudicavi / ad exercicium et eruditionem meam ᵏ questionem inferius proponendam scolastice pertractare, presuppositis 5
tamen quibus ¹ protestationibus. Prima est quod nichil intendo
724, 40 dicere ad iniuriam cancellarii Parisiensis aut alterius cuiuscumque,
sed solum ad tuitionem et deffensionem iusticie ᵐ cause nostre.
Secunda ⁿ, quod nichil intendo determinative aut diffinitive
asserere nisi ea solum que in Scriptura Sacra aut alia authentica seu 10
in doctoribus approbatis continentur, vel ex eis clare sequuntur;
reliqua vero solum probabiliter recitare. Tercia, quod illa que de
hac materia scripsi, eciam in scripto proponere disposui, ne ad-
725 versarii veritatis me aliud dixisse imponant quam dicam. Et / eciam
ut ea que dicturus sum correctioni et emendationi singulorum ad 15
725, 3 quos spectat patenter subiciam. Quibus premissis accedo ad
questionem, que talis est: Utrum hereticum sit dicere quod liceat
pro docendi licencia pecuniam dare vel recipere.

725, 5 Arguitur primo quod sic, quia dare vel recipere pecuniam pro
licentia docendi est symoniacum. Sed hereticum est dicere quod 20
aliquod factum symoniacum sit licitum, igitur etc. Maior patet
quia sic dare vel recipere est commutare temporale pro spirituali,
cum scientia sit spiritualis et licentia docendi scientiam sit potestas
seu auctoritas spiritualis. Nam "scientia donum Dei est, unde vendi
non potest," i. q. iii, *Non solum*.⁶ Sed minor probatur, tum primo, 25
quia sic dicere est expresse dicere contra fidem, que dampnat
symonie vitium tamquam illicitum ᵒ, sicut patet Act. 8, 20. Et per
consequens dicere ipsum esse licitum est hereticum. Tum secundo,
quia symonia est heresis, nam Gregorius in Registro hoc vicium
vocat "symoniacam heresim" ⁷ et iura dicunt quod "inter crimina 30
ecclesiastica, symoniaca heresis primum optinet locum," ut i. q.
ult., *Patet*.⁸ Eciam Magister Sententiarum, libro quarto, distin-

---

ᵏ in eam Ad
ˡ aliquibus N quibusdam d
ᵐ justissime N

ⁿ est (*post* Secunda) *add* N
ᵒ licitum A

---

⁶ *Corpus Juris Canonici*, ed. E. Friedberg, 2 vols. (Leipzig, 1879), I, *Gratiani Decretum*, C.1 q.3 c.11; col. 417.
⁷ *Sancti Gregorii Magni Registri Epistolarum*, Lib. IV, Ep. 13; PL 77, 683.
⁸ Gratian, C.1 q.7 c.27.

ctione 25ᵃ, dicit quod "de symoniacis non est ambigendum quin sint heretici."⁹ Et per consequens, a fortiori, symoniam approbare dicendo aliquod factum clare symoniacum esse licitum est hereticum.

Oppositum tamen arguitur, quia Cancellarius Ecclesie Parisiensis 725, 29
5 dicit quod licenciandi licite dant sibi pecuniam et quod ipse licite recipit eam. Sed quod hoc sit pro licentia docendi patet quia ex eo / quod ipsi iuraverunt nichil dare pro licentia, ipse eos licenciare A. f 75 recusat, exigens eciam cautionem et securitatem de pecunia danda.

Sed ipso notorie sic dicente et faciente, papa et Ecclesia Romana
10 non ignorantes, eum sub dissimulatione permittunt impunitum, quod non facerent si sic dicere esset hereticum aut sic facere symoniacum, igitur etc.

Circa hanc materiam sic procedam. Primo, respondebo ad 725, 41 formam proposite questionis. Secundo reprobabo quasdam frau-
15 dulentas cavillationes et sophisticas responsiones adverse partis, quibus scilicet prefatus cancellarius utitur ad excusandas excusationes in peccatis.

Quantum ad primum principale, pro responsione questionis 725, 50 proposite, tres intendo conclusiones probare. Prima, quod dare
20 vel recipere pecuniam pro licentia docendi theologiam est proprie symoniacum. Secunda, quod sic dare vel recipere pro huiusmodi licentia est contra ius naturale et divinum. Tercia, quod dicere quod sic dare vel recipere sit licitum est hereticum. Ad probationem autem prime conclusionis et omnium sequentium declarationum,
25 tria sunt consideranda ᴾ: primo, quid sit symonia; secundo, quibus rationibus ostenditur esse illicita; tercio, quomodo ex hiis concluditur quod sit symoniacum dare vel recipere pecuniam pro licentia docendi in theologia.

Prima Conclusio Principalis

30 De primo ergo sciendum est quod, secundum Dominum Altis- 725, 70 siodorensem in Somma sua, Libro quarto, et Sanctum Thomam, Secunda Secunde et super Quarto Sentenciarum, d. 25, symonia describitur, quod est "studiosa voluntas emendi / vel vendendi N f. 52

ᴾ declaranda (*ante* consideranda) *del* N

---

⁹ *Petri Lombardi Libri IV Sententiarum*, 2 vols. (ad Claras Aquas, 1916), Lib. IV, d. 25, cap. 2; II, p. 909.

aliquid spirituale vel spi/rituali annexum." [10] Et secundum
726 Raymundum, "non oportet addere 'spirituali annexum', quia
spirituali annexum spirituale est, ut i. q. iii, *Si quis*." [11] Sed in
hoc dicto insistere non curo, quia magis esset difficultas vocalis
quam realis.   5
726, 6 In predicta vero descriptione notantur tria. Primo, illud [q] est
principale in hoc peccato, quia omne peccatum in actu vel habitu
voluntatis principaliter consistit, et ex hoc completur, quod ex
electione procedit. Unde talem actum voluntatis, ex electione
procedentem, prima clausula importat, quia dicitur "studiosa   10
voluntas." Unde concluditur quod, sicut dicit Dominus Altissiodorensis, "illi decretiste erraverunt, qui dixerunt quod non est
symonia, nisi ubi est pactum expressum exterius. Nam in prima
symonia non fuit aliqua pactio [r], sicut patet de Symone Mago [s]
in Novo Testamento et de Giezi puero Helisei prophete in Vetero   15
Testamento, qui primo leguntur symoniam commisisse:" [12] primus,
scilicet, volendo dare, Actuum 8, 18, secundus vero volendo
recipere, sicut patet IV Regum 5, 20. Unde de Symone legitur, non
quod emerit seu pactum fecerit, sed quod optulit apostolis
pecuniam dicens, "date michi hanc potestatem ut cuicumque   20
imposuero manus accipiat Spiritum Sanctum," [13] etc. Et sic apparet
quod peccatum [t] Symonis [v] fuit peccatum [x] voluntatis, qua,
scilicet, emere voluit et precium optulit, scilicet, ex voluntate
deliberata. Ideo, dixit ei Petrus, "Roga Deum si forte dimittatur
tibi hec cogitatio [y] cordis tui." [14] Non enim dixit "hec oblatio,"   25
sed "hec cogitatio," id est, deliberata volitio.
726, 32 Ulterius patet quare hoc peccatum [z] magis denominatur symonia

[q] quod (*post* illud) *add* N   [v] Symonie N
[r] pactio: *ex* compactio *corr* N   [x] pactum d
[s] mago: *interl* A   [y] *in ras* A
[t] pactum d   [z] pactum d

[10] Guillermus Altissiodorensis (William of Auxerre), *Summa Aurea in Quattuor Libros Sententiarum* (Paris, 1500), f. 226ᵛa. Thomas Aquinas, *Summa Theologica*, II, II, q. 100, art. 1, in *Opera Omnia* 25 vols. (Parma, 1852-1872), III, 362. Cf. *Commentum in IV Libros Sententiarum*, IV, d. 25, q. 3, (*Ibid.*), VII, 914.
[11] Raymundus de Peniafort, *Summa . . . de Poenitentia et Matrimonio* (Rome, 1603), 3a, who cites Gratian, C.1 q.3 c.7.
[12] Altiss. f. 229ʳa.
[13] Act. 8, 19.
[14] *Ibid.*, v. 22.

a Symone qui spirituale voluit emere, quam / "giezia" a Giezi qui A f. 75
spirituale voluit vendere. Una enim ratio est, secundum Altissiodorensem, "quia magis peccavit Symon Magus quam Giezi,
eo quod tempore revelate gratie peccavit." [15] Alia est secundum a
5 Thomam, "quia Symon Magus ad hoc spiritualem potestatem
emere voluit, ut b eam postea venderet. Unde dicitur i. q. 3,
quod 'Donum Spiritus Sancti emere voluit ut ex venditione signorum, que per eum fierent, multiplicatam c pecuniam lucraretur.' " [16]
Et sic tam volentes emere quam volentes vendere conformantur
10 Symoni, sed primi conformantur ei in actu, secundi vero in intentione. Illi autem qui spiritualia vendunt in actu imitantur Giezi,
discipulum Helisei, de quo legitur quod accepit pecuniam a
Naaman Syro per Helyseum a lepra mondato. Unde tales non
solum d dici possunt symoniaci, sed eciam giezite.
15 Secundo, principaliter in dicta descriptione notatur materia 726, 5
proxima huiusmodi peccati, seu ipsius actus exterior, circa quem
cadit actus predictus voluntatis interior, scilicet emptio vel
venditio. Ideo dicitur "voluntas emendi vel vendendi." Hic
autem, ut dicit Sanctus Thomas, "nomine emptionis et venditionis
20 intelligitur omnis contractus non gratuitus." [17] Tamen Raymundus
excipit contractum permutationis.[18]
Tercio, notatur materia remota, scilicet obiectum predicte 726, 6(
emptionis vel venditionis per hoc quod dicitur "spirituale vel
spirituali annexum." Hic autem per "spirituale" non intelligitur
25 Spiritus Sanctus, quia nec Symon Magus, a quo symonia dicitur,
Spiritum Sanctum emere voluit, sicut quidam ymaginantur, sed
potestatem dandi Spiritum Sanctum. Unde non dixit "date michi
Spiritum Sanctum," sed "date michi hanc potestatem ut cuicumque
imposuero manus accipiat Spiritum Sanctum."
30 Per spirituale vero, secundum Altissiodorensem, intelligitur 726, 70
illud "quo habetur Spiritus Sanctus, vel quo datur, vel quo haberi
aut dari significatur: quo habetur sicut virtus, quo datur sicut

---

a Sanctum (ante Thomam) add N   c multam d
b ex vendicione signorum (ante eam)   d non solum: solum non N
del N

---

[15] Altiss., f. 229ra.
[16] Tho., II, II, q. 100, art. 1, ad 4, quoting Gratian, C.1 q.3 c.8.
[17] Ibid., art. 1, ad 5.
[18] Ray., p. 5, col. 1.

727 sacramentum, quo haberi significatur sicut donum prophetie / aut potestas faciendi miracula." [19] Unde, secundum eum, ista quatuor tantum proprie sunt spiritualia. Tamen secundum Ricardum, Libro 10, *De Questionibus Armenorum*, convenientius videtur esse

N f. 52ᵛ dicendum / quod non solum illa quatuor sunt spiritualia, sed 5 generaliter omne illud intelligitur esse spirituale quod est "donum Dei gratuitum aut eius effectus sive fructus. Dicitur autem donum Dei gratuitum donum supernaturale, scilicet quod ex puris naturalibus haberi non potest." [20] Et huic consonat responsio Petri quam dedit Symoni Mago, dicens " 'pecuniam 10 tecum sit in perditionem,' et causam subiunxit, 'quoniam donum Dei existimasti pecunia possideri.' Non enim dixit 'hoc donum,' scilicet potestatem dandi Spiritum Sanctum ᵉ, sed generaliter dixit 'donum Dei,' ostendens omnem emptionem seu voluntatem emendi quodcumque donum Dei, scilicet gratuitum et supernaturale, esse 15 peccatum et demeritorium perditionis." [21]

727, 20 Multa autem sunt huiusmodi dona Dei quibus non habetur nec datur nec dari aut haberi significatur Spiritus Sanctus, sicut donum sapientie aut scientie aut prophetie, que dantur multis eciam malis, qui nec habent aut dant Spiritum Sanctum nec potestatem ipsum 20

A f. 76 dandi receperunt. Et tamen illa dona / ponit Apostolus inter dona Dei gratuita, I Cor. 12, 10. Et sic ab illo peccato Symonis non solum voluntas emendi potestatem spiritualem dandi Spiritum Sanctum dicitur symonia, sed eciam voluntas sola, seu voluntas cum oblatione precii emendi vel vendendi donum Dei gratuitum 25 aut eius effectum sive fructum, sicut ab illa specie superbie quam Lucifer ᶠ exercuit totum genus peccati superbie "luciferia" posset dici. Et sic patet quid in proposito per spirituale debet intelligi.

727, 36 Per annexum vero spirituali intelligere possumus omne illud quod alicui competit ratione doni spiritualis, sic quod sublato illo 30 spirituali illud annexum non competeret ei, sicut prebenda aut beneficium ecclesiasticum alicui convenit ratione alicuius potestatis spiritualis, sicut potestatis evangelizandi aut alicuius alterius doni

---

ᵉ Spiritus Sancti Ad   ᶠ Lucifer: *ex* Luci de *corr* A

---

[19] Altiss., f. 226ʳa.
[20] Richardus Armachanus (Richard Fitzralph, Bishop of Armagh), *Summa in Questionibus Armenorum* (Paris, 1511), Lib. X, cap. 9 & 16; ff. 76ᵛb & 78ᵛ a & b.
[21] *Ibid.*, cap. 13, f. 77ᵛb, quoting Act. 8, 20.

spiritualis. Aliter talia non proprie ecclesiastica dicerentur, sicut dicit Ricardus, ubi supra. Qui ergo talia annexa inseparabiliter spiritualibus vendunt vel emunt, spiritualia vendere aut emere concluduntur, quia "quicumque eorum alterum vendit sine quo 5 nec alterum provenit neutrum invenditum derelinquit," ut i. q. iii, *Si quis obiecerit* [22] et habetur Quarto Sententiarum, 25 d.,[23] et sic patet quid sit symonia et hoc de primo.

De secundo vero, scilicet quibus rationibus symonia ostenditur 727, 51 esse [g] illicita, sciendum est quod propter quattuor rationes illicitum 10 est dona Dei gratuita, seu ipsorum effectus vel fructus aut eis inseparabiliter annexa, vendere vel emere, seu velle ea temporali precio commutare. Prima ratio sumitur ex parte Dei principaliter dantis; secunda, ex parte ministri ministerialiter conferentis; tercia, ex parte doni impreciabilis; quarta, ex parte recipientis.

15 Prima ergo ratio est ex parte Dei principalis auctoris, qui est 727, 57 summe potens et summe dives ac nullius egens, iuxta illud Psalmi [15, 2], "bonorum meorum non eges," et ideo lucro mercationis non indiget, nec talis [h] mercatio ei congruit, sed eius gratuitam largitatem quantum in se est, dehonestat. Unde ipse dixit "gratis 20 accepistis, gratis date," Matt. 10, 8, quare, etc.

Secunda ratio est ex parte ministri, scilicet ipsius nuda potestas 727, 71 ministerialis, quia huiusmodi donum suum non est, sed Dei, qui ipsum gratis tribuit. Ideo, si pro illo recipit, cum hoc ad utilitatem do/mini omnipotentis recipere non possit et ipse non sit illius 728 25 dominus sed minister et dispensator, iuxta illud Apostoli I Cor. 4, 1: "Sic vos [i] existimet homo ut ministros Christi et dispensatores ministrorum Dei," sequitur quod ad suum privatum commodum recipit alienum, quia precium, si quod erat, Dei esse debebat, quare etc.

30 Tercia ratio est ex parte doni impreciabilis, quia precio terreno 728, 8 non potest comparari, sicut de sapientia dicitur Proverb. 3, 15, quod "est pretiosior cunctis opibus, et alia desiderabilia ei non valent comparari." Ideo Petrus reprehendebat Symonem "quia donum Dei estimabat pecunia possideri."

---

[g] ens A   [i] vos: nos *Text Vulg* nos *ex* vos
[h] *it* N   *corr* N   nos d

---

[22] Gratian, C.1 q.3 c.7.
[23] P. Lomb., IV, 25, 4; vol. II, p. 910.

28, 14   Quarta ratio est ex parte recipientis, / quia scilicet in collatione
N f. 53 donorum Dei gratuitorum ministri Ecclesie recipienti ea nichil
de suo preter benivolentiam voluntatis impendunt, sed ex lege
nature omni homini [k] benivolentiam tenemur impendere. Ergo,
A f. 76ᵛ qui illam venderet, / vel illam nisi recepto [1] precio retraheret, 5
legem nature de benivolentia proximo impendenda impie violaret.[24]

28, 22   Ex hiis rationibus primo sequitur quod, licet Petrus dixerit [m]
Symoni, "Peccunia tua," etc., "quia existimasti donum Dei pecunia possideri," tamen idem ei dixisset de quolibet alio munere
temporali, cum rationes eciam predicte hoc concludant, quare hic 10
nomine pecunie intelligitur non solum pecunia proprie dicta, seu
nummisma, sed, secundum Sanctum Thomam, intelligitur omne
illud cuius precium pecunia potest mensurari seu nummismate
adequari.[25] Unde a mensurando nummisma dicitur, secundum
Philosophum, IV [n] *Ethicorum*.[26] Et ideo sive propter servitium, 15
vel obsequium, aut preces dominorum, vel favorem humanum,
aut aliquod huiusmodi principaliter darentur dona spiritualia, esset
proprie symonia. Unde secundum Gregorium super illo loco Ysaie,
"Beatus qui excutit manus suas ab omni munere," [27] triplex munus
distinguitur: scilicet munus a manu, sicut pecunia; munus ab 20
obsequio, sicut servitus indebite inpensa [o]; munus a lingua, sicut
favor, ut i. q. i, *Sunt nonnulli*.[28]

28, 42   Secundo. Ex radice secunde rationis potest inferri, secundum [p]
Thomam, *Secunda Secunde* et super *Quatuor Sententiarum*, d. 25, art. 3,
quasi quod "papa potest committere [q] vicium symonie sicut et 25
quilibet alius homo," ymo, secundum eum, "hoc peccatum tanto
in eius persona esset gravius, quanto maiorem optinet locum."
Et ideo, ut dicit, "opinio illa est erronea quorumdam qui dixerunt
quod papa non potest committere symoniam, ex eo quia res

---

[k] recipienti (*ante* homini) *add* A (*post* homini) *add* N *om* d
[1] precepto A percepto d
[m] dixit Ad
[n] V AN 6 d

[o] servitus indebite inpensa: *Ed Gra-tiani* servitus debite impensa A servitus debite non impensa N servitus debitae impensa d
[p] Sanctum (*ante* Thomam) *add* N
[q] *om* N

---

[24] Richardus, Lib. X, cap. 9, f. 76ᵛb.
[25] Tho., II, II, q. 100, art. 2. Cf. in 4º *Sent.*, d. 25, q. 3, art. 3.
[26] Aristotle, *Nichomachean Ethics*, Book IV, Chap. I, 1119b, 26-27.
[27] Isaiah 36, 15.
[28] Gregory quoted in Gratian, C.1 q.1 c.114.

ecclesie sunt sue." Nam quamvis "res ecclesie sint eius tamquam principalis dispensatoris, non tamen sunt eius ut domini et possessoris. Et ideo, si reciperet pro aliqua re ʳ spirituali pecuniam, non careret vicio symonie."[29]

5 Tercio. Ex prima et tercia rationibus sequitur quod licet pro 728, 5ᵇ dono temporalis elemosine Deus det spiritualem thesaurum vite eterne, iuxta illud Mathei 19, 21, "Vade et vende omnia que habes et da pauperibus et habebis thesaurum in celis," non tamen hoc dat pro ipsa elemosina temporali, sed pro merito spirituali, nec 10 dat pro merito quasi pro precio, quia meritum ˢ non est equivalens premio. Et ideo ibi non est emptio vel venditio proprie dicta, sed impropria et methaphorica. Quemadmodum eciam in Ysaia legitur "Omnes sitientes venite ad aquas, venite et emite absque argento et absque ulla commutatione," etc.[30] Unde distinguenda 15 est duplex emptio doni spiritualis: una bona, alia mala. Bona est licet improprie dicta, scilicet, ipsum meritum quod est opus acceptum Deo pro dono spirituali optinendo, sine tamen commutatione offerre, iuxta verbum Prophete. Mala vero est emptio bonum aliquod corporale aut temporale pro spirituali dono cum 20 voluntate commutandi offerre aut dare, vel velle offerre aut dare. Et hanc detestatur Scriptu/ra et non primam. Et sic dampnatur 729 peccatum Symonis non solum quia emere voluit donum Dei, sed quia illicito et incongruo precio per commutationem ipsum voluit possidere.

25 Quarto. Ex radice quarte rationis sequitur quod pro benivolentia 729, 5 voluntatis illius qui confert donum spirituale, licitum est recipienti postea munus offerre vel dare, non tamen conferenti licet exigere scilicet rigorose. Unde, sicut legitur IV Reg. 5, 24, Naaman Syrus Heliseo pecuniam / optulit et Giezi petenti eam dedit. Nec de hoc A f. 77 30 Naaman culpatur, quia ante pecunie dationem aut sponsionem donum Dei recipit, quod vero postea fecit, laudabilis gratitudinis fuit. Sed factum Giezi dampnatur, licet post donum Dei impensum peccuniam receperit. Ratio diversitatis est, secundum Ricardum, libro preallegato, quia "recipiens donum Dei ex dupplici causa

---

ʳ pro aliqua re spirituali: pro aliqua   ˢ nostrum (*post* meritum) *add* N
spirituali A   pro aliquo spirituali d

[29] Tho., II, II, q. 100, art. 1, *ad* 7. Conflated with *Comm. in Sent.*, IV, d. 25, art. 3, *ad* 2.
[30] Isaiah 55, 1.

potest rependere pecuniam sive aliud genus muneris: vel propter
f. 53�v ipsum donum Dei receptum, vel benivolentiam / largientis—
propter benivolentiam potest pro viribus et tenetur vicem rependere, licet non propter donum. Conferens autem nec pro ipso
dono nec pro benivolentia aliquid ᵗ potest exigere," ³¹ ut dictum 5
est, quare etc. Et hec de secundo.

29, 25 De tercio scilicet ᵛ, quomodo ex predictis concluditur quod sit
symoniacum dare vel recipere pecuniam pro licentia docendi in
theologia, sciendum est quod circa hoc quatuor sunt declaranda:
primum est quod theologia est donum Dei spirituale; secundum, 10
quod doctrina, seu predicatio ipsius, est res spiritualis; tercium,
quod licentia seu potestas vel auctoritas docendi vel predicandi
eam est auctoritas spiritualis; quartum ˣ, quod potestas licenciandi
in ea est spiritualis potestas. Ex quibus clare sequitur quod pro
quocumque istorum dare vel recipere pecuniam est proprie 15
symoniacum.

29, 40 Prima propositio patet quia secundum Altissiodorensem ʸ
aliquid donum Dei dicitur spirituale dupliciter secundum quod
Spiritus Sanctus habetur duobus modis. Uno modo habetur ut
inflammans affectum, et sic habetur per virtutes et sacramenta. 20
Alio modo habetur ut illuminans intellectum, et sic habetur per
scientiam. Ideo dicitur spiritualis. Unde ipse concludit quod emere
vel vendere quamcumque scientiam symoniacum est, sed secundum
diversos gradus scientiarum est minor vel maior symonia.³² Sed
quidquid sit de hoc et quidquid dicendum sit de aliis scientiis, 25
tamen non est dubium de theologia quin ipsa sit donum dei
spirituale ᶻ et quin, proprie loquendo, sit symoniacum ipsam
vendere vel emere. Quod clare patet, quia Apostolus, I Cor. 12,
8, ipsam primo loco enumerat inter dona Dei spiritualia dicens,
"Alii autem per spiritum datur sermo sapientie, alii autem sermo 30
scientie secundum eundem spiritum," etc. Theologia, autem,
proprie dicitur sapientia, cum sapientia sit de divinis, secundum
Aristotelem, VI *Ethicorum*.³³ Et ideo non solum in Novo Testa-

---

ᵗ re (*post* aliquid) *del* N   ʸ *in ras* A
ᵛ *om* N   ᶻ proprie (*ante* spirituale) *add* N
ˣ est (*post* quartum) *add* N

---

³¹ Richardus, Lib. X, cap. 22, f. 80ʳa.
³² Altiss., f. 230ʳa.
³³ Chap. 7, 1141b, 3-7.

mento sed eciam in Veteri prohibitum est ipsam vendere vel emere
juxta illud Prov. 23ᵃ, 23: "Noli vendere sapientiam," etc. Igitur, etc.

   Secunda propositio, scilicet quod doctrina seu predicatio 729, 6.
theologie est res spiritualis, patet ex hoc, quia Christus, Matt.
5 10, 8, ubi dicit, "gratis accepistis, gratis date," immediate ante
premisit illa spiritualia gratis danda, et inter illa primo ponit
doctrinam seu predicationem theologice sapientie cum dixit
apostolis: "Euntes autem predicate dicentes quoniam appro-
pinquabit regnum celorum. Infirmos curate" ³⁴ etc. Unde clare
10 patet doctrinam seu predicationem huiusmodi non esse venalem,
sed gratis exhibendam. Ideo Sapiens, postquam dixit "Noli vendere
sapientiam," addidit "neque doctrinam," ³⁵ clare innuens quod,
sicut divina sapientia, sic eius predicatio seu doctrina nullatenus 730
est vendenda, quia est res spiritualis nullo terreno precio com-
15 parabilis, eodem dicente quod "Sapiencia preciosior est cunctis
opibus," etc. Prover. 3, 15. Quare etc. ᵇ /   A f. 77

   Tercia propositio, scilicet quod licentia seu potestas vel auctoritas 730, 5
docendi vel predicandi theologiam est auctoritas spiritualis, patet
quia actus huiusmodi potestatis vel auctoritatis, scilicet doctrina
20 vel predicatio, est res spiritualis, ut iam dictum est. Ergo huiusmodi potestas vel auctoritas est spiritualis. Unde dicit Altissiodorensis quod "predicatio est spiritualis et eciam annexa spirituali.
Spiritualis quia scilicet ᶜ per eam ᵈ datur Spiritus Sanctus, et est
annexa spirituali, scilicet ordini, quia sacerdotum est proprie ᵉ
25 predicare, vel ad minus ordinatorum," ³⁶ quod ᶠ intelligo non
solum de ordinatis in Ordine Sacro sed eciam in ordine Ierarchico,
id est, missorum et approbatorum ad predicandum auctoritate
Apostolica pro universali Ecclesia, juxta illud Apostoli, "Quomodo predicabunt nisi mittantur?" Rom. 10, 15. Et ideo patet quod
30 huiusmodi missio ad predicandum, que nichil aliud est quam
licentia ad docendum, est potestas spiritualis, que ᵍ non potest

---

ᵃ 24 AN
ᵇ Quare etc. *it* A
ᶜ scilicet *om* N
ᵈ ipsam N

ᵉ proprie: *Ed Altiss om* Ad
ᶠ non (*post* quod) *del* N
ᵍ quare N

---

³⁴ Matt. 10, 7.
³⁵ Prov. 23, 23.
³⁶ Altiss., f. 226ᵛb.

esse licite venalis. Unde Altissiodorensis,[37] querens utrum cancellarius vendens potestatem docendi sit symoniacus, respondet quod

◁ f. 54 sic, quod maxime verum est de potestate do/cendi in theologia, ut patet ex dictis. Quare etc.

▶30, 29   Quarta propositio est quod potestas licenciandi in theologia est 5 potestas spiritualis, que patet [h] ex hoc quia Christus [i] in Novo Testamento hanc potestatem exercuit, quando Apostolos in theologia licenciavit dicens, "Ite, docete omnes gentes," etc. Math. 28, 19, et prius, Math. 10, 7, "Euntes autem predicate," etc. ubi subdit "Gratis accepistis, gratis date." Unde Apostoli 10 ibidem receperunt a Christo non solum licentiam seu potestatem docendi et predicandi, sed eciam pro se et suis successoribus receperunt potestatem alios licenciandi ad docendum theologiam et predicandum. Et ibi docuit eos Christus et eorum successores, scilicet papam et eius commissarios in hac parte, quod huiusmodi 15 potestatem spiritualem non poterant vendere, sed sicut eam gratis acceperant [k], ipsam tenebantur gratis dare.[38] Quare patet quod pro ea pecuniam dare vel recipere est proprie symoniacum. Unde super predicto verbo "Euntes predicate" etc. dicit Glossa Ordinaria, "Ne Iudas, qui loculos habebat, de predicta potestate pecuniam 20 congregare vellet, nequiciam eius supprimit Dominus, dicens: 'Gratis accepistis' etc. et dampnat hic perfidiam symoniace hereseos." [39] Et sic apparet clare prima conclusio.

Secunda Conclusio Principalis

▶30, 53   Secunda conclusio principalis [l] quod dare vel recipere pecuniam 25 licentia docendi theologiam est contra ius naturale et divinum. Et ista probatur, primo, quia hoc est symoniacum, ut patet ex prima conclusione, igitur est contra jus naturale et divinum. Consequencia tenet quia symonia est contra ius naturale et divinum, ut patet ex dictis. Et quod ipsa sit contra ius divinum satis notum 30 est, sed quod sit contra ius naturale specialiter probari potest,

[h] potest A
[i] quia Christus *om* A   quod Christus d

[k] acceperant: accipiant *in* acceperant (*sic*) *corr* A   accipiant d
[l] est (*post* principalis) *add* N

---

[37] *Ibid.*, f. 229va.
[38] Cf. Richardus, Lib. X, cap. 8; f. 76vb.
[39] G. O., Matt. 10, 7, *ad verb.* "Gratis accepistis."

quia Num. 22, 22-24 legitur ᵐ quod reprobatus est a Domino et
dampnabilis iudicatus Balaan, qui de Balath, Rege Moabitarum,
precium sue prophetationis accepit. Unde de quibusdam impiis
imitantibus eum scribitur in secunda Epistola Petri et in Epistola
5 Iude.⁴⁰ Et sic iste vendens donum prophetie, vel pocius effectum / A f. 7⁸
doni ipsius, dampnabilis iudicatur, et tamen ipse nec legem Dei
novam nec antiquam receperat. Et per consequens, istud vicium
ex lege nature reprehensibile et dampnabile erat. Unde et hoc
vicium ab ipso Balaan, eius primo actore, Balaamia ⁿ posset
10 congrue nominari. Nominatur tamen a Symone, quia rationem
huius criminis Christus in Novo Testamento clarius expressit
quan/do dixit "Gratis accepistis, gratis date." Ideo magis peccant 731
contra hoc venientes in Nova Lege. Tamen, et sub Lege Moysi
et sub lege nature, ratio quam Christus hic innuit omnium hominum
15 cordibus naturaliter debebat esse impressa.⁴¹ Quare etc.

Secundo. Ex predicta radice probatur conclusio quia donum 731, 6
theologice sapientie et eius effectus ac potestas eis correspondens
non minus ymmo magis sunt spiritualia quam donum prophetie
et eius effectus ac potestas eisdem ᵒ correspondens. Nam Apostolus,
20 I Cor. 12, 8, enumerans dona gratuita et spiritualia, preposuit ᵖ
donum sapientie, dicens "Alii autem datur per spiritum sermo
sapientie," et postposuit donum prophetie, dicens "alii prophetia"
et concludit, "Hec autem �q omnia operatur unus atque idem
spiritus," etc. Ergo, si vendere secundum aut aliquid ei insepara-
25 biliter annexum est symoniacum (et non solum contra ius divinum,
sed eciam contra ius naturale, prout iam de Balaan dictum est),
sequitur quod eciam vendere primum aut aliquid ei inseparabiliter annexum etc. Et per consequens, vendere vel emere potestatem docendi sapientiam, seu pro ea dare vel recipere pecuniam, est
30 contra ius divinum et naturale. Et sic apparet conclusio.

Ex qua conclusione et ʳ eius probatione primo sequitur quod 731, 2⁸
dare vel recipere pro licentia docendi theologiam iuramentum de
reverentia et honore illi qui eam ministrat impendendum, vel eius
aut sui officii iuribus deffendendum, non minus est contra ius

---

ᵐ *om* Ad   ᵖ proposuit Ad
ⁿ Balaamina Ad   �q *interl A*
ᵒ eisdem *ex* eis *corr* A   eis d   ʳ ex (*post* et) *add* N

---

⁴⁰ II, Petr. 2, 2; Iude, 11.
⁴¹ Richardus, Lib. X, cap. 9; f. 76 b.

naturale et divinum quam dare pecuniam. Patet quia non minus
‹ f. 54ᵛ est symoniacum, ut patet ex dictis / in secundo puncto prime
conclusionis, nam tale iuramentum et eius effectus, sive illud
super quo prestatur, potest pecunia comparari et sub nomine
pecunie comprehendi. Eciam est munus ab obsequio, ut notum 5
est. Igitur, etc.

731, 37   Et ideo, licet recipiens licentiam ad talem reverentiam de con-
gruentia teneatur, tamen dans licentiam pro illa exhibenda iuramentum exigere non potest, ratione licentie conferende, sicut et
episcopus pro ordinibus conferendis talem iuramentum non posset 10
exigere, licet dignum sit, ut ei ab ordinatis honor exhibeatur juxta
illud Apostoli, "Qui bene presunt presbiteri duplici honore digni
sunt," I Thim. 5, 17. Ulterius sequitur ex conclusione quod
prohibitio que habetur *Extra, De Magistris*, 1, 2, et 4 capitulis,
qua scilicet prohibetur "ne pro licentia docendi exigatur aliquid 15
aut eciam promittatur ˢ,"⁴² quantum ad hoc et in quantum respicit licentiam docendi in theologia, non est proprie loquendo ius
humanum, sed ius naturale et divinum, licet huiusmodi constitutiones, quantum ad aliquas penas ibidem expressas possint dici iura
humana.   20

731, 54   Et ideo dicerent / aliqui ex hoc posse inferri, quod non solum
A f. 78ᵛ iudex spiritualis, sed eciam piinceps aut iudex temporalis transgressores predicte prohibitionis in hiis quibus sunt ei subiecti
potest iudicare et penis iuriditioni sue competentibus cohercere.
Ita quod istud crimen, quantum est de se, non est exemptum a 25
seculari juriditione, ex eo scilicet quia est contra ius naturale,
sicut eciam dicerent de usura, licet sit iure canonico prohibita.

731, 63   Ulterius, quinto sequitur quod previlegium Gregorii Universitati Parisiensi concessum, quod incipit *Parens Scientiarum*, quantum
ad illam clausulam "Nec cancellarius a licentiandis magistris 30
iuramentum vel obedientiam seu aliam exiget cautionem, nec
aliquid emolumentum seu promissionem recipiet pro licentia concedenda," ⁴³ scilicet in quantum respicit licentiam in theologia,

---

ˢ permittatur A

---

⁴² *Corpus Juris Canonici*, ed. E. Friedberg, 2 vols. (Leipzig, 1879), II, *Gregorii
IX Papae Decretalium Libri V*, X. 5, 5, Chaps. 1, 2, & 4; cols. 768-770. *Decreta-
les* abbreviated henceforth as "X."
⁴³ *Chartularium Universitatis Parisiensis*, ed. H. Denifle & E. Châtelain,
4 vols. (Paris, 1889-97), I, no. 79, p. 138. (Henceforth "Chart.")

non est proprie privilegium, quasi privans legem, vel quasi privata
lex, sed est ius commune, non solum humanum, sed naturale et
divinum.

Et ideo, sexto sequitur quod hoc non potest aliqua prescriptione   731, 73
5 vel contraria consuetudine abrogari. Nec / contra hoc potest   732
prescriptio ^t aut iusta consuetudo acquiri, quia consuetudo non
preiudicat iuri naturali vel divino. Unde, propter hoc, contraria
consuetudo, seu potius corruptela, que dudum erat in gallicana
Ecclesia sub anathemate prohibetur, *Extra, De Magistris, Quanto,*
10 ubi eciam dicitur quod "hec prava consuetudo a cupiditatis
radice processit et decorem ecclesiastice honestatis confundit." [44]
Et hec de secunda ^v conclusione.

Tercia Conclusio Principalis

Tercia conclusio principalis est quod dicere quod dare vel   732, 10
recipere pecuniam pro licentia docendi theologiam sit licitum est
15 hereticum. Et ista probatur sic, quia omnis illa assertio est proprie
heretica que fidei seu Catholice veritati est contraria. Sed dicere
quod dare vel recipere pecuniam pro licentia docendi theologiam
est licitum est asserere contra fidem seu veritatem Catholicam.
Igitur etc. Consequentia clara est. Et minor satis patet ex dictis
20 in declaratione prime et secunde conclusionis, quia sic dicere est
asserere illud esse licitum ^x, quod tamen secundum fidem et
Catholicam veritatem est symoniacum et quod est contra ius
naturale et divinum, ut clare ostensum est.

Sed maior apparet quia, licet in iure canonico heresis multi-   732, 24
25 pliciter sumatur et multis modis dicatur aliquis hereticus, tamen
in theologia heresis, a qua aliquis proprie hereticus dicitur, est
error in fide, et assertio heretica est assertio erronea in fide. Unde
ab Augustino diffinitur hereticus, quod est ille "qui falsam de fide
opinionem vel gignit vel sequitur," [45] ut 24, q. 3, *Hereticus,* quod
30 intelligendum ^y est de illo qui in fide pertinaciter errat.

Ex quibus sequitur quod qui pertinaciter assereret quod licitum   732, 33

---

^t perscriptio A   *in ras* N   praescrip-   ^x *ex* illicitum *corr* A
tio d   ^y *in ras* A
^v tercia (ante conclusione) *del* N

---

[44] X. 5, 5, 3.
[45] Augustine quoted in Gratian, C.24 q.3 c.28.

est licentiare in theologia pro pecunia, seu pro quocumque alio
N f. 55 quod potest pecunia appreciari, seu aliquid dare vel recipere / pro
huiusmodi licentia, non solum assereret heresim, sed eciam esset
hereticus censendus et tamquam hereticus puniendus.

732, 40   Secundo sequitur quod, licet licentiare in theologia pro tali 5
precio temporali, seu huiusmodi precium dare vel recipere pro
tali licentia sit symoniacum et grave peccatum et per consequens
in moribus erroneum, tamen hoc non est heresis, nec hoc faciens
A f. 79 ex hoc est hereticus. / Verbi gratia, licet fornicatio sit peccatum,
tamen fornicari non est hereticum, nec fornicator ex hoc est here- 10
ticus. Sed dicere quod licitum est fornicari est hereticum, et hoc
pertinaciter asserens hereticus est censendus. Et ita in proposito.

732, 50   Ex quo tercio ^{z} sequitur quod auctoritates in principio quasi ^{a}
allegate, que sonare videntur quod symonia sit heresis et quod
symoniaci sunt heretici,[46] non sunt intelligende secundum propriam 15
nominis significationem, scilicet secundum propriam heresis accep-
tionem, sed secundum exteriorem operis protestationem, quia in
hoc quod aliquis vendit vel emit spirituale, vel ostendit exterius se
velle vendere vel emere, quodammodo protestatur licet non in
mente tamen in opere, se esse aut velle esse dominum rei spiritualis, 20
et quod ipsa sit precio comparabilis: hoc autem est hereticum.

732, 62   Secundo, eciam ex alia causa symoniaci dicuntur heretici, quia
Symon Magus, preter hoc quod ab Apostolis donum Spiritus
Sancti emere voluit, eciam dixit quod mondus non erat a Deo
creatus, sed a quadam superna virtute, ut dicit Ysidorus, *Libro* 25
Ethimologiarum,[47] et secundum hoc inter alios hereticos symoniaci
computantur, ut patet per Augustinum, *Libro De Heresibus*.[48]

732, 70   Sed ad hoc ^{b}, tercio, ex alia causa symoniaci heretici dicuntur,
quia Symon Magus non solum habuit errorem voluntatis, volendo
emere spirituale pro temporali, sed eciam errorem intellectus, 30
733 existimando donum Dei pecunia possideri, id est pre/cio pecunie

---

^{z} *om* N ^{b} huc N
^{a} questionis N

---

[46] *Supra*, pp. 197-200.
[47] Isidorus Hispalensis, *Originum sive Etymologiarum Libri XX*, ed. Lindsay,
2 vols. (Oxford, 1911), VIII, 5, 2.
[48] "The 'De Haeresibus' of Saint Augustine," Liguori J. Müller, ed., *The
Catholic University of America Patristic Studies*, vol. XC (Washington, D. C.,
1956), pp. 62-64 and p. 135 note.

comparari. Et ista existimatio erat heretica. Et qui in hoc essent
Symonis imitatores pertinaciter hunc errorem credendo essent
heretici. Et ad hunc intellectum dicitur 1, q. 1: "tollerabilior est
Mathedonii impia heresis quam symoniacorum," etc. [49] Ex quo
5 ulterius patet quod existimare seu credere licentiam docendi in   **733, 6**
theologia pro pecunia seu precio temporali posse comparari vel
possideri non solum esset symoniacum, sed eciam proprie hereticum. Et hoc [c] de tercia conclusione et primo articulo principali.

SECUNDUS ARTICULUS PRINCIPALIS

10   Quantum ad secundum articulum, in quo reprobabo quasdam   **733, 13**
fraudulentas cavillationes quibus utitur pars adversa ad excusa-
tionem sui erroris, primo sciendum est quod dictus cancellarius
contendit quod pro licentia docendi in theologia non recipit nec
exigit aliquid a bachalariis licenciandis, sed alias causas assignat
15 sue receptionis.

Una est quam ponit in articulis per eum domino Pape in Romana   **733, 20**
Curia [d] presentatis, scilicet quod bachalarii licentiandi, receptis
cedulis illis que Parisius communiter signeta vocantur et per quas
de eorum licentia obtinenda securi redduntur et certificati, cancel-
20 lario a predictis [e] bachalariis, nec per se nec per alium quidquam
petente, singuli bachalarii [f], scilicet trium facultatum Theologie,
Decretorum, et Medicine, in signum virtuose recognitionis et
gaudiose congratulationis, de ipsorum libera et mere spontanea
voluntate, consueverint [g] cancellario per nuntios qui eis dicta
25 signeta portaverunt remittere, seu [h] in pecuniis aut aliis enceniis,
aliqua munuscula tanta et talia, sicut eorum gratuite libertati
expedire videtur, quos postea licentiat, nullum super eo quod
parum misit calumpniando, et hec in 8º et 9º articulis.[50]   **A f. 79ᵛ**

Alia est causa sue receptionis quam proposuit coram regia   **733, 37**
30 Parlamenti Curia, scilicet quod bachalarii in theologia licentiandi,
ex laudabili consuetudine et usu hactenus observatis, debent et

---

[c] hec Nd   [f] *in ras* A
[d] in (*post* Curia) *add deinde del* A   [g] consueverunt N
[e] dictis N   [h] sive N

---

[49] Gratian, C.1 q.1 c.21.
[50] For the *signetum* see *Chart.*, III, no. 1520, pp. 404-6, items 12-20.

tenentur sibi dare et mittere post dictam receptionem signetorum
et ante licentiam ad minus decem francos auri, et ultra liberum
◁ f. 55ᵛ est / eis plus mittere sibi prout eorum placet voluntati. Et hoc dicit
esse sibi licitum recipere ratione sui laboris, quem habet occasione
dicte licentie conferende.⁵¹   5

733, 46 Et hanc rationem eciam proposuit in dictis articulis, scilicet
articulo 10, in quo dixit quod dictus usus laudabilis est et similiter
in aliis universitatibus observatus, scilicet quod bachalarii licenciandi donaria faciunt, quandoque maiora premissis, illi a quo
licentiam optinent, tam ratione supratacta, quam ratione laboris 10
quem pro eis in eorum examine et aliis habuit sustinere.

733, 55 Et quod sit licitum et iustum sic dare et recipere pro labore
videtur posse probare aliquibus rationibus et auctoritatibus
Scripture Sacre. Prima est quia potestas vel officium predicandi
non minus est spiritualis quam potestas ⁱ vel officium cancellarii. 15
Sed Paulus predicabat pro temporalibus, ut fierent collecte pauperibus, ut patet I Cor. 16, 1.

733, 62 Similiter Christus docuit Apostolos recipere necessaria vite ab
hiis quos docebant et hoc ostendit esse iustum, dicens "dignus
est enim operarius mercede sua," Luc. 10, 7. Unde Apostolus, ex 20
hoc fundamento, dicit, I Tim. 5, 17, "Qui bene presunt presbiteri,
duplici honore digni habeantur, maxime qui laborant in verbo et
doctrina." Dicit enim Scriptura "Non infrenabis os bovi tritu-
ranti" ⁵² et "Dignus est operarius," etc.ᵏ ⁵³ Similiter eandem
sententiam ponit pluribus aliis locis, specialiter I Cor. 9, 7, ubi 25
dicit "Quis militat suis stipendiis" etc. et ibi concludit "Si nos
vobis spiritualia seminavimus, non magnum est si nos carnalia
vestra metamus." Si ergo Apostolus predicabat et spiritualia
734 ministrabat pro tem/poralibus, vel saltem pro labore in amministratione spiritualium temporalia recipiebat, et specialiter pro 30
labore ¹ predicandi, sequitur quod eciam cancellarius hoc potest
pro labore licentiandi.

ⁱ cancellarii (*post* potestas) *del* N   ¹ in amministratione . . . pro labore
ᵏ etc.: mercede sua N   *om* d

---

⁵¹ For the chancellor's testimony before the Parlement of Paris, see: C. E. Du
Boulay, *Historia Universitatis Pariensis*, 6 vols. (Paris, 1665-73), IV, 606-14,
and for these arguments, see p. 607.
⁵² I Tim. 5, 18.
⁵³ Luc. 10, 7.

Item. Usus prophetie non minus videtur esse spiritualis quam 734, 4
usus potestatis licenciandi. Sed pro usu prophetie olim licitum
erat dare et recipere, nam I Reg. 9, 8-10, legitur de Saul et III ᵐ
Reg. 14, 3, de uxore Jeroboam, quod attulerunt precium sanctis
5 prophetis. Igitur pro usu seu labore sui officii licitum est cancellarius recipere a licentiandis.

Item. Ministri Ecclesie pro labore in amministratione sacra- 734, 11
mentorum et celebratione missarum et aliorum officiorum
ecclesiasticorum licite recipiunt redditus annuos et proventus
10 temporales sicut et in Lege Veteri ut patet Num. 18, 21, ubi ⁿ
scribitur quod filii Levi recipiebant ex ordinacione et dono Dei
"omnes decimas Israelis pro ministerio quo serviebant in tabernaculo federis," et infra ⁵⁴ dicitur "comedetis eas" etc. "quia
precium est pro ministerio quo servitis in tabernaculo" etc. Ergo, a
15 fortiori, licitum est / cancellario recipere precium pro suo ministerio. A f. 8ᵛ

Item. Licitum est omni jure alicui locare operas suas, eciam in 734, 24
rebus spiritualibus, sicut magistris docentibus pueros pro officio
docendi et advocatis pro consilio ᵒ et officio patrocinandi, ergo
et cancellario pro officio licentiandi.

20   Sed premissis non obstantibus, dico quod predicte due re- 734, 28
sponsiones stare non possunt. Et primo declarabo quod una
illarum aliam interimit; secundo, quod prima responsio in se falsa
est et quod evidentia facti ei contradicit; tercio, quod secunda
responsio eciam falsa est et multa inconvenientia includit. Prius,
25 respondebo ad predictas rationes.

Quantum ad primum, quod una dictarum responsionum aliam 734, 37
interimit et cum ea stare non possit, patet quia in prima dicitur
quod bacalarii libere et mere spontanee gratuite et liberaliter dant
quod volunt, et in secunda dicitur quod debent et tenentur dare
30 decem francos et ᵖ ad hoc obligantur ratione laboris dicti cancellarii. Modo ista clare repugnant eciam quia illud quod debetur
pro labore non datur mere libere et �q / gratuite. Nam illi qui N f. 5ᵛ
operatur, et cui pro labore merces debetur, merces huiusmodi seu
stipendium laboris, secundum sententiam Christi et Apostoli, non

---

ᵐ IV Reg AN   ᵖ quod (*post* et) *add* N
ⁿ *om* AN   et d   �q aut N
ᵒ concilio A

---

⁵⁴ Num. 18, 31.

impenditur secundum gratiam, sed secundum debitum et iusticiam, quia "Dignus est operarius mercede sua." [55] Igitur [r] etc.

734, 51 Quantum ad secundum, scilicet quod prima responsio falsa sit, patet nam evidentia facti satis ostendit quod bacalarii non mere gratuite et liberaliter dant, quia secundum Raymundum in *Summa*, 5 *Responsio de Symonia*: "Si dubitetur utrum gratis vel ex corrupta voluntate datum sit, tria sunt maxime attendenda: scilicet qualitas dantis vel [s] recipientis, videlicet utrum a paupere diviti vel econverso, sive a divite locupleti; secundo, quantitas muneris, si magni vel parvi precii res data existit; tercio, tempus donationis, an 10 scilicet instante necessitate seu alio tempore conferatur. Et secundum hoc est habenda presumptio, ut *Extra*, [*De Symonia*,] *Etsi Questiones*." [56]

734, 65 Et ideo, ratione primi, est evidens presumptio quod bacalarii non gratis dant, quia communiter sunt pauperes, et ut plurimum 15 mendicantes, qui vivunt de elemosinis et nichil habent proprium unde dare possint. Ratione secundi idem patet, quia nullatenus est presumendum quod [t] pauperes gratis dant talia munera magna que [v] ipse recipere satagit, licet vocet ea munuscula et imponat preciosa nomina culpe. Munus eciam [x] decem francorum non est 20 uni pauperi munusculum. Ratione tercii patet idem, quia non 735 dant [y] post licentiam, sed immediate ante / et adhuc [z] instante necessitate, quia, licet receptis signetis essent securi de licentia, non tamen de loco seu ordine locorum. Ideo presumendum est quod non gratis dant, sed ut plus danti locus honestior assignetur. Et 25 hoc ostendunt abusus commissi, quare etc.

735, 7 Quantum ad tercium, scilicet quod secunda responsio [a] non valet et quod multa inconvenientia continet, tres conclusiones sunt declarande. Prima est quod cancellarius non potest licite recipere, vel saltem non potest exigere, a bacalariis licentiandis 30 ratione sui laboris; / secunda, quod non potest licite tantum exigere quantum exigit pro labore; tercia, quod esto quod pro labore exigere possit, tamen non taliter qualiter exigit. Primam conclu-

f. 80ᵛ

---

[r] *ex* et quare *corr* A
[s] et N
[t] quia Ad
[v] quia A

[x] enim N
[y] dantur N
[z] ad hoc Ad
[a] racio (*ante* responsio) *del* N

---

[55] Luc. 10, 7.
[56] Ray., p. 6, col. 2 citing X. 5, 3, 18.

sionem declarabo, primo ex iure divino, secundo ex iure humano, tercio ex speciali privilegio Universitati Parisiensi concesso.

Prima ergo ratio principalis, que fundatur in iure divino, talis 735, 19 est: quia papa non posset licite recipere, vel saltem exigere, a 5 licentiandis ratione sui laboris, si ipse huiusmodi licenciandos in propria persona licentiaret, ergo nec cancellarius hoc potest. Consequentia tenet quia suppono pro claro quod cancellarius in hac parte gerit personam pape et est eius commissarius b. Nam ipse licentiat apostolica auctoritate et, per consequens, in hoc 10 officio non habet potius c quam papa, cuius ipse est commissarius, tanquam iudex ordinarius, ut ipsemet dicit. Sed antecedens probatur ex Evangelio, quia papa super omnes alios tenetur pascere spiritualiter gregem Christi, et maxime pastura spirituali predicationis seu doctrine salutaris, quia Petro, pro se et suis successoribus, 15 specialiter dictum est: "Pasce oves meas," Joan. 21, 17.   735, 35

Sed quia grex est magnus et per se ipsum totum gregem pascere non potest, alios, quos scit esse ad hoc ydoneos, ad pascendum gregem mittere et licentiare debet, vel per se, vel per alium, iuxta illud Matt. 9, 37: "Messis quidem multa, operarii autem d pauci. 20 Rogate ergo dominum messis, ut mittat operarios in messem suam," id est, "predicatores e ad congregandum electorum Ecclesiam," secundum Glossam.57 Et super eodem Luc. 10, 2, "Messis est turba credentium, operarii sunt Apostoli et sequaces. Et licet messis verbo Dei sit sata, tamen culture laborem sollicitum re- 25 quirit, ne aves celi sparsa f semina dissipent." 58

Ex quibus patet quod papa licentiando aliquos in theologia, 735, 48 sive per se, sive per alium, mittit eos ad pascendum gregem sibi commissum et ad messem Ecclesie colendum et, per consequens, mittit eos ad opus suum. Sed absurdum est dicere, et omnino / N f. 56ᵛ 30 contra jus naturale et divinum, quod aliquis mittendo alium ad opus suum, pro labore mittendi eum possit ab eo mercedem recipere, vel saltem exigere. Ymmo, magis tenetur, si hoc potest,

---

b *ras in fine* A
c non habet potius: *ras* (*post* potius) A
non habet pocius ius N   non habetur potius scilicet d

d aut A
e ad (*ante* predicatores) *add* A
f sparsa *Ed G. O.* dispersa Ad sper-
sa N

---

57 G. I., Matt. 9, 37, *ad verb.* "operarios."
58 G. O., Luc. 10, 2, *ad verb.* "Messis quidam."

sui operis et sui laboris premium ei ^{g} reddere, juxta parabolam Evangelicam de illo qui misit operarios in vineam suam. Non enim dicit, "Pro labore meo, michi dabitis," sed "quod iustum fuerit dabo ^{h} vobis." Math. 20, 4.

735, 61   Et ideo sequitur quod papa, ^{i} licenciando aliquos in theologia, 5 quod nichil aliud est quam eos mittere ad pascendum gregem ^{k} seu ad colendum messem vel vineam Ecclesie sibi commisse, non solum non debet pro labore mittendi vel licentiandi ab eis recipere vel exigere; ymmo debet eos pro suo labore iusta mercede quantum potest remunerare, et de fructibus vinee et lacte gregis, id est, de 10 bonis Ecclesie, tenetur eis, saltem necessaria vite, concedere, juxta illud Apostoli, "Quis plantavit vineam et de fructu eius non edit ^{l}? Quis pascit gregem et de lacte eius non manducat?" I Cor. 9, 7.

735, 73   Confirmatur eciam antecedens predictum exemplo Christi, cuius
A f. 81 papa est vicarius et quem tenetur in hoc imitari./ Nam Christus, 15
736   quando licenciavit / Apostolos dicens: "Euntes predicate," etc. Matt. 10, 7, pro labore licenciandi nichil ab eis recepit aut exegit, sed omnino gratis dedit. Et eam gratis dare docuit, eciam quoad laborem, quia dixit "Euntes," in quo notatur labor eorum. Unde subdit, "Gratis accepistis," etc., quasi dicens, prout ait glossa 20 interlinearis, "Sicut ego sine precio vobis do talem potestatem, et vos date gratis, ne Evangelii gratia corrumpatur," quia, ut ibidem dicitur, "bona spiritualia precio vilescunt." ^{59} Ille autem non gratis nec sine precio daret talem potestatem, qui reciperet, et maxime ^{m} qui exigeret precium laboris. Igitur, etc.   25

736, 12   Dico autem notanter "qui exigeret precium laboris," quia licet in casu liceret aliquid recipere pro labore, non tamen exigere nec recipere quasi precium, sed sicut gratis oblatum. Unde, super eodem verbo, Luc. 10, 7, dicit Glossa, "Ecce qui saccum et peram prohibuit, sumptus ex predicatione concedit, sic tamen ut oblato 30 cibo et potu sint contenti." ^{60}

736, 20   Tercio. Ex hoc confirmatur propositum, quia pro effectu illius potestatis seu auctoritatis, scilicet licencie in theologia, hoc est

---

^{g} *om* N	^{k} grege A
^{h} *ex* da *corr* A	^{l} dedit A
^{i} propter Ad	^{m} surface smeared over first two or three letters of lines 7-28 A

---

[59] G.I., Matt. 10, 7, *ad verb.* "Gratis accepistis."
[60] G.O., Luc. 10, 7, *ad verb.* "In eadem."

pro doctrina vel predicatione, nec pro labore ei inseparabiliter
annexo potest aliquid exigi quasi precium, ymmo nec recipi, nisi
sicut gratis oblatum, nisi forte in casu necessitatis extreme, ut
patet ex predicta glossa et ex dictis Augustini, sermone tercio
5 *De Verbis Domini* [61] et diffuse libro *De Opere Monachorum*.[62] Igitur,
a fortiori, nec pro medio, scilicet pro labore seu alio inseparabiliter
requisito ad conferendam talem potestatem, quia iste labor non
minus est spiritualis, vel spirituali annexus, quam primus.

Ex quo sequitur quod pro tali labore seu auctoritativa in- **736, 33**
10 quisitione super sufficientia licentiandorum, aut pro predicatione
seu [n] labore sermonis [o] vel collationis in licentia theologorum, non
est licitum cancellario precium exigere, seu ipsum in iudicio con-
tentiose petere. Et dicere hoc esse licitum videtur esse hereticum.

Quarto. Hoc idem confirmatur quia symoniacum est dare, recipere **736, 40**
15 aut exigere pecuniam, aut aliud precium, pro beneficio ecclesiastico
habendo aut habito, vel pro ministerio seu labore in eius collatione
impenso, iuxta capitulum primum, *De Symonia, In Antiquis*.[63] Sed
insanum est in fide dicere quod auctoritas docendi in theologia et
predicandi Evangelium non sit spiritualior et maior auctoritas in
20 Ecclesia Dei quam potestas resultans ex beneficii non curati collatione. Ergo sequitur quod symoniacum est / pro ministerio, **N f. 57**
seu labore adhibito in illius auctoritatis collatione, precium petere **736, 50**
seu modo [p] predicto exigere. Et per consequens, hoc approbare
est hereticum.

25   Quinto. Aliter sequeretur quod cuiuslibet potestatis administra- **736, 54**
tio, quantumcumque spiritualis, esset licite acquisibilis pro pecunia,
saltem in ratione laboris. Et sic nullus posset symoniacus convinci.
Ymmo, nec Symon Magus potuisset de symonia convincibiliter
reprehendi, quia Scriptura dicit quod obtulit pecuniam dicens,
30 "Date michi hanc potestatem," etc.[64] Et sic non habetur quod
obtulerit pecuniam pro illa potestate, quia potuisset dicere quod

---

[n] pro (*post* seu) *add* N   [p] *om* Ad
[o] Symonis Ad

---

[61] PL, 38, 272-3.
[62] *Ibid.*, 40, *passim*.
[63] Cf. X. 5, 3, 43, which corresponds to De Simonia, cap. 1 (5, 1, 1) in the
"Quinta Compliatio Decretalium," ed. E. Friedberg, *Quinque Compilationes
Antiquae* (Leipzig, 1882), p. 181.
[64] Act. 8, 19.

f. 81ᵛ offerebat eam pro labore / et negasset Petro quod existimasset donum Dei pecunia possideri.

736, 65   Sexto. Quia sicut patet Num. 22, 22-35, Balaam a Domino per angelum reprehensus est �q, qui pro muneribus arripuit iter et laborem ut ʳ iret ad utendum potestate spirituali, scilicet prophetice 5 benedictionis vel ˢ maledictionis. Ergo, multo magis sub lege Evangelica dampnandus est cancellarius, qui pro lucro assumit laborem, ad finem licentie concedende seu benedictionis spiritualis conferende. Et per consequens, pro huiusmodi labore non potest aliquid exigere. Quare, et cetera. Et pro ista conclusione est ᵗ 10
737   expresse Durandus, in 4º *Sententiarum*, et ibi dicit quod alle/gare quod recipitur aut exigitur pro labore est cooperimentum Symone, etc.⁶⁵

737, 3   Secundo. Hoc idem probatur ᵛ principaliter ex jure humano, scilicet per iura canonica, *Extra*, *De Magistris*, "Ne exigatur 15 aliquid pro licentia docendi." ⁶⁶ Nam intentio iurium est prohibere non solum exigere pro licentia, sed ˣ pro labore seu quacumque occasione licentie annexa. Et licet hoc sit clarum cuilibet ʸ non male affectato, tamen hoc multipliciter ostenditur.

737, 11   Primo, quia aliter huiusmodi iura imponerent legem verbis et 20 non rebus. Nam nullus unquam diceret se exigere pro licentia, ex quo posset honeste et inreprehensibiliter ᶻ exigere pro labore, et sic frustra fuissent ista iura condita et pene inutiliter ibidem expresse. Item, cum de ᵃ iure divino sit clarum quod non licet exigere pro licentia, maxime in theologia, ista iura nichil adderent, 25 quantum ad hoc, ultra ius divinum, nisi excluderent eciam exigere pro labore, etc.

Item. Ibidem dicitur in capitulo *Quanto*, ubi dampnatur consuetudo Gallicana, quod "digni sunt animadversione illi qui sine certo

---

 q *om* Ad
ʳ et A
ˢ et A
ᵗ *om* Ad
ᵛ *om* Ad

ˣ eciam (*post* sed) *add* N
ʸ cuibus N
ᶻ re (*ante* inreprehensibiliter) *add* N
ᵃ *ins interl* A

---

⁶⁵ Durandus a Sancto Porciano, *In Petri Lombardi Sententias Theologicas Commentariorum Libri IV* (Venetiis, 1571), Lib. IV, d. 25, q. 3, nos. 10-14; if. 365ʳb-365ᵛa. Here I cite Durandus' refutation of the whole argument that payments may be demanded for labor. The expression "cooperimentum Symone" does not occur.
⁶⁶ X. 5, 5.

precio docendi alios licentiam non impendunt." [67] Et sic indistincte
sive pro labore, sive pro alia occasione, negat precium impendenti
licentiam. Hoc autem capitulum factum fuit contra Cancellarium
Parisiensem, qui "a quolibet docente marcam unam exigebat," ut
5 dicit Glossa Vincentii in Antiqua Compilacione.[68]

Item. Sequitur ibidem, "quicumque viri ydonei et literati 737, 29
voluerint legere studia literarum, sine molestia et exactione
qualibet permittantur," ubi negat exactionem quamlibet sive pro
licentia, sive pro alia causa licentie annexa, etc.[69]

10   Item, in capitulo *Quoniam Ecclesia* dicitur quod "pro licencia 737, 34
docendi nullus [b] precium exigat, vel sub obtentu alicuius consuetudinis ab eis qui docent aliquid querat nec docere quemquam [c]
qui sit ydoneus interdicat." [70] Ubi non solum negat pro licentia
precium exigere, sed eciam alia occasione a docentibus aliquid
15 querere, quacumque consuetudine non obstante. Et, per consequens, ex quo consuetudo est dampnata, postea non potuit fieri
licita.

Item. Raymundus in *Somma*, querens "quid de cancellario 737, 43
Parisiensi vel Bononiensi, qui cupiditate vel consuetudine longa
20 nolunt aliquando dare licentiam docendi, nisi aliquo sibi dato,"
respondet simpliciter, non distinguendo / sive pro licentia sive pro **N** f. 57ᵛ
labore detur. Et dicit quod "nec / magister qui petit licentiam **A** f. 82
debet aliquid dare vel promittere [d], nec aliquis supradictorum
aliquid exigere." Et hoc tenet per iura predicta, quare, etc.[71]

25   Tercio. Principaliter probatur propositum ex speciali previlegio 737, 52
Universitati Parisiensi concesso, quia in previlegio supra allegato,
quod incipit *Parens Scienciarum*, non solum dicitur quod cancellarius nichil exigat, sed eciam quod nichil recipiat pro licentia

---

[b] nullo N   [d] permittere A
[c] quemquem A

---

[67] X. 5, 5, 3.
[68] Commenting *Quanto Gallicana*, X. 5, 5, 3, Bernard of Parma says: "Hoc
capitulum, ut ait Vincentius, fuit impetratum contra Cancellarium Parisiensem,
qui marcham unam, a quolibet docente exigebat, quod est notandum pro
intellectu huius capituli et praecedentis." *Gregorii Pape IX Libri V Decretalium*
(Rome, 1582), col. 1651. See Vincentius Hispanus, "Apparatus ad Compilationem Primam," Vat. lat. 1377, in 1 *Comp.* 5. 4. 3. Cf. *Chart.*, I, intro., no. 4,
n. (p. 5).
[69] X. 5, 5, 3.
[70] X. 5, 5, 1.
[71] Ray., p. 31, col. 2.

concedenda.[72] Et sic ultra jura predicta, que solum exprimit de exactione, privilegium addit et declarat de receptione.

737, 60   Item. Quia de iure divino clarum est quod non est recipiendum pro licentia in theologia, ut patet ex dictis in primo articulo, previlegium addit quod nec eciam pro labore in licentia ministranda. 5 Et hoc notat ille terminus "concedenda," in quo notatur labor, qui est pro concedendo seu ministrando licentiam. Aliter enim, quantum ad licentiam theologie, previlegium fuisset frustra datum, quia non adderet ad jus divinum.

737, 69   Item. Idem patet ex previlegio quod incipit *Servus Crucis*, in quo 10 dicitur "nullus incipiat licenciatus a cancellario vel ab alio, data ei pecunia, vel fide prestita, vel alia conventione habita." [73] Et in fine, contra contumaces transgressores, fertur excommunicationis sententia. Unde per hoc quod dicitur, "data ei pecunia," sine quacumque additione, clare ostenditur quod nec pro licentia, nec 15 **738** pro labore seu alia occasione est pecunia danda. Et ita dico de fide, seu iuramento, vel conventione, quare etc. Et sic patet prima conclusio.

738, 4   Secunda conclusio est quod, esto quod cancellarius posset exigere aut recipere pro labore, non tamen tantum quantum exigit, 20 vel quantum se posse recipere asserit. Et hoc probatur tripliciter: primo ex conditione recipientis [e], secundo ex consideratione dantis, tercio ex comparatione doni [f] et laboris.

738, 11   Prima, ergo, ratio fundatur ex consideratione [g] recipientis, scilicet ipsius cancellarii, qui est in hac parte iudex ordinarius, ut 25 suppono. Sed constat quod talis iudex non debet pro iusta sententia ferenda precium recipere vel exigere, et maxime talia et tam magna munera que possent eius iudicium verisimiliter pervertere. Et istud patet primo ex Scriptura Divina, nam Exo. 23, 8, dicitur judici, "Non accipies munera, que eciam excecant [h] prudentes 30 et subvertunt verba iustorum." Et Deu. 16, 18: "Judices et magistros constitues," etc. et sequitur: "Non accipies personam nec munera, quia excecant [i] oculos sapientum et mutant verba

---

[e] dantis (*post* condicione) *del* N
[f] doni: has marks of emphasis above and below in A
[g] ex consideratione: in condicione N
[h] execant A
[i] excaecant: *ed. Vulg.* execant AN

---

[72] *Chart.*, I, no. 79, p. 138.
[73] *Chart.*, I, no. 20, p. 79.

iustorum." Et Eccles. 20, 31: "Encenia ᵏ et dona excecant oculos
iudicum." Unde contra oppositum facientes dicitur Michee 3, 11:
"Principes eius in muneribus iudicabant," etc.

    Secundo. Idem patet secundum iura, quia, sicut dicit Ray- 738, 28
5 mundus: "Ordinarii iudices non debent petere eciam expenssas,
cum propter iusticiam tenendam suas habeant dignitates et
redditus assignatos." ⁷⁴ Ad istos enim extenditur illud: "Neminem
concuciatis, neque calumpniam faciatis, et contenti estote stipendiis
vestris." Luc. 3, 14. Ubi glossa Ambrosii et Augustini: / "Ne dum A f. 82ᵛ
10 sumptus queritur, predo crassetur." ⁷⁵ Moderata tamen encenia
possunt recipere sponte oblata, non tamen nisi consideratis tribus
circumstantiis quas supra recitavi, ut per hoc mala suspicio vitetur ¹.
Et hoc probatur ex juribus, quibus eciam concordat ratio moralis.

    Et ideo licet iudici spirituali sit licitum aliquod munus accipere, 738, 40
15 ut *Extra. De Symonia, Etsi Questiones*,⁷⁶ tamen, sicut dicit Sanctus
Thomas, 4º *Sentenciarum*, d. 25: hoc ibi conceditur, "ubi non est
probabile quod animus iudicis spiritualis flectatur ad aliquid
faciendum pro parvo munere, aliter non. Et propter hoc in parvis
muneribus iudici datis, Ecclesia, cuius iudicium est secundum
20 exteriora, non iudicat symoniam committi, sed / apud Deum, qui N f. 58
cor videt, symonia est sive in magnis sive in parvis muneribus, si
animus judicis ex eis flectatur."⁷⁷ Et hoc si sit spiritualis iudex,
aliter non committit symoniam, sed graviter peccat. Modo Cancellarius est ᵐ judex spiritualis et ordinarius ⁿ, quia eciam mortuo papa,
25 non expirat eius º potestas iudiciaria. Sequitur ergo quod non
potest sine periculo symonie recipere magna munera, et per consequens, nec exigere. Quare, etc.

    Item. Secundum jura, et ut tenet Raymundus, "Si aliquis 738, 58
magister habet beneficium, qui ex officio teneatur docere, certum
30 est exigere aliquid propter hoc symoniacum esse," ut *Extra. De*

ᵏ Encenia: Xenia *ed. Vulg.* enxenia N   ⁿ quia eciam (*post* ordinarius) *del* N ut
¹ *ex* videtur *corr* A   ipsemet dicit (*post* ordinarius) *add* N
ᵐ *om* A   º cuius A

---

⁷⁴ Ray., p. 209, col. 2.
⁷⁵ Ambrosius Mediolanensis, *Expositio Evangelii Secundum Lucan*, II, 77
(CSEL XXXII, 83) and Augustinus, *De Verbis Domini*, Ser. XIX. Both quoted
by Ray.
⁷⁶ X. 5, 3, 18.
⁷⁷ Q. 3, art. 3, ad 1.

Symonia, Nemo.[78] Unde Gregorius [p]: "Vendentes in templo sunt qui hoc quod quibusdam iure debetur, ad premium vel precium largiuntur." [79] Cum ergo cancellarius habeat beneficium, et ei ratione officii competat licentiare, si licentiam que dignis iure debetur non sine precio largiatur, symoniacus est. 5

738, 68   Item. Secundum Sanctum Thomam, super 4º *Sentenciarum*, d. 25[q]: "In actibus [r] qui spirituales sunt," quantum ad suum principium, id est, qui [s] competunt alicui ex aliquo spirituali dono vel officio, "nullo modo potest sine [t] symonia aliquis locare actus suos" vel operas suas.[80] Sic est in proposito, quare ex hac et 10
739   precedente [v] ratione sequitur quod / tam ratione beneficii, quam ratione officii spiritualis, cancellarius non potest exigere pro operis suis seu laboribus, etc. et per consequens, nec recipere, precipue magna munera. Alioquin bis solvetur [x] pro eadem opera, cum ex beneficio ecclesiastico habeat laboris stipendium, juxta illud quod 15 habetur, *Extra. De Magistris, Quoniam Ecclesia*, ubi de illo qui sub obtentu [y] alicuius consuetudinis aliquem ydoneum non sine precio docere permittit, dicitur quod "ab ecclesiastico fiat beneficio alienus," et causa subditur, "quia dignum est ut in Ecclesia, fructum laboris sui non habeat, qui ecclesiasticum profectum 20 nititur impedire." [81] Et sic beneficium ecclesiasticum quod habet cancellarius est [z] fructus laboris sui, quo fructu debet privari si pro labore alium fructum exigat, maxime si propter hoc dignos a predicatione et doctrina fidei impediat vel retardet.

739, 18   Item. Predicatoribus [a] non licet ab illis quibus predicant recipere 25 ad habundantiam sive voluptatem, saltem non eis licet hoc petere, juxta illud Apostoli: "Habentes alimenta et quibus tegamur, hiis contenti simus," I Thim. 6, 8, eciam quoniam [b] omnes glose et
A f. 83   omnes doctores locuntur solum de vite / necessariis, et per consequens, nec hoc licet illis qui licentiant eos seu mittunt ad pre- 30

---

[p] Nemo unde Gregorius *in marg*   [v] precedenti N
   A   Unde Gregorius *om* d   [x] solveretur N
[q] 5 Ad   [y] *ex* obtentum *corr* A
[r] Apostolorum (*post* actibus) *del* N   [z] *om* A
[s] quia N   [a] Quia (*ante* predicatoribus) *add* N
[t] *om* A   [b] quia N   *om* d

---

[78] Ray., p. 30, col. 2 citing X. 5, 3, 14.
[79] Gregorius, *XL Homiliarum in Evangelia Libri II*, Hom. 39; PL 76, 1297.
[80] Q. 3, art. 2, solutio 2.
[81] X. 5, 3, 14.

dicandum, maxime quando illis est per beneficium ecclesiasticum, de competenti victu provisum. Quare, etc.

Secundo, principaliter probatur propositum ex consideratione 739, 28 dantis, scilicet bachularii licentiandi, a quo ipse exigit. Nam
5 bachalarius ᶜ cui licentia denegatur, pro cuius examine cancellarius laboravit, pro eius labore non tenetur ei, saltem ad tantum quantum ipse petit, igitur nec pro eodem labore ad tantum obligatur bachalarius licentiatus. Antecedens videtur notum et consequentia patet, quia tantum et plus communiter laborat cancellarius pro examine ᵈ
10 bacalarii non admissi, sicut bacalarii licentiati.

Item. Secundum Augustinum in quadam epistola ad Macedo- 739, 39 nium, "Non ideo iudex debet vendere iustum iudicium, aut testis verum testimonium, quia vendit advocatus iustum patrocinium, aut iurisperitus iustum consilium." Et rationem subdit, "illi
15 enim," judex scilicet et testis, "inter utramque partem ad examina adhibentur. Isti ex una parte consistunt," scilicet advocatus et jurisperitus, et per consequens, ex illa ratione, si liciteᵉ iudex in aliquo casu posset recipere pro labore, deberet ab utraque parte recipere.⁸² Cum ergo cancellarius sit iudex in hac materia, ut dictum
20 est, patet quod una pars, scilicet bachalarius licentiandus, non plus debet ei pro labore / quam alia pars, scilicet bachalarius non N f. 58 admissus, a quo tamen nihil recipit. Quare, etc.

Tercio. Probatur intentum ex comparatione doni et laboris, 739, 54 quia donum seu precium quod cancellarius petit est multo maius
25 quam deceat, si comparetur ad parvitatem laboris, ut satis notum est. Et maxime quia sicut ipse qui est iudex laborat pro iusto iudicio dando, sic magistri eciam laborant pro fideli testimonio perhibendo de bacalariis licentiandis, et tamen pro isto labore, nichil omnino recipiunt aut exigunt. Quare indecens est quod
30 cancellarius pro suo labore tam magna stipendia recipiat aut exigat, maxime cum ipse pro hoc officio exercendo habeat beneficium, et ipsi non. Igitur, etc.

Item. Omnino absurdum videretur quod cancellarius pro tali 739, 66 labore posset quantumlibet recipere, sic, scilicet, quod non esset

---

ᶜ *ex* bacharius *corr* N   ᵉ si licite: *ed. Aug.*   scilicet A   si N
ᵈ licentia Ad

---

⁸² A. Augustinus, *Epistulae*, ed. A. Goldbacher, CSEL, 44 (Vindobonae & Lipsiae, 1904), no. 153, p. 423, 5.

aliqua determinata mensura ultra quam non posset recipere, sicut
ipse proposuit in iudicio quod aliqua est determinata mensura,
scilicet decem florenorum, citra quam bacalarii theologie non
debent dare. Nam, cum labor suus non sit infiniti valoris [f], sed
est precio nummismatis appreciabilis, in politia bene ordinata, 5
740 oportet quod apprecie/tur sub iusta mensura. Ideo enim [g] conceditur actio illi qui proponit in appreciatione alicuius rei, se esse
deceptum ultra medium iusti precii. Quare, etc.

740, 5   Tercia conclusio est [h] quod, esto quod cancellarius pro labore suo
exigere posset, non tamen per modum per quem exigit. Et ista 10
probatur, nam modus per quem exigit est iste: quia [i], eo quod
bacalarii fecerunt certum iuramentum de non dando cancellario,
ipse impedit vel differt eorum licentiam. Et proponit in iudicio
quod hoc licite potest. Sed ad reprobandum istum modum, tres
A f. 83[v] sunt propositiones declarande: prima est quod iste modus / est 15
illicitus et multipliciter scandalosus; secunda [k], est proprie symoniacus; tercia, quod si cancellarius hunc modum pertinaciter approbet,
ipse est hereticus censendus.

740, 19   Prima propositio patet, nam secundum doctrinam Sancti Thome,[83]
que in hoc omni iuri et rationi consonat, ad hoc quod evitetur 20
symonia, vel saltem ad hoc quod evitetur [l] peccatum, cum in
dispensatione sacramentorum seu aliorum spiritualium aliqua
recipiuntur, primo requiritur quod hoc fiat ex concessione iuris
divini vel humani, aut saltem pie consuetudinis; secundo, quod sit
intentio pura, non corrupta; tercio, quod sit forma honesta, 25
scilicet quod non requiratur aliquid ante pii officii exhibitionem,
ne pactum intervenire videatur.

740, 30   Primo, ergo, apparet dictum modum exigendi esse illicitum
ratione prime conditionis, quia ad sic exigendum pro licentia
theologie, que est potestas vel auctoritas spiritualis, ut patet ex 30
primo articulo, cancellarius non habet concessionem iuris divini.
Ymmo, hoc magis est contra ius divinum, ut patet ex dictis in
prima conclusione huius articuli. Etiam si ius divinum sibi con-

---

[f] laboris (*ante* valoris) *del* A   [i] ex (*post* quia) *add* N
[g] non Ad   [k] est quod (*post* secunda) *add* N
[h] *om* Ad   [l] symonia . . . evitetur *om* d

[83] II, II, q. 100, art. 2, *ad* 4 and art. 3, *responsio*, which d'Ailly paraphrases
to draw these principles or "conditions." Cf. this same passage quoted at
length, below, p. 235, l. 1-9.

cederet posse recipere pro labore licenciandi, papa non posset hoc
sibi negare quod ius divinum sibi concederet. Et tamen papa
prohibet sibi recipere pro labore ab artistis licentiandis, quorum
tamen licentia non est sic spiritualis sicut licentia theologie. Item.
5 Nec hoc habet ex concessione iuris humani, sicut patet ex secunda
conclusione m eiusdem articuli et eciam ex secunda probatione
prime conclusionis, quia iura prohibent exigere. Item. Nec ex
concessione pie consuetudinis, quia iura dampnant consuetudinem
quam allegat. Eciam privilegia universitatis prohibent dare et
10 recipere, et per consequens, exigere, ut patet ex dictis in fine dicte
secunde conclusionis.⁸⁴ Igitur, etc.

Secundo. Patet propositum ratione secunde conditionis, scilicet **740, 52**
quod intentio pura, non corrupta. Nam, que sit recta intentio in
proposito, ostendit Sanctus Thomas, in IIᵃ, IIᵉ, scilicet quod non / **N f. 59**
15 exigatur quasi precium rei spiritualis, cum intentione vendendi vel
emendi, nec ab invito, sed quod accipiatur quasi stipendium, et
quod intentio refferatur ad observantiam consuetudinis, et precipue
quando quis ⁿ voluntarie solvit.⁸⁵ Hec autem non sunt in proposito,
ut notum est. Quare, etc.

20   Item. Raymundus, in responsione de symonia, distinguit quando **740, 62**
aliquid datur in collatione spiritualis rei, scilicet utrum principaliter
detur propter illud an non, ita quod aliter esset daturus. In primo
casu tenet, et ᵒ esset symonia, et per consequens corrupta intentio,
sed non in secundo casu,⁸⁶ ut *Extra.*, eodem [*De Symonia,*] *Etsi*
25 *Questiones.*⁸⁷ Cum ergo cancellarius publice confiteatur et in
iudicio quod aliter non est ᵖ daturus licentiam, nisi sibi detur
pecunia, patet quod non est in eo pura intentio, sed corrupta et
symoniaca. Constat eciam quod bacalarii aliter non essent daturi,
nisi essent licentiandi. Ideo non gratis dant, sed coacti / et per **A f. 84**
30 exactionem. Quare, etc.

Tercio. Patet intentum ex racione tercie condi/tionis, scilicet **741**
quod sit forma honesta, sic quod nichil prius exigatur. Nam

ᵐ *om* A   ᵒ quod N
ⁿ aliquis N   ᵖ *in ras* N

---

⁸⁴ *Chart.*, I, nos. 20 & 79. Cf. *supra*, pp. 222, 25 - 223, 18.
⁸⁵ Q. 100, art. 3.
⁸⁶ Ray., p. 17, col. 1.
⁸⁷ X. 5, 3, 18.

secundum Sanctum Thomam et Raymundum, ubi supra,[88] exactio in hac materia omnino damnatur, maxime ante exhibitionem pii officii. Licet autem receptio in aliquibus casibus concedatur pro labore vel stipendio, tamen, ut ipsi dicunt, in hiis omnibus q sollicite cavendum est omne illud quod habet speciem symonie 5 vel cupiditatis. Ideo r non solum a malo, sed ab omni specie mali abstinendum est, secundum Apostolum, I ad Tess., 5, 22.[89]

741, 12   Cum ergo in proposito, in sic exigendo non solum sit species mali ymmo grande scandalum fidei et offendiculum Evangelii: tum, primo, quia per talem exactionem datur occasio Gentilibus 10 et Judeis dicendi quod doctrina fidei Christiane et s auctoritas ipsam docendi est venalis, sicut iam de facto aliqui Judei in Tholosa dixisse traduntur t quod rabi fidei nostre fiunt per pecuniam (quod tamen valde cavendum est, quia bonum testimonium querendum est, secundum Apostolum, I Thim. 3, 7, "non solum 15 a domesticis, sed eciam alienis," scilicet "Judeis et gentilibus," ut ibidem dicit glossa);[90] tum, eciam, quia per hoc datur occasio licentiatis, ut sicut eis exigitur pecunia aliter non licentiantur v ad docendum et predicandum, sic eciam sine exactione pecunie non doceant neque predicent. Et sic ipsi et doctrina ac predicatio 20 eorum scandalizabuntur et vilipendentur x, juxta illud Michee 3, 11; "Sacerdotes eius in mercede docebant," ubi dicit Jeronimus quod "quia pecuniam accipiebant, prophetia eorum facta est divinatio." [91] Et sic eciam doctrina et predicatio theologica reputabitur divinatio, et forte deceptio, propter turpem questum. 25

741, 36   Ideo, hiis attentis, quamvis cancellarius de iure in casu posset aliquid recipere, cessante tali scandalo, tamen non debet in scandalum fidei, ubi occasio malignandi et species mali notorie et publice suspicatur et presumitur, non solum exigere, ymmo nec recipere, exemplo Apostoli, qui, licet de iure divino potestatem 30 haberet ab illis quibus predicabat recipere, tamen dicebat "sed non

---

q casibus (*post* omnibus) *add* N
r Idem A et d
s et: (In N, there is a reference to a marginal comment or addition that has been lost.)

t creduntur N
v licentiatur A
x vilipendetur A

---

[88] Pp. 227-8, notes 83, 84, 86 and especially Ray., pp. 16-17.
[89] Cited also by Tho., II, II, q. 100, art. 2, *ad* 4.
[90] G. O., I Thim. 3, 7, *ad verb.* "oportet autem."
[91] *Commentariorum in Michaeam Libri Duo*, I, iv; PL 25, 1183.

sumus usi hac potestate, ne aliquod offendiculum daremus
Evangelio Christi." I Cor. 9, 12. Igitur, etc.

Secunda propositio, scilicet quod predictus modus exigendi est   741, 46
proprie symoniacus, patet satis ex immediate ʸ dictis in ᶻ declara-
5 tione prime propositionis, tamen specialiter declaratur, pro quo
supponitur quod juramentum dictorum bachalariorum fuit licitum.
Nam, secundum veritatem, ipsi nichil aliud iuraverunt, nisi solum
quod cancellario nichil darent, iuxta formam et intentionem
privilegiorum universitatis superius ᵃ allegatorum ᵇ. Sed tale
10 juramentum fuit licitum, nec est in aliquo contra dictum cancellarium, cum dicta privilegia sint iusta, sancta, et licita, prout ipsemet
cancellarius non negat cum eciam ipsemet eadem juraverit.

Item. Dare aliquid cancellario est bachalariis prohibitum / ut   741, 59
patet ex clausula previlegii *Servus Crucis*, superius allegata.⁹² Ergo,   A f. 84ᵛ
15 peccatum inobedientie esset dare. Et per / consequens licitum est   N f. 59ᵛ
iurare non dare.

Item. Licitum est iurare non participare criminoso in crimine.   741, 64
Sed cancellarius exigendo est criminosus, ut ex dictis patet. Et
ille qui daret sibi sic exigenti, participaret secum in hoc crimine,
20 iuxta illud quod habetur, *Extra.*, *De Symonia*, *Non Satis*, ubi
dicitur: "Tam ille qui dat, quam ille qui recipit vel consentit,
partem [se cum] Symone non dubitet habiturum." ⁹³ Igitur, etc.

Item. Istud iuramentum habet utilitatem spiritualem et causam   741, 72
rationabilem, tum quia factum est ad providendum saluti et dantis
25 et recipientis, ut peccandi ᶜ tollatur occasio, et presumptio male
sus/cipiendi ᵈ, et iustum iudicium pervertendi, et pro vitandis   742
iniustis promotionibus, ac pauperibus sublevandis ᵉ; tum, eciam,
quia factum est ad vitandum confusionem Ecclesie, quia "prava
consuetudo" dandi et recipiendi in materia nostra "Decorem eccle-
30 siastice honestatis confundit," ut supra allegatum est, *Extra. De
Magistro*, *Quanto*. ⁹⁴ Igitur, iuramentum non solum est licitum, sed
meritorium.

ʸ tactis (*post* immediate) *del* N
ᶻ *ex* ne *corr* A
ᵃ superiorus *ex* superiorum *corr* A
male
ᵇ universitatis superius allegatorum:
universitatis superiorus (*sic*) allega-

torum A Universitatum superiorum allegatorum d
ᶜ peccandum A
ᵈ suspiciendi Nd
ᵉ sublevandum Ad

⁹² *Chart.*, I, no. 20, pp. 78-79.
⁹³ X. 5, 3, 8.
⁹⁴ X. 5, 5, 3.

742, 9   Hoc ergo presupposito, arguitur sic: negare dignis tempore
debito licentiam docendi in theologia vel eam differre, quia iuraverunt licitum iuramentum de non dando cancellario, est proprie
symoniacum, quia hoc est negare spirituale nisi detur temporale,
quod est species venditionis, hoc est eciam propter commodum 5
temporale principaliter impedire opera caritatis, scilicet opera
doctrine et predicationis. Sed hoc facit cancellarius, ut patet,
et per consequens, symoniam incurrit, ymmo eciam ultra hoc,
incurrit periurium, quia iuravit dignis, tempore debito, licentiam conferre, ut patet ex previlegio *Parens Scientiarum*.[95] Igitur, 10
etc.

742, 22   Item. Si dicatur quod dictum iuramentum non fuit licitum, quia
bachalarii non solum iuraverunt ut prefertur, sed ultra hoc aliquid
in dicti cancellarii preiudicium, licet hoc sit falsum, tamen supposito quod ita esset, adhuc per hoc non deffenditur a symonia. 15
Nam secundum Sanctum Thomam, super 4⁰ *Sententiarum*, d. 25,
et Raymundum, ubi supra, et communiter omnes doctores,
theologos et iuristas, quando in administratione spiritualium, ex
pia consuetudine fidelium aliquid datur, sicut in sepulturis vel
exequiis mortuorum aut huiusmodi, hoc tamen non debet a 20
sacerdotibus exigi, et si negatur, non propter hoc debent spiritualia
differri, sed ex post facto potest per superiorem correctio adhiberi
in illos qui denegant dare quod consuetudo exposcit, sicut patet
Extra. De Symonia, Ad Apostolicam.[96]

742, 38   Et ideo, cum licentia theologie sit ita vel magis spiritualis sicut 25
sepultura, vel huiusmodi, licet universitas vel bachalarii dictum
cancellarium gravassent per dictum iuramentum, eciam supposito
quod esset illicitum et illicite in preiudicium eius factum, tamen
propter hoc non debet dignis negare licentiam vel differe, nec ante
eam aliquid exigere, sed ante omnia tenetur licentiare, et postea 30
poterit agere contra transgressores consuetudinis, vel super hoc
A f. 85   auxilium ᶠ iudicis / implorare. Et ideo, quia alio modo exigit,
symoniam incurrit.

742, 50   Item. Licet hoc satis sit clarum de iure, tamen probatur ratione,
quia nisi sic esset, nunquam aliquis posset de symonia convinci. 35

ᶠ auxilia N

---

[95] *Chart.*, I, no. 79, p. 138.
[96] X. 5, 3, 42 quoted by Ray., p. 18, col. 2. See also Tho., in 4⁰ *Sent.*, d. 25,
q. 3, art. 2, sol. 2 *ad* 2.

Unde potest sic argui: quandocumque ista propositio verificatur:
"nisi dederis michi, vel promiseris, aut securum feceris de dando
A, non dabo tibi B," ibi est venditio, sive contractus non gratuitus.
Et per consequens, si A sit temporale et B spirituale, ibi est symo-
5 nia. Aliter enim nullus posset convinci quod venderet vel commu-
taret A cum B. Modo, sic est in proposito, quod dicta propositio
verificatur, quia cancellarius dicit bachalariis quod, nisi ei dederint
aut promiserint vel securum fecerint de dando pecuniam, non
dabit eis licentiam in theologia, / que tamen licentia est res spiri- **N f. 60**
10 tualis, ut dictum est. Et per consequens incurrit symoniam modo
predicto exigendo et sic differendo ᵍ bachalariorum licentiam.
Igitur, etc.

Tercia propositio, scilicet quod si cancellarius predictum modum **742, 67**
exigendi, cum circumstantiis premissis, pertinaciter approbaret,
15 sustinendo ipsum esse licitum, ipse esset ʰ hereticus reputandus,
patet ex predictis, quia hoc esset pertinaciter approbare crimen
symonie, vel saltem crimen concussionis ⁱ, et multa alia crimina,
scilicet inhoneste cupiditatis et scandalose ᵏ exactionis, et eciam
crimen periurii, et insuper esset approbare quod licitum esset
20 im/pedire opera misericordie et caritatis, scilicet doctrine et **743**
predicationis. Sed constat quod omnia talia approbare tamquam
licita includit multas hereses. Igitur, etc. Et sic patet conclusio
principalis.

Tunc respondendum est ad rationes que videntur esse contra **743, 5**
25 predicta et pro parte adversa.⁹⁷

Ad primam ergo rationem negatur minor. Unde dico primo
quod Paulus nunquam predicavit pro temporalibus. Nam Altissiodorensis ˡ ponit hanc regulam generalem, quod "non licet
predicare pro lucro temporale vel favore humano," ⁹⁸ quia, ut
30 dicit, *li* " 'pro' ᵐ ⁹⁹ notat causam principalem," quando proprie

---

ᵍ *ex* defferendum *corr* A   ᵏ studiose N
ʰ est A   ˡ *in ras* A
ⁱ *ex* concassionis *corr* A   ᵐ li pro: Hieronymus d

---

⁹⁷ *Supra*, pp. 214-6.
⁹⁸ Altiss., f. 226ᵛb.
⁹⁹ Here I take "li" as the Old French masculine, singular, definite article,
referring to the preposition "pro," which is then analyzed. The passage cited
greatly clarifies d'Ailly's meaning: "Hec dictio 'pro' notat causam primam,
principalem, et immediatam." Altiss., f. 227ʳa.

accipitur. Et sic accipio hic et in omnibus dictis precedentibus, modo nunquam licitum est spiritualia principaliter dare pro temporalibus. Aliquid autem dare principaliter pro temporali, secundum Raymundum, ubi supra, est sic dare quod sine illo non esset daturus ille qui dat.[100] Et sic non licet principaliter predicare 5 pro temporalibus. Unde Augustinus: "Non enim debemus evangelizare ut manducemus, sed manducare ut evangelizemus. Ut cibus non sit premium quod appetitur, sed necessarium quod additur."[101] Aliquis tamen potest predicare, eciam principaliter, ut moveat homines ad opera pietatis. Ad huiusmodi autem finem conse- 10 quitur datio temporalium, ut sic consecutive predicat Apostolus pro temporalibus, ut fierent collecte pauperibus. Nam hoc erat opus pietatis, ad profectum spiritualem dantis et ad sublevandum deffectum temporalem recipientis.[102]

743, 31 Secundo. Dico pro[n] solutione aliarum auctoritatum quod 15 Apostoli et alii predicatores licite receperunt et recipere possunt
A f. 85v mercedem / sive stipendium ab illis quibus predicant[o], ad sustentationem vite pro ministerio, sive potius, pro labore in ministrando, vel adhuc magis proprie loquendo, non pro labore, sicut probat[p] Durandus, ubi supra,[103] sed pro victus necessitate, "ne, scilicet, 20 cogantur relinquere verbum Dei et circa procuranda sibi necessaria occupari."[104] Et sicut dicit Sanctus Thomas, "Ista non debentur eis quasi precium predicationis, nec sicut merces dispensationis, sed sicut stipendium necessitatis."[105] Unde super illo verbo, "Qui bene presunt,"[106] etc., dicit glossa Augustini: "Accipiant susten- 25 tationem necessitatis a populo, mercedem dispensationis a Domi-
743, 47 no."[107] Ex hiis tamen non probatur quod eodem modo sit licitum cancellario recipere a bachalariis. Ratio diversitatis est quia hoc predicatoribus expresse conceditur a iure divino, sed[q] non sic conceditur cancellario, ymmo negatur, ut patet ex dictis in prima et secunda 30

---

[n] quod A
[o] *om* A

[p] dictus (*post* probat) *del* A   *add* d
[q] licet Ad

---

[100] Ray., p. 17, col. 1 and cf. Durandus, IV, d. 25, q. 4, no. 7.
[101] Quoted by Altiss., f. 227ra.
[102] Altiss., 227ra.
[103] Durandus, IV, d. 25, q. 3, no. 10.
[104] Tho., In 4o Sent., d. 25, q. 3, art. 2, sol. 2, *ad* 5.
[105] Tho., II II, q. 100, art. 2, resp.
[106] I Tim. 5, 17.
[107] Sermo XLVI, cap. 2, 5; PL 38, 273. Quoted by Durandus, f. 365va.

conclusionibus huius secundi articuli. Licet ^r forte per hoc proba[re]tur quod, in casu necessitatis scilicet ubi ^s aliter non haberet unde vivere posset recipere a populo cui licentiandi predicabunt, et cui mittit eos ad predicandum vel docendum; sed non ab ipsis
5 quos ipse mittit: exemplum de episcopo, qui mittit Mendicantes ad predicandum, etc.

Tercio. Dico quod licet predicatores modo predicto possint **743, 59** vite necessaria recipere tamquam eis iure divino concessa, non tamen possunt saltem ultra necessitatem vite exigere, seu com-
10 pulsive petere, sed gratiose, sine compulsionis rigore, petere solum necessaria vite, juxta illud Augustini, *Libro de Opere Monachorum*: "Constituit Dominus quod ex Evangelio viventes panem gratuitum manducarent ab eis ^t quibus gratuitam gratiam predicabant." ¹⁰⁸ Ideo, si eis vite necessaria denegarentur ^v, que eis / **f. 60�v**
15 debentur, non tamen propter hoc licite possent denegare vel differre predicationem petentibus doctrinam, si aliunde, eciam propriis manibus laborando, possent vivere, exemplo Apostoli, etc. Unde patet quod, licet ex predictis auctoritatibus probaretur quod cancellarius posset recipere pro labore, non tamen quod
20 posset exigere compulsive, nec bacha/lariis non dare volentibus, **744** licentiam denegare. Quare, etc.

Ad secundam rationem, dicendum est, sicut dicit Jeronimus **744, 3** super Micheam, quod talia munera sponte exhibebantur bonis prophetis, non quasi ad emendum prophetie usum, sed ad susten-
25 tationem ipsorum, ut spiritualibus vacarent liberius. Tamen pseudoprophete illud retorquebant ad questum. Unde super illud Michee 3, 11, "Sacerdotes eius in mercede docebant populum," dicit glossa interlinearis de talibus, quod "non nisi accepto precio docebant populum, nec responsa Dei nisi pro mercede proferebant, qui
30 prophetare debuerant." ¹⁰⁹ Ideo dicit ibi Jeronimus, quod "prophetia talium facta est divinatio." ¹¹⁰ Et ita est in proposito. Quare, etc.

Ad terciam. Conceditur antecedens, sed negatur consequentia. **744, 16** / Et licet ratio satis pateat ex dictis, tamen adhuc dico cum Sancto **A f. 86**

---

^r sicut (*ante* licet) *del* A   ^t ab eis *ins interl* A
^s *om* A   ^v denegarent N

---

¹⁰⁸ PL 40, 555.
¹⁰⁹ G.I., Mica, 3, 11, *ad verb.* "prophete," "divinabant."
¹¹⁰ *In Micheam*, I, iv; PL 25, 1183.

Thoma, II^a IIe, quod "Accipere vel dare aliqua pro sustentatione ministrantium spiritualia, secundum ordinationem Ecclesie et consuetudinem approbatam est licitum. Ita tamen quod desit intentio emptionis et venditionis spiritualium, et quod ab invitis non exigatur per substractionem spiritualium que exhibenda sunt, quia hoc haberet quandam venditionis speciem. Sed spiritualibus prius gratis exhibitis, possunt statute et consuete oblationes vel quicumque alii proventus exigi a nolentibus et valentibus solvere auctoritate superioris interveniente." ^111 Verbi sunt Sancti Thome. Sed constat quod ista clare sunt contra cancellarium, quia non est sibi concessum, ymmo prohibitum, recipere, ut ostensum est. Eciam notum est quod ipse exigit contra formam predictam. Quare, etc.

744, 36   Ad quartam. Licet ^x satis responsum sit ex predictis, tamen adhuc dico cum Sancto Thoma, II^a IIe, quod "Ille cui committitur spiritualis potestas, ex officio obligatur ad usum potestatis sibi commisse in spiritualium ^y dispensatione, et eciam pro sua sustentatione statuta stipendia habet ex redditibus ecclesiasticis. Et ideo, si aliquid acciperet pro usu spiritualis potestatis, non intelligeretur locare operas suas, quas ex debito suscepti officii debet impendere, sed intelligeretur vendere ipsum spiritualis gratie usum. Ille autem qui habet scientiam, ideo, non suscipit officium ex quo obligetur aliis usum scientie impendere, et ideo licite potest precium sue doctrine vel consilii accipere, non quasi veritatem aut scientiam vendens, sed quasi operas suas locans. Si autem ex officio ad hoc teneretur, intelligeretur ipsam veritatem vendere, unde graviter peccaret ^z, sicut patet in illis qui instituuntur in ecclesiis ad docendum clericos, etc." ^112 Hec Sanctus Thomas. Ex quibus et aliis supra dictis, patet quod cancellarius non potest recipere vel saltem exigere pro labore licentiandi, sicut advocatus pro labore patrocinandi, etc. Et sic ex omnibus predictis apparet quod pars questionis affirmativa est vera.

744, 61   Unde ad rationem in oppositum, dicendum quod Papa et Curia Romana non sunt super hoc adhuc sufficienter informati—sed quan-

---

^x hoc (*post* licet) *add* N   ^z peccant A
^y concessione (*post* spiritualium) *del* N

---

^111 Q. 100, art. 3, resp.
^112 Q. 100, art. 3, *ad* 3.

do constabit eis de veritate que Parisius est notoria, ipsi super hoc
salubriter providebunt et Universitatis Parisiensis veracem opinionem nullatenus condempnabunt, advert[ent]es [a] illud quod dixit
Augustinus contra Donatistas: "Non facile pro uno vel paucis
adversus multos religionis et unitatis viros, et magno ingenio et
libera doctrina preditos, nisi pertractatis pro viribus atque per-
spectis rebus, ferenda sentencia est."[113] Et hec de questione.

[a] advertes AN

[113] Not found in Augustine's anti-Donatist works.

"SUPER OMNIA VINCIT VERITAS"

f. 86ᵛ   "Super omnia vincit veritas," [1] ut dicit propheta, sed quia "non
est victoria sine pugna," [2] et "ubi pugna fortior, ibi victoria
gloriosior," [3] ideo, ut veritas fortius impugnata gloriosius [a] vincat,
intendo, prout promisi, veritatem, quam in quadam questione alias
declaravi, pluribus rationibus tunc contra me factis et quibusdam 5
aliis impugnare, et easdem pro posse solvere. Ac eciam non solum
ipsis, sed aliis nunc faciendis [b], illo adiuvante, qui coronam glorie
legitime pro veritate certantibus pollicetur, aliqualiter respondere,
premissis tamen et presuppositis protestationibus alias per me
factis.   10

745, 13   Igitur in questione alias per me tractata, qua querebatur "utrum
hereticum sit dicere quod liceat pro docendi licencia pecuniam
dare vel recipere," [4] quantum ad primum articulum, tres fuerunt
conclusiones declarate: prima fuit quod "dare vel recipere pecuniam
pro licentia docendi theologiam est proprie symoniacum," [5] ad 15
cuius declarationem quibusdam premissis circa materiam symonie
tandem posite fuerunt quatuor propositiones et per ordinem declarate, prima fuit quod "theologia est donum Dei spirituale;" [6]
secunda, quod "doctrina seu predicatio ipsius est res spiritualis;" [7]
tertia, quod "licencia seu potestas vel auctoritas docendi vel 20

---

[a] gloriosus A   [b] interficiendis d

---

[1] Considered an anonymous Latin proverb, but cf. "Magna est veritas,
et praevalet," III Esdras, 4, 41; "In omni re vincit imitationem veritas,"
Cicero, *de Oratore*, III, 57, 215; "Veritas vincit," Hans Walther, *Proverbia
Sententiaeque Latinitatis Medii Aevi. Lateinische Sprichwörter und Sentenzen des
Mittelalters in alphabetischen Anordnung* 5 vols. (Göttingen, 1963), no. 33157s.
"Veritas semper triumphat de putri mendacio," *Ibid.*, 33157 al.

[2] Cf. "Nulla sine adversario corona victoriae," Ambrose, Epist. 18, 28;
"Nemo athleta sine sudore coronatur." Cited in A. Otto, *Die Sprichwörter und
sprichwörtlichen Redensarten der Römer* (Leipzig, 1890), p. 290.

[3] Cf. "Tanto periculosior eorum pugna sit quanto frequentior, et tanto
victoria clarior quanto difficilior." P. Abelard, *Ethics*, ed. Luscombe, Oxford
Mediaeval Texts (Oxford, 1971), p. 4. "Ubi pugna dura, ibi clarior victoria."
Walther, 32066 f.

[4] I.e. Radix omnium.

[5] Radix, pp. 200-9.

[6] *Ibid.*, pp. 200-4.

[7] *Ibid.*, p. 208.

predicandi eam est auctoritas spiritualis;" [8] quarta, quod "potestas licentiandi in ea est eciam potestas spiritualis." [9] Ex quibus clare sequitur conclusio, scilicet quod "dare vel recipere pecuniam pro licentia docendi theologiam, seu pro quocumque predictorum, est
5 proprie symoniacum." [10]

Contra primam propositionem arguo sic: theologia non est **745, 35** gratuitum donum Dei, seu donum supernaturale, id est, quod ex puris naturalibus non possit haberi. Igitur non est donum Dei spirituale. Consequentia tenet ex dictis in eodem articulo, in
10 declaratione tertie partis descriptionis symonie.[11] Antecedens probatur quia aliquis infidelis vel hereticus posset esse theologus, et theologiam pure naturaliter acquirere. Et per idem arguitur contra secundam propositionem, quia talis theologus infidelis vel hereticus potest, ex puris naturalibus, scire theologiam docere et
15 predicare. Et sic talis doctrina vel predicatio non est spiritualis vel supernaturalis.

Et confirmatur argumentum, quia ex hoc quod theologia est **745, 46** sapientia, seu donum sapientie, probatum est quod ipsa est res spiritualis vel supernaturalis et quod non debet esse venalis. Sed
20 sapientia est unus de quinque habitibus intellectualibus, de quibus tractat Aristoteles, VI° *Ethicorum*, qui sunt habitus mere naturales.[12] Eciam secundum eundem, *Libro Methaphysice* in pluribus locis, methaphysica est theologia et est sapientia, et tamen non est supernaturalis, nec ex illo sequitur quin ipsa vel ipsius doctrina possit
25 esse venalis.[13] Igitur nec valet probatio illius propositionis. Quare, etc. /   **746**

Ad primum, nego antecedens, loquendo de theologia proprie dicta, de qua hic intelligo. Unde pro materia, dico primo quod theologia, proprie loquendo, est habitus acquisitus, vel plures
30 habitus acquisiti, ex discursu proprie theologico vel ex discursibus theologicis. Vocatur autem / discursus proprie theologicus, qui **f. 87** constat ex dictis seu propositionibus in Sacra Scriptura contentis, vel ex hiis, vel saltem ex altero [c] huiusmodi [d]. Et [e] principia theo-

---

[c] altera A   [e] sic (*post* et) *add* A
[d] sequentibus (*post* huiusmodi) *add* d

[8] *Ibid.*, pp. 208, 17 - 209, 4.
[9] *Ibid.*, p. 209, l. 5-23.
[10] See note 5, p. 237.
[11] Radix, pp. 202-4, esp. p. 203, l. 17-21.
[12] Book VI, Chap. 3, 1139b 14-18.
[13] Book VI, Chap. 1, 1026a 17-33.

logie sic sumpte sunt sacri canones, id est Sacre Scripture veritates, distinguendo autem conclusiones contra principia. Conclusiones theologice dicuntur omnes veritates non secundum se formaliter in Sacra Scriptura contente, sed ex contentis in ipsa de necessitate sequentes, et non alie. 5

746, 16 Secundo dico quod talis theologia, de huiusmodi conclusionibus et per huiusmodi principia, modo predicto acquisita, in animo illius qui dat fidem Sacre Scripture, est quedam fides, seu f habitus creditivus. Et ideo, theologia sic accepta et proprie dicta est quedam fides acquisita. Quare sequitur quod non potest ab in- 10 fideli acquiri, ipso manente infideli, nec est possibile aliquem infidelem esse theologum, loquendo de infideli simpliciter, qui nulli parti Scripture fidem daret. Si vero accipiatur theologia magis large, pro illo vel illis habitibus quo vel quibus aliquis novit sensum Sacre Scripture, et unum dictum per aliud exponere et probare, 15 talem theologiam potest infidelis acquirere et ipsam docere.

746, 30 Tercio dico quod theologia primo modo dicta, cum sit quedam fides, est quoddam Dei donum gratuitum. Nam fides enumeratur inter gratias gratis datas, I Cor. 12, 9, et ad Ephes. 2, 8, dicitur: "Gratia salvati estis per fidem, et non ex vobis, ne quis glorietur. 20 Dei enim donum est." etc. Unde dicit Sanctus Thomas, II, II, q. 6, art. 1, quod "cum homo ad assentiendum hiis que sunt fidei, elevetur supra naturam suam, oportet quod hoc insit ei ex supernaturali principio interius movente, quod est Deus. Et ideo fides," secundum eum, "quantum ad assensum, qui est principalis actus 25 fidei, est g a Deo interius movente per gratiam."

746, 42 Similiter, Guillielmus Parisiensis, in prima parte tractatus sui De Fide et Legibus, concludit ex multis racionibus, "fidem esse gratiam, hoc est divine h largitatis et beneficentie gratuitum donum, qua i scilicet intellectus vincit se et k credit contra se l vel m saltem 30 supra se, et est lumen vincens naturalia lumina intellectus humani, et ideo est gratia, quia n est media inter gloriam et naturam." 14 Et idem dicendum est de theologia sic accepta. Quare, etc.

---

f ex se corr in marg A
g om d
h dre A
i quia d

k vincit se et in ras A
l credit contra se: concludit quia in se d
m et ideo est gratia (post vel) del A
n quae d

---

14 Guillielmus Parisiensis, De Fide et Legibus, 2 vols. (Paris, 1674), I, 6.

Quarto dico quod, licet theologia secundo modo dicta, vel 746, 52
eciam secundum aliquos qui non tenerent opinionem predictam,
licet theologia primo modo dicta posset naturaliter acquiri, pre-
supposita prima revelatione Scripture Sacre, tamen ad istum
5 sensum potest dici supernaturaliter haberi, quia obiectum seu
principium theologicum, scilicet ipsa Scriptura Sacra naturaliter
non habetur ex supernaturali revelatione, juxta illud: "Spiritu
Sancto inspirati locuti sunt sancti Dei homines." etc.[15]

Et ad eundem sensum, theologia utroque modo sumpta, et 746, 62
10 ipsius predicatio seu doctrina, dicitur res supernaturalis et
spiritualis[o]. Satis enim notum est quod predicatio seu doctrina
theologie, seu predicare et docere, est quidam actus corporalis,
et per consequens naturalis. Et tamen, alia consideratione, dicitur
spiritualis et supernaturalis, quia est, respectu Sacre Scripture,
15 supernaturaliter inspirata [p], sicut eciam baptismus et alia sacramenta, quantum ad materiam, sunt quedam corporalia / et per f. 87ᵛ
consequens naturalia, et tamen dicuntur spiritualia et super-
naturalia quantum ad effectum, scilicet quantum ad sacramentalem
gratiam, vel eciam quia supernaturaliter et divini/tus instituta.   747
20 Unde, generaliter in proposito, illa dicuntur spiritualia et super-
naturalia que respiciunt regimen humani generis, non solum in hiis
que sunt ex puris naturalibus humanitus adinventa, sed ex speciali
revelacione divinitus inspirata. Sic autem est de theologia, quocumque modo sumpta, et eius predicatione vel doctrina. Quare, etc.
25 Ad confirmationem, dico quod theologia est sapientia. Nam 747, 8
Deuteronomio, in principio legis, dicitur: "Hec est vestra sapientia
et intellectus coram populis." [16] Similiter, secundum Augustinum,
12, *De Trinitate*, "Sapientia est divinarum rerum cognitio." Et
secundum eum ibidem, "Superior pars rationis sapiencie deputatur;
30 inferior autem scientiis [q]." [17] "Superior autem ratio," ut ipse in
eodem libro dicit, "intendit [r] rationibus supernis [s], id est divinis
et conspiciendis et consulendis." [18] "Conspiciendis" quidem,

---

[o] supernaturalis et spiritualis: et spiritualis *in ras* A supernaturalis et *om* d
[p] inspirate Ad

[q] scientiae d
[r] *om* d
[s] deputatur (*post* supernis) *add* d

---

[15] II Pet. 1, 21.
[16] Deut. 4, 6.
[17] Book 12, Chap. 15; PL 42, 1012. Quoted by G. O., I Cor. 12, 8.
[18] Cf. *Ibid.*, Chap. 24 passim.

secundum quod divina in seipsis contemplantur, "consulendis" [t] autem, secundum quod per divina iudicat de humanis, ut per divinas regulas actus humani dirigantur. Utrumque autem horum convenit theologie, primum secundum illam partem, in qua ipsa est speculativa, secundum vero, secundum illam partem in qua 5 est practica. Quare patet quod ipsa proprie est sapientia.

747, 25 Tamen distinguenda est duplex theologia et duplex sapientia, secundum quod duplex est cognitio divinorum. Una est de veritatibus que ex puris naturalibus humanitus possunt sciri, et de ista loquitur Aristoteles in libro *Methaphysice* et [v] 6⁰ *Ethicorum*.[19] Alia 10 est de veritatibus que supernaturaliter et divinitus inspirantur et revelantur, et de ista ad presens loquimur. Nec talis theologia vel sapientia est venalis, nec eius predicatio vel doctrina, sine symonia, ut satis probatum fuit ex dicto Christi: ["Gratis accepistis, gratis date."] Math., 10, 6, et glossa ibidem. Quare, etc. 15

747, 36 Secundo, principaliter arguo contra terciam propositionem, probando quod licentia theologie non sit aliqua potestas vel auctoritas spiritualis, quia habenti scientiam theologie non est prohibenda ipsius predicatio seu doctrina. Sed quilibet sciens theologiam permittendus est predicare et docere sine speciali 20 missione vel licentia. Igitur ad hoc non requiritur aliqua spiritualis auctoritas vel potestas. Consequentia videtur nota. Antecedens probatur quia predicare et docere sunt opera misericordie. Ergo non sunt alicui prohibenda, sed multitudo predicancium et docentium, cum sit ad salutem fidelium, est multum appetenda, 25 iuxta illud Sapi., 6, 26, "Multitudo sapientium," id est "cetus predicatorum," secundum glossam, "sanitas est orbis terrarum."

747, 52 Item. Confirmatur quia Num. 11, 28, legitur quod cum in castris filiorum Israhel quidam preter [x] mandatum Moysi prophetarent et ob hoc Iosue dixisset: "Domine mi Moyses prohibe eos." Ipse 30 non [y] prohibuit, sed respondit: "Quid," inquit, "emularis? Quis **f. 88** tribuat ut omnis populus prophetet [z]?" Igitur / videtur a simili, quod nullus sciens predicare est prohibendus.

---

[t] consulendum A   [y] tamen d
[v] et 6⁰: 26⁰ d   [z] prophetiset d
[x] propter d

---

[19] Aristotle, *Metaphysics*, Book VI, Chap. 1, 1026a 17-33 and *Nichomachean Ethics*, Book VI, Chap. 3, 1139b 14-18.

Item. Ad Philip. 1, 18, dicit Apostolus, "Sive per occasionem, 747, 60
sive per veritatem, Christus annuntietur, et in hoc gaudeo et
gaudebo." Ubi glossa, "Ideo Apostolus non prohibet mercenarios,"
scilicet eos qui predicant Christum per occasionem terrenam, "sed
5 eos permittit quia et ipsi ᵃ utiles sunt ad aliqua." Ergo nullus
utiliter predicans, eciam si non sit missus, est prohibendus, sed de
eius predicatione gaudendum est.

Item. Luc. 9, 50. Cum prohibuissent Apostoli quemdam 747, 67
facientem in nomine ᵇ Christi miracula, ne amplius ea faceret, eo
10 quod non sequebatur eos, ait eis Christus: "Nolite prohibere: qui
enim non est adversus nos, pro nobis ᶜ est. Ergo a simili videtur
quod habens scientiam predicandi non debet a predicatione
prohiberi.

Item. Actuum, 18, 24 legitur quod "Apollo Judeus Alexandrinus, 747, 74
15 cum esset eloquens et potens in Scrip/turis," etc. "docebat diligen- 748
ter ea que sunt de Jesu, sciens tantum Baptisma Johannis," id est
nundum baptizatus baptismate Christi, sed baptismo Joannis
tantum. Non tamen fuit eius predicatio a discipulis repulsa. Ergo,
quicumque est potens in Scripturis, eius predicatio non est pro-
20 hibenda. Etc.ᵈ

Ad istam rationem respondeo negando principale antecedens, 748, 7
et pro declaratione dico primo quod nullus quantumcumque
sciens in theologia licite potest exercere officium publice et auctori-
tative predicationis seu doctrine sine speciali missione vel licencia,
25 juxta illud Apostoli ad hoc probandum ᵉ allegatum: "Quomodo
predicabunt nisi mittantur." Rom. 10, 15, ubi dicit Glossa: "Non
sunt veri Apostoli nisi ᶠ missi, nec predicabunt nisi mittantur."
Unde eciam, cum ᵍ Christus sciret messem esse multam, operarios
vero paucos, non tamen eos precipitanter ʰ multiplicavit, nec eos
30 indifferenter premisit ⁱ, sed dixit Apostolis ᵏ: "Rogate ergo
dominum messis, ut mittat operarios in messem suam." ²⁰ Ipsi
autem rogaverunt eum, ut legitur xxi. d. cap. *In Novo*.²¹ Et ipse

---

ᵃ et ipsi *om* d
ᵇ meo (*post* nomine) *del* A
ᶜ nos, pro nobis: vos, pro vobis *text*
    Vulg et d
ᵈ Etc. *it* A
ᵉ praedicandum d

ᶠ *interl* A
ᵍ *interl* A
ʰ precipitantur A
ⁱ permisit A
ᵏ Apostolus A

---

²⁰ Matt. 9, 38.
²¹ Gratian, D.21 c.2.

rogatus eos misit dicens, "Ecce, ego mitto vos." etc. Luc. 10, 3. Hoc autem totum plenum est misterio [1] et doctrinali exemplo, cum omnis Christi actio nostra sit instructio. Et ideo, per hoc, instruimur quod nullus debet publice predicare nisi missus.

748, 28 Secundo, dico quod illorum qui mittuntur, quidam mittuntur 5 a Deo tantum, id est, non per hominem, quidam vero a Deo per hominem, [m] ut dicit Augustinus ad Orosium, "Missi fuerunt a Deo et non per hominem Moyses et Johannes Baptista, qui missi fuerunt per angelum, vel per divinam revelationem." [22] Tales autem sic missi probare debent suam missionem, aut per miraculum 10 sibi ad indicium sue missionis iniunctum, sicut Moyses probavit per conversionem virge in colubrum, et econverso, sicut Dominus ei iniunxerat Exo., 7, 9, aut per specialem prophetiam de ipsis dictam, sicut Johannes probavit suam missionem per prophetiam Ysaye, quam exposuit de seipso dicens: "Ego vox clamantis in 15 deserto." etc. Johan. 1, 23. Aliter enim non [n] est credendum ipsis dicentibus se missos, quoniam [o] idem dicerent heretici, sicut legitur *Extra. De Hereticis, Cum Ex Iniuncto.*[23]

f. 88ᵛ

748, 45 Missi autem a Deo per hominem, sicut [p] / Josue per Moysem, et prelati per Ecclesiam, vel aliqui non prelati per Ecclesie prelatos 20 canonice mittuntur, sicut eciam Paulus, quando non sufficiebat [q] omnibus, mittebat discipulos suos sibi experimento probatos, unde I ad Cor [r]., 4, 17, dicit, "Misi ad vos Thymotheum." etc. Et talis missio probari debet per canonica documenta, sicut et alia que per Ecclesiam fiunt, secundum jura. Unde a Deo mitti 25 creditur, qui canonice mittitur et rite ab Ecclesia ad hoc eligitur. Nam super illo verbo Hebr. 5, 4: "Nec quisquam assumit sibi honorem, sed qui vocatur a Deo tanquam Aaron," dicit glossa quod "a Deo vocatur qui recte eligitur."

748, 58 Tercio dico quod, illorum qui mittuntur a Deo per hominem, 30 seu per Ecclesiam, quidam sunt ordinarie instituti, sicut episcopi, loco Apostolorum, ut 68. d. *Quorum Vices,*[24] et minores, seu par-

---

[1] misterio: mi[ni]sterio A
[m] quidam vero . . . hominem *om* d
[n] *interl* A
[o] cum d

[p] sicut (*post* hominem) *it* A
[q] sufficebant A
[r] Thim A

---

[22] Nothing of the sort in *Ad Orosium*, PL 42, 669-78. Cf. *Contra Faustum Manichaeum*, XVI, 12; PL 42, 322.
[23] X. 5, 7, 12.
[24] Gratian, D.68 c.6.

rochiales presbiteri, loco lxxii discipulorum, ut xxi. d. *In Novo* [25] et secundum glossam Luc. 10, 2.[26] Isti duo ordines ab initio Ecclesie fuerunt principaliter constituti, sed postea archidyaconi et archipresbiteri seu alii, secundum diversos ritus ecclesiarum, ad
5 animarum regimen additi [s] sunt, qui "opitulationes," id est, "opem maioribus ferentes [t]" appellati sunt, secundum glossam I Cor [v]., 12, 28.

Quidam autem sunt extraordinarie missi, sicut generaliter dici **748, 71** possunt, extraordinarie opitulationes, illi quos episcopi, in aliis
10 occupationibus impediti, mittunt per suas dyoceses, ad exercendum vice ipsorum predicationis officium, seu aliud [x] regimen ani/marum, **749** sicut eis videtur expedire, ut legitur *Extra., De Officio Judicis Ordinarii, Inter Cetera*,[27] quod eciam, eadem ratione, dici potest de minoribus prelatis, sicut sunt plebani et alii rectores ecclesiarum,
15 qui videlicet possunt per suas parrocias predicatores mittere, vel vocare, vel mutare, ut vii. q. i. *Episcopi vel Presbiteri*.[28]

Quarto dico quod, quia papa est summus episcoporum, et **749, 8** ordinarius singulorum, ex certis causis, secundum quod iudicaverit expedire, potest mittere aliquas personas ad predicandum vel
20 aliud regimen [y] animarum, ut *Extra., De Hereticis, Cum ex Iniuncto*,[29] et hoc modo ab eo mittuntur illi qui auctoritate apostolica in theologica licentiantur [z]. Sed, cum "ars artium sit regimen animarum," ut dicit Gregorius,[30] ideo non passim cuilibet est predicationis officium permittendum [a], sed solis ydoneis et probatis,
25 juxta illud I Thim. 3, 10, "Hii autem probentur primum [b] et sic ministrent." Etc. Etc.

Hiis premissis, respondeo ad obiecta et primo ad probationem **749, 20** principalis antecedentis, dicendo quod quidquid sit de secreta

---

[s] addicti d
[t] ferentibus A
[v] *ex* Thim *corr* A
[x] ad d

[y] al (*post* regimen) *del* A
[z] licentiatur A
[a] premittendum A
[b] *interl* A

---

[25] *Ibid.*, D.21 c.2.
[26] *Decretum Gratiani cum Glossis Bartholomei Brixiensis* (Venetiis, 1496), f. 17[rb]. The *Decretum* cites Luke 10, 2, "videntes messe esse multam et operarios paucos," ad verbum *operarios*: "hic signaverunt doctores." Here again, this time implicitly, the doctors are "sent."
[27] X. 1, 31, 15.
[28] Gratian, c.7 q.1 c.38.
[29] X. 5, 7, 12.
[30] S. Gregorius Magnus, *Regulae Pastoralis Liber*, Pars I, cap. 1; PL 77, 14.

predicatione, correctione, seu doctrina, tamen publica predicatio, sicut nec publica correctio, est opus misericordie, nisi prout fit cum debitis circumstantiis, inter quas una est quod ille qui eam facit sit ad hoc missus. Nec publica doctrina cuilibet permittitur, cum dicat Apostolus "Mulierem docere in Ecclesia non permit- 5 to." [31] Nec multitudo sapientium, id est predicatorum, est utilis, nisi debite instituta et approbata, maxime cum non debeat assiduari predicatio ne vilescat, quia super illud Hebr. 6, 7, "Terra [c] super
f. 89 se venientem sepe bibens ymbrem [d]" / dicit glossa: "Doctrina Sacra ad instar ymbris, si rara est non sufficit, si assidua, vilescit." [32] 10 Et de actoribus [e] seu predicatoribus [f] Sacre Scripture, dicit Augustinus, li. xviii, *De Civetate* [*Dei*], cap. xxxix, "Ipsi sane pauci esse debuerunt, ne multitudine vilesceret quod religione carum esse oporteret." [33] Ideo, si predicatores multiplicarentur sine missione vel licentia, eorum predicatio non esset appe[ten]da [g], 15 sed prohibenda.

49, 42 Ad primam confirmationem antecedentis, dico quod Moyses sciebat illos duos esse de illis viris electis, quibus dederat Dominus spiritum ad prophetizandum. Ideo illos tanquam a superiori, scilicet a Deo missos, noluit prohibere. Hoc eciam argumentum 20 non cogit, quia non sumitur ibi "prophetare" pro "predicare," sed "pro laudes Deo canere." Quare, etc.

Ad aliam dico quod ibi loquitur Apostolus de mercenariis, qui predicant propter questum, sicut patet per glossam allegatam. Quidam autem eorum sunt missi, ideo tollerandi quamdiu Evan- 25 gelio proficiunt. Dico tamen quod predicatio (actio), id est actio predicationis, illorum qui predicabant [h] Christum occasione ter- rena, ut dicit glossa, non placebat Apostolo, quia, cum illi pec- carent, Apostolus, gaudendo de peccato, peccasset. [34] Sed predicatio (passio), id est effectus vel profectus predicationis illorum, qui 30 Deo auctore inde proveniebat Apostolo placebat, et hoc notat [i]

---

[c] cum (*post* Terra) *add* d
[d] ymbrum A
[e] auctoribus d
[f] predicationibus A

[g] approbanda d
[h] predicabunt A
[i] non d

---

[31] I Tim. 2, 12.
[32] G. O.
[33] Aurelius Augustinus, *De Civitate Dei Libri XXII*, in Corpus Christiano- rum, Series Latina, vol. XLVIII (Turnholt, 1955), p. 636, Lines 21-23.
[34] G. O. in Philip. 1, 17-18, *ad verb.* "sive per veritatem."

glossa, 16. q. 1, *Addicimus*, [35] sicut de crucifixione Christi dicitur
"actio displicuit, passio grata fuit."

Ad terciam dico quod opera miraculorum permissa eciam sunt   749, 63
malis et a Deo non missis, ad dampnationem eorum et utilitatem
5 aliorum. Publica vero predicatio nulli permittitur, quantumcumque predicet in nomine Christi, nisi a Deo tantum, vel a Deo per
hominem mittatur, ut dictum est. Eciam [k] ratio diversitatis est,
quia facientes in nomine Christi miracula nullius usurpant officium,
sed publice predicantes non missi usurpant officium prelatorum et
10 sacerdotum ac aliorum missorum.

Ad ultimam dico quod licet forte ille Apollo non esset missus   749, 73
ab homine, tamen missus erat a Deo, quia dicitur ibidem quod
"doctus erat viam Domini et / fervens spiritu loquebatur," [36] et   750
aliqui discipuli habentes discretionem spirituum, cognoverunt [1]
15 quod ductus erat a Spiritu Sancto, ideo eum non piohibuerunt,
quia "qui Spiritu Dei [m] ducuntur, non sunt sub lege." Gal. 5, 18.
Similiter, eciam, quia nundum tunc distincta et distributa erant
officia ecclesiastica, ideo nullius prelati officium usurpabat. Quare
non sic prohibendus erat, sicut modo, quando distributio officio-
20 rum facta est in Ecclesia, per quam aliqui sunt prelati et alii subiecti,
ut legitur ii. q. vii. *Hiis Itaque*.[37] Unde, licet tunc essent Apostoli
et Apostolatus officium, non tamen sic se habebat illius Apostolatus
discursus sicut modo se habet, ut dicit Augustinus, et per hoc
ultimum dictum posset responderi ad omnia obiecta. Ex quibus
25 omnibus patet quod ad predicationis officium requiritur auctoritas
vel potestas seu missio vel licentia. Quare, etc.

Tercio principaliter argumentatum fuit contra me una ratione,   750, 19
que simul facere videtur contra terciam et quartam [n] propositiones,
/ probando quod licentia docendi, vel auctoritas licenciandi, licet   f. 89v
30 sit aliqua potestas, non tamen potestas spiritualis, quia talis potestas
potest committi et convenire layco, et merito matrimonio coniugato, ergo talis non videtur potestas spiritualis, sed magis civilis
et temporalis.

Ad istam rationem alias respondi, negando consequentiam, et dixi   750, 2

---

[k] Et jam d   [m] *om* d
[1] cognoverant d   [n] secundam d

---

[35] Glossa Ordinaria (Johannes Teutonicus) in C.16 q.1 c.19 *ad verb*. "sacerdotes."
[36] Act. 18, 25.
[37] Gratian, C.2 q.7 c.39.

quod asserere talem consequentiam esse bonam esset hereticum, quia hereticum est dicere assertive quod potestas episcopalis vel sacerdotalis non sit spiritualis et talis posset aut potuisset convenire alicui matrimonio coniugato. Nam quandoque sacerdotes verum matrimonium contrahebant, ymo eciam episcopi, juxta il- 5 lud Apostoli I Thim. 3, 2, "Oportet episcopum esse unius uxoris virum," et adhuc eciam sacerdotes Grecorum, secundum doctores, contrahunt ᵒ verum matrimonium. Ymo, dicunt aliqui, quod non repugnat eciam ᵖ episcopos plures antiquitus habuisse uxores et quod intelligitur dictum Apostoli "Oportet episcopum esse unius 10 uxoris virum," et illud quod ad Titum, primo, 5-6, quod presbyter �q debet esse "unius uxoris vir," scilicet post baptismum,quia si ante baptismum habuerat unam, post baptismum poterat ducere aliam, nam baptismus tollebat illam irregularitatem secundum Jeronimum, et ut ibi dicit glossa.³⁸ 15

⸠50, 49 Item. Mirum esset quod matrimonium potestati sacerdotali aut alteri spirituali repugnaret, cum infidelitas vel heresis ei non obstet. Potest enim aliquis esse sacerdos, et fieri infidelis vel hereticus, manente in eo sua spirituali potestate. Quare, ex hoc quod aliquis matrimonio coniugatus, vel quod maius est, ex hoc quod aliquis 20 infidelis vel hereticus, potest esse theologus et habere licenciam docendi vel potestatem licentiandi, concludere quod huiusmodi non sint spiritualia est puerilis consequentia. Nec esset sanum talem consequentiam sustinere, exemplum de prophetia et potestate prophetizandi ʳ, que convenit infideli. Quare, etc. Et ex hoc eciam 25 apparet solutio prime rationis principalis superius facte, etc.

⸠50, 64 Item. Nulli dubium est quin potestas excommunicandi sit potestas spiritualis, et tamen talis potestas potest committi et convenire layco, quia sicut dicit Bartholomeus, xxxii. d. in glossa super cap. *Verum* ³⁹ et eciam secundum Huguccionem,⁴⁰ papa ˢ tam 30

ᵒ contrahant A   contrahebant d
ᵖ *om* d
�q probatur d

ʳ prophetandi d
ˢ Huguccionem, papa: Hugonem Papam d

³⁸ G. O. *ad verb*. "unius uxoris vir." Jerome is quoted by G. O. *in* I Tim. 3, 2.

³⁹ Bartholomeus Brixiensis on C.32 q.6 c.3 in: *Decretum Gratiani* una cum Glossis domini Joannis theutonici . . . et annotationibus Bartholomei brixiensis (Venetiis, 1514), f. 51ʳa.

⁴⁰ Huguccio on D. 32, pars 3, para. 1, *ad verb*. "utrum," in: *Summa ad Decretum* (Firenze, Bib. Laurenziana, ms. Pluteo I, Sin. IV), f. 40ʳa, lines 28-39. The following marginal comment appears: "Et sit pocius excommunicare iu[ri]sdictionis quam ordinis."

excommunicationem quam absolutionem, que pertinet ad potestatem juridicionis, scilicet in foro contentioso, potest committere seu
delegare layco. Et sic, de facto, hiis temporibus, huiusmodi
potestas, ut dicitur, commissa est in certis casibus Parisiensi Pre-
5 posito, qui est judex laycus et irregularis. Quare, etc. /   751
    Item. Quod maius, secundum aliquos, et sicut tenet Johannes
in *Summa Confessorum*,[41] laycus si ordinaretur, reciperet ordinem
et potestatem sacerdotalem et ipsius caracterem, ex quo baptizatus
esset, quia baptismus est ianua omnium sacramentorum, xxxii. d.
10 § *Verum* [42] et illud quod videtur esse contra hoc in ca. *Omnes*,   751, 5
xxxviii. d.,[43] refferendum est ad ordinis executionem, et idem tenet
Hostiensis.[44] Et per consequens, ex hoc quod aliqua potestas
committitur [t] layco, non infertur quod non sit potestas spiritualis.
Quare, etc.
15   Quarto principaliter potest argui contra conclusionem in se, per   751, 1
quamdam rationem iuristarum. Nam in iure canonico, post rubrica
"De Symonia" [45] sequitur rubrica de quadam specie symonie, /   f. 90
scilicet, "Ne prelati vices suas sub annuo censu concedant," [46]
et deinde ponitur rubrica specialis [v] "De Magistris, Ne aliquid
20 exigatur pro licentia docendi," [47] in qua, postquam dictum est
"qualiter spiritualia prohibeantur acquiri" in precedentibus rubri-
cis, consequenter tractatur "de hiis que spiritualium instar [x] habent,
scilicet de licentia docendi," secundum Raymundum, ibidem.[48] Ergo
sequitur quod licentia docendi non sit proprie potestas spiritualis,
25 nec ipsam vendere aut pro ipsa aliquid exigere, est proprie symo-

---

[t] committi A   [x] se (*post* instar) *add* d
[v] spiritualis d

---

[41] Joannes de Friburgo, *Summa Confessorum*, Lib. 3, tit. 5, q. 3 (Lugduni,
1518), f. 100[v]a.
[42] D.32 c.6. D'Ailly erroneously cites D.27, but John of Friburg, to whom
he is referring, and Ray. (p. 262, col. 2), upon whom John draws in turn,
refer the saying "Baptismus est ianua omnium sacramentorum" to Gratian,
D.32, which says in c.6 pars 3, § 4, "Baptisma . . . et ordine prior, et necessarior
sit." Goffredus, f. 163[v]a, also associates these sayings.
[43] Gratian, D.38 c.6.
[44] Henricus de Segusio, Cardinalis Hostiensis, *Summa*, Lib. I, De temp. ord.
et qual. ord., Quarta regula. § Sed numquid (Lugduni, 1537, reissue 1962)
f. 30[r]a.
[45] X. 5, 3.
[46] X. 5, 4.
[47] X. 5, 5.
[48] Ray., p. 30, col. 1.

niacum, nec symoniam committit exigens aliquid, sed crimen concussionis, secundum Hostiensem et alios doctores juris canonici.
Aliter enim tale crimen debuisset in rubrica "De Symonia" prohiberi. Alioquin iste rubrice ᵞ non essent convenienter distincte.
Quare, etc.   5

751, 32 Ad istud dico quod non est generaliter verum de qualibet
licentia docendi quod sit res spiritualis, sicut nec quelibet doctrina est spiritualis, ut de spirituali hic loquimur. Et ideo non
quamlibet licenciam docendi vendere aut pro ea exigere est proprie
symoniacum, sed in pluribus est solum crimen concussionis,   10
propter quod, post materiam de symonia, rationabiliter ponitur
specialis ᶻ rubrica, "Ne Pro Licentia Docendi" etc., que quidem
licentia, licet spiritualium instar ᵃ habeat, tamen in pluribus
scientiis secularibus et humanitus adinventis non est proprie
spiritualis. Unde, a maiori fit denominatio illius rubrice, de hiis   15
que spiritualium instar ᵇ habent.

751, 45 Tamen, cum hoc stat quod licentia docendi in theologia, sicut
et ipsa doctrina theologica, est spiritualis, ita ᶜ quod de ipsa
speciale ᵈ est, quod eam vendere, vel pro ipsa aliquid exigere,
proprie symoniacum est. Nec propter hoc necesse fuit hoc ᵉ crimen   20
in rubrica "De Symonia" prohiberi: tum primo, quia hoc crimen
satis est prohibitum iure naturali et divino, ut ostensum fuit in
questione et in solutione prime rationis principalis nunc facte,[49]
quare non neccesse fuit de hoc specialem prohibitionem fieri in
iure canonico; tum secundo, quia in dicta rubrica, non tractatur   25
de qualibet specie symonie, sed specialiter de illa que fit in sacra-
mentalibus vel in beneficialibus, ut patet intuenti rubricam, unde
etiam ibidem aliqua prohibentur que non sunt proprie symoniaca
a iure divino.

751, 61 Nam in capitulo primo dicitur, sicut non debet episcopus ma- 30
nuum impositionem, ita nec minister vel notarius in ordinatione
eius vocem vendere, vel calamum vel cartam,[50] et tamen ista non
sunt proprie spiritualia aut spiritualibus annexa, nec de iure divino

---

ᵞ Canonice (*post* rubrice) *add* d   ᶜ juxta d
ᶻ spiritualis d   ᵈ spirituale d
ᵃ se (*post* instar) *add* d   ᵉ *om* d
ᵇ se (*post* instar) *add* d

---

[49] Radix Omnium, pp. 209, 25 - 212, 12; Super Omnia, pp. 238, 6 - 241, 15.
[50] X. 5, 3, 1.

[prohibita], in talibus proprie committitur symonia. Similiter, in
capitulo *In Tantum*, ne pro ecclesiarum investitura peccunia
postuletur,[51] et in capitulo *Audivimus*, ne pro sepultura aliquid
exigatur,[52] expresse tanquam symoniacum, prohibitum est, et **751, 70**
5 tamen ista non sunt proprie spiritualia, vel saltem non sunt magis
spiritualia quam licentia in theologia, seu predicatio vel doctrina
theologica, de quibus non tamen tractat ibi ius canonicum, hoc
relinquens tanquam clarum per ius di / vinum, cum etiam in illa **752**
rubrica magis tractetur de symonia positiva, que est a jure humano,
10 quam Henricus Boich[53] vocat "symoniam canonicam," / in capi- **f. 90ᵛ**
tulo *Significasti*, *De Electione*, quam de symonia proprie dicta, que
est a jure divino. Quare, etc.

Secunda principalis conclusio fuit quod dare vel recipere pecu- **752, 7**
15 niam pro licentia docendi theologiam est contra jus naturale et
divinum, que probata fuit principaliter per istud medium, quia
symonia est contra jus naturale et divinum, ut ibi fuit ostensum.
Ex qua conclusione, inter alia corollaria, fuit illatum istud [f] corollarium, quod dare vel recipere pro licentia docendi theologiam
20 juramentum de reverentia vel honore, illi qui eam [g] ministrat im-
pendendis, vel eius aut sui officii iuribus deffendendis, non minus
est contra jus naturale et divinum quam dare vel recipere pecuniam, quia tale juramentum obsequiosum est munus ab obsequio,
in quo committitur symonia sicut in munere a manu, ut dictum
25 fuit.[54] Quare, etc.
Sed contra ista arguitur sic: Papa licite potest pro licentia do- **752, 22**
cendi theologiam recipere pecuniam vel iuramentum obsequiosum.
Igitur talia dare vel recipere etc. non est contra jus naturale et
divinum. Consequentia patet quia papa non potest licite facere
30 contra jus naturale vel divinum, cum non sit a tali iure exemptus
plus quam quicumque alius. Sed antecedens probatur quia si
papa non posset hoc licite, hoc maxime esset pro tanto quia istud
est symoniacum, sicut patet ex probatione conclusionis. Sed hoc

---

[f] *ex* estud *corr* A   [g] eum d

---

[51] *Ibid.*, c.36.
[52] *Ibid.*, c.41.
[53] *In Quinque Decretalium Libros Commentaria* (Venetiis, 1576), p. 37, col. a, §9.
[54] Radix Omnium, pp. 209-12, 227-8, 230-2.

non obstat, quia papa, secundum quosdam, non potest committere
symoniam, ex eo quod res Ecclesie sunt sue. Quare, etc.

752, 36   Confirmatur quia papa recipit seu mandat recipi iuramentum
obsequiosum, [h] scilicet iuramentum fidelitatis ab episcopis consecrandis et ab archiepiscopis in palii [i] traditione, ca. *Significasti*, 5
De Electione.[55] Si ergo licite detur et recipiatur tale juramentum
pro consecratione episcopali, seu episcopali ordine, multo magis
hoc poterit pro licentia theologie, et per consequens neutrum est
contra jus divinum vel naturale. Quare, etc.

752, 45   Ad primum, potest negari antecedens, capiendo *li* "pro" sicut 10
ego dixi in questione.[56] Et ad probationem respondet Sanctus
Thomas in *Secunda Secunde* et etiam super *Quarto Sententiarum*, d.
25, art. 3, quasi quod papa potest committere vitium symonie,
sicut quilibet alius homo. Ymmo, secundum eum, hoc peccatum
tanto in eius persona esset gravius, quanto maiorem optinet locum. 15
Et ideo, ut dicit, opinio illa est erronea quorumdam, qui dixerunt
quod papa non potest committere symoniam ex eo quia res Ecclesie
sunt sue. Nam quamvis res Ecclesie sint [k] eius, tanquam principalis
dispensatoris, non tamen, ut dicit, sunt ipsius tamquam domini
et possessoris.[57] Et ideo, si reciperet pro aliqua re spirituali pec- 20
cuniam, non careret vicio symonie. Et ad hoc facit secunda ratio [l]
quam feci in secunda parte primi articuli, ad ostendendum quare
symonia est illicita.[58]

752, 62   Aliqui tamen iuriste distingunt de dupplici symonia. Nam quedam sunt prohibita quia symoniaca, sicut vendere vel emere 25
sacramenta, et breviter omnia que in Veteri et Novo Testamento
symoniaca erant; quedam autem sunt symoniaca quia prohibita,
scilicet illa que per constitutionem Ecclesie tantum sunt symoniaca,

f. 91   ut si quis / renuntiet Ecclesie, eo pacto, ut detur nepoti suo. Hec
autem distinctio est intelligenda, quod quedam est symonia proprie 30
dicta, que est prohibita iure naturali et divino, alia improprie et
similitudinarie [m] dicta, que sunt prohibita iure humano, scilicet
ab Ecclesia [n] instituto, sicut tactum est in solutione quarte rationis

---

[h] obsequium A   [l] responsio d
[i] et . . . palii: *in ras* A   [m] similitudinare A
[k] sunt A   [n] Ecclesiae d

---

[55] X. 1, 6, 4.
[56] Radix Omnium, pp. 232-3.
[57] Tho. II, II, q. 100, art. 1, *ad* 7, and 4⁰ *Sent.*, d. 25, art. 3, *ad* 2.
[58] Radix Omnium, pp. 204-5.

prius facte.[59] Loquendo er/go de symonia proprie dicta, de qua hic **753**
loquimur, papa potest esse symoniacus, sicut quilibet alius. Sed
loquendo de symonia secundo modo, papa non potest symoniam
committere, scilicet symoniam canonicam, ut dicit Henricus Boich,
5 ubi supra,[60] et hoc verum est, [o] sic quod incurrat penam a iure
taxatam, aliter non, secundum Durandum,[61] quia, cum sit caput
Ecclesie, non est subiectus iuri humano, scilicet ordinationi seu
constitutioni ab Ecclesia institute, ut ix. q. iii. *Cuncta*.[62]

Tamen, quidquid sit de hoc, [dico] quod [p] non potest licite vendere **753, 9**
10 licentiam docendi theologiam, seu eam dare pro pecunia, seu alio
munere ab obsequio, nam hoc esset [q] symoniacum primo modo,
quia prohibitum iure divino, ut in probatione prime conclusionis
probavi ex glossa super illo verbo "Euntes ergo predicate," etc.
Math. 10, 7, ubi sequitur "Gratis accepistis, gratis date." [63]

15   Ad confirmationem dico quod concesso antecedente, scilicet **753, 17**
quod papa licite recipiat iuramentum obsequiosum, scilicet fidelitatis ab episcopis consecrandis, non tamen sequitur illud quod
infertur, scilicet quod illud recipiat, seu licite recipere possit, pro
consecratione seu episcopali ordinatione. Et ideo nec sequitur
20 quod hoc possit licite recipere pro licentia theologie, licet posse
tale iuramentum licite recipere vel ordinare aut statuere quod
reciperetur ab ipsis licentiandis, sicut et ab ipsis ordinandis, maxime post electionem, seu provisionem, ut infra dicam.

Et si queratur si non recipit [r] pro ipso ordine episcopali, vel **753, 28**
25 pro tali licentia, pro quo ergo recipit talia iuramenta? Ad hoc
dico [s] quod ipse in tali casu huiusmodi iuramenta recipit pro eo
quia papa est capud Ecclesie, et Romana Ecclesia caput omnium
ecclesiarum, et ideo, ratione istius superioritatis, omnes inferiores
ecclesie et persone, specialiter ecclesiastice, tenentur ei [t] ad fidelita-
30 tem et obedientiam, propter quod papa, pro se et Ecclesia Romana,

---

[o] ut dicit . . . verum est *om* d   [r] decipit A
[p] *om* d   [s] *om* A
[q] est d   [t] eis A

---

[59] Super, pp. 248, 15-250, 12.
[60] *In Quinque Decretalium Libros Commentaria*, p. 37, col. a, § 9 and *supra*,
p. 250, l. 10.
[61] Durandus a Sancto Porciano, *In Petri Lombardi Sententias Theologicas Libri
IV*, IV, d. 25, q. 5 (Venetiis, 1571), f. 365ᵛb in fine.
[62] Gratian, C.9 q.3 c.17, cited by Durandus.
[63] Radix Omnium, p. 209.

potest licite recipere iuramentum a suis inferioribus, de illo ad
quod tenentur, et precipue hoc potest ab illis qui sunt in dignitati-
bus et altioribus gradibus ecclesiasticis, sicut sunt episcopi consecrandi. Et hec ratio ponitur in ca. *Significasti, De Electione.*[64]

753, 43 Et si dicatur quod ergo, pari ratione, episcopus posset licite, 5
ab illis quibus confert sacros ordines, recipere iuramentum fidelitatis
et reverentie, quia, licet non pro ipsis ordinibus conferendis, tamen
pro eo quia est eorum superior, et ipsi sibi ad huiusmodi fidelitatem
et reverenciam tenentur; dico quod, quidquid sit de consequente,
tamen illud non sequitur ex dictis. Ratio diversitatis est quia 10
multa licent pape, qui est supremum capud, que non licent cuilibet
superiori respectum suorum inferiorum, sicut multa licent regi
que non duci, et duci que non comiti, etc. Unde talia iuramenta
obsequiosa de fidelitate, reverentia, vel honore servando [v] non
debent recipi vel exigi in administratione rerum spiritualium nisi 15
a superiori, nec quolibet, sed a solo papa, vel de eius speciali auc-
f. 91ᵛ toritate vel licentia, aut ex consuetudine per ipsum tacite / approbata. Et sic credo quod aliqui archiepiscopi et episcopi ab aliquibus abbatibus, per eos consecratis, certa iuramenta recipiunt,
vel forte ratione alicuius temporalitatis, in qua eis temporaliter 20
subiciuntur, sicut eciam rex ab pluribus episcopis et abbatibus de
novo consecratis huiusmodi [x] iuramenta recipit. De hac autem
materia iuramentorum inferius magis dicam. Ideo hec sufficiant
circa secundam [y] conclusionem.

753, 68 Tercia conclusio principalis fuit quod dicere vel asserere quod 25
dare vel recipere pecuniam appreciative pro licencia docendi theologiam sit licita est hereticum. Probatio autem huius conclusionis
principaliter in hoc fundabatur, quia hoc est asserere illud esse
licitum quod secundum fidem et Catholicam veritatem est symonia-
754 cum et contra / ius naturale et divinum, ut patet ex duabus prece- 30
dentibus conclusionibus. Quare, etc.

754, 3 Ex qua conclusione, inter alia corollaria, inferebatur istud corollarium, scilicet quod existimare vel credere licentiam docendi in theologia pro pecunia seu precio temporali posse comparari vel possideri,

---

[v] servandum A   [y] tertiam d
[x] huius A

---

[64] X. 1, 6, 4.

non solum esset symoniacum, sed eciam proprie hereticum. Et hoc
fuit declaratum ex tercia causa que data fuit ᶻ,⁶⁵ propter quam Symon
Magus et symoniaci ab eo sic vocati dicuntur heretici, scilicet quia
existimavit donum Dei pecunia possideri, ut dicitur Act. 8, 20.

5   Sed contra hoc arguitur: quia non est hereticum asserere quod **754, 13**
licitum sit dare pecuniam pro Spiritu Sancto, seu pro habendo
Spiritum Sanctum, ergo, a fortiori, non est hereticum asserere
quod licitum est dare pecuniam pro licentia docendi theologiam,
seu pro habendo huiusmodi licentie gradum. Consequentia est
10 satis clara, sed antecedens nuper in publico sermone posuit et
concessit quidam Magister, ut michi relatum est, qui tamen de
hoc non est tanquam de heresi reprehensus. Unde circa hanc
materiam tria dogmatizavit et publice asseruit sub hac verborum
forma.

15   Primo enim, quasi nescio quid grande intonans, ait, "Symon **754, 25**
Magus," inquit, "habere voluit Spiritum Sanctum quia nemo dat
quod non habet." Et adiunxit quod in hoc non peccavit quod
Spiritum Sanctum habere voluit.

    Secundo dixit quod nec in hoc peccavit quod voluit dare pecunias **754, 30**
20 suas pro habendo Spiritum Sanctum. Et probacionem subdidit:
nam licet dare temporalia pro spiritualibus, nec hoc est symonia,
iuxta illud: "Vade et vende omnia que habes, et da pauperibus,
et habebis thesaurum in celo." ⁶⁶

    Tercio dixit quod peccatum Symonis, unde symonia nomen ac- **754, 36**
25 cepit, solum fuit in ᵃ hoc, quod voluit habere Spiritum Sanctum
ut venderet aliis. In hoc symonie peccatum commisit et non in
hoc quod voluit dare temporalia sua pro habendo Spiritum
Sanctum.

    Ex quibus patet quod ipse dogmatizavit licitum esse ᵇ dare **754, 41**
30 pecuniam pro habendo Spiritum Sanctum. Et cum *ly* "pro" denotet
appreciationem, seu commutationem, secundum communem ᶜ
modum loquendi doctorum, licitum est, secundum eum, emere
Spiritum Sanctum et emere spiritualia pro temporalibus et, per
consequens, licentiam theologie et alia spiritualia / pro pecunia **f. 92**
35 seu precio temporali commutare et possidere. Et per hoc sequitur

---

ᶻ fuerit (*ante* fuit) *del* A   ᵇ esset A
ᵃ *om* d   ᶜ *om* d

---

⁶⁵ Radix, pp. 213-4.
⁶⁶ Matt. 19, 21.

quod sic asserere vel credere non est hereticum, quod est contra conclusionem et corollarium, cum ipse ex huiusmodi dictis et publice dogmatizatis non sit reprehensus, etc. etc.

754, 54   Ad istam rationem respondeo negando principale assumptum. Et ad illa que dixit ille magister, nisi esset propter reverentiam 5 magisterii, sufficeret pro omni responsione dicere illud Satiricum Persii:

> Folle premis ventos, et clauso murmure raucus,
> Nescio quid tecum grave cornicaris inepte [d]. [67]

Tamen per singula eius dicta censui discurrendum.   10

754, 64   Quoniam [e] ergo primo dicit quod Symon Magus habere voluit Spiritum Sanctum, quia nemo dat quod non habet, aut hoc omnino non est ad propositum, aut ipse per hoc intelligit quod nemo potest dare Spiritum Sanctum, nisi ille qui habet ipsum, quemadmodum nemo dat denarium, nisi qui habet denarium. Et in hoc 15 manifeste includitur heresis, nam, licet solus Deus proprie et principaliter dare possit Spiritum Sanctum, tamen, loquendo de datoribus mediatis qui dicuntur dare Spiritum Sanctum ministerialiter, secundum quem modum Symon Magus dari voluit

755 Spiritum Sanctum ab Apostolis, et qualiter Aposto/li ipsum dare 20 poterant, et eorum successores, scilicet prelati et sacerdotes, certum est quod sic dare possunt Spiritum Sanctum, scilicet ministerialiter in ipsis sacramentis, aliqui qui non habent ipsum, quia sunt in peccato mortali; alioquin soli ministri Ecclesie qui essent in gratia dare possent Spiritum per sacramenta, quod est hereticum, 25 ut posset ostendi.

755, 9   Quantum vero ad illud quod secundo dixit, scilicet quod Symon Magus in hoc non peccavit quod voluit dare pecunias suas pro habendo Spiritum Sanctum, contra hoc expresse videtur esse textus Scripture, quia Petrus ei respondit, "Pecunia tua tecum sit in 30 perditionem, quia existimasti donum Dei pecunia possideri." Act. 8, 20. Sed velle dare pecunias pro habendo Spiritum Sanctum, seu velle habere Spiritum pro peccunia, est velle ipsum pecunia possidere, quod Petrus reputabat dampnabile. Quare, etc.

755, 19   Et per idem respondeo ad probationem illius dicti, quando enim 35

---

[d] ex inempte *corr* A   [e] Cum d

---

[67] Satura V, 11-12.

subiungit quod licet dare temporalia pro spiritualibus, nec hoc
est symonia. Istud nego loquendo secundum communem usum
doctorum. Et ad illam auctoritatem quam allegat, "Vade et vende"
etc.,[68] satis responsum est in uno corollario partis secunde primi
5 articuli.[69] Tamen adhuc dico quod, cum dicitur aliquid temporale
dare pro [f] spiritualibus, sicut pro vita eterna, vel huiusmodi, sicut
dicitur Danielis 4, 24, "peccata tua elemosinis redime," ibi *ly*
"pro" non capitur proprie, prout, scilicet notat appreciationem
vel proprie dictam emptionem, sed secundum Sanctum [g] Thomam
10 et Joannem [h] in *Summa* et alios doctores omnes, ibi accipitur
meritum pro emptione vel redemptione, et est impropria et methaphorica [i] locutio.[70]

Si ergo sic intelligat quod licitum est dare temporalia pro 755, 34
spiritualibus, scilicet per modum meritorie actionis, hoc modo
15 constat quod Symon Magus non voluit dare pecuniam pro Spiritu [k]
Sancto / vel eius dono, et per consequens, non est hoc ad propo- f. 92ᵛ
situm de symonia, sed est inducere eos [l] qui nesciunt quid sit
symonia, ut generaliter credant fore verum quod pro spiritualibus
licet dare temporalia, que doctrina est mala. Cum talis propositio
20 secundum se et iuxta communem modum loquendi falsa sit, quia
in hac materia *ly* "pro" apud doctores capitur prout notat appreciationem, sicut eciam expresse notavi in conclusione, vel eciam
prout notat causam motivam principalem, prout dixi circa finem
questionis, in solutione cuiusdam rationis.[71] Nam sicut dicit Do- 755, 49
25 minus Altissiodorensis [m], *ly* "pro" notat causam principalem quando
proprie accipitur.[72] Et sic in nullo casu licitum est dare temporalia
pro spiritualibus, nec sic dare debemus elemosinam *pro* vita
eterna, seu *pro* nostra beatitudine, sed principaliter propter Deum, f. 92ᵛ
seu pro Dei bonitate, licet possimus [n] licite dare elemosinam pro

[f] *om* A
[g] *om* d
[h] Jeronymum d
[i] metaphysica d

[k] Spiritu *ex* Spiritum *corr* A
[l] *om* A
[m] Altissimus *in* Altiss *corr* A   Altissi-
    mus d
[n] possumus d

[68] Matt. 19, 21.
[69] Radix, p. 206.
[70] Tho. II, II, q. 100, art. 1, ad 3. Joannes de Friburgo, *Summa Confessorum*,
Tit. I, q. 10; f. 2ʳa.
[71] Radix, pp. 232-3. Cf. Super, p. 254.
[72] *Summa Aurea* (Paris, 1500), f. 227ʳa.

vita eterna, sed *ly* "pro" denotet causam motivam minus principalem.

'55, 58 Sed quantum ad illud quod tercio dixit, scilicet quod peccatum Symonis, unde symonia nomen accepit, solum fuit quod in hoc voluit habere Spiritum Sanctum ut venderet aliis, et in hoc pec- 5 catum symonie commisit, et non in hoc quod voluit dare temporalia, etc. Ista propositio innuit, ymmo quasi clare exprimit, quod peccatum Symonis non fuit in hoc quod voluit emere Spiritum Sanctum, sed in hoc solum, quod voluit vendere ipsum. Ita quod si voluisset emere ipsum, absque hoc quod ipsum ⁰ voluisset vendere, 10 non peccasset, nec peccatum quod symoniam vocamus commisisset, quod est contra Augustinum, super Joannem, secundo, ubi ᵖ dicitur quod "que honeste ᵠ emuntur non illicite venduntur." [73]

Hoc ergo manifeste falsum est et, ut credo, simpliciter hereticum. Nam, licet verum sit quod Symon Magus ad hoc spiritualem 15 potestatem emere voluit ut eam postea venderet, ut dicit Sanctus **756** Thomas,[74] et sicut habetur i. q. iii. *Salvator*,[75] / propter quam causam, tam ʳ volentes emere quam volentes vendere, communiter dicuntur symoniaci, sicut dixi in secundo corollario prime partis descriptionis symonie in primo articulo questionis ˢ.[76] 20

756, 4 Tamen prout dicit idem ᵗ Sanctus Thomas, 25 d., quarti *Sententiarum*, si distincte loqui volumus, ementes dicuntur symoniaci et ᵛ vendentes giezite, quia Giezi spiritualia vendere voluit, IV Reg. 5, 20.[77] Sed quod Symon Magus ea ˣ vendere voluit, licet hoc verisimiliter presumatur, ut dixi, tamen hoc ex textu Biblie, Act. 25 8, 18-19, expresse non habetur, sed solum quod ʸ ea emere voluit. Et hec emptio seu cogitatio, id est deliberata volitio emendi, ibi tanquam dampnabilis ab Apostolo reprehenditur, que eciam

---

⁰ peccatum A
ᵖ ideo A
ᵠ quod est ... honeste *in ras* A
ʳ *om* A
ˢ quasi d

ᵗ *om* d
ᵛ *om* d
ˣ eam A
ʸ quia d

---

[73] Aurelius Augustinus, *In Iohannis Evangelium Tractatus CXXIV*, tr. 10, cap. 4 (in Joh. 2, 14-16), ed. R. Willems, in *Corpus Christianorum, Series Latina*, vol. 36 (Turnholti, 1954), p. 102. "Quae enim honeste emuntur, non inclite venduntur."

[74] II, II, q. 100, art. 1, *ad* 4.

[75] Gratian, C.1 q.3 c.8.

[76] Radix, pp. 201-2.

[77] Tho. in 4º *Sent.*, d. 25, q. 3, art. 1, ad 4.

dampnabilis et reprehensibilis erat, eciam supposito quod non
habuisset voluntatem vendendi, sicut clare patet ex dictis in secunda
parte, primi articuli questionis ᶻ, et specialiter ex secunda ratione ibi
facta, quia, scilicet dona Dei spiritualia sunt impreciabilia, etc.[78]
5 Et per consequens, non solum in volendo vendere, sed eciam in
volendo emere consistit peccatum symonie. Et principaliter
denominatur ab ipsa emptione, sicut patet ex textu Sacre Scripture
et per omnes doctores. Quare, etc.

Item. Ostendo quod tertium dictum non stat cum secundo quia, **756, 25**
10 si Symon Magus in hoc solum commisit peccatum symonie, quod
Spiritum Sanctum voluit aliis vendere, tunc arguo sic: quia / per **f. 93**
secundum eius dictum, ipse in hoc non peccavit, quod voluit dare
pecunias pro habendo Spiritum Sanctum. Vel ergo Apostoli peccassent dando seu volendo ei dare Spiritum Sanctum pro suis
15 peccuniis vel non. Si ᵃ dicat quod sic, ergo eciam ipse peccasset
volendo pro suis peccuniis ab eis habere vel sibi dare Spiritum
Sanctum, quia in hoc particeps fuisset peccati ipsorum, quod est
contra eius secundum dictum. Si dicat quod non, ergo nec ipse
Symon peccasset volendo aliis vendere Spiritum Sanctum, seu
20 volendo eum dare aliis pro pecuniis, quod est contra tertium eius
dictum, nec prelati aut sacerdotes peccarent, volendo dare sacramenta et alia dona Dei spiritualia, pro pecuniis, seu pro temporalibus, volendo vendere spiritualia. Et sic evacueretur omnis symonia,
et per consequens patet quod eius dicta simul non concordant, nec
25 consonant modo loquendi Sacre Scripture et doctorum. Quare sunt
male sonantia in fide et merito revocanda ᵇ vel saltem exponenda.

Unde evidenter apparet qualiter aliqui, nescio quo zelo ducti,
ferventi animo contra Matrem Nostram Universitatem, pro eius **756, 4⁇**
adversario, veritatem persecuntur, dum falsam et perniciosam doc-
30 trinam, sub quadam verborum obscuritate de mentibus hominum
educere, et in publico dogmatizare conantur. Nec latet quam
libenter tales in angulis et latenter contra veritatis declarationem
murmurant, dum in favorem falsitatis talia obscura et inepta dog-
mata, in fide male sonantia, patenter asserere et predicare publice
35 non formidant. Et hec circa tertiam conclusionem et totum primum
articulum sufficiant.

ᶻ Quasi d   ᵇ est (*post* revocanda) *del* A
ᵃ si *ex* sic *corr* A

---

[78] Radix, p. 204, l. 30.

756, 62 Quantum ad secundum articulum, reprobavi duas cavillosas [c] responsiones, quibus cancellarius nititur sustinere quod pro licentia docendi in theologia non recipit nec exigit aliquid a bachalariis licentiandis. Una est quam dedit in articulis Domino Pape presentatis, in qua dicit quod bachalarii de ipsorum libera et mere sponta- 5 nea voluntate gratuite et liberaliter dant quod volunt. Alia est quam dedit in Parlamento, ubi proposuit quod bachalarii in theologie licentiandi tenentur sibi dare ad minus decem Francos, et hoc ratione laboris quem habet occasione licentie conferende.[79] Et pro ista secunda via feci quatuor rationes et induxi aliquas auc- 10

757 toritates Scripture Divine, quibus videretur [d] / posse probari quod sit licitum dare et sic recipere pro labore.[80] Sed postea ad illas clare respondi et, illis non obstantibus, declaravi quod dicte due responsiones stare non possunt. Et primo ostendi quod una illarum alia interimit,[81] secundo quod prima responsio falsa est,[82] et tertio 15 quod secunda multa inconvenientia includit.[83]

757, 10 Probavi primum quia repugnat quod bachalarii gratis et libere dant quod volunt, sicut dicit prima responsio, et quod teneantur [e] ratione laboris dicti cancellarii sibi dare decem Francos, sicut dicit secunda responsio. Et ibi dixi quod illud quod debetur alicui pro 20 labore non datur ei mere libere et gratuite, nam illi qui operatur et cui pro labore merces debetur, merces huiusmodi seu stipendium laboris non impenditur [f] secundum gratiam, sed secundum debitum iusticie, juxta dictum Christi et Apostoli, "Dignus est operarius mercede sua." 25

757, 21 Sed / contra hoc obicitur, quia ex hac auctoritate Christi, et
f. 93ᵛ aliis pluribus Apostoli, patet quod predicatoribus, ex debito iusticie, debetur victus ab illis quibus predicent [g]. Et hoc expresse dicit Sanctus Thomas in II [a] II [e], Questione de Religiosis Predicatoribus, Articulo 5,[84] et tamen, secundum Augustinum, huiusmodi victus 30 predicatoribus gratis datur, unde ipse dicit in *Libro de Opere Mona-*

---

[c] cavillosas *in ras* A
[d] videtur d
[e] tenantur d

[f] impeditur A
[g] predicant d

---

[79] Radix, pp. 214-5.
[80] *Ibid.*, pp. 215, 12 - 216, 19.
[81] *Ibid.*, pp. 216, 26 - 217, 2.
[82] *Ibid.*, p. 217, l. 3-26.
[83] *Ibid.*, pp. 217, 27 - 230, 2.
[84] Tho. II, II, q. 187, art. 5, *ad* 5.

chorum: "Constituit Dominus quod ex Evangelio viventes, panem
gratuitum manducarent ab eis quibus gratuitam gratiam predicabant." [85] Ergo huiusmodi panis, in quo eorum victus intelligitur,
licet [h] eis debeatur, tamen est gratuitus, et gratis datus. Et per
5 consequens stat aliquid esse gratis datum et tamen debitum.

Ad hoc potest dupliciter responderi. Primo, quia predicatoribus **757, 35**
debetur victus. Non dico tamen quod pro labore, sed pro vite
necessitate, ut alias tetigi et magis infra declarabo. Et ideo, proprie
loquendo, eis non datur gratis, sed tamen dicitur gratuitus, quia,
10 licet eis a populo debeatur, tamen, ex eo quod non est determinata
certa quota que ab isto singulari supposito vel ab illo debetur,
ideo quod datur ab aliqua singulari persona, gratuitum seu gratis
dari dicitur.

Alio modo, et magis ad intentionem Augustini, potest responderi **757, 45**
15 quod panis predicatorum, licet sit debitus, tamen dicitur gratuitus,
non quia gratis datus, sed quia sine corporali labore recipitur. Et
hoc dicit Augustinus in eodem libro, sub hiis verbis: "ut [i] tamen [k]
spiritualiter operantes, scilicet predicando, manducet panem a
corporali labore gratuitum." [86] Ideo patet quod, non obstante illa
20 auctoritate, non stat aliquid esse gratis datum et de jure debitum.

Quantum vero ad primam viam, probavi quod ipsa non stat, et **757, 54**
quod falsum est quod bachalarii gratis dant. Et hoc ostendi ex
tribus conditionibus quas ponit Raymundus in *Summa* et habetur
Extra., *De Symonia*, *Etsi Questionis*, per quas concluditur utrum
25 gratis vel ex corrupta intentione datur. Prima est qualitas dantis
et recipientis; secunda, quantitas muneris; tertia, tempus donationis.[87] Unde, ex hiis, concludebam verisimiliter presumendum
quod bachalarii licenciandi non dant gratis, etc.

Sed contra hoc secundo obicitur [l] quia non obstantibus predictis **757, 69**
30 conditionibus, a magno tempore et tanto quod quasi non est
memoria de contrario, omnes bachalarii licenciandi dederunt. Ergo
omnes corrupta intentione et non gratis dederunt et, per consequens, omnes symoniaci fuerunt et merito a suis gradibus depo-
nendi, vel non fuerunt ve/re graduati, quod est absurdum, cum **758**

[h] liceat A	[k] tantummodo A
[i] *interl* A	[l] *in ras* A

[85] PL 40, 555.
[86] *De Opere Monachorum*.
[87] Ray., p. 6, col. 2, citing X. 5, 3, 18.

etiam multi, ratione huiusmodi graduum, sepe fuerint in Ecclesia
ad summas dignitates promoti.

758, 4 Ad hoc respondeo et dico primo quod falsum est antecedens,
scilicet quod omnes dederunt, quia scio quod aliqui, et de tempore
istius cancellarii et aliorum, nichil dederunt. Secundo dico quod 5
licet multi dederint, non tamen in omnibus predicte conditiones
f. 94 concurrerunt. Quare stare / potuit quod gratis dederunt. Tercio
758, 11 dico quod, licet in multis tres predicte conditiones concurrerint
tamen non sequitur quod omnes tales corrupta intentione
dederint. Et ratio est quod, licet predicte conditiones faciant 10
presumptionem iuris ad concludendum quod corrupta intentione
datum sit, et hoc in foro exteriori. Nam ᵐ secundum Guillelmum,[88]
ille conditiones intelligende sunt in foro causarum, ubi accipitur
presumptio de symonia ex multis circumstantiis, quod non obstantibus predictis conditionibus, aliqui qui dederunt habuerunt 15
conscientiam et intentionem interiorem rectam, vel saltem non
corruptam.

758, 23 Pro cuius declaratione, ulterius dico quod aliqui sic dederunt
non advertentes Iura Canonica in ista materia, nec eciam privilegia
universitati concessa, et ex illa inadvertentia dabant, non pro ipsa 20
licentia, seu pro maiori ⁿ sui honoris promotione per muneris cor-
ruptelam inducenda ᵒ aut procuranda, sed credentes quod sic dare
esset licitum et honestum. Et licet tales haberent intentionem in
hoc erroneam, et per illam inadvertenciam, opinionem falsam, non
tamen intentionem mala affectione corruptam. 25

758, 34 Quinto dico quod aliqui dederunt, qui in dando habuerunt intentionem rectam quia, scilicet, ᵖ dederunt ad redimendam vexationem suam. Et hoc maxime potuit esse tempore istius cancellarii,
qui non dantibus vexationes multas intulit: aufferendo vel diffe-

---

ᵐ tamen d   ᵒ indurenda A
ⁿ maioris d   ᵖ si d

---

[88] Guillelmus Rhedonensis, *Apparatus in Summam S. Raimundi*, in: *Summa
Raymundi de Peñafort de Poenitentia* (Rome, 1603), p. 16, col. b, *ad verb.* "exacta
vel extorta.*" The editor of the 1603 edition of Raymund's *Summa* attributes
the gloss to John of Freiburg. This error was exposed by Quetif and Echard
(*Scriptores Ordinis Praedicatorum*, 2 vols., Paris, 1719-1721), I, 131, who show
Vincent of Beauvais, Henry of Ghent, and Nicholas of Lyra attributing the
commentary to William of Rennes. In his *Summa Confessorum*, even John of
Freiburg praises the *Apparatus* under William's name, according to Quetif
and Echard. Pierre d'Ailly calls it the "Glossa Guillelmi" or just plain "glossa."

rendo ius suum. Quando autem aliquis sic vexatur iniuste in suo
spirituale jure, licitum �q est dare pro vexatione sua redimenda,
Extra, De Symonia, ca. *Dilectus* I [89] et juxta illud Apostoli, "Redi-
mentes tempus quoniam ʳ dies mali sunt," [90] ut i. q. iii. *Quesitum,*[91]
5 et *Extra. De Magistris, Prohibeas.*[92] Hoc tamen, secundum glossam
et secundum Guillelmum [93] et Sanctum Thomam in *Summa,*[94] non
habet locum super iure spirituali, nisi quando redimenti pro certo
constat de iure suo, aliter non.

    Et si dicatur quod nulli potest pro certo constare quod habeat **758, 49**
10 ius ad licentiam theologie, quia hoc de se credere esset superbe
presumere, quare etc., ad hoc respondeo, negando antecedens, quia
ex illo sequeretur quod nullus posset ˢ licite appetere seu petere
licentiam theologie, quod est falsum. Nam, sicut dicit Sanctus
Thomas in quadam questione de Tercio Quolibet, "petere huius-
15 modi licentiam quantum est in se, nullam videtur turpitudinem
continere. Potest tamen quandoque turpitudinem continere, ratione presumptionis que esset si ille, qui non est ydoneus ad docendum, peteret docendi officium. Sed hec presumptio," ut dicit,
"non equaliter est in petentibus licentiam ad docendum et in
20 petentibus pontificatum." Et rationem subdit, que est ad propositum. "Nam scientiam, per quam aliquis est ydoneus ad docendum,
potest aliquis scire per certitudinem se habere; caritatem ᵗ autem,
per quam aliquis est ydoneus ad pastorale officium, non potest
aliquis scire per certitudinem se habere. Et ideo semper est viciosum
25 pontificatum petere. / Non autem semper est viciosum petere licen- **f. 94ᵛ**
tiam docendi." [95] Quare patet quod multi absque superba presum-
ptione possunt credere, ymmo de certo scire, se habere ius ad licentiam theologie, et tales quandoque licite potuerunt dare pro redimenda vexatione, vel saltem sine corrupta intentione.

30   Dico tamen ulterius. Si aliqui non fuerunt ydonei / ad docendum, **759**
sive hoc crediderint, sive oppositum, et illi dederint ad licentiam

---

�q licite A   ˢ potest (*ante* posset) *del* A
ʳ cum d   ᵗ charita d

  [89] X. 5, 3, 28.
  [90] Ephes. 5, 16.
  [91] Gratian, C.1 q.3 c.4.
  [92] X. 5, 5, 2.
  [93] Glossa Guil. in Ray., p. 21, *ad verb.* "simoniam commissam."
  [94] II, II, q. 100, art. 2, ad 5.
  [95] Tho., *Quaestiones Quodlibetales,* III, q. 4, art. 9.

theologie obtinendum [v], tales corruptam intentionem habuerunt et symoniam commiserunt, nec per redemptionem vexationis excusati sunt.

759, 6 Dico septimo, quod stat aliquos non gratis dedisse, sed in dando corruptam intentionem habuisse, et tamen symoniam non com- 5 misisse. Patet si aliqui fuerint ydonei ad docendum et securi de licentia habenda, qui tamen dederint, non pro ipsa licentia, sed ad honestiorem locum licentie obtinendum. Tales enim non comisissent crimen symonie, sed vicium concussionis vel ambitus, seu ambitionis. Et ideo, licet peccassent, tamen fuissent vere graduati 10 et licentiati. Secus autem de illis, qui fuissent ad licentiam symoniace promoti. Exemplum potest poni de illo qui digne esset ad sacros ordines promovendus, et de sua promotione esset securus, si daret episcopo pecuniam, non pro ipsis ordinibus, sed ut inter alios esset primo loco ordinatus, in casu quo tali primevitati esset aliquis 15 honor annexus. Talis enim non esset symoniacus, sed ambitiosus, nec a gradu vel officio removendus.

759, 25 Ultimo dico quod licet bachalarii qui tempore retroacto dederint modis supradictis, vel quibusdam aliis, possent [x] a symonia excusari, et ab omni crimine vel vicio [y], tamen non sic excusari pos- 20 sunt illi qui modo darent cancellario. Ratio diversitatis est, quia ipse ab eis pecunias et quedam iuramenta obsequiosa symoniace exigit, et in sic exigendo, est manifeste symoniacus, ut alias probavi et inferius declarabo. Igitur illi qui sibi sic exigenti darent, secum in crimine symonie participarent, et sicut ipse, symoniaci essent, 25 nec possent propter redemptionem vexationis excusari.

759, 36 Sui vero predecessores non sic exegerunt, sed solum tamquam gratis oblata receperunt, quod patet de Magistro [z] Joanne de Calore, suo immediato predecessore, qui, a clerico suo, quem mittebat ad portandum signeta, recipiebat iuramentum quod nichil 30 exigeret, et quod non portabat signeta animo aliquid recipiendi. Et ipsum, ut audivi, instruebat [a] quod sibi oblata, prima vice, in signum quod essent gratis data, cum quadam honesta modestia refutaret. Scio eciam quod aliquas pecunias sibi missas et gratis datas, quandoque reddere obtulit. 35

759, 46 Et si dicatur quod saltem ipse excusari non possit, de hoc quod recepit, quia fecit contra privilegium *Parens Scientiarum*, in quo

---

[v] obstinendam d
[x] possint d
[y] vicio *in ras* A

[z] *om* d
[a] inferebat A

dicitur quod "nichil recipiat pro licentia concedenda," [96] respondeo
quod istud privilegium solum prohibet recipere pro licentia, vel
eciam pro labore annexo inseparabiliter in ipsa / licentia conce- f. 95
denda, sicut alias dixi, in tertia probatione, prime conclusionis
5 principalis, secundi articuli,[97] sed non videtur prohibere recipere
gratis data.

Et si iterum dicatur quod privilegium *Servus Crucis* prohibet 759, 56
gratis dare, quia simpliciter dicit, "Nullus incipiat licentiatus a
cancellario [vel] ab alio, data ei pecunia," etc.,[98] respondeo quod
10 istud solum prohibet bachalariis dare, sed non cancellario recipere,
saltem expresse. Quia tamen si bachalarii illicite dant, cancellarius
illicite recipit, quia in sic recipiendo cum eis in peccato participat
et consentit. Ideo dico quod licentiatus qui gratis dat non illicite
dat, nec in hoc peccat, dumtamen non incipiat, quia in hoc pri-
15 vilegio, non incipere est pena dantis. Ideo, si talem penam subeat,
videtur quod culpam non incurrat, iuxta notam [b] Joannis Monachi,
ca. *Cupientes, De Electione. Libro Sexto,* § *ad hoc.*[99]

Aliter potest dici quod istud previlegium simpliciter prohibet 759, 71
dare, eciam gratis, et implicite prohibet cancellario recipere a
20 bachalariis, secundum mentem legislatoris, et ideo tam cancellarii,
quam bachalarii, qui contra fecerunt, saltem contumaciter, sententiam excommunicationis incurrerunt, ut ibidem dicitur. Credo tamen
quod ipsi, vel saltem multi ipsorum, ignoverunt [c] hoc privilegium.
Ideo non intelligitur contumaci/ter fecisse contra ipsum, quia, 760
25 licet ignorantia iuris communis, et maxime iuris divini, non excuset, ignorantia tamen iuris privati, sicut talis privilegii, bene
excusat, dum tamen non sit ignorantia crassa et affectata. Qualis
esset illa ignorantia, que modo est in quibusdam, qui, non obstante quod sciant privilegium, tamen, ex inordinata affectione, non
30 credunt quod sit illicitum dare vel recipere, et ex tali ignorantia
dant vel recipiunt. Et sic, ex omnibus predictis, clare patet responsio
predicte rationis principalis et excusatio quorumdam, qui dederunt
et receperunt temporibus retroactis, et eciam accusatio aliquorum
in casibus certis.

---

[b] M d   [c] agnoverunt d

[96] *Chart.*, I, no. 79, p. 138.
[97] Radix, pp. 222, 25 - 223, 18.
[98] *Chart.*, I, no. 20, p. 79.
[99] Johannes Monachus, *Glossa Aurea Super Sexto Decretalium*, 1, 6, 16
(Paris, 1535), f. 92ra.

760, 18   Sed quia nos sumus in materia de dando gratis, ad hoc tertio
principaliter arguitur contra illud quod modo dictum est de privilegio *Servus Crucis*, scilicet quod simpliciter prohibet dare, eciam
gratis. Nam videtur quod non potest prohiberi quin licite possit
gratis dari ^d, nam quidam non ^e [dant] pro licentia aut labore vel 5
pena in ipsa licentia concedenda, sed pro benivolentia voluntatis
ipsius licentiam conferentis, juxta illa que dixi in ultimo corollario,
secunde partis, primi articuli,¹⁰⁰ quia sic dare gratis est actus virtutis, scilicet liberalitatis, vel gratitudinis, sicut dictum fuit de
Naaman Syro, etc. Sed actus virtutum non sunt prohibendi, nec 10
possunt illicite fieri, quia, secundum Philosophum, virtutibus non
contingit male uti.¹⁰¹ Igitur, etc.

760, 33   Ad hoc posset dupliciter responderi, uno modo, modificando illud quod dictum est quod illud privilegium simpliciter prohibet
dare eciam gratis, scilicet ante licentiam et inceptionem. Et hoc 15
notatur cum dicitur "nullus incipiat data pecunia" etc., sed non
prohibet dare gratis post inceptionem, sicut eciam Naaman Syrus
dedit Giezi pecuniam, vel ^f dare optulit post doni spiritualis
receptionem, ut dixi in corollario preallegato. Sic autem dare, in
f. 95^v collatione doni spiritualis / est actus virtutis et laudabilis gratitu- 20
dinis, alias non.

760, 43   Si quis vero omnino dicere velit, quod illud privilegium simpliciter prohibet dare pecuniam, et ante et post inceptionem, potest
consequenter respondere quod recipiens licentiam, pro benivolentia voluntatis ipsius conferentis, potest bene aliud reprehendere 25
quam pecuniam, scilicet reciprocam benivolentiam et honorem et
reverentiam. Et ideo privilegium non prohibet sibi actum virtutis,
scilicet gratitudinis, sed solum prohibet secundum quid, scilicet
circa certam materiam, id est pecuniam, et hoc non est inconve-
760, 55 niens. Insuper potest dici quod virtutibus et earum actibus inte- 30
rioribus non contingit male uti. Sed quia earum actus exteriores
secundum se non sunt boni vel mali, sed prout procedunt ex actu
interiori. Ideo talibus actibus exterioribus contingit male uti, et
propter hoc, vel quandoque ex alia causa rationali aliquibus
personis, et in casibus certis possunt prohiberi. Verbi gratia, 35

---

^d *ex* dare *corr* A   ^f *interl* A
^e *om* A

---

¹⁰⁰ Radix, pp. 206, 25 - 207, 26.
¹⁰¹ Cf. Aristotle, *Nichomachean Ethics*, II, 5; 1105b, 5-12.

publice docere est actus virtutis et tamen hunc actum prohibet
Apostolus mulieribus, ut supra dixi.[102] Similiter, elemosinam dare 760, 64
est actus virtutis, et tamen prohibetur aliquibus religiosis, quia
religioso cui non est rerum dispensatio commissa non licet ele-
5 mosinam facere [g], ut dicit Sanctus Thomas, in quadam questione
de tercio quolibet. Sic ergo in proposito, gratis dare potest non
solum religiosis, sed eciam aliis prohiberi, et hoc ex causa rationali,
scilicet ad tollendum omnem speciem mali et omnem suspicionem
corruptele. Et hec sufficiant circa primam responsionem partis
10 adverse.

Quantum ad secundam responsionem cancellarii / in qua dicit 761
quod potest licite a bachalariis licentiandis recipere et rigorose
exigere ad minus decem Francos pro suo labore, contra hoc declaravi tres conclusiones. Prima fuit quod cancellarius non potest
15 licite recipere, vel saltem non potest exigere, a bachalariis licentiandis, ratione sui laboris. Et hanc probavi primo ex iure divino,
secundo ex iure humano, tercio ex speciali previlegio Universitati
Parisiensi concesso.[103] Prima autem probatio continebat sex rationes, in quarum prima et principali dixi quod papa non posset
20 licite recipere, vel saltem exigere, a licentiandis, ratione sui laboris,
etc., et per consequens nec cancellarius, etc. etc.[104] Sed contra hoc 761, 16
quarto arguitur. Nam ista ratio fundatur in hoc, quia papa, licenciando aliquos in theologia, mittit eos ad opus suum, scilicet [h]
ad pascendum gregem Ecclesie. Et ideo, pro labore sic mittendi,
25 non debet ab eis exigere, sed magis eos remunerare, etc.[105]

Contra hoc arguitur autem, quia sicut se habebat Aaron, sacer- 761, 22
dos summus, ad sacerdotes inferiores legis Moysi, sic papa ad
licentiatos et alios gradus ecclesiasticos legis Christi. Sed summus
sacerdos a minoribus sacerdotibus, licet eos mitteret ad opus
30 suum, sicut papa quando mittit aliquem ad docendum, poterat
ab eis, pro suo labore, exigere decimam decime, sicut patet Numer.
18, 24. Ergo, et propter hoc, licite posset [papa] ab eis, quos
licentiat ad docendum vel predicandum. Quare, etc. Confirmatur

---

[g] non licet elemosinam facere *it* A   [h] sed A

---

[102] I Tim. 2, 12.
[103] Radix, pp. 217, 27 - 223, 18.
[104] *Ibid.*, pp. 218, 3 - 221, 13.
[105] *Ibid.*

quia, licet forte predicta ratio haberet locum, vel aliquam ap-
f. 96 parenciam,/ in illis licentiatis quos papa motu proprio mitteret ad
opus suum, pro necesitate Ecclesie, non videtur tamen valere de
illis qui requirunt et procurant ut ab eo mittantur, eciam quandoque importune et absque ulla Ecclesie necessitate. Igitur, saltem 5
a talibus licite posset exigere.

761, 40 Ad primum dico primo quod sicut inferius plenius declarabo,
nec summus sacerdos, nec alii Levitici generis recipiebant decimas
pro labore suo in spiritualium administratione, sed pro neccesi-
tatibus vite. Unde ibidem dicitur, "decimarum oblacione contenti, 10
quas in usus eorum et necessaria separavi." [106] Ideo minor rationis
est falsa.

761, 47 Secundo dico quod summus sacerdos ab aliis inferioribus decimam decime non exigebat, sed per modum oblationis gratuite Deo
facte eam recipiebat. Unde sequitur ibi, "Cum acceperitis decimas 15
a filiis Israel, primitias earum afferte [i] domino, id est decimam
partem decime," etc. "et date Aaron sacerdoti," etc.[107] Et ideo
iterum minor est falsa.

761, 54 Tercio dico quod summus sacerdos, licet ab aliis sacerdotibus
immediate reciperet illam decimam decime, tamen mediate reci- 20
piebat eam a populo, cui ipse et alii ministrabant in tabernaculo.
Et hoc est quod ibi premittitur [k] cum inquit, "acceperitis decimas
a filiis Israhel." Et sic eciam papa potest licite recipere, ymmo
qualibet die exigit decimam a viris ecclesiasticis de redditibus
beneficialibus, quos loco decimarum habent a populo Christiano. 25
Et hoc modo, si illi quos ipse per se vel per alium licentiat, ratione
huius licentie [l], haberent redditus a populo, posset ab eis recipere
vel exigere decimam decime, et tunc magis censeretur [m] eam recipere per medium ipsorum a populo quam ab eis. Quare, etc.

761, 68 Ultimo dico quod quia huiusmodi licentie [n] non est annexa 30
opitulatio [o] ordinaria, ratione cuius ipsi licenciati habeant vel
recipiant certos redditus vel proventus a populo. Ideo papa vel
alius loco pape, eos licentians et mittens ad opus doctrine vel
predicationis, non potest licite exigere decimam decime, vel aliud

---

[i] offerte d   [m] censerentur A
[k] permittitur d   [n] licentia d
[l] ratione huius licencie *om* d   [o] apitulatio A

[106] Numer. 18, 24.
[107] Numer. 18, 28.

temporale emolumentum, ratione sui laboris et sue missionis. Quare, etc. / 762

Ad confirmationem, dico quod ratio mea habet locum in omnibus licentiatis, tam in illis quos papa motu proprio mittit, quam
5 in illis qui procurant et requirunt ut mittantur, quia illi qui ᴾ procurant et petunt ut licentientur, vel sunt ad hoc digni, vel non. Si sunt digni, tunc licite petunt licentiam, secundum opinionem Sancti Thome, ut supra dixi in secunda ratione principali huius articuli,¹⁰⁸ dum tamen ea non petant importune et inhoneste, et
10 quod hoc faciant pro utilitate Ecclesie, quia velle per licentiam pape scientiam suam aliis communicare laudabile est et ad caritatem pertinens, juxta illud Sapientie 8, 13, "Quam sine fictione didici, et sine invidia communico," et I Petri, 4, 10, "unusquisque, sicut accepit gratiam, in alterutrum illam administrantes�." Et ideo se
15 ad opus doctrine vel predicationis offere talibus non est vituperabile, cum Ysayas ad hoc se optulerit, dicens "Ecce ego, mitte me." Ysa. 6, 8. Quare ex hoc quod tales / pape se offerunt ad f. 96ᵛ faciendum opus suum, non potest ab eis licite exigere, pro labore eos mittendi, lucrum et ʳ emolumentum, sed magis eos pro hoc
20 remunerare.

Si vero tales sunt indigni ad tale officium, tunc presumptuose **762, 23** petunt, nec mittendi aut licenciandi sunt, et a talibus recipere vel exigere haberet speciem mali, quia probabilis suspitio esset quod tales indigni essent propter lucrum temporale promoti. Quare
25 patet quod nec a dignis nec ab indignis licentiam petentibus, potest aliquid papa exigere, ratione sui laboris.

Quinto ¹⁰⁹ principaliter arguitur contra predictam conclusionem **762, 31** in se, et simul contra premissam probationem eius, quia episcopus, pro quibusdam operis ˢ spiritualibus, ad quas tenetur a suis sub-
30 ditis, ad quos pascendos mittitur, licite potest recipere et exigere, puta cum ipse consecrat ecclesiam, vel visitat episcopatum, potest exigere procurationem, *Extra., De Symonia, Cum sit Romana;*¹¹⁰

ᵖ *om* A   ʳ est A
� administrare A   ˢ operibus d

---

¹⁰⁸ Super, p. 262, 13.
¹⁰⁹ D'Ailly's numbering is difficult to follow. At the end of this speech (296,6), d'Ailly claims he has refuted twenty arguments, yet in his text he enumerates only fourteen.
¹¹⁰ X. 5, 3, 10.

x. q. iii, *Relatum*,[111] et dicit Gaufredus quod non audet dicere quod pro actu consecrandi vel visitandi episcopus aliquid exigat, sed pro labore vie.[112] Cum ergo episcopus auctoritate iuris, et per consequens auctoritate pape, sic possit exigere pro suo labore, sequitur quod eciam papa, et cancellarius, qui ab eo mittitur ad ipsos bachalarios, et pro ipsis licentiandis, pro suo labore potuerint exigere ab eis, quia non apparet ratio dissimilitudinis, etc.

762, 53   Ad istud dico primo quia hic est magna dissimilitudo, quia episcopus exigit ab illis ad quos principaliter mittitur[t]. Cancellarius autem non, quia ipse non mittitur ad bachalarios licentiandos principaliter pro ipsis, sed pro illis ad quos ultimate mittuntur, scilicet principaliter pro populo docendo, et in favorem tocius Ecclesie. Et ideo Ecclesia, et non ipsi bachalarii, debet eum remunerare. Et idem dico de papa, in casu quo propter hoc aliquid vellet recipere vel exigere, sicut alias tetigi, exemplum de illis, quos papa mittit in guerram suam vel Ecclesie, etc.

762, 60   Secundo dico quod opinio Gaufredi non est vera, qui[v] dicit quod episcopus, in predictis casibus, exigit[x] procurationem pro labore vie. Unde Bernardus, in glossa super ca. *Cum Sit Romana*, dicit expresse quod nec pro labore, sed potius quia "ista procuratio a iure permissa est." Ymmo etsi ecclesia propter paupertatem procurare non posset episcopum, ipse, suis sumptibus, ecclesiam deberet consecrare, x. q. iii, *Cavendum*. Hec Bernardus[y].[113] Et idem tenet Hostiensis ibidem.[114] Quare, etc.

762, 70   Tercio dico quod ex predicta opinione Bernardi[z] et Hostiensis, et communiter omnium doctorum, apparet quod in administratione operarum spiritualium, ad quas ex officio quis tenetur, nunquam est licitum exigere, nisi bonum[a], hoc est expresse permissum a jure. Et ideo, cum licentiare in theo/logia sit opera spiritualis,
763 ut declaravi, non est cancellario licitum in illius administratione,

---

[t] mittetur A
[v] que d
[x] exigat d

[y] *om* d
[z] *in ras* A
[a] boni A

---

[111] Gratian, C.10 q.3 c.9.

[112] Gottofredus da Trani, *Summa super titulis decretalium* (Lugduni, 1519), f. 200.

[113] *Compilatio Decretalium Gregorii Pape IX cum Glossis Bernardi Parmensis* (Venetiis, 1486), f. 219[v], where Bernard cites Gratian, D.10 q.3 c.7.

[114] Host., *Summa*, Lib. V, De Simonia, Qualiter Committatur, § Sed pro labore vie; f. 232[r]a: "Melius est, ut dicamus, quod hoc ius habet."

cum ad hoc ex officio teneatur, aliquid exigere, quia hoc non est
sibi a iure permissum, ymmo expresse prohibitum. *Extra.*, *De
Magistris*, *Quanto*,[115] quod capitulum, ut dicit glossa, propter
Cancellarium Parisiensis [b] Ecclesie fuit factum.[116] Quia cum hoc
5 sit a iure permissum episcopo in visitando et non cancellario
licentiando, patet clare ratio dissimilitudinis, et [c] ex secundo [d]
dicto patet / quod ratio non est ad propositum conclusionis.   **f. 97**

Sexto arguitur contra illud quod dictum est, quod non est **763, 12**
licitum exigere pro labore, sicut eciam nunc tactum est, secundum
10 Bernardi opinionem et Hostiensis. Unde quidam alias arguebat sic,
quia in administratione rerum minus preciosarum licitum est
laborem suum vendere, seu pro eo exigere, sicut patet de labore in
administratione rerum corporalium, ergo similiter in administratione rerum magis preciosarum, scilicet rerum spiritualium. Quare,
15 etc. [e] Et confirmatur ex parabola Evangelica, Matt. 13, 45, de
homine negotiatore qui, "inventa una preciosa margarita, vendidit
omnia que [f] habuit, et emit eam," ut dicit glossa quod illa preciosa **763, 23**
margarita est "scientia Salvatoris." [g] [117] Si ergo scientia salutis,
scientia theologica, propter suam preciositatem licite potest
20 emi [h], multo magis labor in sui administratione, ratione sue
preciositatis, maiori precio potest vendi quam labor in administratione rei vilioris, scilicet rei corporalis. Quare, etc.

Ad hoc dico primo, negando consequentiam, quia non est simile **763, 32**
de labore in rebus corporalibus et in spiritualibus. Nec preciositas
25 rerum spiritualium concludit quod talis labor sit licite venalis,
ymmo magis concludit oppositum, sicut patet ex tertia ratione,
quam posui in secunda parte, primi articuli questionis [i],[118] et hic
nunc magis declaro, scilicet ex comparatione rei vendite ad precium.

Nam sicut dicit Durandus, prima questione de symonia, super **763, 39**
30 quarto [libro *Sententiarum*], d. 25, "Illa venditio est de se illicita,
in qua res vendita non potest per precium comparari vel compensari.
(Hoc enim habet natura emptionis et venditionis, quod res empta

---

[b] par d
[c] *om* A
[d] *om* d
[e] *del* A

[f] et A
[g] salutis d
[h] *ex* eum *corr* A
[i] quod d

---

[115] X. 5, 5, 3.
[116] Cf. Radix, p. 222, n. 68.
[117] G. O., Matt. 13, 45, *ad verb.* "preciosa."
[118] Radix, p. 204, 30.

vel vendita compensetur precio.) Sed res spiritualis non potest
terreno vel temporali precio compensari, iuxta illud Proverbiorum
3, 15, quod dicitur de sapientia, quod 'preciosior est cunctis opibus,
et omnia que desiderantur ei non valent comparari.' Et eadem
ratione, hoc verum est de aliis donis spiritualibus, sicut tetigit 5
Petrus, Act. 8, 20, dicens Symoni, 'Pecunia tua' etc. 'quia existimasti.' etc." [119] Unde concludo [k] quod, quia res spiritualis propter
sui preciositatem non est licite venalis propter hoc, nec labor in
eius administratione inseparabiliter annexus, qui eciam per at-
tributionem spiritualis dicitur, nunquam licite venditur, quid- 10
quid sit de labore in administratione rei corporalis, que propter
minorem preciositatem est precio comparabilis, et ideo labor ei
annexus potest dici licite venalis.

763, 60   Tamen adhuc dicit predictus doctor ibidem, in eadem questione,
quod non solum "concomitantia illa, maxime que inseparabilia 15
sunt ab amministratione sacramentorum, ut labor corporalis, qui
est in administrando sacramenta, vel in consecrando ecclesias, nullo modo vendi possunt sine vicio symonie," ymmo reddendo
causam huius, subdit generaliter quod "labor operantis nunquam cadit sub venditione [l], sed solum opus, eciam in pure 20
corporalibus." [120]

763, 69   Et hoc declarat sic, "quia sicut operarius, sicut carpentator vel
fossor vinearum, posset opera sua exercere sine labore quocumque, nichilominus posset vendere ea. Et si laborando exerceat
predicta opera, et ea vendat plus propter laborem, tamen emens 25
non emit plus propter laborem, sed propter fructum operis [m],

f. 97ᵛ ad quem nichil facit labor operantis,/quia, si sine labore fierent,

764 equalis fructus/fieret ementi predicta opera. Unde labor nunquam
secundum se emitur ex intentione mentis, sed solum opus, cui
annexus est labor." [121]   30

764, 3   Et ideo concludit quod "si opus administrationis sacramentorum, et aliorum spiritualium, non potest cadere sub venditione sine
vicio symonie, nec per consequens vendi potest labor qui est in
tali opere, nisi symoniace. Et dicere [n] oppositum est ridiculum, et

---

[k] concedendo d   [m] sed . . . operis *in ras* A
[l] conditione d   [n] est (*post* dicere) *add* A

[119] Durandus, *In 4º Sent.*, d. 25, q. 3; f. 365ʳa.
[120] *Ibid.*
[121] *Ibid.*

prestans velamentum excusationis symoniacorum, qui possent dicere, 'non vendimus sacramenta, sed laborem quem habemus in administratione sacramentorum.' " [122] Et ideo ulterius concludit quod "si aliquid licite recipit minister ecclesiasticus dispensando
5 sacramenta, non recipit illud ut precium operis vel laboris, sed ut sustentationem ministri," [123] sicut eciam alias dixi. Et idem ᵒ tenet ᵖ P. Aureoli, libro 4, d. 25, q. 3, art. 2, eiusdem.[124] Et ad hunc intellectum vera est opinio supradicta Bernardi et Hostiensis. Quare, etc.

10 Ad confirmationem vero dico quod in illa parabola Evangelica, **764, 18** Christus loquitur si[mi]li[tudina]rie �q et capitur ibi emptio, non proprie, sed methaphorice ʳ, sicut eciam supra dixi.[125] Regnum Celorum emi, eciam margaritam scientie ˢ Christi, simili[tudina]rie ᵗ et mistice dicitur emi, omnibus aliis venditis, quia pro
15 ea, homo omnibus misteriis Veteris Legis et observationibus renunciat, sicut fecit Paulus, ut ibidem dicit glossa.[126] Quare, etc.

Septimo arguebatur contra illud quod dictum fuit in tercia **764, 27** probatione principali, dicte conclusionis, scilicet quod per previlegia universitatis cancellarius non solum non potest licite exigere,
20 sed eciam nec recipere peccuniam, aut iuramentum obsequiosum, etc.[127] Nam si papa per huiusmodi previlegia voluit prohibere dationem et receptionem pecunie ᵛ, scilicet quia inductive sunt ad corruptionem, ergo, similiter prohibere debuit recipere preces seu litteras precum, cum tales possint corrumpere iudicem. Eciam
25 munus a lingua consistit in precibus, et in tali munere potest committi symonia, sicut in munere a manu, vel ab obsequio, ut dictum est. Quare, etc.

Ad hoc dico quod papa rationabiliter magis debuit prohibere **764, 41** pecunie receptionem quam precum, quia receptio pecunie, quantum est de se, magis est corruptiva iudicii, et magis habet speciem mali.

ᵒ idem: *ex* ad hunc *corr* A
ᵖ intellectum (*ante* tenet) *del* A
�q similarie d
ʳ metaphysice d

ˢ eciam margaritam scientie: scientiam margaritam scientia d
ᵗ similarie d
ᵛ pecuniarum d

---

[122] *Ibid.*, f. 365ʳb.
[123] *Ibid.*
[124] Petrus Aureolus Verberius, *Commentariorum in Quartum Librum Sententiarum* (Romae, 1605), d. 25, q. 1, art. 2; p. 166.
[125] *Super*, pp. 255, 27 - 256, 12.
[126] G. O. in Matt. 13, 45, *ad verb.* "preciosa."
[127] *Radix*, p. 222, 25.

Unde eciam quandoque preces non corrumpunt iudicem, sed sepe instruunt et informant de sufficentia illius pro quo fiunt. Tamen sicut dicit Durandus, ubi supra, questione quarta ˣ, et communiter alii doctores, distinguendum est, "quia preces vel sunt pro digno, vel pro indigno. Si pro indigno, tunc bene apparet clare quod 5 nichil aliud movet ad exaudiendum tales preces, nisi favor precantis, aut periculum quod timetur, nisi preces potentis exaudiantur, que preces dicuntur 'armate.' Et ideo in hoc casu semper est symonia, cum ad tales preces aliquid spirituale datur. Si vero preces fiant
f. 98 pro digno / quantum ad judicium hominum, probabile est quod 10 dans magis moveatur ʸ intuitu dignitatis persone, quam favore precum, verumptamen si principaliter moveatur favore precum vel timore rogantis, quantum ad iudicium Dei, symoniam committunt, et rogatus qui dat, et rogans, si hoc intendat," ut dicit iste doctor,[128] et idem Sanctus Thomas,[129] et Hostiensis,[130] et alii. Et 15 similiter, secundum eum, dicendum est de obsequioso quantumcumque sit honestum, quod symonia est, si pro eo detur principaliter spirituale donum.[131]

764, 67 "Ratio autem istorum est, quia idem est iudicium de pecunia, et de omni precio temporali, quod potest per pecuniam comparari. 20 Sed favor persone et quodcumque obsequium quantumcumque honestum est commodum temporale, quod potest pecunia comparari. Ergo sicut est peccatum symonie conferendo aliquid spirituale digno vel indigno pro pecunia, similiter est symonia, si
765 conferatur digno vel indigno aliquod spirituale pro mune/re a 25 lingua, id est pro favore precum, vel pro ᶻ munere ab obsequio, si ad hoc principaliter habetur respectus. Habetur principaliter autem respectus, quando sine ᵃ hiis non esset aliter collatum." [132] Hec ille. Et concordat cum hiis que dixi in primo corollario, secunde partis, primi articulis questionis ᵇ.[133] Et per hec patet solutio 30 predicte rationis. Et hoc circa primam conclusionem.

ˣ secunda Ad   ᵃ si A
ʸ moveat A   ᵇ quasi d
ᶻ *om* d

---

[128] Durandus, *In 4º Sent.*, d. 25, q. 4, § 6; f. 365ᵛa-b.
[129] Tho. II, II, q. 100, art. 5, ad 3.
[130] Host. V, De Simonia, Qualiter, § Ubi autem; 232ᵛb.
[131] Durandus, *In 4º Sent.*, d. 25, q. 4, § 7; f. 365ᵛb.
[132] *Ibid.*
[133] Radix, p. 205.

Secunda conclusio fuit quod esto quod cancellarius posset ali-   765, 9
quid exigere aut recipere pro labore, non tamen tantum quantum
exigit, vel quantum se posse recipere asserit et proponit.[134] Et hec
conclusio probabitur tripliciter: primo ex conditione recipientis,
5 secundo ex consideratione dantis, tertio ex comparationi doni et
laboris.

Prima ratio fundatur in hoc, quia cancellarius habet in hac parte   765, 18
iudicis officium. Et pro hoc officio, habet ecclesiasticum beneficium,
ratione quorum, scilicet officii et beneficii, tenetur ad licentiandum,
10 quare non debet recipere magna munera, sicut est munus decem
Francorum, etc., juxta notas c Raymundi,[135] Sancti Thome,[136] et
aliorum doctorum, etc.

Contra hanc conclusionem arguebat quidam sic, quia Archydya-   765, 26
conus Tholosanus, qui ex officio licentiat in theologia, plus recipit
15 quam Parisiensis cancellarius. Unde, quia ipse quandoque volebat
exigere viginti Francos, ut solitus erat, lis super hoc fuit in Romana
Curia, et tandem illa summa fuit ad duodecim Francos reducta. Et
tamen ille non habet tantum laborem sicut cancellarius Parisiensis,
quia nec ipse facit collationem in licentiis, nec arguit in magisteriis,
20 ut iste asserit. Igitur, etc. Ad hoc eciam facit illud quod cancellarius
allegat in suis articulis, scilicet articulo 10, ubi dicit quod predictus
usus laudabilis est, et similiter in aliis universitatibus observatus,
scilicet quod bachalarii licentiandi donaria d faciunt quandoque
maiora premissis, etc.

25 Ad hoc dico primo quod ille usus seu abusus in Tholosa generavit   765, 42
scandalum fidei, quia ibi dixerunt Judei quod rabi fidei nostre, id
est doctores et magistri, fiunt per pecuniam. Et ideo, propter
speciem mali tollendam e, eciam si non esset alia ratio, papa deberet
illum abusum dampnare, sicut patet ex dictis in tertia conclusione,
30 in probatione prime propositionis.[137]

Secundo dico quod non credo quod papa vel Romana / Curia   765, 50
illum usum in Tholosa approbaverit per sententiam diffinitivam,   f. 98v
sed forte partes litigantes in hoc consenserunt per communem con-

---

c nota A   e tollendum d
d dona omnia d

---

[134] *Ibid.*, pp. 223-7.
[135] Ray., p. 30, col. 2.
[136] Tho., II, II, q. 100, art. 3, ad 3.
[137] Radix, pp. 228, 31 - 230, 2.

cordiam. Et si papa hoc diffinisset ^f, videnda esset forma mandati. Aliter de hoc nescirem certitudinaliter loqui.

765, 57 Tertio dico quod illa diffinitio vel declaratio pape magis esset contra cancellarium quam pro eo, quia ille Archidyaconus Tholosanus reciperet vel exigeret auctoritate pape, et ex speciali previlegio. 5 Cancellarius autem ^g non, ymmo contra ius commune, et contra privilegium universitatis et mandatum pape, ut dictum est.

765, 64 Quarto idem dico de aliis universitatibus, in quibus ille usus servaretur. Non tamen servatur in omnibus, nam Aureliani nichil datur, et eciam Parisiis, in artium facultate, expresse ^h papa prohibet 10 recipere, eciam pro labore. Et si ita sit in hiis, multo magis debet servari in theologia, cum ipsa sit magis spiritualis, et magis debeat esse libera et liberalis quam scientia legum, vel artium liberalium, ut notum est. Quare, etc.

765, 73 Nono ⁱ, sic arguitur contra predictam conclusionem et eius 15 probationem, sive ex eius probatione contra eam, quia per proba-
766 tionem, ideo, non est li/citum cancellario exigere, quia pro tali officio exercendo, habet beneficium ^k. Si ergo non haberet beneficium pro officio, vel si beneficium non sufficeret ad victum suum vel statum, videtur quod posset exigere, sicut magister, licet habeat 20 beneficium, si tamen ipsum habeat et non pro officio docendi, vel si beneficium sit officio docendi annexum et non possit commode illo beneficio sustentari, potest exigere, secundum Raymundum ¹³⁸ et Hostiensem,¹³⁹ argumento: xii. q. ii, *Quicumque*; et ca. *Ecclesiasticis*; et ca. *Caritatem*.¹⁴⁰ Modo cancellarius dicet quod non habet 25 beneficium cancellarie pro officio licentiandi, quia beneficium cancellarie fuit antequam forte esset cancellario commissum officium licentiandi. Dicet eciam quod, licet haberet talem beneficium pro huiusmodi officio, tamen non potest de illo commode sustentari, ut ipse in Parlamento proposuit, et per consequens poterit exigere 30 pro supplemento victus sui, etc.

766, 21 Ad istud dico primo quod non est simile in proposito de magistro docente et de cancellario licentiante ^l, quia in casu predicto con-

---

^f diffinivisset d
^g aut A
^h *om* d

ⁱ *in ras*
^k officium (*ante* beneficium) *del* A
^l *in ras* A

---

¹³⁸ Ray., *Summa*, p. 31, col. 1.
¹³⁹ Host., *Summa*, V, De Magistris, Utrum a Scholaribus, f. 235rb.
¹⁴⁰ Gratian, C.12 q.2 cc. 4, 67, & 45, cited by Ray. and Host.

cessum est a jure quod magister docens recipiat vel exigat, ut patet per iura allegata. Sed in proposito ^m non est sic cancellario a iure concessum vel permissum, ymmo expresse prohibitum, ut alias dictum est et ostensum. Dicunt eciam aliqui, sicut Guil-
5 lelmus in glossa, quod illi magistri, qui ab Ecclesia habent stipendium non sufficiens, possunt inopiam suam scolaribus exponere et insinuare quod libenter reciperent si gratis darent, sed non licet extorquere ab invito, nec debent eos repellere a scolis, vel spolia eorum accipere, si non velint sponte promittere, sed postquam
10 promiserint, promissa possint exigere.[141] Et sic, ut credo, intellexit Raymundus, quod si sua non sufficiunt, eis competenter et honeste possunt licite exigere moderate,[142] et consimiliter dici posset in proposito de cancellario, nisi esset sibi omnino prohibitum tam exigere quam recipere, sicut patet ex speciali previlegio supra
15 allegato.

Dico secundo quod cancellarius habet beneficium propter offi-   766, 43
cium licentiandi. Nam papa habenti beneficium ecclesiasticum sufficiens ad victum honestum potest ex causa rationabili, et pro utilitate Ecclesie, committere aliquod officium oneris ⁿ, maxime
20 quando est honoris ^o, absque hoc quod augeat eius beneficium, vel quod ei dat ^p auctoritatem / ad ^q recipiendum novum stipen-   f. 99
dium, maxime quando ipsi non contingit extra suum domicilium proficisci, iuxta ca. *Statutum, De Rescriptis, Libro Sexto*,[143] et iuxta ca. *Cum Ab Omni, De Vita et Honestate Clericorum, In Anti-*
25 *quis*.[144] Et potest poni exemplum in materia nostra, de Cancellario Sancte Genovefe, etc. Pro hoc eciam faciunt no[tari] ^r per Hostiensem, in dicto ca. *Cum Ab Omni* ubi dicit quod delegatus pape, sufficienter beneficiatus, vivens de bursa litigantium, inhoneste vivit et peccat.[145] Et ratio est quia stipendia sui beneficii sunt de
30 patrimonio Christi, et debet esse illis contentus, sicut iudex secularis

---

^m propositio d   ^p det d
ⁿ *om* d   ^q *om* A
^o operis (*ante* honoris) *del* A   ^r notata d

---

[141] Guil. Rhed., *Glossa in Ray.*, p. 31, col. 1, *in verb.* "licet exigere."
[142] Ray., p. 31, col. 1.
[143] *Liber Sextus Decretalium Domini Bonifacii Pape VIII*, I, 3, 11, 4 (ed. E. Friedberg, *Corpus Iuris Canonici*, Leipzig, 1879), II, 942.
[144] X. 3, 1, 10.
[145] Host., *Summa*, III, De Vit. et Hon. Cle., Et In Quibus, § Item consistit; f. 135vb.

de hiis que dantur a fisco. Et sic a fortiori dico de cancellario,
cum sit iudex ordinarius, et tunc talis censetur habere huiusmodi
beneficium propter officium, eciam supposito quod prius habuerit
beneficium ante illud officium. Et sic cancellarius censetur habere
beneficium cancellarie propter officium licentiandi.   5

766, 69 Dico tertio quod cancellaria Parisiensis sufficit ad victum
honestum cancellarii, et si non, tamen ˢ habet alia ecclesiastica
beneficia, de quibus potest honeste sustentari. Et hoc sufficit,
quia cum ipse exercendo officium licentiandi, non solum serviat
universitati, nec ecclesie Parisiensi, nec uni regno vel patrie, sed 10
767 toti Ecclesie Universali. / Sufficit eciam quod sustentetur de bonis
ecclesie cuiuscunque et in hoc debet contentari, sicut a simili
dicitur de illo qui servit principi pro re publica, quod debet et
potest recipere stipendium de aliqua alia ecclesia particulari, licet
eidem specialiter non serviat, ut ᵗ in ca. *Cum Dilectus, De Clericis* 15
Non Residentibus, cum suis similibus.¹⁴⁶

767, 8 Dico quarto quod esto quod ipse non haberet de bonis ecclesiasticis ad sufficientiam sui status, tamen in ᵛ hoc non debet
esse iudex, nec ad ipsum, sed ad papam, vel alium iudicem superiorem, pertinet iudicare et determinare quid et quantum sufficeret 20
ad sui status honestatem. Nec propter indigentiam deberet exigere
vel recipere, cum sit sibi prohibitum, nec propter hoc licite posset
sui officii exercitium denegare, sed teneretur suum officium exercere
aut beneficium dimittere, exemplo pauperum curatorum, qui, licet
habeant pauperrima beneficia, tamen tenentur eis deservire vel ea 25
dimittere. Quare, etc.

767, 21 Decimo (*sic*) arguebatur contra eandem conclusionem quia
magistri recipiunt vestes a bachalariis magistrandis, et has ˣ licite
recipiunt racione sui laboris, ergo cancellarius similiter poterit
licite recipere a bachalariis licentiandis, quia non minorem videtur 30
habere laborem ratione licentie, quam magistri ʸ ratione magisterii
conferendi, et tamen, vestes que dantur magistris regulariter plus
valent quam illud quod petit cancellarius. Ergo in hoc non videtur
reprehendendus, etc.

767, 31 Ad hoc dico quod hic est magna dissimilitudo et multiplex ratio 35

ˢ et si non, tamen: et si tamen non d   ˣ hoc d
ᵗ et d   ʸ magister Ad
ᵛ *om* A

---

¹⁴⁶ X. 3, 4, 14.

diversitatis. Primo, quia magisterium non est quid spirituale, sicut licentia theologie, ut infra dicam. Et ideo recipere aliquid in ipsius administratione non habet speciem symonie, sicut recipere in administratione licentie. Non dico tamen quod magistri recipiant
5 pro ipso magisterio, nec eciam pro labore in ipsum administrando, saltem / proprie et principaliter, licet forte aminiculative et f. 99ᵛ occasionaliter.

Secundo, quia magistri circa suos bacalarios magistrandos non 767, 42 habent post licentiam iudicialiter cognoscere, nec de eorum suffi-
10 cientia iudicare. Et ideo talium vestium aut aliorum munerum receptio vel oblatio non corrumpit aut pervertit in eis iudicium. Secus autem est de cancellario, cum sit iudex, etc., ut alias dictum est.

Tercio, quia magistri, ex officio suo, non tenentur ad illos labores 767, 48 seu actus exercendos quos habent circa bachalarios per eos magi-
15 strandos; cancellarius autem, ex officio, tenetur ad licentiandum licenciandos ᶻ.

Quarto, quia magistri pro predictis laboribus et actibus exer- 767, 53 cendis non habent beneficium seu publicum stipendium, sicut cancellarius, et ideo pro stipendio possunt vestes recipere seu aliud
20 genus muneris et non ipse, aliter ipse, ut alias dixi ᵃ, pro eadem opera, haberet duplex stipendium, contra capitulum *Quoniam Ecclesia, Extra. De Magistris*.¹⁴⁷

Quinto, quia magistris non est prohibitum sic recipere, sicut 767, 60 cancellario, ymmo hoc est a iure permissum seu concessum, saltem
25 aliis quam theologis concessum est quod possunt operas suas locare, theologis quod recipiant sustentationem vite ex doctrina vel predicatione, quia, secundum Raymundum et Hostiensem, si magisterio non sit annexum beneficium, potest collectam pro suis laboribus accipere, et in hoc omnes conveniunt. Ymmo, quod plus
30 est, dicit Hostiensis, et concordat Raymundus, quod si sit annexum magisterio beneficium ecclesiasticum aut publicum salarium sic sufficiens ad vitam quod nullam habeant indigentiam, licet tunc ᵇ non debeant aliquid exigere, tamen gratis oblata et sponte possunt suscipere, x. q. iii *Priscis*.¹⁴⁸ Cum ergo magistri huius

---

ᶻ licentiatos d   ut dixi d
ᵃ aliter ipse, ut alias dixi: alias ipse,   ᵇ tamen d

---

¹⁴⁷ X. 5, 5, 1.
¹⁴⁸ Ray., p. 31, col. 1; Host., V, De Magistris, Utrum a Scholaribus, f. 235ʳᵇ, where he cites Gratian, C.10 q.3 c.2.

768 universitatis ra/tione magisterii non habeant beneficia annexa vel
publica stipendia, et ipsi, maxime in tribus Facultatibus, scilicet
Theologie, Decretorum, et Medicine, a scolaribus vel bacalariis
collectas non recipiant vel exigant, non est illicitum si a bacalariis
magistrandis vestes percipiant, maxime gratis et sponte oblatas.   5

768, 8   Sexto, quia hoc cedit ^c ad honorem ipsorum bachalariorum, et
non solum ad utilitatem ipsorum magistrorum recipientium. Secus
autem esset, si peccunias reciperent, sicut vult facere cancellarius,
quia in hoc non honorantur bachalarii, sicut ex vestibus magistri,
ymmo potius dehonestantur, et inde est quod huiusmodi pecunie 10
clandestine dantur et recipiuntur, quod non est signum liberalis et
gratuite donacionis, sed est occasio male suspicionis. Quare, etc.
Et hoc circa secundam conclusionem.

768, 19   Tercia conclusio principalis fuit quod esto quod cancellarius, pro
labore suo, aliquid exigere posset, non tamen per modum per quem 15
exigit.[149] Et ista probatur quia modus per quem tunc exigebat,
quando predictam questionem tractavi, erat iste: nam ex eo quod
bachalarii fecerant certum iuramentum de non dando cancellario,
f. 100 ipse impediebat et differebat eorum licentiam. Postea vero / de malo
in peius procedendo, modum predictum aggravavit, quia licet 20
dictos bachalarios ad aulam episcopi vocaverit, et eosdem tamquam
dignos recommendaverit, et approbaverit pro licentia concedenda,
ex eo tamen quia ab eis certum iuramentum obsequiosum exegit,
quod ipsi prestare noluerunt, ipse eisdem licenciam denegavit, et
eos licentiare recusavit et recusat.   25

768, 35   Sed ad reprobandum istum modum exigendi, tres propositiones
declaravi. Prima est quod iste modus est illicitus et multipliciter
scandalosus.[150] Secunda, est proprie symoniacus.[151] Tercia, quod
si cancellarius hunc modum pertinaciter approbet, ipse est hereticus
censendus.[152]   30

768, 43   Principale autem fundamentum omnium istorum stat in hoc,
quia in administratione rerum spiritualium, ante ipsius rei spiritualis
administrationem, exigere aliquod precium temporale, sicut peccuniam vel iuramentum obsequiosum, seu aliud quod potest
pecunia appreciari, et hoc sic rigorose ^d exigere, quod non volenti 35

---

^c cedat A   ^d rigoroso A

[149] Radix, pp. 227, 19 - 230, 2.
[150] *Ibid.*, pp. 227,19-230,2.
[151] *Ibid.*, pp. 230, 2 - 232, 12.
[152] *Ibid.*, p. 232, l. 13-23.

dare denegetur ipsum donum spirituale, est illicitum et scandalosum
et proprie symoniacum. Et hoc pertinaciter approbare est hereticum. Modo sic est in proposito, ut probavi diffuse. Igitur, etc.
Pro hiis clare facit, ca. *Ad Apostolicam, De Symonia*,[153] et causa
5 redditur in ca. *In Tantum*, supra eodem, ubi dicitur quod "expres-
sius exprimit venditionis speciem, qui prius recipit precium, quam
rem 'conferat' e preciosam." [154]

    Contra hoc arguebatur quia ex hiis sequitur quod Universitas **768, 58**
Parisiensis esset symoniaca, et quod rector et omnes facultates
10 ipsius multipliciter committerent vicium symonie. Consequens
videtur absurdum, et consequentia declaratur per simile. Nam
rector et universitas ab ipsis bachalariis licentiatis, ad magisterium
admittendum, ante magisterium preexigant f certa emolumenta
peccuniaria et certa iuramenta obsequiosa, sicut de honore rectoris
15 et de secretis celandis, de previlegiis observandis g, et huiusmodi.
Unde si bachalarii magistrandi talia non vellent dare, non essent
admissi ad magisterium in dicta universitate. Quare, etc.

    Confirmatur specialiter de Facultate Theologie, que, sicut et alie **768, 71**
facultates, non solum predicta exigit a bachalariis magistrandis, sed
20 eciam a bachalariis ad lecturam cursuum, vel eciam Sententiarum
admittendis. Nam tales non h admitterentur ad hu/iusmodi lecturam **769**
nisi solverent certas bursas, et facerent certa iuramenta obsequiosa,
scilicet de honore decani, facultatis, et magistrorum, etc. Et tamen,
in i sic admittendo bacalarios facultas est iudex, et habet iudicis
25 officium, unde et talis admissio ad legendum videtur esse quedam
licentia docendi in theologia, quare omnino simile videtur, sicut
supra dictum est de cancellario. Igitur.

    Secundo confirmatur, quia in ecclesiis cathedralibus et pluribus **769, 10**
collegiatis, communiter nullus recipitur nisi prius solvat quedam
30 jura ecclesiarum solvi consueta, et iuret quedam iuramenta / ob- **f. 100ᵛ**
sequiosa, sicut de honore decani k, et de secretis et previlegiis ac l
juribus capituli servandi, vel huiusmodi. Igitur, a simili, vel omnes
tales ecclesie erunt m symoniace, quod est absurdum, vel cancellarius sic exigendo non est symoniacus. Quare, etc.

---

e *sic in* A   i non d
f pre-: interl A   si exigant d   k dacani A
g observandum A   l de d
h *om* A   m erant d

---

153 X. 5, 3, 42.
154 X. 5, 3, 36.

769, 20   Tercio confirmatur, quia in quibusdam locis, ab illo qui excommunicatus est, preexigitur ante pecunia, et quandoque eciam
iuramentum de parendo mandatis Ecclesie vel iudicis, antequam
absolvatur, nec aliter absolutionis beneficium ei daretur. Igitur in
proposito, a simili, vel a fortiori, cancellarius in sic exigendo de 5
symonia non convincitur. Quare, etc.

769, 28   Pro solutione istorum argumentorum, dico aliqua. Et primo
quod non est simile de Rectore Universitatis, vel de ipsa Universitate, aut de quatuor Facultatibus eius, respectu bacalariorum
suorum magistrandorum, et de cancellario respectu bacalariorum 10
licentiandorum. Unde in hoc est multiplex dissimilitudo. Prima
est, quia licentia docendi in theologia, a cancellario data, est
potestas seu auctoritas spiritualis, ut dictum est. Sed magisterium,
eciam in theologia, non est, ultra licentiam predictam, aliqua
auctoritas spiritualis, sed solum quidam honor, seu quidam honoris 15
gradus politicus seu civilis. Unde magisterium huiusmodi se habet
ad licentiam, sicut nuptie ad sacramentum matrimonii. Et licet
huiusmodi sacramentum sit spirituale, non tamen huiusmodi nuptie, sed sunt quedam sollempnitas ad honorem et decorem sacramenti, et sic in proposito. Ideo patet quod Universitas, vel aliqua 20
facultas, eciam si venderet magisterium, non posset in hoc symoniam committere, sed solum crimen concussionis vel ambitus. Non
enim debet vendi magistratus, secundum [n] jura, quia non est licitum
vendere gradus honoris, qui debentur virtuosis in signum virtutis,
secundum Philosophum, quarto *Ethicorum*.[155]   25

769, 54   Secunda dissimilitudo est, quia Rector, Universitas [o], et Facultas
quelibet, respectu suorum [p] bacalariorum, et generaliter respectu
omnium suorum suppositorum, habet quemdam politicum ordinem
et ordinatam superioritatem, racione cuius potest recipere et exigere a suis suppositis illa que sunt utilia et expedientia ad con- 30
servationem et tuitionem sue politice communitatis. Nam quelibet
rite ordinata et approbata [q] communitas, ab illis quos in suum consortium admittit, potest, secundum sui status, exigentiam, onera
rationabilia sive pecuniarum sive iuramentorum, sicut suis subiectis
imponere, recipere, et exigere. Arguitur ca. 1, *De Iureiurando, Libro* 35

---

[n] seu d   [p] *om* d
[o] Universitatis d   [q] approbatas A

---

[155] Cf. Aristotle, *Nichomachean Ethics*, V, 3; 1131a, 24-27.

Sexto.[156] Et sic in proposito exigit Universitas vel facultas quelibet a
suis bacalariis, non pro ipso bacalariatu vel magisterio, sed pro ipsius
conservatione et tuitione. Hoc eciam modo, et pro eadem ratione,
exigunt quedam ecclesie certa iuramenta et alia emolumenta ab
5 illis qui volunt suum collegium introire. Cancellarius vero, respectu
Universitatis seu eius suppositorum, non habet talem politicum
ordinem seu superioritatem, alioquin / essent in corpore Universi- **770**
tatis plura capita / non subordinata, quod est monstruosum. Unde **f. 101**
postquam bachalarii sunt licentiati, ipse, ratione licentie huiusmodi,
10 nullam habet superioritatem super eosdem. Quare nec ab eis potest
talia onera exigere.

Tercia dissimilitudo est quia Universitas predicta, ad premissa **770, 7**
onera exigenda, habet privilegium, scilicet de collectis vel contributionibus levandis et certis iuramentis exigendis. Cancellarius
15 autem non. Primo r contra hoc, Universitas, ultra ius commune s,
habet speciale privilegium, ut dictum est.[157] Quare, etc. Dico
secundo, quod nec Universitas, nec Facultas Theologie, quidquid
fiat in aliis facultatibus, a licentiandis de novo magistrandis in
theologia preexigit aliqua iuramenta officiosa, sed solum post
20 magisterium, quando volunt intrare ad eorum congregationem
vel consortium. Cuius tamen oppositum assumitur in primo argumento. Secus autem est de cancellario. Quare, etc. etc. Dico tercio,
quod in exactione iuramentorum in ipsa administratione rerum
spiritualium, quantum ad propositum sufficit, possunt tres con-
25 ditiones considerari.

Prima. Utrum exactum iuramentum detur ante vel post rei **770, 27**
spiritualis administrationem, et utrum exigatur a superiori vel
non. Unde, secundum Raymundum, *De Symonia*, quidam dicunt
(et bene, sicut dicit glossa) "quod ante electionem nulla cautio
30 sive t pactio peti potest (scilicet ab illo qui eligendus est per suos
electores, secundum glossam), et, si prestatur, symonia est, quia
videtur facere propter hoc, ut eligatur, viii. q. iii *Talia.*" [158] Et,
ut notat Huguccio, super eodem capitulo, hoc exigere est symo-

---

r Dico (*ante* Primo) *add* d   t seu d
s generale d

---

[156] *Liber Sextus Decretalium*, 2, 11, 1.
[157] The reference is to *Servus Crucis, Chart.*, I, no. 20, p. 79, cited in Radix,
p. 223.
[158] Ray. et *Glossa* Guil. p. 9, col. 2. Ray. cites Gratian, C.8 q.3 c.1.

niacum.[159] Et idem tenet Archidyaconus, *De Iureiurando*, ca. 1, *Libro Sexto*.[160] Similiter dicit Hostiensis, quod "ante promotionem non potest cautio exigi, sed [v] bene post," scilicet illa que iure vel antiqua consuetudine approbatur, et que est licita et honesta, 8. q. iii, ca. *Artardus*; i. q. 2, *Quam Pio*,[161] et ut notant [w] predicti doctores. 5 Et hoc verum est, dum tamen ante promotionem pactum non precesserit de prestando talem cautionem, ut in dicto capitulo *Artardus*, et ut notat Hostiensis in *Summa, De Symonia*, § iii, usque [ad] ultima[m] [x], ubi excipit superiorem, qui [y], secundum eum et alios doctores, ante confirmationem et post, bene potest cautionem 10 debitam exigere, non solum nudam, sed iuratoriam, ut in ca. *Significasti, De Electione*.[162] Sed, ut dicit, non ante electionem seu promotionem, arguitur *De Electione, Officii*.[163]

770, 53   Quod autem dicit Raymundus, quod illa opinio magis placet, que dicit quod per superiorem potest peti honesta cautio, et ante 15 et post electionem, ut 28 d., *De Siracusane*, x. q. iii.[164] Glossa non concordat cum Raymundo, ad hoc quod possit ante electionem cautio exigi, sed dicit "quod nec prelatus nec alius potest exigere aliquam cautionem ab illo, qui eligendus est, ante electionem, et iura que inducuntur ad contrarium, locuntur de iam 20 electis, non elegendis," [165] ut in dicto capitulo *Significasti*;[166] *De Iureiurando, Nullus*;[167] 23. d, *Quamquam*;[168] et aliis, que locuntur de iam electis seu [z] confirmatis. Et hec opinio verior est, secundum Hostiensem.[169]

---

[v] *om* d	[y] quia d
[w] non d	[z] sed A
[x] usque ad ultimam: Visi ultra Ad	

---

[159] Huguccio, *Summa ad Decretum*, Firenze, Bibl. Laurenziana, ms. Pluteo I, Sin. IV, in 8. q. 3, 2. "Ego credo esse illicitum et praestare et exigere ante electionem vel receptionem, nisi forte superior exigat, et credo esse simoniacum." f. 128[rb], lines 22-23.

[160] Guido de Baysio (called Archidiaconus), *In Sextum Decretalium Commentaria, ad* 2, 11, 1 (Venetiis, 1577), f. 67[v].

[161] Host., *Summa*, V, De Simonia, Quid si iudex, § Sed numquid; f. 233[ra], § 9 where he cites Gratian, C.8 q.3 c2. and C.1 q.2 c.2.

[162] Host., *ibid.*, citing X. 1, 6, 4.

[163] *Ibid.*, citing X. 1, 6, 38.

[164] Ray., p. 9, col. 2, citing Gratian, D.28 c.13 and C.10 q.3 c.10.

[165] Guil., *Glossa in Ray.*, p. 9, col. 2.

[166] X. 1, 6, 4.

[167] X. 2, 24, 5.

[168] Gratian, D.23 c.6.

[169] Cf. note 161.

Et ideo, ex hiis sequitur quod cancellarius non potest sine 770, 66
symonia exigere huius cautionem iuratoriam ante ipsorum bachalariorum promotionem, scilicet ante licentiam, eciam supposito /
quod ^a esset eorum superior, et quod huiusmodi iuramentum non **f. 101ᵛ**
5 esset contra ius commune vel previlegium speciale, quod tamen
falsum est, ut dixi.

 Secunda conditio, que in proposito potest circa huiusmodi
iuramentum considerari, est utrum illud / de quo exigitur iura- 771
mentum sit ipsi rei spirituali, que confertur, annexum, ut in dicto
10 ca. *Significasti* notat Glossa Antiqua Vincentii,[170] et allegat ca.
Significatum, De Prebendis,[171] et xxviii. d. *Dyaconi.*[172] Sic enim licite
exigit cancellarius iuramentum a bachalariis licentiandis, quod
fidele testimonium perhibebunt de futuris bachalariis licentiandis,
quia hoc onus perhibendi tale testimonium est rationaliter an-
15 nexum eorum licentie, et hoc interveniente auctoritate pape, ut
patet ex previlegio *Parens Scientiarum.*[173] Et licet honestius esset
tale iuramentum exigi post licentiam quam ante, tamen, si ante
exigitur, non habet aliquam speciem symonie, ex eo quod non est
in favorem exigentis, sed totius rei publice.

20 Tercia conditio que potest hic considerari, est utrum tale iura- 771, 16
mentum sit obsequiosum, per quod intelligitur illud iuramentum
quod est ad ipsius exigentis personale commodum, sicut est iuramentum illud quod exigit cancellarius a bachalariis, scilicet quod
servabunt honorem ^b suum, jura, libertates, et laudabiles consue-
25 tudines cancellarii et officii. Unde, licet tale iuramentum deberetur
cancellario, non tamen ante licentiam potest illud ab invitis exigere
sine vicio symonie, quoniam ^c in talibus iuramentis obsequiosis
maxime habent ^d locum illa ^e que dicta sunt, quia vero ei non
debetur huiusmodi iuramentum, eo quod talis exactio est sibi a
30 iure interdicta in Capitulo, *Quanto, De Magistris,*[174] nec ante, nec

---

^a *om* A   ^d habet A habeant d
^b hominem A   ^e illum A
^c cum d

---

 [170] Cf. Bernard of Parma on the same chapter, X. 1, 6, 4, *ad verb.* "conditione": "hoc onus annexum est dignitati. infra, *De Prebendis, Significatum* et
18 q. ii, *Eleutherius.*" *Compilatio Decretalium,* f. 18ʳa.
 [171] X. 3, 5, 11.
[172]Gratian, D.28 c.8.
 [173] *Chart.,* I, no. 79, p. 138.
 [174] X. 5, 5, 3.

post, potest huiusmodi iuramentum obsequiosum exigere. Secus
autem est de iuramentis non obsequiosis, que non dantur in favorem persone sue, seu ad commodum temporale vel personale, sicut
est predictum iuramentum de fideli testimonio perhibendo, vel
iuramentum de pace servanda inter religiosos et seculares, et si 5
que sunt similia, que dantur in favorem rei publice, vel in favorem
dantis, sicut est iuramentum de non expendendo ᶠ ultra tria millia ᵍ
Grossorum in magisterio, iuxta ca. *Cum Sit Nimis, De Magistris,*
in *Clementinis,*[175] que exiguntur auctoritate iuris, vel legislatoris.
Unde ipse quasi non censetur ista exigere, sed magis hoc exigit 10
ius commune ʰ, ut 18. q. 2. *Elutherius,* et ut notat dictus Vincentius,
ubi supra, in ca. *Significasti.*[176]

Ex premissis ergo patet multiplex solutio ad primum argumentum et eciam aliqualiter respondeo ad confirmationem primam
et alias sequentes. 15

771, 49 Tamen ad primam ⁱ confirmationem, dico ulterius, quod Facultas
Theologie, licet aliquo modo sit iudex, in congnoscendo de sufficientia bachalariorum admittendorum ad lecturam, tamen talia
f. 102 emolumenta que ab eis exigit, vel eciam iuramenta, / si obsequiosa
dici debeant, non sunt munera de quibus presumatur quod cor- 20
rumpant iudicium, sicut illa que cancellarius petit, quia talia non
sunt ad singularem utilitatem magistrorum, sed tocius communitatis, eciam aliquo modo ad utilitatem dantis, sicut recipientis,
quia pro conservatione ᵏ tocius ipsius communitatis vel facultatis,
cuius ipsi bachalarii sunt membra. 25

771, 61 Nec eciam talis admissio, qua facultas admittit bacalarios ad
legendum, est talis licentia docendi, sicut illa licentia que datur
per cancellarium, sicut videtur presupponere argumentum. Nam

ᶠ exponendo Ad
ᵍ tria millia: materiam d
ʰ Ecclesie d

ⁱ secundam Ad
ᵏ et (*post* conservatione) *add* A

---

[175] *Constitutiones Clementis Pape V*, V, 1, 2, in *Corpus Iuris Canonici,* ed.
E. Friedberg (Leipzig, 1879), II, 1180.
[176] Cf. Bernard of Parma on the same chapter, X. 1, 6, 4, *ad verb.* "conditione": "... vel refert a quo apponatur conditio, quia si a superiore non
symonia, vel potest dici, et melius, quod ius commune est quod hic exigitur.
Compilatio Decretalium, f. 18ʳa. Bernard then cites the same chapter of Gratian,
C.18 q.2 c.30. I conclude on the basis of the three references to Vincent,
here, p. 222, and p. 284, that Bernard's standard gloss on the Decretals was the
source of d'Ailly's quotations of Vincent.

licentia docendi, que datur bacalariis, non est aliqua potestas vel
auctoritas spiritualis, sicut nec doctrina eorum est [1] auctoritativa,
sed solum examinatoria et temptativa sive probativa. Ideo non
datur eis licentia docendi generalis, sed in certo loco et particularis.
5 Secus autem de licentiatis per cancellarium, quare patet ratio
diversitatis, etc.

Ad secundam confirmationem, dicendum est, sicut dicit Hos-   771, 73
tiensis, et post eum Joannes in *Summa Confessorum*, quod "ubi est
consuetudo quod ca/nonicus de novo receptus det cappam vel   772
10 aliquod simile, consuetudo est servanda tamquam laudabilis, argu-
mentato capitulo *Significatum, De Prebendis.*" [177] "Non tamen
retinere debent prebendam loco pignoris, vel dici potest, quod
eciam retinere possit, si hec sit consuetudo, et ibi exigitur loco
Dei spirituale pro spirituali, et non queritur utilitas privata." [178]

15 Dico eciam quod ibi decanus, vel capitulum, exigentes talia   772, 9
emolumenta vel iuramenta, non ea exigunt ante rei spiritualis collationem, quia papa, vel collator, iam contulit canonicatum et
prebendam, et sic isti non dant aliquam rem spiritualem, sed solum
possesionem corporalem, quare ibi non potest esse symonia. Secus
20 autem de cancellario in materia nostra, quare, etc.

Ad terciam [confirmationem], dicendum [est], secundum Sanc-   772, 17
tum Thomam,[179] et Joannem post eum in loco preallegato,[180] quod
in absolutione ab excommunicatione, "non exigitur pecunia
tamquam precium absolutionis, quia hoc esset symoniacum, sed
25 quasi pena culpe precedentis, pro qua fuit excommunicatus." Et
idem Hostiensis, *Libro* 5, rubrica, *De Excessibus Prelatorum*, et addit quod excommunicatus "absolvi debet libere, et eo absoluto
cogi potest ad satisfaciendum de pena, sed ante non potest exigi,
cum nec pro illo fuerit excommunicatus." [181] Et consimiliter dico
30 de iuramento obsequioso, et si oppositum [m] fiat alicubi, censeo
quod non videtur [n] consuetudo, et ita in proposito. Quare, etc.

---

[1] *om* d   [n] videt A
[m] propositum d

---

[177] Host., *Summa*, V, De Simonia, Qualiter, § Quid ergo; f. 232rb. citing
X. 3, 5, 11.
[178] Jo. de Friburgo, *Summa Confessorum*, Tit. I, q. 31; f. Vra.
[179] Tho., II, II, q. 100, art. 2, ad 3.
[180] Jo. de Friburgo, *Summa Confessorum*, Tit. I, q. 37; f. Vrb.
[181] Host., *Summa*, V, De Excessibus Prelatorum, Qualiter, § Quid si petitur;
f. 259va.

772, 31   Duodecimo arguitur principaliter quia in quibusdam locis, curati non dant, nec suis parrochianis ministrant sacramenta, nisi prius eis detur [o] pecunia. Similiter, nec quidam episcopi ministrant ordines, nisi prius peccunia recepta. Unde, ut quidam dicebat, in Anglia eciam est consuetudo quod non ministrantur Corpus 5 Christi parrochianis, nisi prius iurent quod bene solvent decimas
f. 102ᵛ illo anno. Sed absurdum esset dicere / quod omnes tales essent symoniaci, et per consequens consuetudo loci vel patrie facit illum modum exigendi esse licitum, et ita poterit dici in proposito. Nam cancellarius dicit se habere consuetudinem laudabilem de sic 10 exigendo huiusmodi iuramentum a tanto tempore quod non est memoria de contrario.

772, 46   Confirmatur quia decime debentur [p] ministris Ecclesie de [q] iure divino, ut patet Num. 18, 21, et tamen, ut quidam arguebat, in quibusdam locis, est consuetudo quod decime non solvuntur. Unde 15 absurdum esset dicere quod omnes qui non solvunt ibidem essent in peccato mortali, et per consequens, consuetudo loci vel patrie excusat eos. Si ergo consuetudo potest acquiri contra ius divinum, multo magis contra ius humanum, et per consequens cancellarius potuit acquirere consuetudinem exigendi per modum supradictum. 20 Quare, etc.

772, 57   Ad primum dico quod curati in administratione sacramentorum, et episcopi in collatione ordinum, licet quandoque petant pecunias, seu alia iura eis de iure vel consuetudine debita, de quibus iuribus ad presens non disputo, nec ea approbo vel reprobo, tamen non 25 possunt talia sic exigere, quod non dantibus temporalia denegent spiritualia. Aliud est simpliciter petere, et aliud predicto modo rigorose exigere, quia in casu primum posset licite [r-t] fieri, non secundum, nec sic exigere posset aliqua consuetudine excusari, cum sit contra ius divinum et proprie symoniacum. Nec credo 30 quod in Anglia sit consuetudo sic exigendi, salva reverentia dicentis. Si tamen esset ibi talis consuetudo, seu potius corruptela, non esset approbanda, nec faceret illum modum exigendi contra ius divinum esse licitum.

    Sic ergo dico in proposito, quod cancellarius non habet, nec 35 habere potest, laudabilem consuetudinem, vel iustum possessionem

---

[o] datur d   [q] ex d
[p] debent A   [r-t] *om* d

exigendi tale / iuramentum per modum predictum. Et hoc probo 773
multipliciter.

Primo quia talis modus exigendi est contra ius divinum, cum
sic exigere sit proprie symoniacum, ut patet ex dictis. Sed contra
5 ius divinum consuetudo non habet locum, nec prescriptio, nec
contra ipsum potest haberi iusta possessio. Igitur, etc.

Secundo, quia esto quia sic exigere non esset contra ius divinum, 773, 9
quod tamen omnino falsum est, tamen per ius canonicum exactio
quelibet in proposito expresse prohibetur cancellario, in capitulo
10 *Quanto, De Magistris*.[182] Et ibi dampnatur consuetudo tanquam
prava et inhonesta, pretextu cuius Cancellarius Parisiensis volebat
exigere. Si ergo huiusmodi consuetudo ante ius conditum erat
prava et dampnatur tanquam corruptela, multo magis post ius
conditum ipsa est dampnabilis et [v] repudianda; maxime quia, ex
15 [eo] quo aliqua consuetudo est a iure [x] expresse prohibita, supposito quod prius fuisset iusta vel licita, tamen post nunquam fiet
consuetudo iusta, aliter esset frustra iure dampnata. Ideo non
dicitur amplius "consuetudo", sed "corruptela", arguitur notanter
per Joannem Monachum, *De Bigamia*, capitulo unico, *Libro*
20 *Sexto*.[183]

Tercio, quod esto [y] quod non esset iure prohibita, tamen cancel- 773, 25
larius, qui est Magister in Artibus et in Theologia, sicut et alii
magistri, iuravit servare privilegia Universitatis "ad quemcumque
statum devenerit," [184] inter que iuravit / servare previlegium *Parens* f. 103
25 *Scientiarum*,[185] in quo prohibetur non solum exigere, ymmo eciam
recipere huiusmodi iuramentum, et per consequens, ipsum sic
exigendo agit contra proprium iuramentum. Nec ipse, sicut forte
aliqui predecessores sui, potest in hoc per ignorantiam vel inadvertentiam excusari. Quare ex hoc videtur incurrere periurium.
30 Sicut autem ipse dicit quod sui predecessores receperunt iuramentum huiusmodi, a tanto tempore quod non est memoria de contrario, licet hoc forte sit falsum, sicut quidam dicunt, nec illud

---

[v] om A   [y] ista A
[x] me A

---

[182] X. 5, 5, 3.
[183] Johannes Monachus "Cisterciensis", *Glossa Aurea Super Sexto Decretalium ad* 1, 12 (Paris, 1535), f. 138vb.
[184] *Chart.*, I, no. 501, p. 587.
[185] *Ibid.*, no. 79, pp. 136-139.

videtur verissimile, cum illud iuramentum non inveniatur scriptum in aliquo scripto ᶻ vel ᵃ libro antiquo. Quidquid tamen sit de hoc, dico eciam quod sui predecessores a tanto tempore quod non est memoria de contrario, vel saltem a maiori tempore quam facta fuerit dicti iuramenti exactio, fuerunt magistri et dicte Universitatis 5 iurati, et per consequens, sic exigendo contra Universitatis previlegium, fecerunt contra proprium iuramentum. Sed actus vel usus ab aliquo, contra suum iuramentum factus, non acquirit sibi iustum consuetudinem vel possessionem, nec iustum dominium seu prescriptionem ᵇ. Non concederem, sed potius negarem, sibi quod 10 predecessores sui valentiores eo exegissent contra sua iuramenta; ymmo concedo, sed per ignoranciam quantum ᶜ ad ᵈ previlegium *Servus Crucis*.

773, 57 Quarto, si forte dicatur quod illud iuramentum generale, scilicet de servando previlegio ᵉ etc., non sufficit ad concludendum ipsum 15 periurium, vel ipsum aut suos predecessores non habere vel habuisse usum iustum, induco adhuc iuramentum speciale, quia ipse ᶠ, sicut et ᵍ ceteri cancellarii, quando primo recipitur ad huiusmodi officium, specialiter iurat dignis tempore debito licentiam conferre, ut patet in predicto previlegio, *Parens Scientiarum*. Ergo denegando 20 modo licentiam bachalariis ad hoc dignis, ipse incurrit ʰ periurium. Et supposito quod illud iuramentum, et alia que petit a bachalariis, sibi de iure vel consuetudine deberentur, quod est falsum, tamen non potest licite ⁱ eis licentiam denegare, seu huiusmodi licentiam eis debitam retinere per modum pignoris, sicut rector ecclesie, sup- 25 posito quod debeat aliquid habere, puta vestes defuncti, pretextu consuetudinis, si tamen ei non satisfiat de illa, non debet retinere,

774 loco pignoris, e/xequium, quod conferri debet gratis, ut notat Hostiensis in *Summa, De Symonia, Qualiter Committatur.*¹⁸⁶ Quare, etc.

774, 4 Si vero dicatur, sicut quidam alias arguebat, quod cancellarius 30 non denegat licentiam dignis, nec retinet eam per modum pignoris, sed ex eo denegat, quod isti bachalarii reddunt se indignos, et ostendunt se male morigeratos ᵏ, quia, scilicet, denegant sibi

---

ᶻ aliquo [?] (*post* scripto) *in ras* A antiquo d
ᵃ aliquo (*post* vel) *add* d
ᵇ perscriptionem A
ᶜ quam d
ᵈ p- (*ante* ad) *del* A

ᵉ previlegia A
ᶠ ipsi A
ᵍ *om* A
ʰ *in ras* A
ⁱ *ex* eicite *corr* A
ᵏ moriginatos A

¹⁸⁶ § Quid si consuetudo, f. 232ᵛa.

iuramenta et alia ei de iure vel consuetudine debita, quod est
iniustum et illicitum. Quare, etc.

Ad hoc respondeo quod de hoc non potest se cancellarius iuvare, 774, 11
cum ipse huiusmodi bacalarios in aula episcopi publice vocaverit
5 et sollempniter recommendaverit tamquam dignos ad licentiam
recipiendam. Et tamen ante iuraverant sibi nichil dare, iuxta
tenorem previlegiorum Universitatis. Secundo dico, quod illud 774, 17
iuramentum non ¹ fuit illicitum, sed meritorium, ut alias dixi.¹⁸⁷ Et
supposito quod fuisset illicitum, tamen hoc non est clarum sed
10 sibi dubium, nec in hoc debet esse iudex in facto proprio ᵐ. Tercio
dico, quod esto quod illud iuramentum esset clare illicitum, et f. 103ᵛ
quod bachalarii hoc iurando, vel ea que petit denegando peccassent, tamen non quodlibet peccatum reddit aliquem ⁿ indignum
habendi licentiam ad docendum. Quare, etc.
15   Quinto,¹⁸⁸ si cancellarius acquisivit possessionem et consue- 774, 27
tudinem exigendi dictum iuramentum etc., ut dicit, constat quod
hoc acquirere non potuit, nisi ex donatione bacalariorum. Sed
ostendo quod non fuit iusta donatio inter eos, nam ad iustam donationem, quatuor conditiones requiruntur, quas ponit Doctor
20 Subtilis, in *Quarto* [*Sententiarum*], d. 15, q. 2, art. 2, in materia de
translatione dominiorum. "Primo, requiritur liberalis translatio ex
parte dantis; secundo, voluntas recipiendi, scilicet iusta, ex parte illius cui fit donatio; tercio, libertas ex parte amborum, huius dandi,
et illius recipiendi; quarto, quod nulla lege superiore prohibeantur
25 iste dare vel ille recipere, nec per actum alterius, scilicet superioris,
prohibeantur, a quo dependeant in ista translatione." ¹⁸⁹

Propter defectum secunde conditionis, dicit quod "non potest 774, 43
quis donare pecuniam Fratri Minori, quia ille non vult iuste esse
dominus, et propter eandem causam, dico quod non potest aliquid
30 iuste dare. Propter defectum tercio et quarto conditionis, dico

---

¹ *interl* A   ⁿ aliquid A
ᵐ in facto proprio: ut in secundo pro-
    posito d

---

¹⁸⁷ Radix, p. 230, 3-32. Note that the subject has shifted here. Now d'Ailly
is defending the bachelors' oath not to pay or swear obedience to the chancellor,
as opposed to the oath of obedience demanded by the chancellor prior to the
licence.
¹⁸⁸ Taking up from "Quarto," p. 289.
¹⁸⁹ Joannes Duns Scotus, *Quaestiones in quartum librum Sententiarum*, in *Opera
Omnia* (26 vols.; Parisius, 1891-95), 18, p. 277b.

quod nec monachus, preter abbatis licentiam, nec filius familias, preter voluntatem parentis, nec clericus in casu, sine voluntate pape, ut habetur *Libro Sexto* o, *De Censibus, Romana*,[190] ad cuius capituli observationem penam ponit Gregorius X, *Libro Sexto Decretalium*, ca. *Exigit*,[191] scilicet quod visitantes p a visitatis nulla 5 recipiant munuscula, et si recipiant, teneantur duplum restituere, etc." [192]

774, 56   Sic ergo dico in proposito, quod licet prima condicio, quandoque fuerit in bachalariis dantibus, et secunda q, in aliquibus cancellariis recipientibus, quia per ignorantiam vel inadvertentiam, 10 poterant ab iniusta voluntate dandi vel recipiendi excusari. Tamen tercia et quarta non sunt in proposito, quia tam a lege superiore, scilicet a iure commune, quam ex previlegio pape, a quo iste dependent in huiusmodi donatione, tam donantes quam recipientes erant prohibiti, et sic non habebant iustam libertatem dandi vel 15 recipiendi. Et quandoque eciam due prime conditiones deffuerunt, quare patet quod non fuit ibi iusta donatio, nec per consequens iusta possessio aut consuetudo. Quare, etc.

774, 70   Sexto, supposito quod sic exigere non esset cancellario iure divino, vel humano, vel a papa ex speciali previlegio prohibitum, 20 nec esset contra eius iuramentum, et quod dare vel recipere esset bachalariis, vel ipsi cancellario permissum vel concessum, que
775 omnia falsa sunt, ut dixi, tamen / adhuc dico quod non potest habere consuetudinem sic exigendi, sicut modo exigit, per usum predecessorum suorum. Quod patet quia predecessores sui nun- 25 quam habuerunt usum exigendi ab invitis, nec est a seculo auditum
f. 104 quod a nolentibus dare iuramentum,/ per denegationem licentie ipsum exigerent r, seu involuntarie extorquerent, sed solum a libere volentibus receperunt. Et in signum huius, antequam huiusmodi iuramentum reciperent, petebant ab eis: "Vultis vos ista iurare?" 30 Et per consequens, ex talibus actibus non habuerunt usum vel consuetudinem extorquendi huiusmodi iuramentum involuntarie. Exemplum de illo qui qualibet die transiret per domum meam, petendo a me: "Vis quod transeam?" Non est dicendum quod

---

o *Extra* A
p usitantes A

q *om* d
r exigerentur A

---

[190] *Liber Sextus Decretalium*, 3, 20, 1.
[191] *Ibid.*, 3, 20, 2.
[192] Scotus, 277b-278a.

iste acquireret usum, possessionem, vel consuetudinem transeundi per eam, me invito, et me nolente et contradicente sibi. Quare, etc.

Ad confirmationem, dicendum est cum Sancto Thoma, in 775, 19
5 *Secunda Secunde,* quod preceptum de solutione decimarum partim erat morale, et partim ⁸ iudiciale. Quod enim illis qui divino cultui ministrabant ad salutem populi totius ᵗ, populus victus necessaria ministraret, hoc dictat ratio naturalis, et quantum ad hoc, illud preceptum ᵛ morale. Sed determinatio certe partis, scilicet decime,
10 non erat de iure naturali, sed fuit introducta ex institutione divina, secundum conditionem illius populi. Et quia "omnia in figura contingebat illi ˣ," ut dicit Apostolus, ideo non solum precepta cerimonialia, sed eciam iudicialia ʸ, erant alicuius futuri figurativa. In hoc, tamen est inter ea differentia, quia multa ᶻ, tempore legis
15 gratie illicitum esset cerimonialia observare; iudicialia vero, etsi non obligent tempore gratie, scilicet virtute institutionis legis antique, tamen possunt observari absque peccato, et ad eorum observantiam possumus obligari, si statuantur auctoritate illorum, quorum est legem condere. Et sic determinatio decime partis
20 solvende, amplius non est auctoritate legis divine, sed solum auctoritate Ecclesie instituta, que tamen pensatis oportunitatibus temporum et personarum posset aliam partem determinare solvendam.¹⁹³ Et ideo dico quod ex parte iuris divini, si non obstaret aliud, scilicet institutio Ecclesie, consuetudo loci vel patrie, posset
25 eciam aliam partem, scilicet terciam vel quartam, partem decime determinare. Nec ex hoc sequitur quod consuetudo possit acquiri contra ius divinum. Quare, etc.

Tredecimo. Principaliter arguitur contra unum quod dixi in 775, 49 probatione prime propositionis, tercie conclusionis, scilicet quod
30 si ius divinum concederet cancellario quod posset recipere pro labore licentiandi, papa non posset hoc sibi negare, quod sibi ius divinum concederet. Et tamen papa prohibet sibi recipere pro labore ab Artistis licenciandis, etc.¹⁹⁴

ˢ et partim: partim erat d   ˣ illa A
ᵗ totius: *Text. Tho.* totus Ad   ʸ sed . . . iudicialia *om* d
ᵛ est (*post* preceptum) *add* d   ᶻ multo A

---

¹⁹³ Tho., II, II, q. 87, art. 1, *ad* 1, where Thomas also quotes I Cor. 10, 11.
¹⁹⁴ Cf. Super, p. 266; Radix, p. 218.

775, 57   Contra hoc quidam arguebat sic: quia archydyaconus, et in quibusdam ecclesiis decanus, visitat subditos suos, et in sic visitando, de iure divino, debet recipere visitationem seu procurationem, scilicet ad victum suum et vestitum. Et tamen papa [a] potest inhibere, ne aliquid recipiat, contentus eius beneficio et fructibus 5 eius. Igitur papa alicui potest negare illud quod sibi ius divinum concedit. Quare, etc.

775, 66   Ad hoc dicendum est, sicut immediato tactum fuit et / sicut
f. 104ᵛ ibidem dicit Sanctus Thomas, quod licet de iure naturali et divino, ministris Ecclesie debeantur victus necessaria, sicut et hiis qui com- 10 muni [b] utilitati invigilant, ut principibus et militibus debentur stipendia vite, unde et Apostolus hoc probat I Cor. 9, 7, per humanas consuetudines, dicens: "Quis militat suis stipendiis? Quis plantat vineam et de fructibus eius non edit?" etc.[195] Tamen, in
776   iure divino, saltem in Novo Testamento, non est deter/minatio 15 certe quantitatis, nam Apostolus solum generaliter dicit: "Habentes alimenta et quibus tegamur, hiis itaque contenti simus." I Tim. 6, 8. Et ideo dico quod papa, secundum qualitatem locorum et statum personarum, potest quantitatem determinare. Et quidquid est ultra alimenta et vestimenta necessaria, non est de iure divino 20 vel naturali, sed de iure humano. Unde episcopo vel archidyacono, habenti beneficium unde potest habere vite necessaria, visitationes seu procurationes quas recipit in visitando, non habet iure divino, sed ex permissione iuris humani, scilicet quia ista procuratio "a iure permissa est," sicut dicunt Bernardus et Hostiensis, ut supra 25 allegavi, in solutione quinte rationis principalis huius articuli.[196] Et ideo papa potest inhibere ne aliquid recipiat, maxime si habeat beneficium, unde possit merito contentari. Hoc autem non posset ei negare, si esset concessum iure divino vel naturali. Et sic in proposito. Quare, etc. 30

776, 20   Decimoquarto. Arguitur contra unum dictum in probatione tercie propositionis, scilicet [c] quod quandocumque [d] ista propositio verificatur: "Nisi dederis michi, aut promiseris, vel securum feceris de dando A, non dabo tibi B. Et si dederis, dabo," ibi est

---

[a] *om* A
[b] eorum d

[c] *om* d
[d] quantumcumque d

---

[195] A more concise statement of the passage paraphrased on p. 292, with the same scriptural authorities.
[196] Super, p. 269, l. 16-24.

venditio, seu contractus non gratuitus. Et per consequens, si A
sit temporale et B spirituale, ibi est symonia, etc.[197]

Et ad hoc facit illud quod dicit Scotus, Doctor Subtilis, loco   776, 28
preallegato, in duodecima ratione huius articuli,[198] scilicet quod
5 "Quedam est translatio dominii non mere liberalis [e], que distinguitur contra proprie dictam donationem, in qua transferens ex-
pectat aliquid pro illo quod transfert, et dicitur proprie contractus,
quia ibi simul trahuntur voluntates partium. Trahitur enim iste ad
transferendum in alium pro aliquo commodo." Et ista translatio
10 vel contractus exprimitur, secundum eum, dicendo "'Do ut des,
vel si des,' et debet esse solum rei utilis pro re utili et quasi equi-
valentis pro equivalenti," sicut declarat iste doctor.[199] Et per consequens, patet quod non debet esse rei spiritualis pro temporali.

Sed contra, quia si hec vera essent, sequitur quod omnes sacer-   776, 43
15 dotes et religiosi mendicantes, qui celebrant missas recipiendo an-
nalia, et omnes curati tradentes curas suas capellanis mercenariis
sub firma, ex certa conventione prehabita [f], essent symoniaci, quia
ibi habet locum "Do ut des." Et per consequens, contractus non
gratuitus. Quare, etc.

20   Ad hoc respondeo quod, secundum Raymundum, *De Symonia*,   776, 50
dicens, causa, "Si desunt ei sumptus, potest eos licite recipere." [200]
Et concordant in hoc Hostiensis [201] et Gaufredus.[202] Similiter, Innocentius, in ca. *Non Satis*.[203] Et addit postea Raymundus, quod
"si talis / aliunde habet sumptus, aut debet cantare gratis, aut ces-   f. 105
25 sare; alias videtur facere ex avaritia, licet forte hic non esset
symonia." [204] Et idem tenet Gaufredus.[205] Sed glossa hic dicit
quod "in omni casu, gratis debet cantare, quia sive detur ei pecunia

---

[e] liberalitatis d   [f] prohibita d

---

[197] Radix, p. 232.
[198] Super, p. 290, l. 15-26.
[199] Scotus, *In Quarto Sententiarum*, d. 15, q. 2, art. 2; p. 282b.
[200] Ray., p. 19, col. 1.
[201] Host., *Summa*, V, De Simonia, Qualiter, § Et sunt hec; f. 232[r]a-b.
[202] Gottofredus, f. 203[r]b.
[203] Innocentius IV Pont. Max., *In Quinque Libros Decretalium*, 5, 4, 3, *ad verb.*
"regimen" (Turin, 1581), f. 208[r]a. This passage, on *Quoniam enormis*, is better
than the one cited by d'Ailly, for here Innocent says: "Ille qui locat operas
suas spirituales non peccat, si aliunde sumptus non habet."
[204] Ray., p. 19, col. 1.
[205] Gottofredus, f. 203[r]b.

pro sumptibus, sive dentur ei sumptus in domo illius quo iuvat ᵍ
officiando ecclesiam, sive habeat ecclesiam ad firmam, de qua reddit certam pensionem et residuum retinet, ex pacto, pro sumptibus.
Gratis tamen debet impendere officium, et quod datur ei, gratis
debet dari: sicut dicit Augustinus 'quod apostoli gratuitum panem 5
accipiebant ab illis quibus gratuitam predicationem impende-
bant.' " ²⁰⁶ Et hiis satis videtur concordare Thomas in *Summa*.²⁰⁷

776, 68   Similiter, secundum Raymundum, Titulo *Ne Prelati Vices*, in
principio, "Nec episcopus, nec archidyaconus, nec alius prelatus
potest, sub precio vel annuo censu, concedere alicui vices suas, id 10
est, prelationem vel iuriditione, vel aliquod ius spirituale, *Extra.*,
eodem titulo, 1, 2, et 3." ²⁰⁸ Et concordant in hoc Gaufredus ²⁰⁹
et Hostiensis, eodem titulo.²¹⁰ Sed tamen licet prelatis et aliis

777   clericis ʰ / vendere, vel ad pensionem tradere fructus temporales
beneficiorum suorum, scilicet ad tempus, dum tamen, sub tali 15
venditione, nichil spirituale interveniat, secundum Raymundum,
ibidem.²¹¹ Et quamvis possint ⁱ huiusmodi prelati, vel rectores ecclesiarum, conductitiis ᵏ presbiteris, vel eciam conductori fruc-
tuum, ad tempus, curam animarum vel aliud ius spirituale committere, secundum eundem, tamen, sicut dicit glossa hic, "non 20
habet in talibus locum locatio et conductio, sed gratis debet fieri."²¹²
Et Hostiensis dicit quod "gratis et sine pactione aliqua." ²¹³

777, 13   Et sic ex omnibus predictis patet, quod sine vicio symonie non
potest in talibus prehaberi conventio, que sit contractus per "do
ut des," et hoc si huiusmodi conventio vel contractus cadat super 25
re spirituali. Potest tamen contractus cadere de temporali ad
temporale, quare, etc. Et talem intentionem debent habere sacer-

---

ᵍ domo illius quo vivat *Text Ray et*   ʰ Ecclesiasticis d
gloss: dono (*ex* domo *corr*) illius quam   ⁱ possent d
iuvat A   dono illius quia juvat d   ᵏ conductarum d

---

²⁰⁶ Guil. Rhed., *Glossa in Ray.*, p. 19, col. 2. Quoting Augustine, *De Opere Monachorum*, PL 40, 555.
²⁰⁷ Tho., II, II, q. 187, art. 5, ad 5.
²⁰⁸ Ray., p. 28, quoting X. 5, 4, caps. 1, 2, & 3.
²⁰⁹ Gottofredus, f. 203ᵛb.
²¹⁰ Since d'Ailly here refers to the whole tenor of this Title, it is hardly surprising that these authorities agree, but for Host. see especially *Summa*, V, Ne Prelati, § Supra posuit; f. 234ʳb.
²¹¹ Ray., p. 29, col. 1.
²¹² Guil. Rhed., *Glossa in Ray.*, *ibid*.
²¹³ Host., *Summa*, V, Ne Prelati, § Item fructus; f. 234ᵛa.

dotes, qui pro pecuniis cantant missas, vel qui tradunt aut qui recipiunt ad firmam parrochiales aut alias ecclesias. Aliter non habent conscientias rectas, nisi actualiter, vel saltem habitualiter, hoc intendant. Et forte contra hoc multi, per ignorantiam, pec-
5 cant, de quo dolendum est.

Patet igitur [1] responsio ad viginti [m] rationes principales, in 777, 25 primo et secundo articulis factas, ex quarum solutione et argumentorum plurium [n] eis annexorum, potest ad multa alia responderi.

Pro fortificatione vero, et confirmatione illorum que dixi in
10 tribus conclusionibus principalibus secundi articuli, et in solutione quatuor rationum in fine questionis, ultimate, per modum recollectionis, notandum est, quod Ecclesia, seu ministri Ecclesie, in spiritualium administratione, tribus de causis temporalia recipiunt, quas ponit Altissiodorensis, Libro Tercio, in materia de
15 symonia, questione tercia. "Prima causa est propter devotionem; secunda, propter ministrorum Ecclesie stipendium, vel sustentationem; tertia, propter correctionem." [214]

Primo modo debet ecclesia facere anniversarium, non pro red- 777, 40 ditibus, sed pro devotione dantis, et in signum devotionis / debet f. 105�v
20 dari pecunia vel redditus; et ita in aliis similibus. Et concordant [o] in hoc Raymundus,[215] Glossa Guillelmi,[216] Sanctus Thomas,[217] et alii doctores theologici; similiter Innocentius [218] et Hostiensis, in ca. *Quoniam Enormis, Ne Prelati Vices Suas*, etc.[219]

Secundo modo, sacerdotes recipiunt ecclesias ad firmam, et 777, 47
25 episcopi ac archidyaconi procurationes ab illis quos visitant. Tercio modo, episcopus recipit ab excommunicato, non pro excommunicatione, sed pro ipsius pena et correctione. Et diffuse hec tria prosequitur iste doctor, sed numquam invenitur quod ipse, vel

---

[1] ergo d	[n] principalium d
[m] vigesimas d	[o] concordat A

---

[214] Altiss., f. 227ʳb.
[215] Ray., p. 19.
[216] Guil. Rhed., *Glossa in Ray.*, *ibid.*
[217] Tho. *In 4º Sent.*, d. 25, q. 3, art. 2: "Anniversarium celebrare est spiritualis actus primo modo; et ideo nullo modo licet pacisci pro eo celebrando; si tamen cum devotione aliquid detur Ecclesiae, Ecclesia tenetur celebrare pro illis pro quibus rogatur."
[218] Innoc., f. 208ʳa.
[219] Host., *Summa* V, context unclear, but at § *Sed quare non*, Host. comments generally: "Ubi pecunia intercedit, gratificatio removetur, nec ad eterne retributionis premium habetur consideratio." f. 234ᵛa.

alius doctor theologus antiquus dicat quod sit recipiendum pro labore. Et si aliquis novellus hoc dicat, habet pro eodem dicere pro labore, sicut pro sustentatione vite, non advertens ᵖ differentiam.

777, 58   Secundo notandum est pro �q regula quod ʳ secundum predictum 5 doctorem,²²⁰ et Raymundum in *Summa*,²²¹ et glossam Guillelmi,²²² et communiter omnes doctores, nunquam ˢ datur temporale pro spirituale, vel econtra, sine symonia. Et hec prepositio "pro" notat appretiacionem vel commutationem, sed bene, si notet causam finalem, ut sit sensus: "Iste dedit denarium pro sacramento," 10 id est, pro veneratione sacramenti. Similiter si notet causam efficientem, ut sit sensus: "Iste dedit pro sacramento," id est, pro devotione, quam habuit ad sacramentum, et quod notet causam primam et principalem, seu ᵗ motivam remotam et occasionem, quam Altissiodorensis vocat "causam sine qua non," ²²³ sive "am- 15 miniculantem," ²²⁴ ut cum dicitur aliquid dare pro missa, vel pro visitatione. Et generaliter, sicut ipse [Altissiodorensis] dicit, "si in talibus habeatur respectus ad pecuniam, tanquam ad causam principalem, symonia est. Non autem dicimus quid fiat, sed quid fieri debeat." ²²⁵/   20

778   Tercio notandum quod in talibus, secundum omnes doctores, nunquam sunt exigenda temporalia per substractionem spiritualium. "Et si ante vel post, aliquid optinetur per talem modum, symonia est, nulla consuetudine obstante, iuxta capitulo *Sicut Pro Certo*, *De Symonia*, et capitulo *Apostolicam*." ²²⁶ Et quantum ad 25 hoc, in hiis que allegavi de Sancto Thoma,²²⁷ concordant ᵛ Gaufre-

---

ᵖ admittens d   ˢ quod (*ante* nunquam) *add* d
�q quod A   ᵗ sed A
ʳ *om* d   ᵛ concordat A

---

²²⁰ Altiss., f. 227ʳa, 227ᵛb, and 228ʳb-228ᵛa.

²²¹ Ray., p. 6, col. 2.

²²² Guil. Rhed., *Glossa in Ray.*, *ibid.*, *ad verb.* "pro spirituali," a comment that d'Ailly follows very closely here.

²²³ Altiss., f. 227ʳb, *in fine*.

²²⁴ This term is from Guil. Rhed., *Glossa in Ray.*, p. 19, col. 1, where the phrase "causa sine qua non" is also used.

²²⁵ Altiss., f. 227ʳb.

²²⁶ Jo. de Friburgo, *Summa Confessorum*, 1, 1, 30; f. Vʳa, where he cites X. 5, 3, 39 and 42.

²²⁷ Tho., II, II, q. 100, art. 3, resp.

dus,[228] Raymundus,[229] et glossa.[230] Similiter Innocentius,[231] et Hostiensis,[232] et communiter omnes doctores iuris, secundum Joannem in *Summa*, Titulo i, q. 31.[233]

Et ideo patet, quod cancellarius non potest, sine vicio symonie, **778, 12**
5 nec pro suo labore, nec pro quacumque alia causa, vel occasione, pecuniam vel iuramentum obsequiosum [x] exigere, a [y] licentiandis in theologia per substractionem licentie, non obstante quacumque consuetudine, cum talis licentia sit spiritualis, ut probavi in primo articulo questionis [z]. Et in hoc stat principalis intentio Matris
10 Nostre Universitatis, sub eius correctione hec dicta sunt [a] de presenti questione.

---

[x] officiosum A   [z] Quasi d
[y] a: *in* ad *corr* A *male*   [a] sint A

---

[228] Gottofredus, f. 202[rb].
[229] Ray., p. 16, col. 2.
[230] Guil. Rhed., *Glossa in Ray., ibid.*
[231] Innoc., f. 207[v]a.
[232] Host., *Summa*, V, *De Symonia*, Qualiter, § Verumtamen, et sqq.; f. 232[rb].
[233] Jo. de Friburgo, *Summa Confessorum*, 1, 1, 31; f. V[r]a. John, whom d'Ailly paraphrases here, is responsible for this long list of citations.

INDEX

ERRATA

p. 10, line 13: *instead of* data *read* date
p. 11, n. 44, last line: *instead of* may examples *read* many examples
p. 34, line 12: *instead of* disengenously *read* disengenuously
p. 37, line 15: *instead of* for *read* in
p. 68, line 5 from bottom: *instead of* occured *read* occurred
p. 147, n. 151, line 2: *instead of* is it *read* it is
p. 151, line 10: *instead of* licensed to *read* licensed, to

Alan E. Bernstein, *Pierre D'Ailly and the Blanchard Affair*